AuthorHouse™
1663 Liberty Drive
Bloomington, IN 47403
www.authorhouse.com
Phone: 1 (800) 839-8640

Published by AuthorHouse 07/15/2019

ISBN: 978-1-4918-4572-1 (sc)

Library of Congress Control Number: 2013922698

Print information available on the last page.

authorHOUSE®

LOOKING *into Our* GRANDPARENT'S IMMIGRANT EYES

Photographic Images of Early Immigrant Families to Southeastern Wisconsin

Compiled and edited by Thomas Ramstack

ACKNOWLEDGMENTS

To make a project such as this achieve a qualitative state, takes the assistance of many people. I would primarily like to thank the more than two-hundred and fifty individuals, families, and institutions who provided a vast assortment of wonderful early Wisconsin immigrant "people" photographs, family histories, letters, journals as well as recollections which will hopefully provide us all with a renewed insight into Wisconsin's very unique early immigrant story.

I would like to initially thank Eric Vanden Heuvel, former Archivist for the Waukesha County Historical Society and Museum, for opening up the society's extensive collection of "people" images and allowing me to capture a large assortment of select images to be used in this project. It was this initial contact with Eric which provided a foundation for believing that this project might take on a life which might be both exciting and meaningful. In 2016, Bonnie Byrd, Curator Waukesha County Historical Society & Museum, wrote out a new Rights and Reproductions agreement, likely spending countless hours attaching the images to their collection's location, and finally providing permission to publish many of the society's wonderful "people" images.

I am also indebted to the following reginal historical societies and organizations for providing people photographs or related historical information from their own collections: the Big Bend Vernon Historical Society, the Elmbrook Historical Society, the Hartland Historical Society, Hawks Inn Historical Society, the Muskego Historical Society, the New Berlin Historical Society, Town of Ottawa historian, Carl. L. Borgstram (now deceased), the Sussex-Lisbon Area Historical Society, the Pewaukee Area Historical Society, Wales Village Hall, Wales, as well as the Wisconsin Historical Society.

Next came the notion of requesting permission from genealogists with family connections to southeastern Wisconsin who provided private family photographs found on several commercial genealogical sites. I must have contacted over one hundred families, who displaying wonderful and very useful images. Their response and permission granted was incredibly positive. Images were provided by family genealogists from nineteen states as well as Canada and the U.K. Many of these same families also sent letters, journals, as well as family recollections. At this point the project no longer became mine alone but took on a life of its own as "our project."

Soon thereafter, I made contact with Joan Severa, former curator of textiles for the Wisconsin Historical Society, hoping to acquire her support in the project. Joan had a vast knowledge of historic clothing fashions as exemplified in her landmark work, Dressed for the Photographer: Ordinary Americans and Fashion, 1840-1900, published in 1997. Joan was very generous in providing, for our project, enlightening descriptions of fabric and dress styles focusing on fashion changes from one decade to the next.

What entangled my mind in a constant web of confusion as I began this project, was attempting get a grasp the constant, on the ongoing state of change throughout the period of the German Confederation (1815-1866) throughout the 19th Century. However, over the course of the past twenty-five years, I have found a special friend in Dr. Helmut Treis of Aachen, Rheinland, Germany. First in letter form and later through e-mail messaging, Dr. Helmut very patiently answered my many questions related to political changes, ethnicity, boundary changes, ongoing wars, all of which, in so many ways, continued to change my understanding of Germany during this period. Dr. Treis, as you read what follows, I am certain you will come across a blatant mistake or two. I can only hope that I got most of it right and I will continue to thank you for your ongoing support and friendship!

A special thanks must, also, go to Peter Sjoberg, of Rockford, Illinois, who used his gifted computer skills to digitally repair photographs which might have been damaged to the point that it was difficult to see facial features.

Over the past thirty years, I have had the pleasure of making contact with a large number of individuals who share a similar love for local history. Included are: Libbie Nolan (who for many years served as editor of *Landmark*, the quarterly publication of the Waukesha County Historical Society and Museum); Marilyn Wellauer-Linius (who has pursued a passion for identifying individuals as well as patterns of Swiss immigration to Wisconsin); Martin "Marty" Perkins (Marty, who passed away in November of 2012, was curator of research at Old World Wisconsin, the outdoor museum of rural Wisconsin life. Many of us who worked as interpreters at "Old World" shared in Marty's passion for Wisconsin's rich ethnic history.); and Fred H. Keller (Sussex - Lisbon Area Historian and Museum Curator. Fred is always glad to give a tour of their museum and his love for Sussex-Lisbon history never fails to bubble over.)

Names whom you may or may not recognize who encouraged include: Louis Wassermann, Roy Meidenbauer, Elaine Alane, Mary Stigler, Lynda Thayer, Elaine Moss, Dr. Helmut Treis, John Schoenknecht, Fred C. Smyth, as well as Steve Blattner, who constantly questioned, "Tom, why do you always insist on racing through these projects???" (Lighthearted sarcasm"--I hope!)

In memory and gratitude those who contributed to this project but passed on before it was complete. Including: **Gene Nettesheim, Evelyn J Nicholson, Marion Woelfel, Sally Clarin, Carl L. Borgstram, Joan Severa and Georgia Davis Briggeman.** (My apologies to the families of any others I might have missed.)

INTRODUCTION

The Territory of Wisconsin was organized on July 3, 1836. Possessing fresh, uncultivated land, immigration to the new territory began in earnest from this date forward. New Yorkers and other eastern Americans arrived in Wisconsin by the thousands during the decade of the 1840s. As no passable roads, nor railroads, had not yet existed, immigrants, for the most part, traveled to Wisconsin by way of Great Lakes steamship routes. Referring to the significant numbers of immigrants arriving in Wisconsin during this period, Milwaukee historian H. Russell Austin wrote that immigration to Wisconsin, "was all the rage!"[1]

I wish that I could show you a photograph, but, during this era, photography was yet, somewhat in its infancy. Unlike those wonderful photographs of immigrants arriving at Ellis Island at the turn of the nineteenth century, we have no photographic images to show early immigrant arrivals at Wisconsin. Imagine their feelings: fear, excitement, despair, hope! It is difficult to know with absolute certainty which emotions dominated, as precious few personal accounts portraying the toughts and feelings of Wisconsin's earliest Yankee and European immigration remain.

The Northwest Ordinance (1787) allowed that when the population of a territory reached 60,000, that territory could apply for statehood. Based on this measure, Wisconsin petitioned Congress, and attained statehood on May 29, 1848.[2] It was estimated that 12,000 Germans arrived through the port of Milwaukee that very summer![3] Who could have envisioned that so many families from vastly unrelated locations—the states of New York, Pennsylvania; the western European countries of Ireland, England, Wales, Norway, Germany, Scotland, Alsatians (from France), Dutch (from the Netherlands), as well as numerous other far away locations — would, over a relatively short span, settle in this new home earlier referred to by French explorers as *"Ouisconsin."*

Considering European immigration, we might ask, what husband and father would put his family at such risk? What made them leave? The reality, as you will discover in the pages which follow, life, during this period, was, often, extremely harsh for the large and extremely poor working classes, throughout western Europe, and, in more cases than one might imagine, desperate, for the vast majority of these families.

"Europe endured hard times during much of the 1840s. A series of bad harvests culminating in the potato blight of 1845-46 brought widespread misery and starvation. An economic depression added to the hardship, spreading discontent among the poor and the middle class alike."[4]

In England, parish overseers, resenting the thought of having to support their destitute farm laborers often payed to have them removed to the United States. As the extent of the potato famine, in Ireland, became clearer, Wisconsin

[1] , H. Russell H. Austin. *The Wisconsin Story: The Building of a Vanguard State* 1st Edition. (Milwaukee, Wisconsin, *The Milwaukee Journal*, 1948), p. 17.
[2] https://en.wikipedia.org/wiki/Wisconsin_Territory
[3] Waukesha Freeman Aug. 28, 1846
[4] Area Handbook of the US Library of Congress, University Of Oxford: Global Change Max Roser and Esteban Ortz-Ospina, "World Population Growth"

residents responded with thoughtful, through vastly insufficient relief efforts.[5]

Historian Tyler Anbinder wrote, "The preponderance of Germans emigrated for many of the same reasons as their Irish counterparts. The potato crop also failed in Germany in the late 1840s. Massive unemployment exacerbated these problems, reaching an unprecedented 17 percent by the mid-1850s.[6] The *Milwaukee Sentinel* on Aug. 28, 1846, reported: "The Albany Atlas of the 11th inst says: 'Another large party of respectable Germans emigrants arrived in the city this morning, on their way to Wisconsin. We noticed that some of them had maps of the country, and guidebooks, which appeared to be in their own language'."

Where would their imaginations have taken them when they first laid their eyes on the short, wooden pier at Milwaukee as they stepped off Great Lakes steamers such as the Wisconsin, Empire, Bunker Hill, Missouri, Illinois & Phoenix? What thoughts must have raced through their minds as they immediately viewed the endless lakeshore and a limitless vision of trees? They were risking life and limb on a land with virtually no social structure, nor infrastructure. There were no reasonable roads, there was no practical health care, and there was no guarantee that the land would provide for them.

As the United States was predominately a Protestant country during the 1840s, the fact that so many European immigrants determinedly held onto their old world religions, particularly Catholicism, did not always sit well with many of their new neighbors here in Wisconsin. Thus, there evolved a somewhat miscellaneous assortment of old and new world cultures which, for the most part, filled southeastern Wisconsin's woods and oak openings with tight and, often, uncongenial ethnic settlement patterns during the earliest decades of Wisconsin statehood.

You might ask, "Why should we bother, today, to reflect on their experiences?" That question, I feel, is best answered by looking at their accomplishments. Wisconsin's immigrants of the 1830's through the 1850's, took this fertile land and made a life out of it. We owe them our gratitude for their courage, fortitude, and persistence! Those who had the courage to stay and who were not torn away by the adverse fortunes that did come their way, created a community of people, who, in many respects, formed the foundation of our present way of life as vital families residing in flourishing communities.

Wisconsin's early immigrant story is dramatic and unique in the history of our country. While the great majority of the work focuses on immigration to Waukesha County exclusively, you will find an assortment of accounts from neighboring counties. This work is designed to present an insightful account of southeastern Wisconsin's early immigration story attached to specific families who settled here. In this respect, the two hundred plus families who, unselfishly, provided their own family's genealogies, letters, journals, family histories, to this project; along with useful published as well as unpublished historical accounts, hopefully will provide you with a somewhat new and enriching insight into sensing the courage, persistence as well as the heartbreak experienced by many of Wisconsin's earliest immigrant families.

The variety of photographic styles developed during the 19th century included: Daguerreotypes, Ambrotypes, Tintypes, Cartes de Visite, and Cabinet Cards.[7] The photographs used in this compilation include all five. We can see so many things when studying a face. I hope you might take time and take a good look at each one. These are the faces of our state's earliest immigrants themselves (along with their children). We obviously cannot look inside their minds to understand the various languages many of them spoke; nor can we know the thoughts they held for relatives left behind. Yet, what incredible pondering's must have run through their minds! Their various facial expressions

---

[5]   *Milwaukee Sentinel* June 22, 1847

[6]   Tyler Anbinder, *Nativism & Slavery: The Northern Know Nothings & the Politics of the 1850s* (New York: Oxford University Press, 1992), p. 7.

[7]   https://en.wikipedia.org/wiki/History_of_photography

might suggest an individual who is hard working, sad, sympathetic, fatigued, warm, cold, worried, affectionate, conscientious, sad, or joyful. In studying their faces, we might sense a connection to them as fellow human beings. It is this human connection I most hope that you might sense. As I reported in an earlier work, I am not asking you to look back ten thousand years to some prehistoric world culture. But, merely to peek back over your shoulder one hundred and seventy years ago, or so, to view images and accounts of families, much like our own, but whose lives were set in a backdrop dramatically unlike ours. My greatest hope is that you might find insight as well as joy in what follows!

Beyond the numerous ancestral photographs provided by families from a wide variety of locations throughout the state of Wisconsin, many historic photographs (44 in all) were kindly provided by families from numerous states throughout the country as well as Germany, Canada and United Kingdom. Below is a charting of those providers of family photographs. In many situations, 2nd generation young people, who had nothing to hold them here in Wisconsin, emigrated from their family's homes here to other locations in the U.S., predominately west, to the states the of Colorado, California, Iowa, North Dakota, Montana, Minnesota & Nebraska. (The following information was taken from the more detailed family accounts which follows in the text.)

Provider	Residence as of 2010	ANCESTER'S NAMES	EMIGRATED FROM
Marrialice Blanchard	Salem, Oregon	Emily Rathbun	Massachusetts/NY
Gene Nettesheim	Boulder, Colorado	Johann Nettesheim	Rheinish Prussia/Hanover
Kenneth Eiler	Overland Park, Kansas	Henry Snyder Jr.	Hesse/NY (parents)
Jeannie Brown	Windsor, California	William & Alice Bigelow	Vermont/Canada (parents)
Mark Powers	Woodland, California	Nellie Murphy	Ireland (parents)
Jen Doane	Clinton, Utah	George Barney	NY/Maine
Susan Goodman	Chevy Chase, Maryland	Ole Corfield Family	Norway
Jeanette Pelletier	Bay City, Michigan	Christiana (Pegler) Schrubbe	Prussia (parents)
Judy Lynch	Manhattan, Kansas	John B. Jermark	Prussia (parents)
Lisa Lohry	Waterville, Minnesota	Nathan Baxter	Pennsylvania
Kenneth Eiler	Overland Park, Kansas	Mabel & Alvin Snyder	Hesse/New York
William Joynt	Rockford, Illinois	Gerhard Reinders Family	Nordrhein-Westfalen
Carol Logan	Chico, California	Mary Louis Potter	Saxony
Tricia Dingwall Thompson	Bozeman, Montana	Daniel & Barbara Schley	Bavaria
James Woelfel	Holt, Michigan	Simon Woelfel	Bavaria (genealogy)
Jerry Hartwell	Bowling Green, Ohio	Charles Kreig Family	Saxony & Prussia
Richard LaVerne	Sarasota, Florida	Ferdinand Brunkow	Meck.-Schwerin & Berlin
Terry Haslam-Jones	Rossendale, England	Vogel Brothers	Lower Saxony
Andrew D. Pierce	Eugene Lane, Oregon	Mary Gumm	Prussia (parents)
Debra W. Barham	Clearfield, Utah	Jarvis Porter Boyce	England (parents)

Provider	Residence as of 2010	ANCESTER'S NAMES	EMIGRATED FROM
Betty Ann Kramer	Clovis, California	Albert & Christiana Schrubbe	Pomerania
Fred C. Smyth	Whidbey Island, WA	Best Children	Hesse (parents)
Jonathan Brumfield	Huntsville, Alabama	Behrend Sisters	Prussia (parents)
Linda Cleary	San Francisco, CA	Cleary Family	
Ann Josher	Woodhaven, Queens, New York	George Barney & Julia Washburn	England & Maine
Erica Crom	Rantoul, Illinois	Grudmann Family	Bavaria
Donna H. Grambau	Mount Pleasant MI	William & Clara Bishoff	Saxony & Holland
Roberta Poetsch	Rochester, Minnesota	Charles B. Coleman	New York
Mark J. Kelly	Texas City, Texas	Albert Beecroft Family	England
Georgia Davis Briggeman	Deer Lodge, Montana	Blessinger brother	Baden
Crystal Keslin	Lubbock, Texas	Heinrich Boldt Family	Mecklenburg
Sue Hornbeck Bixby	Troy Michigan	Maria (Boeijink) Bixby	Vermont/Holland
Terry Haslam-Jones	Rosendale, England	Vogel Brothers	Saxony
Jen Doane	Clinton, Utah	Julia Washburn	New York/Maine
Susan Goodman	Chevy Chase, Maryland	Otto & Caspara Rasmussen	Norway
Jerry Hartwell	Bowling Green, Ohio	Charles Krieg	Saxony
Kenneth Eiler	Overland, Kansas	Amelia (Snyder) Putz	Rhineland & PA
Jerry Hartwell	Bowling Green, Ohio	John Christian Dieman	Prussia
Fred C. Smyth	Whidbey Island, WA	John & Eliz. Best Family	Hesse
Georgia Davis Briggeman	Deer Lodge, Montana	Thomas Blessinger	Baden & Ireland
Louise Wasserman	Germersberg, Bavaria	Ulrich Woelfel home	Rollhofen, Bavaria
Carol Logan	Chico, California	Pvt. Clarence Potter	Saxony & NY (parents)
Jennifer Doane	Clinton, Utah	Sebina Barney w/baby	NY & Vermont
Kenneth Eiler	Overland Park, Kansas	Henry Snyder	Hesse/New York

Most of the earliest German families who immigrated to southeastern Wisconsin did so during the period of **the German Confederation (1815-1866)**. The great majority of these German "Kingdom" names might be unfamiliar to most of us today, unless you might be a student of 19th Century European history, which I do not claim to be. For this reason I have a provided a map of Germany along with a listing of German "state" names (both in English & German) from this period. This all might prove confusing to genealogists whose homeland names you associate with your family will appear to be in contradiction to the names presented here. The primary confusion for this might be a result of the fact that many homeland names were changed at the conclusion of the Franco-Prussian War (1871), when Germany became unified under Prince Otto von Bismarck, who became the first Chancellor of the new **German Empire of 1871–1918.** If your family names are identified with these newer names, they may be technically correct in terms of location, but not the locational names most associated with our earliest Wisconsin immigrants. You might want to refer to this page quite often for clarity, as you go through the pages which follow.[8]

Member "Kingdoms" of the German Confederation (1815-1866) most directly associated with early Wisconsin immigration[10]

English Names:	Hanover	Saxony	Hesse	Holstein	Prussia	Mecklenburg Schwerin	Bavaria	Baden	Rhineland/ Rhenish Prussia
German Names:	Hannover	Sachsen	Hessen	Holstein	Preußen	Mecklenburg Schwerin	Bayern	Baden	Rheinisches/ Rheinpreußen

8   Source: https://**en.wikipedia.org**/wiki/**German Confederation**, and https://en.wikipedia.org/wiki/German_Empire

9   https://upload.wikimedia.org/wikipedia/commons/thumb/6/6c/Deutscher_Bund.png/700px-Deutscher_Bund.png

10   en.wikipedia.org/wiki, /List_of_states_of_the_German_Confederation

CHARACTERISTICS OF THE COMMON PEOPLE IN 19ᵀᴴ CENTURY EUROPE

[11] "19th Century Europe referred to the common people as lacking any significant social status, especially those who were members of neither royalty, nobility, the clergy, nor any member of the aristocracy. Working wives, harsh factory conditions, bad housing, poor sanitation, excessive drinking characterized the lives of commoners."[12] "In Germany, peasants continued to center their lives in the village well into the 19th century. In most European countries, serfs were bound permanently to parcels of land. In most of Germany, farming was handled by tenant farmers who paid rents and obligatory services to the landlord—typically a nobleman. In Prussia, the peasants drew lots to choose conscripts required by the army."[13]

[11] https://en.wikipedia.org/wiki/Peasant#Medieval_European_peasant {{PD-US-expired}}

[12] https://en.wikipedia.org/wiki/Commoner

[13] https://en.wikipedia.org/wiki/Peasant

BLEAK CONDITIONS PROMPTS
IMMIGRATION TO WISCONSIN

Heads of households who immigrated with their families to southeastern Wisconsin:	Former homes:	Conditions in their former locations	Year of Immigration:
John & Dorothy Dodge	Vermont	Reduction in wool & sheep economy	1836
Thomas Faulkner Sr.	Ireland/NY	Famine	1848
Thomas Jr. & Nancy Faulkner	New York	Reduction in wheat production	1846
George & Ruth Ferry Family	New York	Worn out soil for agricultural production	(c.1848)
Jeremy & Emily Warner	New York	Reduction in wheat production	(c.1848)
Mary McCormick	Ireland	Famine	(1847)
Maria Amelia Boeijink	Holland	Lack of religious freedom	(c 1848)
August Blodgett	New York	Reduction in wheat production	(1843)
Reiner Nettesheim	Rhineland	Religious, economic & political unrest	(1848)
Jens Jensen Kier	Denmark	Widespread poverty	(1859)
Mathias Kau	Rhineland	Unprofitable farming & political unrest	(c 1859)
John Greer Sr.	Ireland	1st. year of potato blight	(1845)
Thomas D. Jones	Wales	Small & unprofitable tenant holdings	(1842)
John Lumb	England	Landowners abandoned tenant farmers	(1852)
Ferrand Bigelow	Vermont	Worn out soil for agricultural production	(1836)
Dennis Murphy	Ireland	Famine & failure to attain a free Ireland	(c.1848)

Heads of households who immigrated with their families to southeastern Wisconsin:	Former homes:	Conditions in their former locations	Year of Immigration:
Owen Roberts	Wales	Miserable working conditions	(c.1870)
Henry Perry	England	Parish officers refuse to support tenants	(1852)
John Phillips	Prussia	Prussian aggression into trad. kingdoms	(c.1845)
Ephraim Beaumont	England	Terrible conditions in Sheffield steel mills	(1851)
Thomas Cleary	Ireland	Violence directed towards Catholics	(c.1846)
Eliza Tymersen	Holland	English defeat Dutch at New Amsterdam (New York)	(c.1834)
John Howie	Scotland	Presbyterian Covenanters agitate for a free nation	(1841)
Anne Kaarfeld Corfield	Norway	Crop failures compounded by population growth	(1845)
John K. Meidenbaurer	Bavaria	Aristocracy defeated 1848 Revolution	(1848)
John Andrew Schneider	Prussia	Government diminishes the Lutheran Church	(c.1870)
George Wellauer	Switzerland	"People forced to eat clover, nettles & snails"	(c.1848)
August Schaefel	Württemberg	Failure to achieve Democratic rights	(1866)
Wilhelm Bolter	Prussia	Democratic uprising against Prussian rule	(c.1851)
August Erbe	Saxony	Prussia invades Saxony/conscripts their army	(1860)
William Searle	England	Disease, failed economy & peasant revolt	(c.1844)
Alexan Harris	Scotland	Farmers forced off their land, famine & evictions	(c.1852)
Gerhard Reinders	Prussia	Congress of Vienna awards Rhineland to Prussia	(1854)
John Michael Stigler	Bavaria	Population growth, crop failures w/potato blight	(1850)
Ephraim Beaumont	England	Civil unrest resulting from Industrial Revolution	(c.1848)
Thomas Steele	Scotland	Peasants described as a "beggar's mantle"	(c.1858)
Mary Bartlett	Saxony	Greater part of Saxony awarded to Prussia	(1816)
John Small	Scotland	Lack of work for much of the population	(1841)
Daniel Schley Sr.	Bavaria	Fire, pillage & plunder by French armies	(c.1858)

Heads of households who immigrated with their families to southeastern Wisconsin:	Former homes:	Conditions in their former locations	Year of Immigration:
August Bonness	Prussia	Brandenburg-Prussia ravaged during "30 Years War"	(c.1876)
Jesse Smith	Vermont	Wool industry creates disparities in wealth	(c.1860)
George H. Parsons	England	Declining tin mining industry/jobs lost	(1850)
Henry Bliemeister	Mecklenburg-Schwerin	Poor-man's laws & poverty among rural farmers	(1872)
Ernst August Buetow	Pomerania, Prussia	Polish minority suffered extensive oppression	(1871)
Ole Olson	Norway	"Gaunt & hungry children"	(1843)
David Brunkow	Mecklenburg-Schwerin	Cholera devastated the region	(1855)
John H. Phillips	France	Hunger, housing shortages & lack of work	(1842)
John Christian Dieman	Prussia	Determined to avoid military conscription	(c.1851)[14]

---

[14] The documentation presented on this chart comes directly from the material related to European emigration found in the content which follows.

GERMANY TO AMERICA IMMIGRANT SHIPPING LINES

"From the Old to the New World." German emigrants for New York embarking on a Hamburg steamer. Wood engraving in Harper's Weekly, November 7, 1874.[15]

In 1847, the Bavarian Newspaper, *Augsburger Allgemeine*, which remains in major circulation in 2019, reported (below) that German Emigrants, in large numbers, were headed not only for the western Great Lakes, but Milwaukee specifically:

GERMAN EMIGRANTS

"It is indeed frightful to see how the emigration increases. Every day the steamers bring us troops of wanderers, and anyone who at evening visits the now thickly-peopled quay (Rotterdam, Netherlands) on the Rhine, is always sure to find *the same melancholy scenes—mothers seeking to quiet crying children amid the clamor—old people careful about leaving their little worm-eaten chests and boxes*—men and young fellows consulting where they can find shelter for the night. It is also striking to see the successive caravans from the "Upper Country" (Hesse, Baden, Württemberg) appear to be better off, their goods coming in forming larger and heavier wagon loads. The courage, foresight and cheerfulness of the voyagers seem to be kept up under all circumstances. *This morning, though, a severe storm was raging over the roofs and whistling among the spars of the ships, a fearful reminder of the dangers of the sea, three hundred emigrants departed in the highest spirits, a band of music leading them on board ship. Most of them go by way of Antwerp to New York and Milwaukee*."   [*Augsburger Allgemeine*, (General Newspaper), in Bavaria May 17, 1847][16]

16 The *Augsburger Allegemeine* (General Newspaper), published in Augsburg, Bavaria, was a highly circulated German newspaper, beginning its circulation in 1808 and remains in circulation today. Most of the German immigrants who came to Wisconsin during the 1840s, left either through the Dutch port city of Rotterdam, at the mouth of the Rhine River or through the German port of Bremerhaven, at the mouth of the Weser River. As published in the *Milwaukee Sentinel* May 29, 1847.

NEW YORK STATES' ERIE CANAL

"Upon arriving in New York City, among other American ports, *immigrants*, during the late 1830's and through the 1840's, took steamers up the Hudson River to Albany where they *boarded canal boats* which took them to Buffalo on the famous Erie Canal. Once at *Buffalo*, they typically boarded another steamer which took them up through the Great Lakes where they could depart at any one of several port cities built up along the coast of the lakes, including *Milwaukee*.[17] (The map below illustrates the route of the canal across the state of *New York*.)"[18]

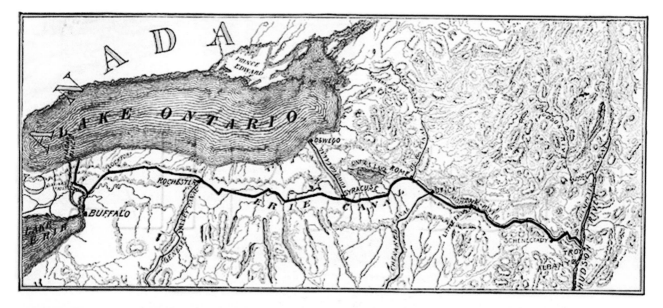

CONSTRUCTION OF THE ERIE CANAL

"Before the 1800s no civil engineering project as ambitious as the Erie Canal had been attempted in this young country. Proposed in 1808, construction began in 1817 on the *363-mile Erie Canal* from Albany to Buffalo. *Between 1800 and 1820 a great migration of Americans—more than a million and a half people—moved from settled areas of the East to the West, beyond the Appalachian Mountains…* The Erie Canal, financed entirely by the state of New York, would connect the ocean port of New York City to the Lake Erie port of Buffalo via the Hudson River, opening travel to the Michigan Territory, which at that time included Wisconsin. By the time of the canal's *completion in 1825*, New York was the largest city in the country. On one day in 1824, *324 ships* were counted in New York Harbor."[19]

---

[17]   Author, *Brookfield: A Fine and Fertile Land—An Early History of Brookfield Township, Waukesha County, Wisconsin* (Collierville, TN: InstantPublisher.com, 2007), vol. 1, p. 61.

[18]   https://upload.wikimedia.org/wikipedia/commons/thumb/0/05/Erie-canal_1840_map.jpg/220px-Erie-canal_1840_map.jpg

[19]   Martha Bergland & Paul G. Hayes. *Studying Wisconsin: The Life of Increase Lapham, Early Chronicler of Plants, Rocks, Rivers, Mounds and All Things Wisconsin* (Madison, WI.: Wisconsin Historical Society Press, 2014), pp. 14 & 15.

A CANAL BOAT ON THE ERIE CANAL

From Norway to Wisconsin on the Erie Canal:

"*Martin Ulvestad was a Norwegian born, American historian and author* whose writings focused on Norwegian-American immigration. He was a pioneer in documenting the early history of Norwegian settlers in America. compiled the *"Norwegian-American Pioneer Stories"* by sending out 163,000 small books and pamphlets along with 450,000 circulars and forms to the early immigrants and their families. The compilations were originally published in 1907 and 1913 in a Gothic script called 1883 Fraktur. *One form went to Dr. J. S. Johnson of Rock County, Wisconsin, who wrote about his grandfather's journey from Norway. After a sixteen-week voyage he arrived in New York*."[20]

View of Erie Canal by John William Hill, 1829. (Watercolor on paper.)[21]

His grandson writes:

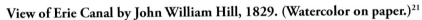

"At the end was New York, where they waited again for a couple of days for the steamship to get ready to go up the Hudson River to Troy, New York, where the Erie Canal had its start. *Arriving there, the chests were transferred onto the canal boat with its horse teams as power, and then began its furious speed of perhaps two and a half miles per hour, when it was not moored.* The baggage and passenger's place were on the deck and since *it became monotonous to sit there on a chest*, they often got off and walked ahead along the canal. When the boat caught up, they readied themselves on the first convenient bridge and then hopped down on the deck as the boat passed under." –**J. S. Johnson, a Norwegian emigrant of Rock County, Wisconsin.**[22]

[20]   https://en.wikipedia.org/wiki/Martin_Ulvestad

[21]   The Miriam and Ira D. Wallach Division of Art Prints and Photographs: Print Collection, The New York Public Library. "View on the Erie Canal." The New York Public Library Digital Collections, 1829. http://digitalcollections.nypl.org/items/510d47d9-7ba7-a3d9-e040-e00a18064a99

[22]   Martin Ulvestad, Translation. *Nordmændene i Amerika* (Minneapolis, MN.: History Forlog, 1907), pp. 19-21.

LARGE LOADS OF STEAMBOAT PASSENGERS JOURNEYED TO WISCONSIN (1839-1860)

STEAMSHIP EMPIRE [23]

GREAT LAKES PASSENGER STEAMBOAT EMPIRE. 1844.

"STEAMBOAT WISCONSIN"

The favorite Steamer *Wisconsin, Capt. SQUIERS*, came into port Saturday morning with one of the largest loads ever brought up the Lakes. She left Buffalo with eight hundred paid passengers, to say nothing of children, and about 200 tons of merchandize. *Of this large load, over 300 passengers and 130 tons of merchandize were landed at Milwaukie. A friend, who came up in the Wisconsin, speaks in high terms of the boat and her popular commander, Capt. SQUIER, and mentioned to us as a specimen of "Life on the Lakes," that on one evening there was a Cotillion in the after cabin, a prayer meeting amidships, and a political gathering forward and a euchre party in the saloon, all in full blast at the same time.* [*Milwaukee Sentinel* May 25, 1846]

The Largest Vessel:

"*The second steamboat for the Troy Line was Empire, Captain R. B. Macey, built in 1843.* The owners feared that travelers would mistake the boat for an Albany liner and the paddle boxes were lettered *"Empire of Troy."* Empire was then the largest vessel in the world, 936 tons, 307 feet length, 30 feet beam and 9 feet depth of hold. W. A. Lighthall built the two inclined beam engines, with cylinders 48 inches' diameter by 12 feet stroke. Empire was in collision with the schooner Mary Brown in Newburgh Bay (just upriver from New York city on the Hudson River), May 18, 1849, when twenty-four lives were lost."[24]

---

23   "Steamship Empire," Courtesy of Maritime History of the Great Lakes Maritime History of the Great Lakes
      Email walter@maritimehistoryofthegreatlakes.ca WWW address http://www.MaritimeHistoryOfTheGreatLakes.ca/

24   Fred Erving Dayton & John Lipton Lochead. *Steamboat Days* (New York: Frederick A. Stokes Company, 1925), p. 48.

Travelling on the Great Lakes:

Once at Buffalo, *immigrants, again, took one of several steamships* onto Lake Erie, through Lake Huron, and into Lake Michigan enroot to Milwaukee or other Wisconsin ports. *The 1913 shipwreck map below, illustrates how deadly travel across the Great Lakes could be.* (The distance over the Atlantic Ocean from Liverpool, England to New York, New York is 2,872.08 nautical miles. The distance over the Great Lakes from Buffalo, New York, to Milwaukee, Wisconsin is 840 nautical miles.)[25]

"Great Lakes 1913 Storm Shipwrecks Map"[26]

Great Lakes Steamboat Travel could be Dangerous

[1840's-1850's] "The **JOURNEY** by steamboat across the Great Lakes was not without its dangers. More men, women, and children were drowned, burned and killed by boiler explosions on their way to the lake settlements than were lost crossing the Atlantic. The losses in ships were heavy. The wooden vessels were powered by engines that exploded all too easily. They burned wood, which was stored on deck, ready to burst into flame when sparks fell among the logs. They were floating firetraps with no firefighting equipment."[27]

---

[25]   Nautical distances courtesy of the U.S. Geological Survey. Visit the USGS at https://usgs.gov

[26]   https://en.wikipedia.org/wiki/File:Great_Lakes_1913_Storm_Shipwrecks.png

[27]   Herbert W. Kuhm, *Historical Messenger of the Milwaukee County Historical Society*, Milwaukee. v. 31, n. 4 Winter, 1975, pp. 111-112.

TENS OF THOUSANDS OF EASTERN U.S. & EUROPEAN IMMIGRANTS LANDED AT THE PORT OF MILWAUKEE (1840's -1860's)

This image of Milwaukee--illustrates a growing metropolis with stone & brick homes, buildings, churches, warehouses and a busy harbor in **1858**, *is in stark contrast to the writings of an **1843** visitor from Boston, Margaret Fuller,* who describes Milwaukee as a small village, with surroundings significantly more primitive than that shown in the below image. *Her focus is on the natural beauty of the location.* The excerpt below is taken from her personal journal describing what she saw during her short stay in Milwaukee. Among other items she recorded, was a colorful description of European immigrants coming ashore to take on the challenges of their new homes in Wisconsin.[28]

Bird's Eye View of Milwaukee[29]

[28]   Author briefly compares & contrasts Margaret Fuller's view of Milwaukee & "Bird's Eye View of Milwaukee"

[29]   Print: "Bird's-eye view of Milwaukee, Wisconsin in 1858," https://commons.wikimedia.org/wiki/File:Milwaukee_1858.jpg

RECALLS THE SIGHT OF THE "REFUGEES" ARRIVING AT MILWAUKEE.

(Summer, 1843) -- "We came to Milwaukie, where we passed a fortnight or more. This place is most beautifully situated. A little river, with romantic banks, passes up through the town. The bank of the lake here is a bold bluff, eighty feet in height…. Approaching the Milwaukie pier, the Great Lakes steamers made a bend, and seemed to do obeisance in the heavy style of some dowager duchess entering a circle she wishes to treat with especial respect. These boats come in and out every day *The TORRENT of emigration swells strongly toward this place* [Milwaukee] and still afford a cause for general excitement… the fine weather, the poor refugees arrive daily, in their national dresses, all travel-soiled and worn. *The night they pass in rude shanties, in a particular quarter of the town, then walk off into the country--the mothers carrying their infants, the fathers leading the little children by the hand, seeking a home where their hands may maintain them… Here, on the pier, I see disembarking the Germans, the Norwegians, the Swedes, the Swiss. Who knows how much of old legendary lore, of modern wonder, they have already planted amid the Wisconsin forests?* --**Margaret Fuller**[30]

The Milwaukee Pier (c. 1848)[31]

An H.W. Bleyer drawing of the old north pier landing at Milwaukee which ran down from Huron Street. Many European immigrants had their first good view of Milwaukee and Wiscosnin from this pier.

[30] Margaret Fuller, *Summer on the lakes, in 1843* . (Boston: Charles C. Little and James Brown; New York, Charles S. Francis and Company, 1844.) Available in digital form on the Library of Congress Web site, pp.68 & 70.

[31] Courtesy of Milwaukee Public Library

SETTLERS TO WISCONSIN FROM NEW YORK

Name: __Alexander Randall__--Birthplace: __Ames Montgomery County, New York__ (31 Oct 1819)–Spouse: __Mary C. Van Vechten/__ deceased (Mary's parents emigrated from the __Netherlands__.) --Residence in 1860: __Waukesha, Waukesha County, Wisconsin__ --Occupation: *attorney* –Residing in Household: *Isaac and Mary Sahn (of New York), Susan Van Vechten, Harriet Van Vechten,* __Mary Van Vechten__ *(of New York) and Mary Coleman (of Ireland).*
(Image and genealogy courtesy of Waukesha County Historical Society and Museum.)

Mary C. (Van Vechten) Randall (c. 1848)[32]

Utrecht, Holland:

"The name of Van Vechten is derived from the Dutch, signifying that those who bore that name and were met on their journeyings or located in other places than on the original estate, came "from the Vechet" river in Holland. Three centuries ago, or about 1600, the Van Vechtens resided in Vechten, province of Utrecht, Holland. For a century and a half prior to the American revolution the name was also very commonly spelled Van Veghten, and this form maybe seen signed on hundreds of the revolutionary records in the state of New York, and on any number of private documents, wills, deeds and family Bible records."[33]

She married a future Wisconsin governor:

"*Alexander Williams Randall was a lawyer, judge and politician from Wisconsin. He served as the sixth Governor of Wisconsin from 1858 until 1861.* He opened a law practice in Waukesha in 1840, where he became postmaster in 1845. Randall was a delegate to the state's first constitutional convention in 1846. There he successfully advocated for a resolution that would put the question of "Negro suffrage" to a statewide referendum. He was instrumental in raising and organizing *the first Wisconsin volunteer troops* for the Union Army during the American Civil War. Once war began Randall raised 18 regiments, 10 artillery batteries, and three cavalry units before leaving office, exceeding Wisconsin's quota by 3,232 men. *The Union Army created a military camp from the former state fairgrounds in Madison, Wisconsin, and named it "Camp Randall" after the governor.*"[34]

---

[32]   "Mary C. (Van Vechten) Randall (c. 1848)," People P-Q-R Box 6:8, Photography Collection, Research Center Library & Archive, Waukesha County Historical Society & Museum, Waukesha, Wisconsin.

[33]   https://en.wikipedia.org/wiki/Utrecht Hudson-Mohawk Genealogical and Family Memoirs, ed. Cuyler Reynolds (New York: Lewis Publishing Company, 1911), v. 1, pp. 202-205.

[34]   https://en.wikipedia.org/wiki/Alexander_Randall

SETTLERS TO WISCONSIN FROM NEW YORK

Name: **_John Dodge_**— Birthplace: **Andover Township, Windsor County, Vermont** (10, Sept. 1813) –Spouse:
Dorothy C. Pierce—Birthplace: **Andover Township, Windsor County, Vermont** (1819)— Residence in 1850:
Vernon Township, Waukesha County—Occupation: farmer--Children: none.
(Image and genealogy courtesy of Waukesha County Historical Society and Museum)[35]

John and Dorothy Dodge (c. 1848) [36]

Emigration west from Vermont:

"_The 1830s and 1840s saw the first widespread 'western fever' in Vermont and New Hampshire. Emigrants began moving to southern Michigan, northern Illinois, and southeastern Wisconsin._ While some Vermont and New Hampshire farmers prospered, the sheep and wool boom was short-lived, and its longer-term consequences were damaging. Environmental degradation, primarily deforestation, and the collapse of the local industry in the 1840s because of cheaper western wool and the end of the tariff, both accelerated westward migration from the region. While fluctuating land values and the difficulties of making a living at farming pushed people to leave, the lure of better opportunities out west pulled people from Vermont."[37]

Earliest immigrants to Vernon Township:

"In 1836, in company with _Orien B. Haseltine, Curtiss B. Haseltine and Prucius Putnam, John Dodge, of Windsor County, Vermont_, immigrated to the Territory of Wisconsin. _They were the first white men in Vernon Township._ His first house was built of logs; in 1851, he built a more comfortable stone house... Though they had no children their house was always open to the young people of the vicinity."[38]

---

35   *Federal Manuscript Sch*edule, Population, Agricultural and Manufacturing Schedules for Waukesha County, Town of Vernon, 1850.

36   John & Dorothy Dodge c. 1848, People C-D-E Box 2:8, Photography Collection, Research Center Library & Archive, Waukesha County Historical Society & Museum, Waukesha, Wisconsin.

37   Vermont Learning Collaborative, flow@learningcollaborative.org

38   John & Dorothy Dodge Family c. 1848, Pioneer Notebook Collection, Research Center Library & Archive, Waukesha County Historical Society & Museum, Waukesha, Wisconsin.

Milwaukee & Watertown Railroad Directors & Contractors (c. 1853)[39]

RAILROAD CREWS FACED POOR WORKING CONDITIONS

"Little documentation has been recorded regarding the immigrant workers who's sweat and toil literally made the Milwaukee & Mississippi Railroad as well as the Milwaukee & Watertown Railroad a reality. In Wisconsin, during the start of the 1850s, there was little legislation in place to support workers. *There were no labor unions organized to protect the rights of railroad laborers. If a worker became injured or sick, he often lost his position, and was left to his own devises to care for himself. The earliest workers on Wisconsin's railroads were young, unmarried Irishmen, followed quickly by young, unmarried Germans.* In both cases, the railroad contractors became negligent in paying their salaries. Laborers who protested were easily replaced by tapping into the constant flow of new immigrants who continued to arrive into the state. These men were young Europeans looking wide-eyed at Wisconsin as a place to start a new life. *For most of them, their initial employment in Wisconsin appears to have been a discouraging and miserable experience.*"[40]

RIOT ON THE
MILWAUKEE & WATERTOWN R.R.

A disturbance, a riot, took place on the section of this road north of the Forest House (on the Milwaukee and Watertown line), on Friday night. Many the hands were driven off by some of those who had, *on a previous occasion, some difficulty concerning their wages.* Sheriff Ellis and Deputy Inman were on their way yesterday morning, to arrest the ringleaders on a charge of riot.

[*Milwaukee Sentinel* Sept. 27, 1853]

[39]   Milwaukee & Watertown Railroad Directors c. 1853, Transportation, Photography Collection, Research Center Library & Archive, Waukesha County Historical Society & Museum, Waukesha, Wisconsin.

[40]   Author, *Brookfield: A Fine and Fertile Land*—vol. 1, p. 61.

SETTLERS TO WISCONSIN FROM MASSACHUSETTS & NEW YORK

Name: **George Ferry**– Birthplace: **Billerica, Middlesex County, Massachusetts** (25 Feb 1813) — Marriage: **Ruth Jane L Olds** (31 Oct. 1838) Spouse's Birthplace: **Brooklyn, Queens, New York** (1818) -- Residence in 1850: Oconomowoc Township, Waukesha County, Wisconsin—Occupation: *farmer*—Children: *Edward, Amos, Julia, Sarah Ann, Vine William, Mary C.*—George Ferry's death: Colby, Marathon County, Wisconsin. (18 Mar. 1884.) (Image and genealogy courtesy of Waukesha County Historical Society and Museum.)[41]

George & Ruth Ferry Family (c. 1853)[42]

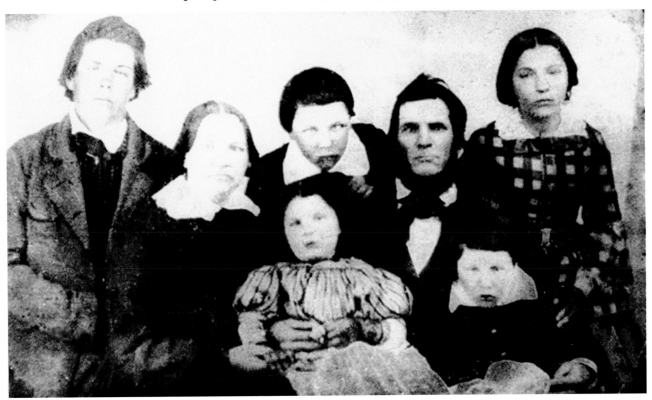

IMMIGRANTS.

Are flowing into Wisconsin beyond all former example. During our sojourn here last summer, great numbers of visitors arrived; no considerable portion of whom, however, came for speculative enterprises, and departed before the season ended. *But those who came this year are generally bona fide "Settlers," prepared to cultivate the soil.*

[*Milwaukee Sentinel* June 27, 1837]

New York settlers arrive in large numbers:

"Thousands of New Yorkers and residents from other eastern states left their farms, along with their soil depleted farmlands after years of continuously planting wheat. Wheat was a good cash crop, but it depletes the soil rather rapidly. Tapping into Wisconsin's virgin & fertile soil, they had a new opportunity to grow large fields of wheat"[43]

---

41   *Federal Manuscript Schedule*, Population, Agricultural and Manufacturing Schedules for Waukesha County, Town of Oconomowoc, 1850.

42   George & Ruth Ferry Family c. 1853, Family Box 3:8, Photography Collection, Research Center Library & Archive, Waukesha County Historical Society & Museum, Waukesha, Wisconsin.

43   Author, *Brookfield: A Fine and Fertile Land, vol. 1*, footnote, p. 6.

IMMIGRANTS TO WISCONSIN FROM NEW YORK & MASSACHUSETTS

Name: **Jeremy Dickinson Warner**—place of birth: **Belchertown, Hampshire, Massachusetts**—Christening: Amherst, Massachusetts (23 May 1813) —spouse: **_Emily Rathbun_**— born: **Aurelius, Cayuga County, New York** (4 May 1841)—Residence in 1850: **Brookfield Township, Waukesha County, Wisconsin**—Occupation: farmer-- Residence in 1880: **Lewiston, Lewis County, Missouri.** —Children: _Frederick, Theodore, Theodore, Charles, Frederick, B.F., George, Sarah & Augusta._ Death: **Salem Township, Lewis County, Missouri.**

(Image and genealogy courtesy of Merrialyce von Krosigk Blanchard of Salem, Oregon.)[44]

Emily Rathbun (c. 1854)[45]

The Yankee element established themselves early:

"_Because they arrived first and had a strong sense of community and mission, Yankees were able to transplant New England institutions, values, and mores._ They established a public culture that emphasized the work ethic, the sanctity of private property, individual responsibility, faith in residential and social mobility, practicality, piety, public order and decorum, reverence for public education, activists, honest, and frugal government, town meeting democracy, and he believed that there was a public interest that transcends particular and stick ambitions by the conditions of frontier life. Regarding themselves as the elect and just in a world rife with sin, air, and corruption, they felt a strong moral obligation to define and enforce standards of community and personal behavior...."[46]

Women's Clothing Styles of the 1850's:

"Emily wears her hair parted in the front & combed to the side with some curling. She is a very beautiful young lady, dressed, not in high fashion, but as someone of modest means. She wears I tight collar around her neck, bowed at the front. During this era many area families purchased home sewing machines from which they could pattern and sow their own family's clothing. Emily likely sowed her dresses while purchasing necessary accessories either threw a mail order catalogue or through an area retailer." **_Joan Severa, "19th Century Clothing & Fashion"_**[47]

---

[44]   _Federal Manuscript Schedule_, Population, Agricultural and Manufacturing Schedules for Waukesha County, Town of Brookfield, 1850.

[45]   Photograph courtesy of Merrialyce von Krosigk Blanchard of Salem, Oregon, e-mail to author, July 9th , 2017.

[46]   John D. Buenker. _The History of Wisconsin, Volume 4: The Progressive Era, 1893–1914_ (Madison: Wisconsin Historical Society Press, 1998), p. 48.

[47]   Joan Severa, of Madison, Wisconsin, e-mail to author, March 16, 2010.

IMMIGRANTS TO WISCONSIN FROM NEW YORK

Name: **Nelson Page Hawks**– Birthplace: **Belchertown, Hampshire, Massachusetts** (13 Mar 1803) —Spouse: **Hannah Crocker**— Birthplace: **Union, Broome County, New York** (22 Feb 1831)—Occupation: proprietor of the "Delafield House"–Residence in 1850: **Village of Delafield, Delafield Township, Waukesha County, Wisconsin**—**Occupation**: *hotel & saw mill*--Children: *Nelson Crocker, **Frances**, Ammi, Parmelia Dubois (Hawks) Sperry*. Death: Delafield, Wisconsin (21 June 1863).
(Image, genealogy, and history courtesy of Hawks Inn Historical Society, Delafield, Wisconsin.)[48]

Frances Hawks (c. 1854)[49]

Nelson Hawks opens an Inn at Delafield:

To the right, stands daughter, Frances Hawks, posing inside her father's inn-- the "Delafield House." Describing the earliest years of the inn, brother Nelson Crocker, in his "scrapbook," wrote: "About 1846 father began building the 'Delafield House' (Hawks Inn) an immense business was done from the start. Emigration was like a tidal wave and the new hotel could not handle all. Our house was packet always and the overflow had to camp on the roadside. People were glad to sleep in the halls and the barn… I can remember those lively days, the jolly teamsters and their songs… *Lead ore was hauled by wagon across the state from Mineral Point to Milwauke*e and our place being a day's journey from Milwaukee and noted for good grub and beds… *Stages came daily, the real articles as you see it in the pictures and the old-time stage driver, just as Mark Twain describes him,* was a great man with lots on his mind. I can sometimes fancy I hear the rumble of the heavy wheels, the sound of his horn as he crested the hill near the village, and the crack of his long whip."—*from the scrapbook of Nelson Crocker Hawks*[50]

Women's Clothing Styles of the 1850's:

"*Frances Hawks wears a very lovely full-length cloak, with the long, wide sleeve of the mid-'50s.* Her bonnet is early '50s, being set far back on the head, and worn very open." **--Joan Severa, "19th Century Clothing & Fashion"**[51]

48   *Federal Manuscript Schedule*, Population, Agricultural and Manufacturing Schedules for Waukesha County, Town of Delafield, 1850.
49   Photograph courtesy of Hawks Inn Historical Society, Delafield, Wisconsin, Germaine Hillmer, e-mail message to author, Dec. 21, 2016.
50   Germaine Hillmer of Hawks Inn Historical Society, e-mail message to author, Jun 13, 2016.
51   Joan Severa of Madison, Wisconsin, e-mail to author, Jan 28, 2010.

IMMIGRANTS TO WISCONSIN FROM IRELAND

Name: **John Faulkner** – Birthplace: **Ireland** (c. 1770)—Spouse: *Mary McCormick* —Birthplace: **Ireland** (c. 1775) —Son: **Thomas Faulkner Jr.**— Birthplace: **Tyrone County, Ireland** (c. 1811) —Married: **Nancy Cheeny**--Place of birth: **New York State**—Parents: **Rufus & Lydia Cheeny**—both of **New Hampshire** –Thomas & Nancy Faulkner's residence in 1860: Prospect Hill, New Berlin Township, Waukesha County, Wisconsin—Occupation: *farmer*–Children: *Viola, Clara & Rufus*—Nancy's parents: *Rufus & Lydia Cheeny*—both of Ireland.
(Image and genealogy courtesy of Cathryn Larsen of Kenosha, Wisconsin.)[52]

Mary (McCormick) Faulkner (c. 1855) [53]

The Irish Potato Blight:

"The Great Famine or the Great Hunger (Irish: An Gorta Mór or An Drochshaol) is the name given to the famine in Ireland between 1845 and 1852. Outside Ireland, it is usually called the Irish Potato Famine. The famine was caused by the blight, "a fungus-like organism which quickly destroyed the potatoes in Ireland, and throughout Europe. The effect was particularly severe in Ireland because potatoes were the main source of food for most Irish people at the time… It is believed that between 500,000 and more than one million people died in the three years from 1846 to 1849 because of hunger or disease. Another million became refugees because of the famine. Many people who left Ireland moved to Great Britain, the United States, Canada and Australia."[54]

To the Committee of the Irish Relief Fund, Milwaukee.

GENTLEMEN: —*I send by bearer for the benefit of Ireland 12 barrels of Flour and 2 barrels of Pork.* You will dispose of them as you see fit. Enclosed is a letter mentioning where some friends would like it to go. Yours, in great haste, E. POTTER. *In behalf of the Committee of Irish Relief Fund in Prairieville (Waukesha).* {The Flour and Pork, accompanying the above, were deposited in DOUSMAN'S Warehouse and will be shipped for their destination the first opportunity.} —*ED. SENTINEL & GAZETTE.*
[*Milwaukee Sentinel* June 22, 1847][55]

---

[52] *Federal Manuscript Schedule*, Population, Agricultural and Manufacturing Schedules for Waukesha County, Town of New Berlin, 1860.

[53] Photograph courtesy of Cathryn Larsen, of Kenosha, Wisconsin, *LinkedIn*, e-mail message to author, Mar 25, 2011.

[54] https://simple.wikipedia.org/wiki/Irish_Potato_Famine

[55] An apparent noble effort from the group from Prairieville (Waukesha) but, in reality, their contribution would not even have meant a pittance in support the massive suffering then going on in Ireland.

IMMIGRANTS TO WISCONSIN FROM NEW YORK AND VERMONT

Name: ___Reuben W. Gibson___—Birthplace: __New York State__—Spouse: __Susan T.__ (1926)—Birthplace: __Vermont__
Residence in 1860: Mukwonago, Mukwonago Township, Waukesha County, Wisconsin---Occupation: *landlord*—
"Mukwonago House" (1855)—daughter: *Lillie.*
(Image and genealogy courtesy of the Waukesha County Historical Society and Museum.)[56]

Reuben W. Gibson (c. 1856)[57]

The "Know Nothing" Movement:

Wisconsin historian Richard Current wrote, "*In 1855, an English-language newspaper appeared that persistently attacked not only the Catholic faith but also its freethinking critics and indeed all foreigners.* This was the ***Milwaukee Daily American,*** the voice of Wisconsin's so-called "Know Nothings," members of an organization so secret they pretended in the presence of outsiders to know nothing about it… Besides taking an oath of secrecy, they had to swear that they were American born of Protestant parents or were American-born and 'reared under Protestant influence,' and that since they were 'In favor of Americans ruling America,' they would oppose anyone of foreign birth or of the Catholic faith running for office."[58]

KNOW NOTHING MEETING!

The Committee of "Know-Nothings" will hold their first annual meeting at the "Mukwonago Grist Mill" on the 1st day of April next, at 11 o'clock A.M. *A general attendance of the Committee is requested.*--TOMUEL REYNOLDS. *Madison, Feb. 5th, 1855*
[*Waukesha Plaindealer* Feb. 7, 1855][59]

56   *Federal Manuscript Schedule*, Population, Agricultural and Manufacturing Schedules for Waukesha County, Town of Mukwonago, 1860.

57   Rueben Gibson, c. 1856, People F-G-H Box 3:8, Photography Collection, Research Center Library & Archive, Waukesha County Historical Society & Museum, Waukesha, Wisconsin.

58   Richard Current, *History of Wisconsin*, v. 2. *the Civil War Era, 1848-1873* (Madison: Wisconsin Historical Society Press, 1976), pp.144.

59   This is not to imply that Reuben W. Gibson was a "Know Nothing." On the other hand, there apparently existed a fairly strong anti-Catholic faction in Mukwonago during this period.

IMMIGRANTS TO WISCONSIN FROM NEW YORK & IRELAND

Name: **Beriah Brown** – Birthplace: **Canandaigua, Ontario County, New York** (1815) —Occupation: *printer* and *publisher* —Spouse: **Jane "Jeanie" McHugh**—Birthplace: **Ireland** (c.1829)– Residence in 1860: **Delafield Township, Waukesha County**–Children: *Elizabeth, Edward,* and *William.*

(Image and genealogy courtesy of Hawks Inn Historical Society.)[60]

Beriah Brown (1856)[61]

Settlers sweep into western New York:

(Beriah Brown was born on Jan. 23, 1815, in Canandaigua, Ontario County, New York.) "The Iroquois fled to Fort Niagara as refugees, and many died that winter of starvation."[62] "*Land-hungry settlers from New England swept into upstate and western New York after the Revolution, as nearly five million acres of new lands were available for purchase since the Iroquois were forced to cede most of their territories to the United States.* Four tribes had allied with the British and were mostly resettled in Canada: the Mohawk, Onondaga, Seneca and Cayuga."[63]

A Newspaper Editor:

"*Beriah Brown* was a newspaper publisher by trade and, later, a member of the first Board of Regents of the University of Wisconsin–Madison. *In 1860, he established the Daily People's Press in Milwaukee, and continued as editor when, after a few months, it was consolidated with the News as the 'Daily People's Press and News'.*"[64]

Men's Clothing Styles of the 1850's:

"*This is a daguerreotype or an Ambrotype of Beriah Brown.* It dates to before 1859 when coat styles changed to a very loose-sleeved style. He wears a somewhat outdated double-breasted jacket with an upright collar, and a scarf bowed at the front. — still, at his age, he might have worn his good old coat well into the 1860's." --*Joan Severa, "19th Century Clothing & Fashion."*[65]

[60] *Federal Manuscript Schedule*, Population, Agricultural and Manufacturing Schedules for Waukesha County, Town of Delafield, 1860.

[61] Photograph courtesy of Hawks Inn Historical Society, Delafield, Wisconsin, Germaine Hillmer, e-mail message to author, Dec. 21, 2016.

[62] https://en.wikipedia.org/wiki/Canandaigua_(city),_New_York

[63] https://en.wikipedia.org/wiki/Ontario_County,_New_York

[64] https://en.wikipedia.org/wiki/Beriah_Brown

[65] Joan Severa, of Madison, WI., e-mail message to author, Feb 7, 2010.

IMMIGRANTS TO WISCONSIN FROM NEW YORK STATE

Name: **_August Blodgett_**—Birthplace: **Buffalo, New York** (1787) — Spouse: **Lucy Pratt**—Birthplace: **New York State** (1791) —Year of immigration: 1843—Residence in 1860: **Brookfield Township, Waukesha County, Wisconsin**—Occupation: *farmer* and *miller*–Children: *Chester.* Death of *August Blodgett*: (16 May 1861) (Image and genealogy courtesy of Isobel Wray of Dousman, Wisconsin)[66]

August Blodgett (c. 1858)[67]

MR. LACHER'S OBSERVATIONS

Compares Names of Towns in New York With Those in Wisconsin.

J.H.A. Lacher, writing for the *Waterford Post*, refers to the repetitions found in names of towns in New York compared with those of southeastern Wisconsin: One of our salesmen having suddenly died, I am now in western New York looking for a man to replace him. Familiar with the nomenclature of southern Wisconsin whenever I visit this beautiful region, I am struck with the similarity of the names of both sections. _This similarity is so striking, that if we had no other evidence, it would be sufficient to prove that a large proportion of the early settlers of Wisconsin hailed from western New York State._ Clustered together in Wayne Co., just east of Rochester, we find **Walworth Township, Walworth and West Walworth, Lyons, Springfield, Lisbon & Palmyra**. In the immediate vicinity of adjacent counties, we are greeted by such names a **Caledonia, Bristol, Vienna, East and West Bloomfield, Como, Geneva, Genesee, Darien, Lima, Mapleton, LeRoy, Byron**. Extending our circle to embrace a few more counties to the east, west and south, these names are disclosed: **Vernon, Eagle, Delavan, Clinton, Fulton, Hartland, Brookfield, New Berlin, Deerfield, Utica, Lodi, Cazenovia, Avoca, Barneveld, Belmont, Ithaca, Richfield, Lebanon, Mayville, Oakfield, Eden, Fredonia, New Fane, Randolph, Omro, Mt. Morris, Westfield, Medina and Friendship**. As we travel eastward, we discover **Arena, Cooperstown, Granville, Albany, Hartford, Hebron, Rome, Milton, Salem, Sharon, Richmond, Sullivan, Kingstown, Windsor, Union Grove, Troy, Watertown, Jefferson County**. A man from southern Wisconsin must surely feel at home in these parts, for not only the names, but the beautiful lakes and fertile soil remind him of his domicile in the west. While admiring the endless orchards and vineyards that cover the plains and overlook the lakes, his mind must wander back to the hardy pioneer who arrived hence a few generations ago to build-up the Badger state.

[*Waukesha Freeman* Nov. 7, 1907]

---

[66] *Federal Manuscript Schedule*, Population, Agricultural and Manufacturing Schedules for Waukesha County, Town of Brookfield, 1860. J.H.A Lacher was Waukesha County's first historian, organized the Waukesha County Museum, as well as being appointed vice-president of the Wisconsin Historical Society.

[67] Photograph courtesy of Isobel Wray, of Dousman, Wisconsin, home visit with author, Oct 13, 2009.

IMMIGRANTS TO WISCONSIN FROM NEW YORK STATE

Name: **August Blodgett**—Birthplace: **Buffalo, New York** (1787) — Spouse: ***Lucy (Pratt) Blodgett***—Birthplace: **New York State** (1791) —Year of immigration: 1843—Residence in 1860: **Brookfield Township, Waukesha County**— Occupation: *farmer* & *miller*–Children: ***Chester***—Death of *Lucy Blodgett*—**Wauwatosa, Wisconsin** (19 Jan 1868) (Image and genealogy courtesy of Isobel Wray of Dousman, Wisconsin)[68]

Lucy Blodgett (c. 1858)[69]

A SUGARING PARTY

Young People Braved the Worst Storm of Winter Visiting Blodgett's Sugar Bush.

Blodgett, March 25. —Last Monday night, perhaps the most boisterous and uncomfortable night of the whole season, witnessed the appearance here in a jolly party of young ladies and gentlemen who came by bus from Waukesha and lighted up the gloom of Blodgett's sugar bush, which was in fact a gloomy place that night save for the good cheer which the visitors brought. The party consisting of Misses Florence Blair, Harriet Sleep, Martha Horning, Julia Sawyer, Henry Lockney & Prof. Nave. On the arrival at the entrance to the sugar bush the darkness and wind which swayed the great trees to the point of almost breaking, made the journey through the woods to the sugaring camp a dangerous undertaking. *However, reluctantly consenting to go to the home of* **Chester A. Blodgett**. *A jollier party has not often enjoyed the hospitality of the Blodgett home, which is noted for good cheer*.

[*Waukesha Freeman* March 26, 1903]

Women's Clothing Styles of the 1850's:

"Lucy Blodgett is dressed conservatively, with her severe hair part. She is wearing a basic bonnet of polished cotton with a soft crown and loose-fitting brim. It ties under the chin, with two rather wide ribbons drooping down from her chin... *She wears a patterned wrap. Her dress is wide at the sleeves and tight at the wrists. This is a no-frills 1850s look, one that would be standard for a middle-aged lady.*" --**Joan Severa**, *"19ʰ Century Clothing Style"*[70]

---

68   *Federal Manuscript Schedule*, Population, Agricultural and Manufacturing Schedules for Waukesha County, Town of Brookfield, 1860.

69   Photograph courtesy of Isobel Wray of Dousman, Wisconsin, home visit with author, Oct 13, 2009.

70   Joan Severa, Madison, Wisconsin, e-mail to author, Feb 7, 2010

IMMIGRANTS TO WISCONSIN FROM NEW YORK STATE

Name: **N. P. Hawks**—Birthplace: <u>**Manlius, Onondaga Co., New York**</u>, March (18 Mar 1803) —Spouse: **Hannah Crocker**—Birthplace: <u>**Union, Broome County, New York**</u> (22 Feb 1831) -- Residence in 1850: <u>Delafield, Waukesha County, Wisconsin</u> —Occupation: *–manager of "Delafield House" tavern and a miller*—Children: *Ammi, Nelson C. & Frances.* Boarders: *J. Sperry (born in New York)*— occupation: *physician*; ***Parmelia Bubois Sperry*** *(born in New York)* —*William Coleman (born in New York)*— occupation: *farmer*; *Morgan, (born in New York)*—occupation: *teacher*; *G. C. Hewit (born in New York)*—occupation: *sawyer*; *Henry Huston (born in Vermont)*—occupation: *blacksmith*; *N. Rockwell (born in Canada)*—occupation: *clerk, Maria Nielson (born in Norge), Wrena Johnson (born in Norge),* and *Granville Coleman*—occupation: *laborer.*
(Image and genealogy courtesy of Hawks Inn Historical Society, Delafield, Wisconsin)[71]

Parmelia DuBois (Hawks) Sperry (c. 1858)[72]

"Grand suppers" were prepared at the Delafield House:

"<u>*(In)1846, emigration from the East and from European countries was in full swing and our hotel was crowded all the time.*</u> We had five girls in the kitchen, three hired men around the house besides the mill and farm hands. Wagon loads of travelers came in profusion and many had to camp on the floor anywhere. Tables were set and reset till late at night. I wonder how dear mother stood the strain. And oh, those grand suppers how mother and <u>*Parmelia used to prepare for those events-gold and silver cakes, Dr. B's loaf, jelly layer, cakes, sugar kisses, etc.*</u> Sometimes the refreshments took the form of oyster suppers. The oysters came from Baltimore in cans and little kegs." --***Nelson C. Hawks letters to his sister Frances (Fannie).***[73]

Women's Clothing Styles of the 1850's:

"<u>*Young Parmelia wears dark curls falling in front of her ears and a hairdo that is pulled tightly back and up behind into a puff or twist, or even a circle of braids.*</u> Her corset is the long-waisted "Elizabethan" style fashion from the mid-forties into the early fifties; it was replaced by a shorter, more curvaceous corset in 1853. The bottom line of the long corset was always set off by a fancy ribbon pinned tight to the low waistline with a brooch. Other ribbons, not usually matching, were worn at the neck, with another brooch." -- ***Joan Severa, 19ᵗʰ Century Clothing Styles.***[74]

71 *Federal Manuscript Schedule*, Population, Agricultural and Manufacturing Schedules for Waukesha County, Town of Delafield, 1860.

72 Photograph courtesy of Hawks Inn Historical Society, Delafield, Wisconsin, Germaine Hillmer, e-mail to author, Dec. 21, 2016.

73 Germaine Hillmer, Hawks Inn Historical Society, e-mail to author, Jun 13, 2016.

74 Joan Severa, Madison, WI., e-mail to author, Jan 23, 2010.

IMMIGRANTS TO WISCONSIN FROM NEW YORK STATE

Name: **_Nelson Page Hawks_**– Birthplace: **Manlius, Onondaga County, New York** (18 Mar 1803) —Spouse: **Hannah Crocker**— Birthplace: **Union, Broome County, New York** (22 Feb 1831)— Residence in 1850: Village of Delafield, Delafield Township, Waukesha County, Wisconsin—Occupation: *hotel & saw mill*--Children: *Nelson Crocker, Frances, Ammi, Parmelia Dubois (Hawks) Sperry. Nelson Page Hawks'* Death: Delafield, Wisconsin (21 June 1863).   (Image, genealogy, and history courtesy of Hawks Inn Historical Society, Delafield, Wisconsin.)[75]

Nelson Paige Hawks (c. 1860)[76]

From New York State to Wisconsin:

"My father, Nelson Page Hawks, was born in Manlius, Onondaga Co., New York, March 18, 1803. His father was a poor man and father left home at an early age to shift for himself. _He was apprenticed to learn the cabinetmaker's trade and was a good mechanic._ When he grew up, he went into general merchandize with Mr. Dunn an also ran a line of stages from Penn Yan, New York to Geneva, New York. While in Binghamton, New York he met our mother, Hannah (Crocker). They were married on February 2, 1830 and went to Elmira, New York where he kept a hotel and where my sister Parmelia was born, 1832. My brother Ammi was born in Binghamton, New York. _Father was the inventor of the first shingle-making machine in 1836_ and I have the old deed on parchment signed by Andrew Jackson"-- *From the Journal of Nelson Crocker Hawk's*[77]

Boats ran on the Great Lakes to Chicago:

"_Now many families of the New England States, New York & Pennsylvania were immigrating westward to Wisconsin, Illinois & Michigan. Wisconsin was a territory and very wild and new. A few boats ran on the Great Lakes from Buffalo, New York to Chicago but there were no railroads_. Deciding to 'Go West' and determining on the Rock River as his future home, father fitted up for the journey with a splendid span of matching horses and strong wagon and in the early spring of 1837 started from Binghamton, New York … The journey was along the southern borders of Lake Erie and Lake Michigan passing through Ohio and Indiana to Chicago and from there through southern Wisconsin and ending in Aztalan. Nelson Hawks sold his land in Atzalan and relocated in Milwaukee in about 1840 and within 2 or 3 years moved again. This time to Delafield, their permanent home." -- *From the Journal of Nelson Crocker Hawk's*[78]

[75]   *Federal Manuscript Schedule*, Population, Agricultural and Manufacturing Schedules for Waukesha County, Town of Delafield, 1850.

[76]   Photograph courtesy of Hawks Inn Historical Society, Delafield, Wisconsin, Germaine Hillmer, e-mail to author, Dec. 21, 2016.

[77]   Germaine Hillmer, Hawks Inn Historical Society, e-mail to author, Jun 13, 2016.

[78]   Germaine Hillmer, Hawks Inn Historical Society, e-mail to author, Jun 13, 2016.

IMMIGRANTS TO WISCONSIN FROM VERMONT & HOLLAND

Name: **Augustus Bixby**– Birthplace: <u>**Essex, Chittenden County, Vermont**</u> (28 Mar 1822)— Second Spouse: <u>*Maria Amelia Boeijink*</u>—Birthplace: <u>Holland</u> (4 Apr 1828)—Residence in 1860: <u>Ottawa Township, Waukesha County.</u>—Occupation: farmer–Children: *John, Maria, Benjamin David, James, George, Marion, Norman, Claude & Augustus.* Augustus Bixby Death: Hudson, <u>St. Croix County, Wisconsin</u> (28 Sept 1899).

(Image and genealogy courtesy of Sue Hornbeck Bixby of Springport, Jackson, Michigan)[79]

Maria Amelia (Boeijink) Bixby (c. 1860)[80]

"A major center of Dutch Immigration:"

"Between 1840 and 1890, Wisconsin was a major center of Dutch immigration. Dutch immigrants to Wisconsin were easily divided into two basic groups based on religious affiliation--Protestants and Catholics. The Protestants were the first to arrive in Wisconsin and settled mainly in Sheboygan, Fond du Lac, Columbia and La Crosse Counties. The Catholics preferred the Fox River Valley. *The first general influx of Dutch began in 1844 with the* **Seceders:** *Dutch who had broken from the Reformed Church of the Netherlands and came to Wisconsin seeking religious freedom.* Beginning in 1848, 40,000 Catholic Dutch came to Wisconsin. Most Dutch immigrants to the Fox River Valley followed the Erie Canal-Great Lakes route, landing in Green Bay where many chose to remain."[81]

Dutch immigrants settle in Milwaukee:

"Dutch emigration to Wisconsin began in earnest in the 1840's. Three main incentives for these families to leave their homeland were economic conditions, the potato famine and religious persecution. Large numbers of Dutch immigrants were Protestant Seceders seeking religious freedom after having broken from the state controlled Reformed Church of the Netherlands. *Significant numbers of these Dutch immigrants began arriving in Milwaukee as early as the mid-1840s and 1850s, most settling in cabins on the hillside northwest of the flats along the Milwaukee River. The neighborhood that grew here, was fondly referred to as Hollandsche berg or "Dutch Hill" by the early settlers. Dutch Hill was home to at least three congregations established to administer to the religious welfare of the Hollanders.* Gijbert Van Steenwijk wrote back to friends in the Netherlands stating that there were now about 700 Dutch living in the Milwaukee area. Dutch settlement in Milwaukee continued to increase up to the 1890s."[82]

Dutch settlements throughout Wisconsin:

(Maria Boijink's family emigrated from Holland to the United States during the 1840's. Maria married Augustus Bixby, and they settled in the town of Ottawa, Waukesha County.)[83] "Larger numbers of Hollanders settled permanently in Sheboygan, Fond du Lac, Columbia and La Crosse Counties. *Dating to as late as the early 1890s, Wisconsin remained home to the 3rd largest Dutch population in the U.S.*"[84]

---

79   *Federal Manuscript Schedule*, Population, Agricultural and Manufacturing Schedules for Waukesha County, Town of Ottawa, 1860.

80   Photograph courtesy of Sue Hornbeck Bixby of Troy, Michigan, e-mail to author, Apr. 23, 2010.

81   "Historical Essay: Dutch in Wisconsin," Cultural Resource Study Units, Wisconsin Historical Society.

82   Megan Daniels, posted in: <u>Following the Plank Road</u> blog, "Hollandsche Berg: MKE'S Dutch settlement," 8 Oct 2012.

83   Sue Hornbeck Bixby, Troy, Michigan, e-mail to author, Apr. 23, 2010.

84   https://en.wikipedia.org/wiki/Dutch_Americans.

IMMIGRANTS TO WISCONSIN FROM RHINELAND/RHENISH PRUSSIA

Name: **Reiner Nettesheim** – Birthplace: **Müddersheim, Königreich Rhineland/ Rheinpreußen** (1797) — Spouse: **Sophia Fuss** —Birthplace— **Friesheim, Rhineland/ Rheinpreußen** – (*Möddersheim and Friesheim are 5-km distance from one another.*) Port of Emigration: *Antwerp, Belgium*—Port of Arrival: New York, 25, August 1848. Residence in 1860: Brookfield Township, Waukesha County.— Occupation: *farmer*–Children: *Walram, Conrad, Catherine & **Johann***.   (Image and genealogy courtesy of Gene Nettesheim of Boulder, Colorado.)[85]

Johann Joseph Nettesheim (c. 1862)[86]

Rheinländers Immigrate to Wisconsin:

"*During most of the 18th Century and into the 19th century, (the Nettesheim family resided in the village of Müddersheim, Rhineland.) like many other families from the Rhineland, the Nettesheims were induced to leave their homes for religious, economic and political reasons.*"[87] "In 1848, the Reiner Nettesheim family set sail for America on the packet ship "*Edwina.*" The Nettesheims, Reiner age 51, Anna Sophia (Fuss) Nettesheim age 46, Conrad age 12, Gertrude age 10, "Johann Joseph" age 5 and Sophia's brother, John Fuss age 48, embarked at Antwerp, Belgium July 19, 1848 for the voyage to New York where they arrived on August 25, 1848. He initially labored as a wheelwright, but, in 1853, Reiner purchased his first 40 acres in the town of Brookfield and began in earnest to clear his land and plant wheat, along with various other crops."[88]

Many soldiers died of disease:

"Enlistment Card: occupation--farmer/Single/ blue eyes//hair & complexion light/ height 5'8'/ stocky build. Took part in the Battle of Helena, July 4, 1863. After a very bad *winter at Helena, Arkansas, Corporal Joseph Nettesheim came down with Typhoid Malaria fever, as so many others did, and died May 23, 1863*. He was first buried near Helena, Arkansas. After the war his body was moved to the Memphis National Cemetery, 3568 Townes Avenue, Memphis, Tennessee. It is said he was engaged to be married to Helena Schmitz, sister to Gene Nettesheim's Great Grandmother, Gertrude, before the war, but that she never did marry."[89]

[85]   *Federal Manuscript Schedule*, Population, Agricultural and Manufacturing Schedules for Waukesha County, Town of Brookfield, 1860.

[86]   Photograph courtesy of Gene M. Nettesheim of Boulder, Colorado—taken from Eugene Nettesheim *The Family Nettesheim* (Boulder, CL: self-published--limited edition, 1984), p. 28.

[87]   https://en.wikipedia.org/wiki/Rhineland

[88]   Nettesheim. *The Family Nettesheim*, p. 2 & 10.

[89]   Nettesheim. *The Family Nettesheim*, p. 2.

IMMIGRANTS TO WISCONSIN FROM SCOTLAND

Name: **John Watson**– Birthplace: **Perthshire, Scotland** (c. 1827) — Spouse: **Mary (Roger) Watson**—Birthplace—**Perthshire, Scotland** (c. 1832) --Residence in 1870: <u>Lisbon Township, Waukesha County, Wisconsin</u>—Occupation: *farmer*–Children: **John A.**, *James, Mary & Katie*. Also residing in this residence are--*Robert Macentine & Mary Rankin*. (Image and genealogy courtesy of Sussex-Lisbon Area Historical Society)[90]

John Watson (c. 1863)[91]

Immigrants from Scotland settle in the Town of Lisbon:

"(John Watson was born near Perthshire, Scotland on December 19, 1827.) John was the fourth of a family of six, born to Andrew and Catherine (Roger) Watson. <u>At age 14, John and an older brother, Gilbert, set sail for New York, embarking from Dundee, Scotland, aboard the sailing ship "Peruvian."</u> It took nine weeks to reach New York, leaving 12 May and arriving 4 July 1841. There were several other Scottish immigrants to the Lisbon area that shipped out with Watson, including nine-year-old Mary Roger (born 16 February 1832). Twelve years later John, 26, and Mary would marry, 15 December 1853. From New York City, the brothers, by way of the Hudson River and the Erie Canal, made their way to Buffalo, N. Y. where they began to work. <u>John worked for nearly two years at $4 a month to earn enough money to head for the newly opened Wisconsin Territory, arriving by steamer at Milwaukee in the fall of 1843.</u> The brothers came directly to Lisbon where they had relatives. When John arrived, he had $10 in his pocket, promptly lost that when he loaned it out and was not repaid. At 16 he started out his life here penniless…" --**Fred Keller** [92]

The Battle at Spanish Fort:

"John Watson and the 28th were assigned to take the massive Spanish Fort. Bombarded from land and sea, its Confederate defenders surrendered April 8 to the 28th's Company C under Capt. Thomas S. Stevens. The first to enter the Fort, the 28th went to assist the attack on Fort Blakely but marched up just as it was surrendering. <u>Shorn of its defenses, the Confederates began to abandon Mobile on April 12, and the Union forces, including the 28th, marched through Mobile to a holding area north of the city</u>. The capture of the Spanish Fort yielded 265 officers, 538 enlisted men, five mortars and 25 pieces of artillery. The capture of Fort Blakely took even more, including 2,400 prisoners." — **Fred Keller**   [*Living Sussex Sun* December 24, 2008]

---

[90]   *Federal Manuscript Census*, Manufacturing Schedules for Waukesha County, Town of Lisbon, 1870.

[91]   Photograph courtesy of Sussex-Lisbon Area Historical Society via Fred Keller, "The Great Civil War—Watson, Soldier and Town Chairman." *Landmark*. v. 32, n. 3, Autumn, 1989, p. 1.

[92]   Fred Keller, "The Great Civil War." *Landmark*., p. 2.

IMMIGRANTS TO WISCONSIN FROM NEW YORK STATE

Name: **Nelson Page Hawks**– Birthplace: **Manlius, Onondaga County, New York** (13 Mar 1803) —Spouse: **Hannah Crocker**— Birthplace: **Union, Broome County, New York** (22 Feb 1831) --Residence in 1850: Village of Delafield, Delafield Township, Waukesha County, Wisconsin—Occupation: *hotel & saw mill*--Children: *Nelson Crocker, Frances,* **Ammi** *& Parmelia Dubois (Hawks) Sperry.* Nelson Hawk's Death: Delafield, Wisconsin (21 June 1863).   (Image, genealogy, and history courtesy of Hawks Inn Historical Society, Delafield, Wisconsin.)[93]

Ammi Doubleday Hawks (c. 1863)[94]

Battle at Helena, Arkansas:

(On July 4, 1863, Ammi Hawks, Co. "C", served as quartermaster during the battle at Helena.) "The greater part stationed on a main road at Helena, Arkansas, near battery "B", where the 28th Wisconsin expected one attack would be made. It was a dark foggy morning, and it was some time before the enemy could be seen. *They had not gone many yards before the Federal's Fort Curtis opened on the Confederates with grape shot and mowed swaths in their ranks,* and they scattered in all directions to get out of the range of the guns. A large number crawled under a church nearby, and many got into hollow out of range. A portion of the 28th Regiment then gathered up one thousand prisoners. *They marched them to the (Mississippi) river and put them on two transports and sent them up the river while the battle was still going on*."[95]

Ammi Hawks' "Housewife":

"Ammi Hawks was a quartermaster with the 28th Wisconsin Regiment during the Civil War and carried a "Housewife" with him in service. *Popularly carried by soldiers during the Civil War to repair torn clothing, a housewife was a sewing case used to store needles, pins, and thread and typically rolled up for transport or storage.* Ammi Hawk's sewing kit in the holdings of the Hawks Inn Historical Society, is described as, 'leather bound with cotton ties and patches, with silk lining. It has an embroidered pocket lined in blue silk, backed with black leather, and trimmed with brown cotton piping and ties. A padded roll at one end holds three pins. A ruffled pocket is embroidered with the initials 'ADH' in white, for Ammi Doubleday Hawks'."[96]

---

93   *Federal Manuscript Schedule*, Population, Agricultural and Manufacturing Schedules for Waukesha County, Town of Delafield, 1850.

94   Photograph courtesy of Hawks Inn Historical Society, Delafield, Wisconsin, Germaine Hillmer e-mail to author, Dec. 21, 2016.

95   Lauren Barker, "Battle of Helena Arkansas, Saturday, July 4, 1863," *Proceedings of the 28th Wisconsin Volunteer Infantry, 31st Annual Reunion* (Milwaukee: Houtkamp Printing Co., 1913), pp. 72-77.

96   Description of Ammi Hawks' *"Housewife,"* from the Collection of the Hawks Inn Historical Society.

IMMIGRANTS TO WISCONSIN FROM DENMARK & HOLSTEIN

Name: ***Jens Jensen Kier***-- Birthplace: <u>**Højer, Sonderjylland, Dänmark**</u> (15 Jan 1805) — Spouse: ***Charlotte Juliana Wilhelmsen***—Birthplace: <u>**Kellinghusen, Holstein, Germany**</u> (29 Sept 1810)—Immigrant ship name: *"Everet"*-- Departure: Liverpool, England—Arrival: New York (1859)—Residence in 1870: <u>Prospect Hill, New Berlin Township, Waukesha County, Wisconsin</u>—Occupation: *carpenter* and *farmer*–Children: *Andreas, Wilhelm & Anna.* (Image and genealogy courtesy of Jean Guthrie Linton, "Landmark" & Waukesha County Historical Society and Museum.)[97]

Jens and Charlotta Kier (c. 1865)[98]

Danish Immigration:

"Most Danes who immigrated to the United States after 1865 did so for economic reasons. By 1865, there had been a large increase in the Danish population in Europe because of the improvement in the medicine and food industries. *It caused a high rate of poverty and ultimately resulted in a significant and rapid increase in Danish migration to other countries.* Another reason for migration was the sale of lands. Many Danes became farmers in the United States. During the 1870s, almost half of all Danish immigrants to the United States settled in family groups."[99]

A skilled Danish cabinet-maker:

"A small, faded picture of a grim-looking couple was in my grandmother's album. On the back of it was a faint, foreign script with a few decipherable dates... *A friend in Racine who could read Danish translated the script to read*: *"Jens Jensen Kier, Born January 15, 1805, in Højer, Denmark; wife, Charlotte Juliana Wilhelmsen, born September 29th, 1810 on Kellinghusen, Schleswig," These dates were confirmed by records in Denmark which further add that Jens signed a petition in 1838 to form a cabinet-maker and carpenter guild in Højer...* Jens and Charlotte had three children, Andreas Lorensen, Wilhelm Hansen, and Anna. Andreas was a cabinet maker and had completed a level of schooling for which he received a certificate. In 1859, Andrea and Anna left together for America. They soon made their way to Wisconsin. The Kier family moved to Prospect Hill (in the town of New Berlin) in 1867, living just north of the hill in a 'Greek Revival' farmhouse set among Norway spruce trees. While he was fascinated by many musical and scientific instruments, his first love remined with wood-working. *He made fancy chests, inlaid with wood or pearl, cabinets, scroll-work shelves and curious, tea-chests, wood goblets, and a dictionary stand with his name and year inlaid*."[100]

---

[97] *Federal Manuscript Schedule*, Population, Agricultural and Manufacturing Schedules for Waukesha County, Town of New Berlin, 1870.

[98] John & Charlotte Kier c.1865, People I-J-K-L Box 4:8, Photography Collection, Research Center Library & Archive, Waukesha County Historical Society & Museum, Waukesha, Wisconsin.

[99] https://en.wikipedia.org/wiki/Danish_Americans

[100] Jean Guthrie Linton, "Genial Kindly Kier." *Landmark*. v. 34, n. 2, Summer, 1991, pp. 18-20.

IMMIGRANTS TO WISCONSIN FROM RHINELAND/RHENISH PRUSSIA

Name: **Mathis Kau (1908)** – Birthplace: **Strassfeld, Kreis Euskirchen, Königreich, Rhineland/ Rheinpreußen** (Germany) (19 Nov 1819)–Spouse: **Agnes (Shaefer) Kau**—Birthplace: **Brauweiler, Rhineland/ Rheinpreußen** (Germany) (1834) – Residence in 1870: New Berlin Township, Waukesha County, Wisconsin—Occupation: *farmer*–Children: *Elizabeth, Joseph, Margaret, Katherine, Balderin, Mary & Clara*. Death: New Berlin, Wisconsin (31 Jan 1882).   (Image & genealogy courtesy of Mary Stigler of Brookfield, Wisconsin)[101]

Agnes (Schaefer) Kau c. 1865[102]

Women's Clothing Styles of the 1860's:

"Agnes Kau's dress style is circa. 1865, with a curved 'Gentleman's style coat sleeve' that appeared after 1860. *She wears a high-waisted hoop skirt* typical of the mid-19th century. She doesn't appear to be dressed as a woman of great wealth but, instead dresses for function—a working dress. Her hair style is also typical of the mid-1860s, and unlike any other 19th style; pulled back and down on the neck, very plain." --*Joan Severa, 19th Century Clothing Styles*[103]

Early European Immigrants to New Berlin:

The following is the second installment on "The German Pioneers of New Berlin" prepared and read by *J. H. A. Lacher*, Wisconsin German Ethnic Historian, at a 1933 meeting of the Waukesha County Historical Society. Mr. Lacher surveyed most of Waukesha County during this period attempting to identify the location of origin of early German as well as other European families into the county. Listed are the family names, country of origin and year of arrival into New Berlin Township: **William Zingsheim** from *Baden* also settled in the town in 1850; 1851-**John Edenharder**, of *Rhenish Bavaria*; **G. and E. Ehrig**, of *North Germany*. Theiss (Tice), Matt. Schneider, Carl and William Schiffmann, M. Stigler, and Chas. Vogel of *Rhenish Prussia*; Bernard Casper of *Alsace, France*; Adam Gruber of *Holstein (Denmark)*; G. Petri; 1852-Mich. Battendorf, Henry Weber, Mich. Zingsheim, all from *Rhenish Prussia*; Franz Elger of *Austria*; 1853-Matt. Oberbillig, John Kau, Bernard Mueller (Miller), Joseph Salentine, and Susan Weber of *Rhenish Prussia*; John Link, of *Austria*; Wm. Thiesenhusen of *Mecklenburg*; Peter Weber, George Walter of *Bavaria*; Robert Zingsheim; 1854-Mary Brunner, Chas. Gigler, George Mueller (Miller), and Jacob Wagner of *Rhenish Bavaria*; John Kimpel, Christian and George Knoepfel (Knipfel) of *Hesse-Cassel*; John Phillips of *Alsace, France*; Peter Graf and Michael Windrath of *Prussia*; Rud. Hauswirth of *Switzerland*; Henry Schwartz of *Saxe-Weimar*; Jacob Jager (Yager), John and Matt. Wecker, Chas. Gigler of *Baden*; Chris. Vogel of *Prussia*; 1855-Peter Lauer, Matt. Kau, Peter Schmidt (Smith), Matt. Johann, and Fred. W. Lucas of *Prussia*; 1856-Chris. Behres of *Holstein (Denmark)*.; George Luber, John Lindner of *Oberhausen, North-Rhine-Westphalia*; L. Lohnerer of *Rhenish Bavaria*; Hans Gosch of *Holstein*.

[*Waukesha Freeman*, January 19, 1933]

[101]   *Federal Manuscript Schedule*, Population, Agricultural and Manufacturing Schedules for Waukesha County, Town of New Berlin, 1870.

[102]   Photograph courtesy of Mary Stigler, of Brookfield, Wisconsin, e-mail to author, June 15, 2011.

[103]   Joan Severa, of Madison, Wisconsin, e-mail to author, Jan 31, 2010.

IMMIGRANTS TO WISCONSIN FROM IRELAND

Name: **John Greer Sr.**—Bithplace: **County Armagh, Ireland** (c. 1729)—Departure: to England (1845)—Departure: to West India Islands (1848)—Depature: to Albany, New York (1850)—Marriage: **Ellen McGuire**—at Albany, New York (15 Oct 1854)—Ellen's birth: **Ireland** (1834)—Departured to California (15 December 1855); Children: *Sarah Johnston, John, Nellie,* (1864) *stillborn*—Death of *Ellen (McGuire) Greer in childbirth*—*John Greer* moved to St. Helena, Napa County, California (21 April 1864)—Marriage: to **Nellie Murphy**, of New Berlin, Wiscosnin, in St. Helena, California (4 Feb 1865)—*John Greer's* occupation: *livery stable.*
(Image and genealogy courtesy of Delbert Greer of Sacramento, California)[104]

Nellie Murphy's wedding day, Feb. 4, 1865[105]

An Irishman with a travel bug:

"*When John Greer was eighteen years of age he went to England and remained there for three years. He then went to the West India Islands, and resided there for two years.* In 1850 he went to to Albany, New York, where he worked in a hotel for five years. He was married in Albany, New York, October 15, 1854, to Anna Tierney (1st marriage), a native of Ireland. Their children were Mary Ann, Michael, Jermiah, Catherine, Bridget Bea, Dennis, Nellie, James, Elis & Elizabeth. *In 1855 he came to California, arriving December 15th. He engaged in various persuits till May 1856, when he came to Napa County, locating at the White Sulpher Springs* and in the following year he took charge of the Springs stables and conducted them for the following fourteen years. He, in company with Mr. Tainter, purchased one hundered acres of land, on which was situated the buisness portion of St. Helena. John Greer married Nellie Murphy, of New Berlin, Wisconsin, in St. Helena, on February 4, 1865 (2nd marriage)."[106]

The Murphy Clan:

"*Nellie Murphy's parents, Dennis Murphy and Catherine Linehan were both born in County Cork, Ireland. Castle Bernard lies west of the town of Bandon, in County Cork.* Castle Bernard became known as one of the most hospitable houses in Ireland and the house parties held by the fourth earl and his wife were legendary."[107] "Murphy, Nellie's father's surname, is the most common surename in Ireland, the fourteenth most common surname in Northern Ireland and the second most common surname in Canada. *The 'Murphy Clan' is steeped in ancient Irish/Celtic tradition.*"[108]

---

[104] *Federal Manuscript Schedule.* Manufacturing Schedules for Waukesha County, Town of New Berlin, 1850.

[105] Photograph courtesy of Delbert Greer of Woodland, California, e-mail to author, Jun 26, 2010.

[106] *History of Napa Valley and lake Counties, California, comprising their geography, geology, topography, climatographic, timber… together with a full record of the Mexican Grants… also separate histories of all the townships… and sketches* (Slocum, Bowen & Co.: San Francisco, 1881), p. 471.

[107] http://en.wikipedia.org/wiki/murphy

[108] http://www.murphyclans.com clan-history, courtesy of Delbert Greer of Sacramento, California.

IMMIGRANTS TO WISCONSIN FROM NEW YORK STATE

Name: **Caroline Robertson**– birthplace: <u>New York</u> (c. 1822) Spouse: deceased—Residence in 1850: owns a 154-acre <u>Brookfield Township, Waukesha County, Wisconsin</u> *farm.* Children: *Mary, Francis &* ***George*** *--assist with farm work. W.W. Bishop resides and labors on this farm.*
(Image and genealogy courtesy of Waukesha County Historical Society and Museum)[109]

George Robertson (c. 1865)[110]

"The greatest 'next year' country on earth"!

"Wisconsin's immigrant farmers had religion, faith, and awareness that they had engaged in a hazardous occupation for who could predict what a year would bring, what disasters upon crops from weather or insects, or what sickness might befall. 'NEXT YEAR" was the term they understood, for next year would be, must be, better, with more land under plow, with more confidence, with more faith, and the optimistic expectation of a bumper crop. In the early days Wisconsin *was the greatest 'next year' country on earth!*"[111]

THE CROPS AND HARVEST.

The Chinch Bug.
We learn from a gentleman just from Waukesha that the farmers on the line of the M. & P. du C. Railroad are proceeding with wheat harvest. He informs us that *the chinch bug*[112] *as of late made fearful havoc with the wheat*; so great indeed, that it will not be likely to turn out more than one third of a crop. Little more than a half crop was anticipated before the bug commenced its ravages. Farmers are cutting it to get out of the way of these destructive insect.*--Madison Argus* [*Milwaukee Sentinel* July 31, 1861]

[109] *Federal Manuscript Census*, Manufacturing Schedules for Waukesha County, Town of Brookfield, 1850.

[110] George Robertson, c. 1865, People P-Q-R Box 6:8, Photography Collection, Research Center Library & Archive, Waukesha County Historical Society & Museum, Waukesha, Wisconsin.

[111] Robert & Milo Gard, *My Land, My Home, My Wisconsin: The Epic Story of the Wisconsin Farm and farm Family from Settlement Days to Present*, Online Computer Library Center, **OCLC**, p. 29.

[112] "The chinch bug, a native to the United States and common in midwestern states, The chinch bug naturally feeds on wild prairie grasses. As the midwestern states were settled in the nineteenth century and crops of wheat, corn, sorghum and other grains were planted, they adapted well to these new species as habitat and food species. Throughout the 20th century, the chinch bug was a major pest to farmers, as it quickly decimated corn or wheat fields" From: https://en.wikipedia.org/wiki/Blissus_leucopterus

IMMIGRANTS TO WISCONSIN FROM NEW YORK & NEW JERSEY

Name: **Albert Van Brunt Dey**— Birthplace: **Varick, Seneca County, New York** (c. 1826) –Spouse: ***Catherine (Opdyke) Day***—Birthplace: **New Jersey** (c. 1826)— Residence in 1870: **Pewaukee Township, Waukesha County, Wisconsin**—Occupation: *farmer*—Children: *Grace, Charles, John & Phoeba*.
(Image and genealogy courtesy of Waukesha County Historical Society and Museum.)[113]

Catherine Dey (c. 1865)[114]

Women's fashion dress styles during the war years:

"(Catherine Dey is wearing a moderately large hoop skirt dress may have been taken from a women's fashion magazine from the 1860's.) The women's magazines, until this time, were essentially a Union feature during the war and continued to be published regularly throughout, mostly in Philadelphia. The illustrations, still taken from the French, show little or no change in presentation from the originals, and the styles seen as elaborate and varied as ever, the use of fabrics as generous, and the trimmings as rich and expense. During war, women read that 'some of the choicest silks… such robes cost two hundred and fifty dollars. Dress patterns of such value are never two made alike. There is another style less expensive… These robes are only one hundred and fifty dollars each. *Of course, only the rich can afford such silks*. There is virtually nothing in the text of Godey's or Peterson's during these war years to indicate the national situation. The only hint of difficulty comes in oblique references."[115]

GODEY'S LADY'S BOOK FOR 1864.

This best of all Magazines for ladies, will commence the new year with a greatly increased subscription list, a large array of literary talent, and with additional attractions, if possible, in its typography and mechanical appearance. The fact that 'Godey's' has more than quadrupled its circulation within the last five years, is sufficient evidence of the high estimate placed upon it by the refined and cultivated women of our country. [*Waukesha Freeman* Nov. 24, 1863]

---

[113] *Federal Manuscript Census*, Manufacturing Schedules for Waukesha County, Town of Pewaukee, 1850.

[114] Catherine Dey, c. 1865, People C-D-E Box 2:8, Photography Collection, Research Center Library & Archive, Waukesha County Historical Society & Museum, Waukesha, Wisconsin.

[115] Joan Severa, *Dressed for the Photographer: Ordinary Americans & Fashion, 1840-1900* (Kent, Ohio & London, England: Kent State University Press, 1995), p. 189.

IMMIGRANTS TO WISCONSIN FROM KENTUCKY

Name: *Alfred L. Castleman*—Birthplace: <u>Shelby County, Kentucky</u> (7 Dec 1808)—Spouse: **Abigail Parmelia Hubbard**—Born: 7 Apr 1809—Residence in 1850: <u>Delafield Township, Waukesha County</u>—Occupation: *physician*—Children: *Margaret, David, Sarah, Virginia Hubbard & Mary Celina*---Death: 2 Aug 1977.
(Image and genealogy courtesy of Hawks Inn Historical Society, Delafield, Wisconsin.)[116]

Dr. Alfred Castleman (1865)[117]

A Civil War Surgeon:

Dr. Alfred L. Castleman was a surgeon in the <u>*Fifth Regiment of the Wisconsin Volunteers,*</u> who maintained a journal throughout the war: The 5th Infantry was assembled at Camp Randall, in Madison on July 12, 1861/ It left Wisconsin for Washington, D.C. on July 24, 1861/ Participated in the battles of: Williamsburg/ Battle of Antietam/Battle of Fredericksburg/Battle of Gettysburg/Battle of the Wilderness/Battle of the Wilderness/Battle at Cold Harbor/Siege of Petersburg/ Mustered out July 11, 1865. [118]

1st Battle of Fredericksburg, December 11–15, 1862:

"To-day we have fallen back on to the same camping ground which we left on the 11th to advance to capture **Fredericksburg.** How different the feelings on that beautiful moonlight morning, whilst they struck and loaded their tents amid their cheering. *Whilst beaten and repulsed, they cherished such visions of glory.*" —*Journal of Alfred L. Castleman*[119]

Union Civil War Hospital at White Oak Church:

(<u>Stafford County, Virginia, *1863 is* app. 6 miles east of Fredericksburg</u>) "April 2nd, 1863—The boxes, and other presents received within the last eight days, have awakened vivid recollections of home, and of 'the girls they left behind them.' I make here a record of some observations in relation to 'hospital fevers,' hospital sores,' 'foul air of hospitals,' and such claptrap. I have lately visited many tent hospitals, in the open field, where *I witnessed cases of hospital gangrenous toes or fingers dropping off,* and heard scientific men, in scientific discussions, attributing it all to the foul air of the hospital! And this, too, in the open field, where the wind swept past them, free as the fresh breezes on the top of the Alleghanies!!!"—*Journal of Alfred L. Castleman*[120]

---

[116] *Federal Manuscript Census*, Manufacturing Schedules for Waukesha County, Town of Delafield, 1850.

[117] Photograph courtesy of Hawks Inn Historical Society, Delafield, Wisconsin, Germaine Hillmer, e-mail message to author, Dec. 21, 2016.

[118] https://en.wikipedia.org/wiki/5th_Wisconsin_Volunteer_Infantry_Regiment

[119] Daily Observation of the Civil War, December 19, 2012. *The American Civil War, The Army of the Potomac—Behind the Scenes from* "The Journal of Surgeon Alfred L. Castleman."

[120] Daily Observation of the Civil War, January 2, 2012, "The Journal of Surgeon Alfred L. Castleman."

IMMIGRANTS TO WISCONSIN FROM NEW YORK STATE

Name: **Thomas Faulkner**— Birthplace: <u>Livingston County, New York State</u> (12 July 1822) —parents: **Thomas and Mary (King) Faulkner** of <u>Ireland</u>--Spouse: **Nancy Moore** – Birthplace: <u>Monroe County, New York State</u> (15 Dec 1820)— Year of Immigration: (c. 1856). Residence in 1860: <u>Prospect Hill, New Berlin Township, Wisconsin</u> —Occupation: *farmer* –Children: *Viola, Clara, Rufus &* ***Frank.***

(Image and genealogy courtesy of Libbie Nolan of Big Bend, Wisconsin.)[121]

Frank D. Faulkner (c. 1866)[122]

Promoting Irish Immigration/ Pre-famine years.

TO IRISHMEN.

THE subscriber as agent for Herdman & Keenan, can receipt fare for passengers from any port in Ireland thr' to Milwaukee or Chicago. Those Irishmen that wish to send home for their friends can make arrangements with the subscriber to have them here by the first of October next, by making appointments soon. J.A. NOONAN Milwaukee.   [*Milwaukee Courier* June 2, 1841]

The Thomas Faulkner Family:

"During the early 1800s, Mr. Thomas Faulkner and his Wife, Nancy, arrived in Milwaukee, then purchasing a farm in Waukesha County. *Mr. Faulkner sold his farm and moved to the village of Waukesha, where he engaged in the manufacture of sash, doors and blinds*, continuing in that business for seven years. At the expiration of that period he located on his present farm in New Berlin, which was known as the 'Rufus Cheney Home.' They were members of the Free Will Baptist Church of the town of New Berlin."[123]

Frank D. Faulkner--Photographer:

"During the 1860s, *Thomas & Nancy Faulkner's* son, *Frank Faulkner,* opened a photography studio in Waukesha. However, as his photography business was not always a dependable source of income, he continued to

farm."[124] "*Frank's images were initially created as tintypes*. A tintype, also known as a melainotype or ferrotype, is a photograph made by creating a direct positive on a thin sheet of metal coated with a dark lacquer or enamel and used as the support for the photographic emulsion. The tintype saw the Civil War come and go, documenting the individual soldier and horrific battle scenes. The tintype's immediate predecessor, the ambrotype, was done by the same process of using a sheet of glass as the support. *One or more hardy, lightweight, thin tintypes could be carried conveniently in a jacket pocket. They became very popular in the United States during the American Civil War.*"[125]

[121]   *Federal Manuscript Schedule*, Population, Agricultural and Manufacturing Schedules for Waukesha County, Town of New Berlin, 1860.

[122]   Photograph courtesy of Libbie Nolan, via Pat Nolan, both of Big Bend, Wisconsin, e-mail to author, Dec. 21, 2016.

[123]   *Portrait and Biographical Record of Waukesha County, 1894*, pp. 305 & 306.

[124]   *Portrait and Biographical Record of Waukesha County, 1894*, p. 306.

[125]   https://en.wikipedia.org/wiki/Tintype

IMMIGRANTS TO WISCONSIN FROMM HESSEN AND NEW YORK

Name: ***Henry Snyder***--Birthplace: <u>Paffenhabenheim, Hessen, Germany</u> (9 Sept 1844)—Spouse—**Mary Elizabeth Eiler**—Birthplace: <u>Troy, Rensselaer, County, New York</u> (3 Mar 1847-24 Mar 1922)—Married—<u>Waukesha, Waukesha County</u> (26 Nov 1865)—Residence in 1870: <u>Waukesha, Waukesha County</u>—Occupation: *shoemaker*—Children: *Martin (1866-1867)—Elizabeth Burlingame (1869-1958)—Rev. Henry Snyder (1874-1954)—Mabel Barbara Perkins (1884-1963)—Gustave (1868-1969)—Amelia Wilhelmina Putz (1872-1926) Alvin — shoe maker's apprentice.*   (Image and genealogy courtesy of Kenneth Eiler of Overland Park, Kansas.)[126]

Henry Snyder Jr. (c. 1866) [127]

The Battle of Shiloh, Tennessee, April 6-7, 1862:

"The 14th, 16th, and 18th Wisconsin Infantry regiments fought at the Battle of Shiloh. Shiloh was one of the bloodiest in U.S. history. Out of 62,000 soldiers engaged, nearly 20,000 were killed or wounded. The 18th Wisconsin Infantry had been out of camp only a week when the battle began. It lost 24 men, including Colonel James Alban who was fatally wounded by a bullet through the lungs. The 14th Wisconsin Infantry arrived the next morning with the reinforcements and took part in the second day's fighting. One lieutenant, who came through the battle unscathed, counted 12 bullet holes through his uniform. <u>Gen. Ulysses S. Grant wrote afterward that the main part of the battlefield was 'so covered with dead that it would have been possible to walk across the clearing, in any direction, stepping on dead bodies, without a foot touching the ground</u>'."[128]

Henry Snyder's shoe shop--furnished with the latest machinery (1900):

"By the late 1850s, the industry was beginning to shift towards the modern factory, mainly in the US. A shoe stitching machine was invented by the American Lyman Blake in 1856 and perfected by 1864. Entering into partnership with McKay, his device became known as the McKay stitching machine. <u>As bottlenecks opened in the production line due to these innovations, more and more of the manufacturing stages, such as pegging and finishing, became automated</u>. By the 1890s, the process of mechanization was largely complete. A process for manufacturing switchless (glued) shoes was developed in 1910." [129]

---

[126] *Federal Manuscript Schedule,* Population, Agricultural and Manufacturing Schedules for Waukesha County, City of Waukesha, 1870.

[127] Photograph courtesy of Kenneth Eiler of Overland Park, Kansas, e-mail to author, Jun 27, 2010.

[128] William D. Love, *Wisconsin in the War of the Rebellion,* vol.1 (Chicago: Church & Goodman, 1866), pp. 482-492.

[129] https://en.wikipedia.org/wiki/Shoemaking

IMMIGRANTS TO WISCONSIN FROM WALES

Name: **Thomas D. Jones**– Birthplace: <u>Llandysil, Cardiganshire, South Wales</u> (c. 1834) — Spouse: *deceased*— Birthplace: <u>Wales</u> (c. 1835)–Year of immigration: 1842—Residence in 1880: <u>Genesee Township, Waukesha County, Wisconsin</u>—Occupation: *farmer*–2nd marriage: **Margaret Roberts**—Children: ***David, Anne***, *Griffith & Sarah*. (Image and genealogy courtesy of Wales Village Hall, Wales, Wisconsin)[130]

David & Annie Jones (c. 1866)[131]

Leaving Wales:

"The reason why the Welsh first went to America, and more specifically to Wisconsin, were partly the same and partly different from the reason that motivated other immigrant groups. "Wales was a small and mountainous land. <u>Farmland was scarce, and farmers there either tenant on land owned by English-speaking Anglican or Welsh landlords, or Welsh framers who had very small holdings of their own.</u> The Welsh language was discouraged by the educational system, and the wealthier were forced to pay taxes to support the Church of England, to which few belonged… The first known Welsh in Wisconsin seems to have been John Hughes and family of seven, who came to Genesee in Waukesha County in 1840. By 1842 there were fifteen families and ninety-nine Welsh people in the community… Many Welsh chapels were constructed in this district—the most famous being Capel Log (The Log Chapel), originally built in 1845. <u>The cemetery associated with it contains an extremely large number of monuments for the Welsh settlers, quite a few of them with inscriptions in Cymraeg.</u> (Cymraeg or y Gymraeg, pronounced [kəmˈraiɡ, ə ɡəmˈraiɡ] is a member of the Brittonic branch of the Celtic languages. It is spoken natively in Wales."[132]

A considerable colony from Wales settle in Genesee Township:

"Mr. Thomas D. Jones, born in South Wales[133], along with his two youngest children lived, during their first summer in Wales, Genesee Township, Wisconsin Territory (1844), on bread and milk for supper, dinner and breakfast, it being eaten on a dry-goods box, brought from Ohio; their coffee was distilled from a berry growing wild in the woods, where deer and wolves were plenty, yet <u>Mr. Jones now avers that some of the happiest days of his life were spent there</u>: the oak shakes for the roof of the house were split with a curious instrument called a **froe** (A froe/frow is a tool for cleaving wood by splitting it along the grain. It is an L-shaped tool, used by hammering one edge of its blade into the end of a piece of wood in the direction of the grain), still kept by him as a relic… after this he operated a threshing machine and a breaking team for many years."[134]

---

130   *Federal Manuscript Schedule*, Population, Agricultural and Manufacturing Schedules for Waukesha County, Town of Genesee, 1880.

131   Photograph Courtesy of Wales Village Hall, Wales, Wisconsin, Gail Tamez, e-mail to author, Dec 21, 2016.

132   Phillips G. Davies, *Welsh in Wisconsin* "Revised and Expanded Edition," (Madison: Wisconsin Historical Society Press, 2006), pp. 9 & 10.

133   "South Wales (Welsh: De Cymru) is the region of Wales bordered by England and the Bristol Channel to the east and south, and Mid Wales and West Wales to the north and west. It is the most densely populated region in the southwest of the United Kingdom." From: https://en.wikipedia.org/wiki/South_Wales

134   "Welsh Immigrant Historical Scrapbook," author visit at Wales Village Hall, Oct. 11, 2010.

"AMERICAN FARMYARD IN WINTER," TAKEN FROM A STEREOPTICON VIEW, (1866)[135]

GEORGE T. LINDEMAN,

"A photographer from Milwaukee, traveled the state of Wisconsin taking, and selling, stereographic views. This scene he entitled *'American Farmyard in Winter,'* which he additionally labelled: *'Taken West of Milwaukee...'*"[136]

Family Clothing Styles of the 1860's:

"*Here we find in the 'American Costume' in everyday use by a woman obviously dressed for utilitarian purposes.* The shortened skirt and the appearance of little or no corseting are evidence of an independent mind, suiting the needs of the frontier... Most women did not use the bloomer dress as their only costume. They were not, in fact, making a statement by wearing the style; rather, they were choosing safe, comfortable adaptations so that they could perform hard, active work efficiently." —*Joan Severa*[137]

Earliest forms of farm technology available in Wisconsin:

Hay Forks, Scythe Snaiths, Cradles, Chains, Harrow Teeth, Picks, Barn Door Hinges, Plough and small Clevises, Hames, Staple and rings, Wedges, Beetle Rings, Axes, Bar Iron and an assortment of Sheep's Grey and other Cloth's. *Just received per Schooner Pennsylvania and for sale by the subscribers on **Walker's Point**.* HOLLISTER & BIGELOW. —*July 10, 1838.*   [*Milwaukee Sentinel July 24, 1838*]

---

[135] Courtesy of Wisconsin Historical Society (WHi-2382) at: https://www.wisconsinhistory.org/Records/Image/IM2382

[136] Descriptor of George Lindeman and his photograph "American Farmyard in Winter," (accompanies photograph) courtesy of Wisconsin Historical Society.

[137] Severa, *Dressed for the Photographer*, p. 279.

IMMIGRANTS TO WISCONSIN FROM ENGLAND

Name: **John Lumb**—Birthplace: <u>**Wrangle, Lincolnshire County, England**</u>— (24 Apr 1840) --Spouse: ***Emily Experience (Snyder) Lumb*** – Birthplace: <u>**Wisconsin**</u> (1847) --Year of Immigration: 1852 — Residence in 1860: Brookfield Township, Waukesha County, Wisconsin—occupation: *farmer*--marriage date: (18 May 1871) -- <u>Granville, Milwaukee County, Wisconsin</u>—Occupation: *farmer* –Children: *Adda, John* — Residence in 1900: <u>Delafield Township, Waukesha County, Wisconsin</u>--Death of *John Lumb*: (16 Jan 1919).
(Image and genealogy courtesy of Libbie Nolan of Big Bend, Wisconsin.)[138]

Emily (Snyder) Lumb (c. 1867)[139]

Emigrants from Lincolnshire, England:

A large number of the earliest English immigrants to Waukesha County came from Lincolnshire County. "Included among these were the families of Richard Doane, Charles Hart, Henry Lumb, Charles Taylor & Samuel Taylor. John Dixon and his wife (Elizabeth Lumb) were, also, natives of Lincolnshire, England, there married, and about 1844 emigrated to America. *They embarked aboard a sailing -vessel from Liverpool, and after a voyage of six weeks' duration dropped anchor in the harbor of New York.* They came direct to Wisconsin by way of the Erie Canal and the Great Lakes and walked out to Waukesha County."[140]

Exposed to Measles:

"At the age of six, in 1923, Libbie Russell (Nolan) was living with Grandma Russell who asked Great Grandmother Emily Lumb to stay with Libbie while she ran an errand. (Emily's husband, John, immigrated to Wisconsin from Lincolnshire, England in 1852.) *Emily apparently was exposed to measles from Libbie while she was with her. Emily Lumb died from measles that year. At the time of her death, in 1923, Emily Lumb was seventy-six while Libbie Russell was only six.*" —— ***Libbie Nolan***[141]

---

[138] *Federal Manuscript Schedule*, Population, Agricultural and Manufacturing Schedules for Waukesha County, Town of Menomonee, 1900.
[139] Photograph courtesy of Libbie Nolan via Pat Nolan, of Big Bend, Wisconsin, e-mail to author, Dec. 21, 2016.
[140] *Brookfield: A Fine and Fertile Land, vol. 1*, pp. 13 & 14.
[141] Author visit with Libbie Nolan, Jan. 15, 2010.

IMMIGRANTS TO WISCONSIN FROM NEW HAMPSHIRE AND VERMONT

Name: ***Abiel Pierce***– Birthplace: <u>Wilton, New Hampshire</u> (1791) — Spouse: <u>Nancy Lovejoy</u>—Birthplace—<u>Andover, Vermont</u> (c. 1790) ---after her death--*Abiel Pierce* married <u>Hannah Manning</u>—Birthplace: (1793) — <u>Andover, Windsor, Vermont</u> --Residence in 1840: <u>Dodge's Corners, Vernon Township, Waukesha County, Wisconsin</u>—Occupation: *brick maker* and *farmer*–Children: none.
(Image and genealogy courtesy of Waukesha County Historical Society and Museum.)[142]

Capt. Abiel Pierce (c. 1867)[143]

Opposition to the War of 1812 was widespread in New England:

"Many New Englanders opposed the conflict on political, economic & religious grounds. When embargo failed to remedy the situation and Great Britain refused to rescind the Orders in Council (1807) and France continued its decrees, certain Democratic-Republicans known as war hawks felt compelled to go to war. Vehement protests erupted in those parts of the country where the opposition Federalist political party held sway, especially in Connecticut and Massachusetts. In the elections that followed in a few months, some members of Congress who voted for war, paid the price. Eight New England congressmen were rejected by the voters, and several others saw the writing on the wall and declined to seek reelection. There was a complete turnover of the New Hampshire delegation. The War of 1812 is less well known than 20th-century U.S. wars, but no other war had the degree of opposition by elected officials. Nevertheless, historian Donald R. Hickey has argued that, 'The War of 1812 was America's most unpopular war. It generated more intense opposition_than any other war in the nation's history, including the war in Vietnam'."[144]

A Captain's Commission:

"During the War of 1812 Abiel Pierce was given a Captain's commission but was never called to active service. <u>His title was retained throughout life owing to leadership in training militia in his hometown Wilton, New Hampshire</u>. He married Hannah Manning, his second wife, of Andover, Vermont in the late 1830s. They immigrated by team to Wisconsin in 1838, locating at Vernon Township, Waukesha County, where he purchased 80 acres. He was an honest and temperate man."[145]

---

[142]   *Federal Manuscript Schedule*, Population of Milwaukee County, Wisconsin Territory, 1840; Frank P. Zeidler Humanities Room, Milwaukee Public Central Library.

[143]   Captain Abiel Pierce, c. 1867, People P-Q-R Box 6:8, Photography Collection, Research Center Library & Archive, Waukesha County Historical Society & Museum, Waukesha, Wisconsin.

[144]   https://en.wikipedia.org/wiki/Opposition_to_the_War_of_1812_in_the_United_States

[145]   Photograph Descriptor of Captain Abiel Pierce Photograph, Photography Collection, Research Center Library & Archive, Waukesha County Historical Society & Museum, Waukesha, Wisconsin.

IMMIGRANTS TO WISCONSIN FROM VERMONT & CANADA

Name: **Ferrand Bigelow**— Birthplace: **Reading, Windsor County, Vermont** (13 Feb 1807)—Spouse: **Caroline M. Hibbard**——Birthplace: **St. Armand, Quebec, Canada** (1812)—Year of Immigration: 1836—Residence in 1840: Prairieville (Waukesha) and then Eagle Township, Waukesha County, Wisconsin— Occupation: *farmer*–Children: *Lucia Ann,* **William**, *Elberton, Franklin, Orpheus, Minerva, Arthur & Sarah. Death*: Eagle, Waukesha County, Wisconsin (Dec 1887).

(Image and genealogy courtesy of Jeannie Brown of Windsor, California.)[146]

William and Alice Bigelow (1868)[147]

Earliest settlers to Prairieville (Waukesha):

"Waukesha was a New England settlement. The original founders of Waukesha consisted entirely of settlers from New England, particularly Connecticut, rural Massachusetts, Vermont, New Hampshire and Maine, as well some from upstate New York who were born to parents who had migrated to that region from New England shortly after the American Revolution. These people were "Yankee" settlers, that is to say they were descended from the English Puritans who settled New England in the 1600s. *They were part of a wave of New England farmers who headed west into what was then the wilds of the Northwest Territory during the early 1800s.* When they arrived in what is now Waukesha County there was nothing but dense virgin forest and wild prairie, the New Englanders laid out farms, constructed roads and erected government buildings."[148]

Sherman's Yazoo Pass Expedition:

(William Bigelow, Co. A, Wisconsin 1st Heavy Artillery, took part in the Yazoo Pass expedition.) "On the eleventh of March 1863, several Wisconsin regiments were landed near Fort Pemberton, at Yazoo Pass, Mississippi, and marched into the woods toward the fort, commanding both the Yazoo and Tallahatchie Rivers. Five companies of the 28th were chosen for this duty, but two guns of the Chillicothe were soon disabled, so that they had to withdraw."[149]

146   *Federal Manuscript Schedule*, Population, Agricultural and Manufacturing Schedules for Waukesha County, Town of Eagle, 1850.

147   Photograph courtesy of Jeannie Brown of Windsor, California, e-mail to author, July 7, 2010.

148   https://en.wikipedia.org/wiki/Waukesha,_Wisconsin

149   Lauren Barker, "Some Incidents Regarding the 28th Regiment," *Proceedings of the Society of the 28th Wiscosnin Infantry*, 15th Annual Reunion (Elkhorn, Wisconsin, June 26, 1902), v. 2, p. 367.

IMMIGRANTS TO WISCONSIN FROM IRELAND

Name: **Dennis Murphy**—Birthplace: **Castletown, County Cork, Ireland** (1810)—1ˢᵗ wife: **Ann Tierney**—Birthplace—**Ireland**—Residence in 1850: New Berlin Township, Waukesha County—Occupation: *farmer*—Children: *Mary Ann, Margaret, Michael, Jeremiah, Catherine, Bridget, Dennis, Nellie, James & Elizabeth*—One of the Murphy's daughter's, Nellie, married John Greer in St. Helena Napa County, California in (4 Feb 1865). John Greer's *1ˢᵗ wife died while in childbirth in 1864*. John Greer's 2ⁿᵈ wife: ***Nellie Murphy***—Dennis Murphy's occupation: *livery stable*—John & Nellie's children: *Mary, John, Thomas, Elizabeth, Thomas, Clarence, infant daughter: stillborn* (1878), *infant daughter: stillborn* (1879), *Ellen: survived 6 days* (1880), *Ellen: stillborn:* (1881), *Kittie: stillborn—* (1882). (Image and genealogy courtesy by Mark Powers of Woodland, California.)[150]

Nellie Murphy (c. 1868)[151]

Dennis Murphy of County Cork:

"In the 19ᵗʰ century, County Cork was the center of the Fenians (Fenian was an umbrella term for the Fenian Brotherhood and Irish Republican Brotherhood (IRB), fraternal organizations dedicated to the establishment of an independent Irish Republic in the 19ᵗʰ and early 20ᵗʰ centuries. and for the constitutional nationalism of the Irish Parliamentary Party from1910 that of the All-for-Ireland Party.) The country was a hotbed of guerrilla activity during *the Irish War for Independence* (1919—1921). Three Cork Brigades of the Irish Republican Army operated in the county and another in the city. Prominent actions included the Kilmichael Ambush in November 1920 and the Crossbarry Ambush in March 1921. On 11 December 1920 Cork City center was gutted by the Black and Tans in reprisal for IRA attacks."[152]

"Soon Angels: Infant and Child Mortality:"

"*The church records of a Wisconsin settlement of Norwegians at mid-century showed that of 194 deaths, 94 had been children under five.* There was an additional cruelty to mothers in the easy trivialization of many of the deaths, for most were from seemingly 'minor' childhood diseases. For some women (like Nellie Murphy), it was more common to have children die than to have them live. One woman married nineteen years had fifteen pregnancies but only five living children while two others were married twelve and thirteen years respectively each had ten pregnancies with only two living children each."[153]

---

[150] *Federal Manuscript Schedule*, Population, Agricultural, fruit production, timber, and manufacturing schedules, the city of St. Helena, Napa County, California, 1870.

[151] Photograph courtesy of Mark Powers of Woodland, California, e-mail to author, Nov 10, 2010.

[152] http://en.wikipedia.org/wiki/County-Cork

[153] Doris Weatherford. *Foreign and Female: Immigrant Women in America, 1840-1930* (New York: Facts on File, 1995), pp. 53 & 54.

IMMIGRANTS TO WISCONSIN FROM ENGLAND

Name: **Henry Perry** — Birthplace: **Wrangle, Lincolnshire, England** (1813)—Spouse: **Eliza Skinner**—Second wife: **Harriet Vintar**—Birthplace: **Village of Wrangle, Civil Parish of Kirton or Kirton in Holland, Borough of Boston, Lincolnshire, England** (c. 1814) --Year of Immigration: c. 1852—Residence in 1860: **Brookfield Township, Waukesha County, Wisconsin**—Occupation: *farmer* – Children: *John, Mary & Sarah*.
(Image and genealogy courtesy of Waukesha County Historical Society and Museum.) [1534]

Perry Family (1868) [155]

(l-r): John, Mrs. John Stewart holding Sarah (baby), Henry (husband) and Harriet (wife). Photograph was taken at the Perry home then located at the northwest corner W. Park and Maple Avenues in Waukesha.

The Lincolnshire colony:

(*Henry Perry* brought his family from Lincolnshire, England (c. 1852) to Wisconsin and settled in Brookfield Township, Waukesha County.) "*A rather large number of English immigrants, the majority from Lincolnshire County, settled in a Brookfield Township* (predominately in sections 14 & 15) beginning in the 1840's. At the center of the community, stood a small settlement including a shoemaker's shop, a blacksmith shop, a sawmill, a grist mill, and the Brookfield Methodist Episcopal Church. Heads of these neighboring English families included: Richard Bingham (farmer); William Booth (carpenter & joiner); George H. Daubner, John Dixon (farmers); Richard Doane (shoemaker & farmer), John Dobner (boot & shoemaker); Charles Hart (farmer & saw mill operator); Henry Lumb (famer); John Wheatly (blacksmith) & Joseph White (farmer)—among others." [156]

English Ministers brought along their Lincolnshire accents:

During the early1880's, young Grant Showerman, and a few other Brookfield boys, attended a service at the new Bible Christian Church into the village of Brookfield. Referring to the service, young Grant recalled, "*They say, 'Yes, Lord!' and 'Oh, Lord!' and 'Lord answer prayer!' The faster and louder the minister prays, the more they all do. We can hear them all over the church. The minister is English. All the Bible Christian ministers are English. We have fun trying to talk their way!*" [157]

---

154 *Federal Manuscript Schedule*, Population, Agricultural and Manufacturing Schedules for Waukesha County, Town of Brookfield, 1860.

155 Perry Family photograph, c. 1868, Family Box 1:3, Photography Collection, Research Center Library & Archive, Waukesha County Historical Society & Museum, Waukesha, Wisconsin.

156 Author, *Brookfield: A Fine and Fertile Land*—vol. 1, pp. 13 & 14.

157 Grant Showerman, *A County Chronicle* (New York: The Century Co., 1916), p. 237.

IMMIGRANTS TO WISCONSIN FROM PRUSSIA

Name: **John Phillips**–Birthplace: **Preußen** (c. 1816) —Spouse: **Katherine Phillips**-- Birthplace: **Preußen**—year of immigration: (circa: 1845)—Residence in 1870—New Berlin, Waukesha County—occupation: *farmer*—in 1873, John Phillips owns a 40 acre (section 18) New Berlin farm[158]--Children: *Magdalen, Bernhard, Mary, Rosanna, Orsa, Martin & Joseph.* (Image and genealogy courtesy of Mary Stigler of Brookfield, Wisconsin.)[159]

John, Joseph and Katherine Phillips (c. 1868)[160]

THE NEW BERLIN FIRE MYSTERY IS SOLVED--PHILLIPS IS GUILTY!

There was a start of surprise in the court room Friday when the name of *John Henry Phillips* was called. It had been generally supposed that he would not be called to testify. He walked to the witness box with long strides, and gave his testimony, in a loud, powerful voice, and without hesitation. His examination was conducted by *Mr. Flanders*. He said he was in the 44th year of his age and had lived in New Berlin all his life; was married and had one child. *His farm had belonged to his father before him.* Mr. Phillips testified that *in October 1887, at the time his first barn burned,* he had three, one double buggy, one center-spring, single buggy, and one received binder. *The fire of 1888 was then taken up in detail.* Witness said the barn was an old one but had been repaired. He had in it 95 bushels old wheat and 275 bushels new wheat, and perhaps 225 bushels oats. He had a meeting with the insurance adjusters in Milwaukee, and they did not allow him the full insurance. *The barn that burned in 1889, said the witness, was wood and built that year; and was 30x40 in size.* He had considerable new machinery. He made out proofs of loss fair, put in 2,535 bushels grain. **(conti-).**

Cross Examined by the Prosecuting Attorney:

Did you set fire to the any of the three barns of yours which burned in 1887, 1888, or 1889?" asked Attorney Flanders. *"No sir"* replied Phillips in a thunderous voice. "Did you or do you know anything about who set those fires?" asked the attorney. *"No sir!"* said Mr. Phillips. "Where those fires set with your knowledge or consent?" pursued the attorney, and for the third time the witness answered, *"No sir!"* with great emphasis. An interesting item of testimony related to conveyance of property by defendant to his wife. He declared that before his arrest he had deeded all the farm to her except 38 acres, which had also been deeded to her at time of his arrest. He had been quiet and unmoved all through the trial. As the jury delivered, much anxiety filled the courthouse. There was a strong feeling against Mr. Phillips by his neighbors and, a belief that he was guilty. Peering at the accused, he looked worn and haggard. *Upon hearing the awful word "guilty" pronounced upon him, he quietly wept.*

[*Waukesha Freeman* June 18, 1891]

---

158   *Atlas of Waukesha County, Wisconsin* (Madison, WI. Harrison & Warner, 1873), Town of New Berlin.
159   *Federal Manuscript Schedule*, Population, Agricultural and Manufacturing Schedules for Waukesha County, Town of New Berlin, 1880.
160   Photograph courtesy of Mary Stigler of Brookfield, Wisconsin, e-mail to author, Aug 8, 2009.

Immigrants to Wisconsin from England

Name: **Ephram Beaumont**—Birthplace: **Huddersfield, Yorkshire, England** (19 Feb 1834)—immigrated to the United Sates (1851) --Spouse: **Deborah A (Wood) Beaumont** (1 Jan 1863)—Birthplace: **Pewaukee, Waukesha County, Wisconsin** (c. 1848)—location of the birth of Deborah's parents: **England**—Residence in 1860: **Merton Township, Waukesha County, Wisconsin** —Occupation: *farmer*—Children: *Saxie, Richard, Hattie, Charles, William, Bessie, & Edith*. Death: Waukesha County (23 Dec 1918).
(Image and genealogy courtesy of Jeanne Pedriana of Elm Grove, Wisconsin)[161]

Deborah A Beaumont (c. 1868)[162]

Labor agitation in Yorkshire, England:

"Huddersfield (the birthplace of Ephraim Beaumont) was a center of civil unrest during the Industrial Revolution. In a period where Europe was experiencing frequent wars, where trade had slumped, and the crops had failed, many local weavers faced losing their livelihood due to the introduction of machinery in factories. Luddites[163] attacks was on Cartwright – a Huddersfield mill-owner, who had a reputation for cruelty – and his Rawfold's Mill. In his book Rebels Against the Future, Kirkpatrick Sale describes how an army platoon was stationed at Huddersfield to deal with Luddites; *at its peak, there were about a thousand soldiers in Huddersfield and ten thousand civilians. The government campaign that crushed the movement was provoked by a murder that took place in Huddersfield.* Although the movement faded out, Parliament began to increase welfare provision for those out of work and introduce regulations to improve conditions in the mills."[164]

Tenants and those living on small farms:

"English settlers provided a steady and substantial influx throughout the 19th century. *Sustained by unrest in the United Kingdom caused emigration to peak in 1842.* Most of these were small farmers and tenant farmers from depressed areas in rural counties in southern and western England and urban laborers who fled from the depressions and from the social and industrial changes of the late 1820s-1840s. *During the last years of the 1860s, annual English immigration increased to over 60,000.* "[165]

Ephram Beaumont of Yorkshire, England, immigrates to Wisconsin:

"Ephram Beaumont, farmer, Sec. 26; P.O. Hartland; was born in Huddersfield, Yorkshire, England, Feb. 19, 1834 and *in 1851, came to the United States, locating in Waukesha Co., Wis., where he made his home until 1854, when he went to California; engaged in mining there until 1862,* he returned to Waukesha County and purchased his present home, was Chairman of the Merton Town Board of Supervisors in 1868-69, and county treasurer during the years 1871-74; and served as Sheriff in 1875-76."[166]

---

[161]   *Federal Manuscript Schedule*, Population, Agricultural and Manufacturing Schedules for Waukesha County, Town of Merton, 1860.

[162]   Photograph courtesy of Jeanne Pedriana, of Elm Grove, Wisconsin, e-mail to author, Apr 23, 2010.

[163]   "The Luddites were a radical group of English textile workers and weavers in the 19th century who destroyed weaving machinery as a form of protest. The group was protesting the use of machinery in a 'fraudulent and deceitful manner' to get around standard labor practices." From: en.wikipedia.org/wiki/Luddite

[164]   https://en.wikipedia.org/wiki/Huddersfield#History

[165]   "British immigrants to the United States," (an open use website), http://immigrationtounitedstates.org/393-british-immigrants.html

[166]   *The History of Waukesha County*. Chicago: Western Historical Co., 1880, p. 948.

IMMIGRANTS TO WISCONSIN FROM ENGLAND

Name: **Henry Thomas Lumb**– Birthplace: **Wrangle, Lincolnshire County, England** (c. 1814)— Spouse: **Harriet (Vinter) Lumb**—Birthplace: **Lincolnshire, England** (1822)-Married: **Boston, Lincolnshire County, England** 18 July 1844--Residence in 1860: **Brookfield Center, Brookfield, Waukesha County**—Occupation: *farmer*— children: *John, John, Sarah Lamb, Sarah Lumb, Vintar,* Thomas, **Thomas**, *Mary E. Smith (born Lumb) & Harriet.*
(Image and genealogy courtesy of Libbie Nolan of Big Bend, Wisconsin)[167]

Henry, Thomas & Harriet Lumb (c. 1868)[168]

A Correction.

Brookfield, Aug 26, 1872

EDITOR FREEMAN: I noticed in your issue of the 22nd inst. A remark that one 'Henry Lamb' had been charged with poisoning the cattle of Charles Hart with *Paris Green*[169]. *The name should be written Henry Lumb.* You will please make the correction in your next issue as no one has ever charged any offense like the above upon Yours Respectfully, JAMES HENRY LAMBE.
[*Waukesha Freeman* Aug. 28, 1872]

"Bad Blood" between Two English Farmers:

Henry Lumb (of Lincolnshire, England) owned 120-acre farm in Brookfield (sections 10 & 15); Charles Hart (also of Lincolnshire, England) owned 110-acre farm neighboring Mr. Lumb's (sections 14 & 15). James Henry Lambe was not a neighbor to either family but merely had a name spelled similar Mr. Lumb's. *What angered Mr. Lumb to such an extent that he felt enticed to poison Mr. Hart's cattle we will likely never know.*[170]

LARGE FIELD OF WHEAT.

Yesterday, Mr. Charles Hart, of the town of Brookfield, Waukesha County, brought to this city samples of a remarkable yield of wheat. *From 23 bushels of seed, on a field of 13 ½ acres, 568 bushels were bagged.* The berries are plump, uniform, and heavy, forming samples finer than yet exhibited yet this season. The wheat is Clauson wheat and the seed was obtained from Genesee County, Mich.   [*Milwaukee Sentinel* Sept. 4, 1879]

---

[167] *Federal Manuscript Schedule*, Population, Agricultural and Manufacturing Schedules for Waukesha County, Town of Brookfield, 1860.

[168] Photograph courtesy of Libbie Nolan, in care of Pat Nolan, both of Big Bend, Wisconsin, e-mail to author, Dec. 21, 2016.

[169] "Paris green (copper(II) acetate triarsenite or copper(II) acetoarsenite) is an inorganic compound . It is a highly toxic emerald-green crystalline powder that has been used as a rodenticide and insecticide, At the turn of the 20th century, Paris green, blended with lead arsenate, was used in America and elsewhere as an insecticide on produce such as apples. The toxic mixture is said 'to have burned the trees and the grass around the trees." From: https://en.wikipedia.org/wiki/Paris_Green

[170] Author, *Brookfield: A Fine and Fertile Land,* vol. 1, p. 13.

IMMIGRANTS TO WISCONSIN FROM ENGLAND

Name: **John Lumb**—*born:* **Wrangle, Lincolnshire, England** *(24 Apr1840)* –*parents:* **Henry & Eliza Lumb** of **Wrangle, Lincolnshire, England** --*John Lumb's* spouse: ***Emily Experience Snyder***— born: **Granville, Milwaukee County, Wisconsin** (26 Apr 1847) —Marriage: **Granville, Milwaukee County, Wisconsin** (18 May 1871) --Residence in 1910: **Menomonee Falls, Waukesha County, Wisconsin**—Occupation: *farmer*--Children: *Adda Stella (Russell)*. *John Lumb's* Death: **Menomonee Falls, Waukesha County, Wisconsin** (20 Jan 1919).
(Image and genealogy courtesy of Cathryn Larsen of Kenosha, Wisconsin)[171]

Emily Experience Snyder Lumb (c. 1868)[172]

Waukesha County Historian Extraordinaire:

Libbie Nolan celebrated her centennial birthday in January 2017.

"For those of you who are not familiar with Libbie Nolan, Libbie has shared her life-time love for Waukesha County history through her long-time role as *editor*, along with her written contributions to "Landmark," the quarterly publication of the *Waukesha County Historical Society*, as a staff writer for *the Waukesha Freeman*, her involvement with *the New Berlin Historical Society*, along with her *gifted artistic work*."—*Tom Ramstack*

Libbie's Great-Grandparents:

"John Lumb died in 1918 falling off a ladder. He was trying to shut the door of the second floor of the barn on a windy day. The wind blew the door knocking him off the ladder. He was trying to help pigeons on that winter day. John Lumb could not read, but his wife Emily Experience (Snyder) Lumb was a teacher."—*Libbie Nolan*[173]

Women's Clothing Styles of the 1860's:

"Emily wears a modest hoop, implying that she is wearing a day dress very likely designed and sown at home. The fabric is a dark and white checked pattern. *Be cautious, all that looks black, in every type of period photograph, is not always black.* In some techniques, green and blue come out jet black. While dress sleeves in the sixties, of this period are typically loose and curved at the elbow, Emily's dress shows very little elbow flair. She wears a small, white collar of lace or linen closed at the neck with a brooch. Her dress is small-waisted and ruffled at the wrists." --*Joan Severa, 19th Century Clothing Styles.*[174]

[171] *Federal Manuscript Schedule*, Population, Agricultural and Manufacturing Schedules for Waukesha County, Town of Menomonee, 1910.

[172] Photograph courtesy of Cathryn Larsen of Kenosha, Wisconsin, e-mail to author, Mar 24, 2011.

[173] Author visit with Libbie Nolan, Jan. 15, 2010.

[174] Joan Severa of Madison, Wisconsin, e-mail to author, Jan. 23, 2010.

SETTLERS TO WISCONSIN FROM NEW YORK AND MAINE

Name: **_George Barney_**– Birthplace: **Adams, Jefferson County, New York** (1825)—Spouse: **Julia Washburn**
Birthplace: **Industry, Maine** (1831)—Residence in 1870: **Waukesha, Waukesha County**—Occupation: *farmer*–
Children: *Sabrina, Denentin, Henry, Carrie, Milton, Harlon, Nellie, Charlie & Lottie*—Other residence in home:
Jefferson Root—*farm laborer* & Ann Wheeler—*domestic*.
(Image and genealogy courtesy of Ann Josher of Woodhaven, Queens, New York)[175]

George Barney (c. 1868)[176]

Steaming through the lakes from New York to Wisconsin:

"Mr. *George Barney* can trace his ancestry back to three brothers. One came from England, one from Wales, and the other from Ireland. Two of the brothers married Holland Dutch women in the Mohawk Valley. George Barney is a native of Adams, Jefferson County, of the old Empire State, born June 22, 1825, being the only child born to Sebina and Polly (Manderville) Barney. *At this point George and his grandfather stepped aboard the steamer "United States."* They touched at Rochester, N. Y., and there visited for a while; they took a packet for Buffalo, then re-shipped on the old steamer, "Ben Franklin," for Detroit, and when *the vessel came to Detroit, she was so badly disabled in breaking the ice that there were only two paddles left on one wheel and three on the other*, which necessitated very slow progress in travel. George Barney, wife and son, came on to Wisconsin, Milwaukee being their objective point. This was in the spring of 1837."[177]

A log cabin at Prairieville:

"There being no stage or transportation of any kind, they walked out to Waukesha, which was then known as Prairieville. Mr. Barney bought a claim of three hundred and twenty acres for $313. The tract of land lay just south of the present village of Waukesha. They moved upon this claim in the spring of 1838, and the first habitation was the veritable log cabin home, about 16x18 feet in dimensions; a projecting roof on the south side formed a shed. The roof was covered with oak shingles twenty inches in length. *Remnants of the tribes of the Menomonee's, Pottawatomie's and Winnebago's had their lodges within a short distance of his home*. The principal market was Milwaukee, and the people hauled their grain there with ox teams."[178]

---

[175]   *Federal Manuscript Schedule*, Population, Agricultural and Manufacturing Schedules for Waukesha County, Town of Waukesha, 1850.

[176]   Photograph courtesy of e-mail to author by Ann Josher of Woodhaven, Queens, New York, July 10, 2011
May 14, 2010

[177]   *Portrait and Biographical Record of Waukesha County, 1894*, pp. 215-216.

[178]   *Portrait and Biographical Record of Waukesha County, 1894*, pp. 217-218.

SETTLERS TO WISCONSIN FROM NEW YORK AND MAINE

Name: **George Barney**– Birthplace: **Adams, Jefferson County, New York** (1825)—Spouse: *Julia Washburn*--Birthplace: **Industry, Franklin County, Maine** (1831)—Marriage: Waukesha, Waukesha County, Wisconsin (13 Mar 1854) --Residence in 1870: Waukesha, Waukesha County —Occupation: *farmer*– Children: *Sabina, De Newton, Henry, Carrie (Tingle), Milton, Harlow, Nellie, Charles, May & Lottie*—Other residence: Jefferson Root—*laborer* & Ann Wheeler—*domestic*.

(Image and genealogy courtesy of Ann Josher of Woodhaven, Queens, New York) [179]

Julia Washburn (c. 1868)[180]

Julia Washburn along with her five daughters were all teachers:

"Mrs. Barney was a native of Industry, Maine, and was born November 6, 1831. Her father was a cousin of Elihu Washburn. *She received an excellent education and was a teacher for ten years.* Her mother was an accomplished lady. There were one son and five daughters in the Washburn family, all the daughters being teachers. Mr. George Barney wedded Miss Julia A. Washburn *and to this marriage have been born ten children,* six sons and four daughters. Seven are living, as follows: Sabina, of Waukesha; De Newton, at home; Henry, deceased, and Carrie B., the wife of A. H. Tingle, of Harlan, Iowa. Milton W., a resident of Zanesville, Wis.; Harlow F., employed at the Industrial School of Waukesha; Nellie is deceased; Charles A.; May is deceased, and Lottie E. The latter has been a student in the Union School of Waukesha for many years and is a graduate of the Spencerian Business College of Milwaukee; she is also a fine stenographer and holds a teacher's certificate in Waukesha County."[181]

19th Century women best suited for the teaching of children:

"By the early 19th century with the rise of the new United States, a new mood was alive in urban areas. *Especially influential were the writings of Lydia Maria Child, Catharine Maria Sedgwick, and Lydia Sigourney, who developed the role of republican motherhood as a principle that United States and family by equating a successful republic with virtuous families.* Women, as intimate and concerned observers of young children, were best suited to the role of guiding and teaching children. By the 1840s, New England writers such as Child, Sedgwick, and Sigourney became respected models and advocates for improving and expanding education for females. Greater educational access meant formerly male-only subjects, such as mathematics and philosophy, were to be integral to curricula at public and private schools for girls. By the late 19th century, these institutions were extending and reinforcing the tradition of women as educators and supervisors of American moral and ethical values."[182]

---

179 *Federal Manuscript Schedule*, Population, Agricultural and Manufacturing Schedules for Waukesha County, Town of Waukesha, 1870.

180 Photograph courtesy of Ann Josher of Woodhaven, Queens, New York, e-mail to author, July 10, 2011.

181 *Portrait and Biographical Record of Waukesha County, 1894*, p. 217.

182 https://en.wikipedia.org/wiki/History_of_education_in_the_United_States

IMMIGRANTS TO WISCONSIN FROM IRELAND

Name: <u>**Thomas Cleary**</u>– Birthplace: at <u>Moyglas, County Galway, Ireland</u> (18 Mar 1819)—Spouse: <u>**Julie Cleary**</u> (1819)— Birthplace: <u>County Galway, Ireland</u> (1819)—Marriage: <u>County Galway, Ireland</u> (1845)— Residence in 1880: <u>Lafayette, Walworth, Wisconsin</u>. Occupation: *farmer*—Residence in 1900: <u>Waukesha, Waukesha County, Wisconsin</u> —Children: *John, James, Thomas, Michael, Francis, Joseph, Julia & Mary*.
(Image and genealogy courtesy of Linda Cleary of San Francisco, California)[183]

Thomas Cleary Family, Walworth County (1868)[184] *--tintype*

Anti-Catholicism in Ireland:

"After the Protestant Reformation and until at least the late 20th Century, the majority of Protestant states (especially the United Kingdom and the United States) made anti-Catholicism and opposition to the Pope and Catholic rituals major political themes, with anti-Catholic sentiment at times leading to violence and religious discrimination against Catholic individuals. Historically, Catholics in Protestant countries were frequently suspected of conspiring against the state in furtherance of papal interests or to establish a political hegemony under the "Papacy", with Protestants sometimes questioning Catholic individuals' loyalty to the state and suspecting Catholics ultimately maintaining loyalty to the Vatican rather than maintaining loyalty to their domiciled countries. In majority Protestant countries with large scale immigration, such as the United States, suspicion or discrimination of Catholic immigrants often overlapped or conflated with nativism, xenophobia, and racist sentiments."[185]

Parish of Balinakill, County Galway, Ireland

Thomas Cleary was born at Moyglas, in the parish of Balinakill, county Galway, Ireland, on the 18th of March, 1819… Mr. Cleary was one of the noblest specimens of that heroic band of brave pioneers who fled from the hardship of their native land, after the never-to-be forgotten days of 1845, and "black '47", and contributed of their splendid qualities of mind and heart, to the prosperity of church and country in this western land more than a half century ago. They hated tyranny, for tyranny had made desolate their native land. *They despised intolerance, and persecution in the name of religion, for religious bigotry and intolerance had consigned their forefathers to ignorance and poverty in Catholic Ireland.*
[*Waukesha Plaindealer* June 22, 1908]

---

183   *Federal Manuscript Schedule*, Population, Agricultural and Manufacturing Schedules for Walworth County, Town of Lafayette, 1880.

184   Photograph courtesy of Linda Cleary of San Francisco, California, e-mail to author, Oct 19, 2011.

185   https://en.wikipedia.org/wiki/Anti-Catholicism

SETTLERS TO WISCONSIN FROM MASSACHUSETTS & RHODE ISLAND

Name: **George Lawrence**— Birthplace: **Village of Shannock, Town of Richmond, Rhode Island** (16 Nov 1839)—Spouse: **Virginia Elizabeth Hall**— Birthplace: **East Wareham, Massachusetts** (13 Feb 1839)—Marriage: East Wareham, Massachusetts (4 Mar 1857) --Year of immigration to Wisconsin: (c. 1860)—Residence in 1870: Town of Waukesha, Waukesha County, Wisconsin —Occupation: *farmer & sheep-breeder* –Children: **George**, Harry, Harriett, and Eliza. —Death: Chicago, Cook County, Illinois (29 Nov 1890).
(Image and genealogy courtesy of Libbie Nolan of Big Bend, Wisconsin.)[186]

Virginia Lawrence (c. 1870)[187]

DEMISE OF CAPT. GEO. LAWRENCE, AN OLD RESIDENT OF WAUKESHA.

Waukesha, July 10. - Capt. Geo. Lawrence, one of the historic men of the county passed peacefully away this morning at the family residence, at 6:30 o'clock. Mr. Lawrence was surrounded by his entire family at the time of his death. Capt. Lawrence was born at Martha's Vineyard, Dukes County, Mass., on Oct. 31, 1812. He began a sailor life when a lad by sailing on the small coasters. _At the age of 16 he shipped with his father who was an old sailor, on a whaling voyage, harpooning two whales before he was 17_. During this voyage he visited China, Japan and the Sandwich Islands and was promoted to boat-steerer. From the position of a steerer he rapidly arose to the position of captain and subsequently became largely identified in the purchase of vessels. _In the fall of 1846 he made Milwaukee his headquarters; in 1847 he built the schooner Lawrence, at a cost of $12,000._ [Milwaukee Sentinel, July 11, 1883]

A Noted Wisconsin sheep-breeder:

"The early dream of the Captain is in a fair way of realization, as he, with his son (**George Jr.**), owned a splendid homestead farm of 330 acres, upon which each has a pleasant and, even elegant home. _These gentlemen for many years were among the most noted of Wisconsin sheep-breeders,_ but, since the founding of the butter and cheese factory in 1877, have given their entire attention to it. They were awarded a pair of nickel-plated scales as a special premium, at the Industrial Dairy Fair, held in New York City, 1878; these scales, worth $100, were awarded for the best tub of butter."[188]

---

[186] *Federal Manuscript Schedule*, Population, Agricultural and Manufacturing Schedules for Town of Waukesha, Waukesha County, 1870.

[187] Photograph courtesy of Libbie Nolan, in care of Pat Nolan, of Big Bend, Wisconsin, e-mail to author, Dec. 21, 2016.

[188] *1880 History of Waukesha County*, pp. 839 & 840.

IMMIGRANTS TO WISCONSIN FROM OHIO

Name: **John Persons Foss Sr.** (1848-1919) --Birthplace: **Boston Township, Summit County, Ohio** ---Parents: **Person's D. Foss** (1814-1884) & **Mary P. Olds** (1803-1870)—Residence: **Oconomowoc, Waukesha County, Wisconsin** (1860) -- Spouse: ***Charlotte Armstrong*** —Birthplace: **Lake Geneva, Walworth County, Wisconsin** (10 March 1853)—Parents: **George Armstrong** (1816-1902) & **Eliza Tymersen** (1814-1895)—John & Mary's Marriage: **Lincoln Township, Monroe County, Wisconsin** (12 Dec 1869)—Charlotte's age: 16--Residence in 1870: **Oconomowoc, Waukesha County, Wisconsin**— Occupation: *farmer*—Children: *Mary, Louis, Laura Dell, Infant-still born (1874), Infant-still born (1876) –Charlotte (Armstrong) Foss (age: 23)—Death: while in labor with the second stillborn.* (Image and genealogy courtesy of Catherine A. Fanara of Madison, Wisconsin)[189]

Charlotte (Armstrong) Foss (1870)

Charlotte's mother came from old Dutch Lineage:

"(*Charlotte Armstrong's mother, Eliza Tymersen, born in Holl in New Ames and, in 1814, was from old Dutch lineageterdam, now lower Manhattan*) dating back to the 1660's. Her father's lineage remains a mystery, but we know they were Irish." — **Allison Fanara**[190]

The old Dutch Settlement captured by the English:

"By 1655, the population of New Netherland had grown to 2,000 people, half of Dutch-Netherlands origin and the other half from Spanish-Netherlands, French-Netherlands, Germanic nations, Sweden, Norway, Finland, Portugal, and other European places, 1,500 living in New Amsterdam… New Amsterdam was renamed New York on September 8, 1664 in honor of the Duke of York (later James II of England), in whose name the English had captured it. *The English kept the island of Manhattan, the Dutch giving up their claim to the town and the rest of the colony*, while the English formally abandoned the island of Run in the East Indies to the Dutch, confirming their control of the valuable Spice Islands. Today much of what was once New Amsterdam is New York City."[191]

New Amsterdam, Wisconsin:

New Amsterdam is an unincorporated community located in the town of Holland, in La Crosse County, Wisconsin, United States. *Settlers from the Netherlands originally settled in the area in 1853.*[192]

---

189 *Federal Manuscript Schedule*, Population, Agricultural and Manufacturing Schedules for Town of Oconomowoc, Waukesha County, 1860.

190 Photograph courtesy of Allison Fanara, of Madison, Wisconsin, e-mail to author, Nov 14, 2011.

191 https://en.wikipedia.org/wiki/New_Amsterdam

192 https://en.wikipedia.org/wiki/New_Amsterdam,_Wisconsin

IMMIGRANTS TO WISCONSIN FROM SCOTLAND

Name: **John Howie**– birthplace: **New Miln, Stewarton County: Ayrshire, Scotland** (10 Dec 1812)—Occupation: *laborer*-- Spouse: **Marion Miller**—Birthplace: **Loudoun, Ayrshire, Scotland** (1814-1875)—Marriage: **Loudoun, Ayr (Ayrshire) Scotland** (13 Mar 1841)—Residence: St Quivox, Ayrshire, Scotland (1841)—Immigration to Wisconsin: (1841) Children: *John* (1843-1863), *William* (1845-1904), *James* (1847-1936) & *Jane* (1850-1889)—Residence in 1850: Waukesha, Waukesha County--Death: Waukesha, Waukesha County (11 Nov 1852)— George Robertson—Birth: Caledonia, Racine County, Wisconsin (1 Aug 1845)--married *Jane Howie* at Waukesha (13 Apr 1870)—Occupation: *farmer*.

(Image and genealogy courtesy of Waukesha County Historical Society and Museum.)[193]

Jane Howie Robertson (c. 1870)[194]

Lowland farmers forced out of Scotland:

"Agriculture in the Lowlands was steadily upgraded after 1700, and standards remained high. *However, after the repeal of the Corn Laws in 1846, when Britain adopted a free trade policy, grain imports from America undermined the profitability of crop production. The result was a continuous exodus from the land—to America...* Emigration from Scotland peaked in the mid-nineteenth century, when more than a million Scots left for the United States."[195]

The Scottish Covenanters:

"The Covenanters were a Scottish Presbyterian movement that played an important part in the history of Scotland during the 17th century. They derived their name from the word covenant meaning a band, legal document or agreement, with reference to the Covenant between God and the Israelites in the Old Testament. In North America Covenanters became known as members of the Reformed Presbyterian Church. *They were among the most vocal agitators for independence from Great Britain and volunteered in large numbers as soldiers in the revolutionary armies.* The Covenanters were opposed to slavery."[196]

The Scots of Vernon:

"A significantly large number of immigrant Scots settled in Vernon Township, Waukesha, County. A Covenanter congregation was organized in Vernon Township by Scottish settlers in October 1848 with Rev. James Milligan at the home of James Wright Sr. *This was the only Covenanter church ever formed in Wisconsin. Although the church was not built until 1857, the cemetery was established in 1855. The first burial was Duncan McNaughton. The cemetery was referred to as Covenanter's Cemetery.*"[197]

---

[193] *Federal Manuscript Schedule*, Population, Agricultural and Manufacturing Schedules for Waukesha County, Town of Waukesha, Waukesha County, 1850.

[194] Jane Howie Robertson photograph c. 1870, People P-Q-R Box 6:8, Photography Collection, Research Center Library & Archive, Waukesha County Historical Society & Museum, Waukesha, Wisconsin.

[195] https://en.wikipedia.org/wiki/Economic_history_of_Scotland

[196] https://en.wikipedia.org/wiki/Covenanter

[197] Courtesy of Jim Olson and the Big Bend Vernon Historical Society.

IMMIGRANTS TO WISCONSIN FROM NORWAY

Name: **Ole Ingebrechsten Kaarfeld Corfield**—*born:* **Østre (eastern) Gausdal Oppland County, Norge**, (8 Jan 1810)—*daughter:* **Martha Olddsatter** -- *Marriage to:* **Elie (Elise) Nilsdatter 'Corfeld' Brendum** --*Born: in* **Follebqu Gausdal, Norge** *(20 Dec 1814)*--Follebu is a village situated in the south of Gausdal.—Children: *Anne, Even Olson & Nicolai*—Emigration—on the *"Praecosia"* (from Norway to New York)—Residence: **Lebanon Township, Dodge County** (1850)— Children: *Caroline, Minnie, Mathia & Mathias*—Residence: **Ixonia, Jefferson County** (1857). Ollie and Elise's fifth child: **Anne Olesdatter Kaarfeld Corfeld**--married: **Nels Gunnarsen Naas Gunderson** of **Ixonia, Jefferson County** (15 June 1861)--Occupation: *farmer*—Children: *Caspera "Cassie", Ella Mathia, Nellie Avida, Nellie, Gunder, Olaf, Tina Marie, Nicholas, "Nettie"& Alma*—Caspera Nels and Anne's ninth child: *Nicholas Gunderson*--born (5 Nov 1876) in **Ixonia, Jefferson County, Wisconsin**.

(Narrative and genealogy courtesy of Susan Goodman of Chevy Chase, Maryland.)[198]

Ole Corfield Family [199]

Østre Gausdal Church in Gausdal (2013)

Østre Gausdal Church:

"It is a long Church of stone from around 1250 in Gausdal municipality, Oppland County, Norway. The Romanesque stone church was built in the period 1250-1300. In the 1700 's it was extended to the East. *It has a carved pulpit with akantusdekor (ornamentation) from the 1700 's.* The Swedes set fire to the Church in 1567 during the 'seven years' war."[200]

The municipality of Gausdal:

"*Gausdal is a municipality in Oppland County, Norway. Follebu is a township and sub-parish in eastern Gausdal.* The source of its name comes from the Old Norse form of the name was *Gausdalr*. The first element is the river name Gausa and the last element is *dalr* which means "valley" or "dale". The municipality of Gausdal was established 1 January 1838. Follebu is the parish of Gausdal in Oppland, Norway. The Follebu stone church was built during the early Middle Ages."[201]

The Corfeld Family Immigration Story:

"*My mother, Anne Kaarfeld Corfeld, was born in Gulbrandsdalen, Norge, March 17, 1839. As a little girl of six years of age, she came to America in the Spring of 1845 with her parents, Ole Ingebrechtsen Kaarfeld Corfeld and Elie Nilsdatter Berndum, who were among the pioneers who braved the frontier life and blazed the way for the future State.* The trip across the Atlantic was made in seven weeks in a sailboat called *"Oleous."* When they reached New York, there was great rejoicing, for they had made the trip in record time and had beaten the *"Presiosa"* which was considered one of the fastest boats, by two days. They reached Milwaukee by way of the Great Lakes August 10th of the same year." — **Nicholas Gunderson (father of Caspara Gunderson, circa--1870).**[202]

---

[198]   *Federal Manuscript Schedule, Population,* Agricultural and Manufacturing Schedules for Waukesha County, Town of Oconomowoc, 1900.

[199]   Østre Gausdal Church source: https://no.wikipedia.org/wiki/Østre_Gausdal_kirke

[200]   https://no.wikipedia.org/wiki/Østre_Gausdal_kirke

[201]   https://en.wikipedia.org/wiki/Gausdal

[202]   *"The Corfeld Immigrant Story,"* courtesy of Susan Goodman of Chevy Chase, Maryland, e-mailed to author, Jun 9, 2016.

IMMIGRANTS TO WISCONSIN FROM SAXONY

Name: **August Thomas Caesar**—*Birthplace:* <u>**Donndorf, Sachsen**</u> *(1820):* —*Spouse:* **Christine Reinhardt** *(1822)*—Birthplace: <u>**Sachsen, Germany**</u> —Port of departure: Bremen, Germany—Ship name: *"F. J. Wichelhausen"*—Port of arrival: New York immigrants to Wisconsin—August & Christine's— residence in 1880: <u>Muskego Township, Waukesha County, Wisconsin</u>—Occupation: *farmer*—Children: *Melinda (1849), Herman (1853), Fredrich (1856), Luis (1859), Anna (1862)* and *William (1867)*---Thomas Caesar's nephew: **Friedrich Franz Caesar**—Birth date: (30 July1854)—Birthplace: <u>**Village of Lossa, Burgenlandkreis District, Sachsen**</u>: "Taufe"--baptism (30 Aug 1854)—<u>*Parish of Donndorf—church: Evangelische Kirche Donndorf (Kr. Eckartsberga.).*</u> The distance between Donndorf and Lossa, Sachsen is 6.7 miles. Both families were members of the parish of Donndorf, Saxony.
(Letter and genealogy courtesy of Elaine Alane of Helensville, Wisconsin)[203]

The Battle of Mars-La-Tour:

"The battle was fought on 16 August 1870, during the Franco-Prussian War, near the town of <u>*Mars-La-Tour*</u> in northeast France. Two Prussian corps encountered the entire French Army of the Rhine in a meeting engagement and, surprisingly, successfully forced the Army of the Rhine to retreat into the fortress of Metz."[205]

Frederick Caesar:

"The Kingdom of Saxony took part in the Franco-Prussian War on the side of Prussia. <u>*Frederick Caesar*</u> was conscripted into the army in the spring of 1869. Frederick's letter (below) provide visions of the horror of war. *Frederick* may have been a nephew to *August Thomas Caesar* who had previously emigrated from Saxony to Muskego Township, Waukesha County, WI."[206]

The Franco-Prussian War (1870)[204]

Pierre-Georges Jeanniot's portrait, depicting The Battle of Mars-la-Tour, fought on 16 August 1870 during the Franco-Prussian War near the town of Mars-la-Tour.

The Horrible fighting in France:

March 22,1871, Ormelle, France
Dear Cousin:
On the 30th in the morning at 5 o'clock we marched and left our Quarters in Bivouac until noon, attack… Now we were laying in the ditches and gave them their daily bread back. Our Artillery behind us shot at them too, now with grenades. <u>*Whole rows of French soldiers just fell to the ground … In the dark we gathered our wounded and brought them here to the flour mill.*</u> The moaning and crying out for pain were terrible. Some of my comrades were terrible crippled and the tears just ran down my cheeks to see this. My regiment had around 500 injured and dead. The French lost a lot more… This little town here, Bourilles, is where the people were so mean to us. They dragged our wounded people into fires and poked their eyes out. Everybody shot at the soldiers, women, children, girls, they all had rifles. And we killed around 70 people (only the ones who shot at the soldiers). First, they had to dig holes in the ground and then they had to stand in front of them. After they got shot, they fell backwards in the holes… This is the same town Napoleon got caught. <u>*Sept. 2, we celebrated our victory. We sang, had music and praised our King.*</u>
Lots of greetings from your cousin—
Fredrich Caesar, Musk. of Comp. & Reg. 31st'" [207]

---

[203] *Federal Manuscript Schedule*, Population, Agricultural and Manufacturing Schedules for Waukesha County, Town of Muskego, 1880.

[204] Pierre-Georges Jeanniot's print source: https://en.wikipedia.org/wiki/1870s#/media/File:Lignedefeu16August.jpg{PD-US}{{PD-US-expired}}

[205] en.wikipedia.org/wiki/Battle_of_Mars-la-Tour

[206] Elaine Allen, e-mail to author, Aug 12, 2010.

[207] Elaine Allen, e-mail to author, Aug 12, 2010.

IMMIGRANTS TO WISCONSIN FROM BAVARIA AND WÜRTTEMBERG

Name: <u>John Michael Meidenbauer</u> – Birthplace: <u>Pruehausen, Landgericht Sulzbach, Oberpfalz, Bayern</u> (11 May 1854) — Spouse: <u>Anna Caroline Schoenwelder</u> —Birthplace— <u>Woeste Goersdorf Kreis, Waldenburg, Württemberg, Germany</u> (23 October 1865)— Year of immigration (1876)—Residence in 1880: <u>New Berlin, Waukesha County, Wisconsin</u>—Occupation: *farmer*– Children: *Lizzie, Willie, Eddie, Sewald, Annie, Emma, Sophia, Harry, Walte, Arthur & Viola.* (Image and genealogy courtesy of Roy Meidenbauer of New Berlin, Wisconsin.)[208]

J. M. Meidenbauer

(Photographed in the Bavarian Army)[209]

Prussia gathers support in war effort:

"The Franco-Prussian War of 1870, sometimes referred to as the Franco-German War, or the 1870 War was a series of battles involving the French Empire under Napoleon III, and Prussia; under King Wilhelm I. Prussia was supported by several German states, including Bavaria and Württemberg. *Because of the Prussian and German victory, the French Empire collapsed, and Napoleon III; the last monarch of France, was deposed. The Germans also took Alsace-Lorraine.*"[210]

Bavaria fought with Prussia: Introduction to letter:

John K. Meidenbauer, a 62-year-old early immigrant to New Berlin, wrote the following letter to his nephew, J. M. Meidenbauer, who had fought with the Bavarian army during the Franco-Prussian War in 1870, in which he, as if in desperate need of support on his farm, encourages his young nephew to come to the United States and join him in New Berlin.

A letter from a New Berlin farmer to his nephew serving in the Bavarian army:

To: John Meidenbauer,
Bayreuth, Bavaria, Dec. 27, 1874
Dear nephew, Your letter of November 16th I received on Dec.12th. You write that you are happy that I wrote to you. Why should I do not do that? You are my beloved brother's son; I have special interest in you. *And that I want you to come or urgently request your coming (to Wisconsin).* In your letter, please write something about your mother and stepfather. How is it with your trade? Where is sister Barbara employed? What are the others doing? In the past you have all written harsh letters to me, but I forgive you because of my dear brother, your late father. Send a picture of you with saber and spurs. I would like to see you like this. *I (will) never forgive your mother for remarrying again. Maybe you could have avoided the army. When your time is up, can you get back to the farm?* I also believe, if your father would be living, you would never have seen Bayreuth. In closing my letter, my sincere wish for you is (that) being a soldier brings you good fortune and good health. Many, many greetings from myself and my wife.
John K. Meidenbauer,
Prospect Hill, New Berlin, Wisconsin[211]

---

[208] *Federal Manuscript Schedule, Population*, Agricultural and Manufacturing Schedules for Waukesha County, Town of New Berlin, 1880.

[209] Photograph courtesy of Roy Meidenbauer of New Berlin, Wisconsin, e-mail to author, Aug 27, 2009.

[210] https://en.wikipedia.org/wiki/Franco-Prussian_War

[211] Roy Meidenbaurer, of New Berlin, Wisconsin, e-mail to author, Aug. 9, 2009.

IMMIGRANTS TO WISCONSIN FROM ALSACE, FRANCE

Name: **Thomas Andrew Schneider (Snyder)**-- Birthplace: <u>Wahlbach, Kries Mulhausen, Elsass</u>[212]<u>, France</u> (7 Jan 1811) — Spouse: **Catherine Casper**--Birthplace: **Kries Mulhausen, Haut-Rhine Department Elsass, France** (1811)—residence of Elsass, although citizens of France, did not speak French, they spoke a dialect similar to Swiss-German--Marriage <u>Buffalo, New York</u> 28 Sept 1841--Residence in 1860: <u>New Berlin Township, Waukesha County, Wisconsin</u>—Occupation: *farmer*–Children: *Anthony, Catherine, Joseph, Mary, Theresa & George*.
(Image and genealogy courtesy of Mary Stigler of Brookfield, Wisconsin)[213]

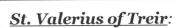

Andrew & Catherine (Casper) Schneider (c. 1871)[214]

Alsace is Occupied by Foreign Forces:

"In response to the restoration of Napoleon, in 1814 and 1815, Alsace was occupied by foreign forces, including over 280,000 soldiers and 90,000 horses in *Bas-Rhin* alone… At the same time, the population was growing rapidly, from 800,000 in 1814 to 914,000 in 1830 and 1,067,000 in 1846. *This combination of factors meant hunger, housing shortages and a lack of work for young people. Thus, it is not surprising that people fled. Many Alsatian began to sail to America.*" — **Benoît Specklin**[215]

St. Valerius of Treir:

"*According to ancient legend, St. Valerius was a follower of Saint Eucharis, the first bishop of Trier. They came to the Rhine and to Ehl (located close to the city of Benfeld in Bas-Rhin, Alsace), where their companion, Maternus, died.* His two companions hastened back to St. Peter and begged him to restore the dead man to life. St. Peter gave his pastoral staff to Eucharis, and, upon being touched with it, Maternus returned to life. After founding many churches, the three companions went to Trier, in Rhineland-Palatinate (Germany), where evangelizing progressed so rapidly that Eucharis chose that city for his episcopal residence. *An angel announced to him his approaching death and pointed out **Valerius** as his successor.*"[216]

A Catholic Church in New Berlin:

"In 1843, *Andrew Snyder (Schneider) Sr.*, came to New Berlin, Waukesha County, bought his present farm, and a *yoke of oxen* with it, for $800; *Mr. Snyder (of Haut-Rhin, Alsace) cleared over a hundred acres, has 60 of timber*; about 1860 built a large and substantial brick house. He married, 1842, in Buffalo, N. Y., Miss *Catherine Casper*. *Mr. Snyder, along with Bernard Casper, of Bas-Rhin, Alsace, initiated the construction of a Catholic Church in New Berlin (1855), to be consecrated in the name of St. Valerius of Alsace.* (*St. Valerius* was the precursor to today's *Holy Apostles Catholic Church*.)"[217]

[212] "At the time of their immigration to Wisconsin, French immigrants from Alsace spoke a language referred to Alsatin which was Germanic in dialect. Hence, they referred to their homeland as Elsass." Courtesy of, Dr. Helmut Treis of Aachen, Rheinland, Germany.

[213] *Federal Manuscript Schedule*, Population, Agricultural and Manufacturing Schedules for Waukesha County, Town of New Berlin, 1860.

[214] Photograph courtesy of Mary Stigler, of Brookfield, Wisconsin, e-mail to author, Aug 29, 2009.

[215] "Brief History of Alsace-Lorrain," http://ourworld.compuserve.com/homepages/Benoit_Specklin/Paul.Reichsl.html by Benoît Specklin, Footnote.

[216] https://en.wikipedia.org/wiki/Valerius_of_Treves. *Trier* is the German pronunciation & *Treves* the French pronunciation for the same city located west of the state of Rhineland-Palatinate (Germany).

[217] *The History of Waukesha County, 1880*, p. 921.

IMMIGRANTS TO WISCONSIN FROM PRUSSIA

Name: **Ludwig-Louis Pegler**– Birthplace: **Cygkomer, Pomerania, Preußen** (1843)—Spouse: **Christiana Beck**— Birthplace: **Waldeck, Preußen** (1853)— Residence in 1870: Milwaukee Ward 9, Milwaukee, Wisconsin— Occupation: *laborer* –Children: ***Christiana***, *Henry, Louis, Eddie, Gretchen, Margaret & Irwin*. **Christiana Pegler** married **Albert Heinrich Schrubbe** on 13 Jan. 1900. Albert & Christina Schrubbe's residence in 1912: Elm Grove, Brookfield Township, Waukesha County, Wisconsin— occupation: *farmer*—Children: *Erna, Albert Jr. & Otto*. Hattie Ohm, *a nurse*, also resides in the household.

(Image and genealogy courtesy of Jeanette Pelletier of Bay City, Michigan)[218]

Christina (Pegler) Schrubbe (c. 1871)[219]

Early Lutheran Immigration to Wisconsin:

"*The first immigration of Germans to Wisconsin in large numbers was that of the so-called Old Lutherans of Pomerania who came between 1839 and 1845, because of the attempt by King Frederick William IV, of Prussia to unite the Lutheran and Reformed faiths.* In a relatively brief time, Lutheranism lost favor in favor of the Reformed faiths. The King no longer tolerated the Lutheran church in this land. *Capt. Von Rohr* was chosen to engage passage for them to go to America and choose places for settlement. *These early settlers were not only the first body of German immigrants to Wisconsin; they were also the beginning of the Lutheran church in the state.*"[220]

Congregations compete for new members:

"American denominationalists saw competition as essential for gaining members; thus, public debates over doctrines ensued. Tensions between specific congregations and their pastors have led to court cases and violence amongst congregations."[221]

Lutherans vs. Catholics in America:

"During the 1930's, Joseph Ramstack Sr., ran a tavern and small farm in the village of Elm Grove in the town of Brookfield. On the east end of the village, stood the farm of Albert Schrubbe. *In the winter of 1940, Albert died in an automobile accident involving 20-year-old, Howard Ramstack, who was charged with manslaughter in causing Mr. Schrubbe's death.* The collision took place on W. North Ave. a quarter mile west of YY in Brookfield." Joe Ramstack Sr. (uncle of Howard Ramstack) helped Mrs. Schrubbe and her sons on their farm after Mr. Schrubbe's death. When Mrs. (Christina) Schrubbe passed away (13 Dec 1940), the Schrubbe children asked Joe Sr. to be a pallbearer at their mother's funeral. But their request had created a dilemma. *The Schrubbe's were Lutheran and the Ramstack's were Catholic.* Joe Sr. had to get special permission from the pastor at St. Mary's Catholic Church, in Elm Grove, to participate in the funeral. *Regrettably, the pastor refused his request. In those days it was almost a 'mortal sin' for a Catholic to attend a Lutheran Church service.* Unfazed, however, Joe Sr. went ahead and took part as a pallbearer at Mrs. Schrubbe's funeral."—***Joseph Ramstack Jr.***[222]

[218] *Federal Manuscript Schedule*, Population, Agricultural and Manufacturing Schedules for Waukesha County, Town of Brookfield, 1920.

[219] Photograph courtesy of Jeanette Pelletier of Bay City, Michigan, e-mail to author, Jun 28, 2010.

[220] Kate A Everst, "Early Lutheran Immigration in Wisconsin," *Wisconsin Academy of Science, Arts and Letters. Transaction 8 images.library.wisc. edu Abstract, 1892,* pp. 289 & 293 - 295.

[221] Bill J. Leonard and Jill Y. Crenshaw, Editors, Encyclopedia of Religious Controversies in the United States, 2nd. Edition. Volume One: A-L, ABC-CLIO (Santa Barbara California, Denver, Colorado, Oxford, England: 2013), preview.

[222] Author interview with his father, Joseph Ramstack Jr, on Aug. 8, 1986.

IMMIGRANTS TO WISCONSIN FROM SWITZERLAND AND BAVARIA

Name: **Benedikt Winzenreid**– Birthplace: **Canton Bern, Schweiz** (c. 1832)—Spouse: **Anna Kunigunda Ramstöck**—Birthplace: **Germersberg, Bayern** (1827)—Residence in 1870: **Brookfield Township, Waukesha County**—Occupation: *farmer*–Children: *Julia Ann, Petar, Christian & Susannah*. (Image courtesy of Elaine Moss of Oconto, Wisconsin; Genealogy courtesy of Maralyn A. Wellauer-Lenius of Winnipeg, Manitoba, Canada.) [223]

Benedict, Julia Anna (daughter) and Anna (Ramstöck) Winzenreid (c. 1871)[224]

Desperate Swiss families immigrate to Wisconsin (1840s-1860s):

"The Wellauer brothers (George, Henry, and Rudolph) who had brought their Swiss born wives and children to Brookfield Township. *They had come to Waukesha County from Wagenhausen, Canton Thurgau where economic conditions were poor, wood and food scarce.* One brother was in debt and the other found it difficult to support their families in their small Rhine River community. *Town chronicles repeat the hard times and suffering. At one time the people were forced to seek 'clover, nettles, wood cabbage (holzkraut) and snails for their sustenance'.*"[225]

The Swiss Colony in Brookfield Township:

"*Jacob Wellauer became the most outstanding figure of then Swiss colony of Brookfield.* Locating there with his parents in 1850, he later went to Milwaukee, where he established one of the largest grocery houses in the state. *Jacob Spycher, a Bernese, likewise came to the town in 1850, almost immediately beginning the successful manufacture of cheese.* Another influential Swiss was Jacob Hengy, who was a tailor in Prairieville as early as 1840 and built in 1845 the famous Exchange Tavern of that place, which he conducted for some years. In the early fifties he bought a farm in the southwestern part of the town of Brookfield. *Other pioneers, who members of the Swiss colony in Brookfield where Brennemann, Braeu, Grub, the Ochsners, Reiss, Maurer, the Schmutz and Winzenreid families.*"[226]

---

[223] *Federal Manuscript Schedule*, Population, Agricultural and Manufacturing Schedules for Waukesha County, Town of Brookfield, 1870.

[224] Photograph courtesy of Elaine Moss of Oconto, Wisconsin, e-mail to author, Dec 7, 2016.

[225] Maralyn Wellauer, "Waukesha County's Swiss Pioneers," *Landmark*, v. 25, n. 4 (Winter, 1982), p. 4. Maralyn Wellauer has continued a comprehensive research of Swiss Immigration to Wisconsin. In progress since 1980, her research is attached to the Foundation for East European Family History Studies (FEEFHS), found online at: http://feefhs.org/resource/switzerland-immigration-to-wisconsin.

[226] J.H.A. Lacher, "German Pioneers of Brookfield," *Wisconsin Domesday Book—Town Studies, vol. 1*: (Madison: Wisconsin Historical Society, 1924), p. 32.

SETTLERS TO WISCONSIN FROM INDIANA & DELAWARE

Name: –**Herbert R. Elderkin**— Birthplace: **Indiana** (c. 1834) –Spouse: **Anna** (c. 1837)—Birthplace: **Delaware**— Residence in 1880: <u>Oconomowoc, Waukesha County, Wisconsin</u>—occupation: *physician*—Children: *Laura, Anna & Philazania.* (Image and genealogy courtesy of Waukesha County Historical Society and Museum.)[227]

H. R. Elderkin M.D. (1871)[228]

19th *Century Treatment for Consumption (Tuberculosis) was generally ineffective:*

Elm Grove, Aug 17, 1868

"Dear Bro (Robert Curran Jr):

We know what change a day may make in our plans. *I went to Waukesha, saw the Indian Dr. & did not think much of him.* Still ordered medicine. Went to Olin's Bro. for dinner. Mr. Olin was a strong believer in little pills & had great faith in Dr. Kendrick, a Dr. of that system. *Finally, I submitted to an examination & brought home a couple of vials. Having been taking the medicine today, I think it has helped me.* Use all haste in money matters. If you can send me some more than mentioned before. I suppose I will spend what I have & don't know what it will cost to lay over.

Yours affectionally,

Charles Curran"[229]

Devastating diseases appeared in Wisconsin during the 1870's:

H. R. Elderkin, M.D., of Oconomowoc had much sickness to tend to during the decade of the 1870's. "Wisconsin settlers in the immediate post-Civil War period found little that resembled the healthful paradise they expected after reading the glowing immigrant reports. True, the peaceful prairies and gently rolling hills presented a welcome contrast to the dirt and clutter of Milwaukee, the city through which many passed on their way northward. *The new arrivals soon enough learned that sickness and disease regularly crossed political boundaries and wrought havoc among those in the hinterland as well as the cities. Typhoid fever, typhus, diphtheria, and small-pox, along with pneumonia, measles, scarlet fever, mumps, and other diseases appeared with appalling frequency.*"[230] — **Dale E. Treleven**

---

[227] *Federal Manuscript Schedule*, Population, Agricultural and Manufacturing Schedules for Waukesha County, Town of Oconomowoc, 1880.

[228] H.R. Elderkin M.D. photograph c. 1871, People C-D-E Box 2:8, Photography Collection, Research Center Library & Archive, courtesy of the Waukesha County Historical Society & Museum, Waukesha, Wisconsin.

[229] Jean Alonzo Curran. "Curran Family History" u/p, 1970. Courtesy of Oconomowoc Public Library—Charles Curran's letter to his brother Robert in Brookfield. Despite good intentions and genuine efforts on the part of doctors, tuberculosis was frequently mis-diagnosed during the mid-19th Century and treatments were, generally, ineffective. Charles Curran died from the effects of tuberculosis in Sept. 1868.

[230] Dale E. Treleven, "One Hundred Years of Health and Healing in Rural Wisconsin." In Numbers, Ronald L. & Judith Walzer Leavitt. WISCONSIN MEDICINE. © 1981 by the Board of Regents of the University of Wisconsin System. Reproduced courtesy of the University of Wisconsin Press, pp. 134 & 135.

IMMIGRANTS TO WISCONSIN FROM WÜRTTEMBERG

Name: **August Shaefle**– birthplace: **Balgheim, Tuttlingen, Württemberg** (c. 1834) — Spouse: **Katherine Henstler**—Birthplace: **Balgheim, Tuttlingen, Württemberg, Germany** (1846) —Emigration: Departed Bremen 9 Oct 1866 aboard *"S.S. Hansa"*. Residence in 1880: **Brookfield Township, Waukesha County, Wisconsin**– Occupation: *physician*— Children: *Sophia, John, Gusta, Kate & Emma*.
(Image and genealogy courtesy of the Williams family of Oconomowoc, Wisconsin)[231]

Sophia Shaefle (c. 1871)[232]

Notice.

THE Public will take notice, that my wife, Caroline Gerl, left on the 29th of January last, without cause or provocation; and I do caution all persons against trusting her on my account, as *I will pay no debts of her contracting.*
HENRY GERL.
[*Waukesha Republic* Feb. 17, 1857]

Horse Whipped:

"Augusts' son, John Schaeffel, was known to remark that his father horse whipped him on several occasions for committing relatively minor offenses (laziness, skipping school, etc.). However, this often-embattled duo were frequent companions. When John was a lad, he was the designated driver when his father went out on his rounds. There could've been a practical reason for this, but I think Mom said that Dr. Schaefle thought it was more dignified to be chauffeured." —*Sue Ellen Williams*[233]

Police Pickings.

Caroline Woelfel is convinced that he better half, Fred Woelfel, requires judicial reproof for his careless exercise of his knuckles. The charge is assault and battery and this forenoon the case is to be brought to notice of Judge Mallory.
[*Milwaukee Sentinel* July 26, 1878]

19th century spousal abuse:

"Probably the most visible difference in the status of American women (as opposed to German women) was the acceptability of open physical abuse. *A German man, for example wrote to a former friend, 'He beat his wife for every little thing, and that's not done here. Here a wife must be treated like a wife and not like a scrub rag...* He who likes to beat his wife had better stay in Germany.' Another German, Christian Kirst, echoed this view in 1881: 'As a man here things are the opposite from over there. 'Here the woman rules the roost, if a man comes home drunk and his wife reports him, he gets put into *Prison*.' The first time for 5 days and then longer and longer if he does it again... she doesn't need witnesses.'"[234]

---

231   *Federal Manuscript Schedule*, Population, Agricultural and Manufacturing Schedules for Waukesha County, Town of Brookfield, 1880.

232   Photograph courtesy of the Williams family of Oconomowoc, Wisconsin, e-mail to author, Jun 28, 2010.

233   The Williams family of Oconomowoc, Wisconsin, e-mail to author, Jun 27, 2010.

234   Weatherford, *Foreign and Female*, p. 345.

IMMIGRANTS TO WISCONSIN FROM IRELAND AND NEW YORK

(1st Generation): Name: **Thomas Faulkner Sr.**—Birthplace: **Lisson, Tyrone County, Ireland** (28 Apr 1793)—Spouse: **Mary (King) Faulkner**--Birthplace: **Monroe County, New York** (22 Oct 1799) -- Member: Reformed Presbyterian Church--(2nd Generation): Son: **Thomas Faulkner Jr.**-- Birthplace: **Livingston County, New York** (12 July 1822)—Spouse: **Nancy E. Cheney**—Place of birth: **New York State**—Residence in 1860: **Prospect Hill, New Berlin Township, Waukesha County**—Occupation: *farmer*—Children: *Viola, Clara & Rufus*--also residing in this household are Nancy's parent's **Rufus & Lydia Cheney**—both of **New Hampshire**. Members: Free Will Baptist Church. Thomas Faulkner Jr.'s Death: 22 Feb 1904.

(Image and genealogy courtesy of Cathryn Larsen of Kenosha, Wisconsin.)[235]

Thomas Faulkner Sr. (c. 1871)[236]

The Royal Scots Guard suppress a rebellion in Ireland:

"The Royal Scots (The Royal Regiment), once known as the Royal Regiment of Foot, was the oldest and most senior infantry regiment of the line of the British Army. The 1st Battalion had returned to the West Indies as a garrison and served there until 1797. The West Indies were hotbeds of disease, and the battalion lost more than half its strength to disease in this period. It was reformed from militia volunteers in Ireland in 1798: *This year saw a major rebellion erupt in Ireland after years of simmering tension. The "Lothian Fencibles" (Lothian is a region of the Scottish Lowlands—fencibles comes from the word defensible) fought with distinction at the Battle of Vinegar Hill, one of the more important engagements of the rebellion.* In February 1812, the regiment was retitled as the 1st Regiment of Foot (Royal Scots), the first official appearance of the popular name."[237]

Thomas Faulkner Sr. enlists in the Scots Guards:

"Thomas Faulkner Sr., was born in Ireland on the 28th of April 1793. Early in life he enlisted at Glasgow, Scotland, in the First Regiment of the Royal Scots and was sent to Lower Canada, where he fought in the War of 1812. After some time had elapsed Mr. Faulkner settle in New York State. There, his son, Thomas Jr., became engaged in the profession of teaching in, and after his emigration to Wisconsin followed that profession for eleven consecutive terms. *On the 28th of May 1846, he was united in marriage with Miss Nancy E. Moore. On the 2nd of July 1846, Mr. Faulkner and his wife arrived in Milwaukee; coming thence to the town of New Berlin, Waukesha County where they purchased eighty acres of wild land, paying $280 for the same. They erected a log cabin and began the task of developing a farm.*"[238]

235 *Federal Manuscript Schedule*, Population, Agricultural and Manufacturing Schedules for Waukesha County, Town of New Berlin, 1860.
236 Photograph courtesy of Cathryn Larsen of Kenosha, Wisconsin, e-mail to author, Mar 24, 2011.
237 https://en.wikipedia.org/wiki/Royal_Scots
238 *Portrait and Biographical Record of Waukesha County, 1894*, p. 305.

IMMIGRANTS TO WISCONSIN FROM NEW YORK

Parents: **Simon & Adeline (Ensign) Faulkner**—Son: **John Seth Faulkner**—born: **New York** (7 Aug 1842)—occupation: *carpenter*— Spouse: **Sarah L. Davis**--born: **New York** (c. 1847)—married: (1865) --birth of son: *Arthur Gilbert* (1865) --another resident: Eva Kelly—*a servant*--Residence in 1880: Waukesha, Waukesha County, Wisconsin—following death of Sarah--**John** married **Juliette Blanche Nelson** in Milwaukee, Wisconsin, (June 1, 1891)—Residence: 1900: Town of Lake, Milwaukee County.

(Image and genealogy courtesy of Cathryn Larsen of Kenosha, Wisconsin)[239]

Romance and History Told.

Across the Fox River on the road one-half mile south of Brookfield Center, were three houses of Alexander Donaldson, Charles Davis and Simon Faulkner. The last named was killed by a falling tree which he climbed after a raccoon. *His son, John Seth Faulkner, placed a couplet upon the tree which remained there for years and which read as follows: 'Simon Faulkner fell from this tree March 1ˢᵗ, 1863.'* --George E. Robinson

[*Waukesha Freeman* May 9, 1923]

John Faulkner's carpentry skills:

"Carpenters normally framed post-and-beam buildings until the end of the 19ᵗʰ century; now this old-fashioned carpentry is called timber framing. Carpenters learn this trade by being employed through an apprenticeship training—normally 4 years. *Traditional timber framing is the method of creating structures using heavy squared-off and carefully fitted and joined structured timbers with joints secured by large wooden pegs* (larger versions of the mortise and tenon joints in furniture). It is commonplace in wooden buildings from the 19ᵗʰ century and earlier. Hewing with broadaxes, adzes, and draw knives and using hand-powered braces and augers"[241]

Sarah (Davis) Faulkner (c. 1874)[240]

Women's Clothing Styles of the 1870's:

"Sarah represents a lady of high fashion. Her ringlet hair style is a little outdated for the mid-1870s. Her ringlets are formed with pined hair in the center; her side hair pulled straight to the back, where it is held with by combs. *Sarah wears long earrings typical to her hairdo style. Her earrings match her necklace and inlaid locket.* Again, you see a wide 'bleach' white neck collar, with short double white fabric running from the neck." --**Joan Severa, "19ᵗʰ Century women's clothing styles**[242]

---

[239] *Federal Manuscript Schedule*, Population, Agricultural and Manufacturing Schedules for Waukesha County, Town of New Berlin, 1860.

[240] Photograph courtesy of Cathryn Larsen, of Kenosha, Wisconsin, e-mail to author, Mar 24, 2011.

[241] https://en.wikipedia.org/wiki/Timber_framing

[242] Joan Severa of Madison, Wisconsin, e-mail to author, Jan. 23, 2010.

IMMIGRANTS TO WISCONSIN FROM EAST PRUSSIA

Name: **Wilhelm Bolter**—Birthplace: **Ostpreußen**: (c. 1843)—Spouse: **Wilhelmina Falk**— Birthplace: **Ostpreußen**: (c. 1846). Year of immigration (c. 1850's)—Residence in 1860: Brookfield Township, Waukesha County, Wisconsin—Occupation: *farmer*—Children: *Charles*, **Henrietta,** *August, Millie, Minnie, Alice & Mamie.*
(Image and genealogy courtesy of Evelyn J Nicholson of West Allis, Wisconsin)[243]

Henrietta "Hattie" (Bolter) Behling (c. 1874)[244]

HAD TO HAVE ARM AMPUTATED

And perhaps a foot—Mrs. Behling's Bad Accident.

Mrs. Henrietta "Hattie" Behling of the town of Brookfield suffered a sad accident near the station Tuesday morning. She was returning from a visit from Prairie du Chein by the early morning train and had nearly reached Brookfield, when the cars slackened speed because the freight train ahead. *Mrs. Behling thought the station was reached and attempted to alight, when she fell and was caught under the wheels.* **(conti. below)**

Mrs. Henrietta "Hattie" Behling:

Henrietta Bolter was the daughter of William & Amanda Bolter, both of Prussia, and residing in New Berlin, Waukesha County in 1900. William was a brother to August Bolter of Brookfield. Henrietta, married Albert Behling of Brookfield. At the time of the accident, the Behling's resided in Brookfield with four children: Elsie, Edith, Florence & Alice.[245]

She was taken out as promptly as possible and Dr. Philler of this village [Waukesha] summoned. *He found one arm crushed so badly that amputation was necessary above the elbow.* One foot also was badly injured, and the doctor is not certain, but it too will have to be taken of. Under favorable circumstances he does not think her injuries will prove fatal, and last accounts she was comfortable as could be expected. Mrs. Behling is 34 years of age and the mother of four children, one of whom, a girl of ten years, was with her at the time. She is being nursed at the home of her parents. [*Waukesha Freeman* Oct. 3, 1889]

---

243 *Federal Manuscript Schedule*, Population, Agricultural and Manufacturing Schedules for Waukesha County, Town of Brookfield, 1860.

244 Photograph courtesy of Evelyn J. Nicholson, of West Allis, Wisconsin, home visit by author, Apr 11, 2009.

245 *Federal Manuscript Schedule*, Population, Agricultural and Manufacturing Schedules for Waukesha County, Town of New Berlin, 1900, Town of Brookfield, 1870.

IMMIGRANTS TO WISCONSIN FROM HESSE

Name: *August Bernhardt Erbe*—Birthplace: **Barchfeld, Hessen** (11-3-1828)—Spouse: *Anna Christina Klinzing*—Birthplace: **Stadtkreis Darmstädt, Hessen**—Year of immigration: 1852—married: 1852—In 1873, August Erbe owns a large 355-acre (sections 17 & 18) **Vermont Township, Dane County farm**-listed Occupation: *farmer*—Children: *Ernest, Henry, Janette, John, August, George, Amelia, Bernard, Caroline, Katherine & Anna*[246]— Mother—*Anna Erbie* died: (05-07-1877) 2nd marriage (1879): **Bertha J. Schoenemann**—Birthplace: **Wisconsin** (1857)—Children: *Louis, Emma & Frederike*—August's Occupation: (1880's): *dairy farming, sheep & cattle breeding, tobacco farming & shoe making*—Residence in 1891: **Dodgeville, Iowa County**.
(Image and genealogy courtesy of Helen Joan Davies Carlson of Palmyra, Wisconsin).[247]

August & Anna Erbe (c. 1875)[248]

Thuringia, Hesse-Darmstadt:

"*Barchfeld (the birthplace of August Bernhardt Erbe) is a district of the community Barchfeld-Immelborn in the Wartburg district in Thuringia and seat of the municipality*. During the Thirty Years' War , the area of Barchfeld belonging to Hesse-Darmstadt was on the side of the Catholic League and was thus enclosed by Protestant-ruled countries. The majority Protestant population suffered immensely specifically in 1634 and 1635 under both warring parties. *As a result of the plague and other introduced diseases, only six families survived in the village. In 1640, the chronicler of the church notes that many of the survivors had gone abroad.* In 1721 Barchfeld became the seat of the Landgraves of Hesse-Philippsthal-Barchfeld. A major fire, in September 1753, destroyed almost all the courtyards and buildings of the village, including the church and rectory. Within three years, the church was rebuilt in the late Baroque style."[249]

A successful Dane County Farmer:

"*The marriage of August Erbe and Anna Christina were engaged before coming to this country, but as they belonged to different provinces it would have cost $40 to consummate their union, so it was deferred until they reached America*. They lived in an old house that was on the property in Vermont Township, Dane County. He built a two-story house from limestone quarried right on his farm. On the opposite side of the road he built a large barn for dairy cattle. It had a 6-foot limestone foundation and a frame supported with huge, hand hewn timbers. *August learned shoemaking in his native Germany as there were several shoemakers among the Erbes in Barchfeld. August made shoes in the evenings and walked all the way to town to sell them.* In later years he operated a mill at Rockwell where he may have contracted his fatal lung condition. In 1891 he moved to Dodgeville in Iowa County. August died on 2-2-1897."[250]

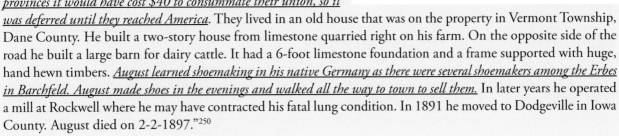

---

246   *Plat Book of Dane County, Wisconsin*. Madison: Harrison & Warner, 1873, Town of Vermont.

247   *Plat Book of Iowa County, Wisconsin*. Madison: Sewyn A. Brant, 1895, Town of Dodgeville.

248   Photograph courtesy of Helen Joan Davies Carlson of Palmyra, Wisconsin, e-mail to author, Jun 25, 2010.

249   https://de.wikipedia.org/wiki/Hessen hilippsthal-Barchfeld

250   *History of Dane County*, 1880, Town of Vermont.

IMMIGRANTS TO WISCONSIN FROM SAXONY

Name: **_August Thomas Caesar_**--Birthplace: **_Donndorf, Sachsen_** (1820): Spouse: **_Christine Reinhardt_** (1822)— Birthplace: **_Sachsen_**— Port of emigrant departure: Bremen, Germany—Ship name: "*F.J. Wichelhausen*"—Port of arrival: New York--August & Christine's residence in 1860: _Muskego Township, Waukesha County, Wisconsin_ — Occupation: *farmer*—Children: *Melinda* (1849), *Herman* (1853), *Frederick* (1853), *Louis* (c. 1859), *Anna* (1862) & *William* (1867). Death of Christine (Reinhardt) Caesar: _Muskego, Waukesha County_ (1890).

(Image, letter and genealogy courtesy of Elaine Alane of Helenville, Wisconsin.)[251]

August and Christine Caesar (c. 1875)[252]

Lack of Education:

During the <u>majority of the 19th century rural farm children did not always complete basic schooling</u> as their work was needed on the farm. Hence, their *English grammatical skills were often poor.*

Letter from James Sullivan of Muskego to Fred Caesar of Waseca, Minnesota:

Muskego, March the 30, (c. 1878)
well fred with pleasure I sit down to answer your welcom letter which i received the 21 of march i had ought to answer it Sooner but I was wating until we got through with the crops but we aint dun yet i thought we might beat ye up ther aint any oats Sowed here yet i was down to your house Sunday your folks are all well and Shafers are well too you felows ware lucky to get work So Soon and So near to gether *i Suppose John has work by this time to--Buttonhogans* (neighbors to the Caesar farm, correct spelling Bodenhagen.) two boys was burried this week with dipteriah** (**Diphtheria**,* is an acute contagious infection that chiefly affects children, caused by a bacillus and characterized by the formation of a false membrane in the air passages, and by fever and great weakness.)[253] *Was took henery and rudolph and willy aint esepected to live that is purty hard on A poor man fred but what is loted can't be bloted i tell you fread ye felows put a hole in our crowd--it looks kind of thin around here now-- the Snow is* Just more than coming down here today-- well fred I guess i will have to close for this time for paper is mighty Scarce --you must write to one often good bye fred--**_James Sullivan_**[254]

Diphtheria outbreak ravages the state:

"A disease which continued to rampage across Wisconsin through the turn of the (19th) century, _Diphtheria proved to be especially troublesome. In an outbreak in the early 1880s, of an estimated 10,000 persons affected across the state of Wisconsin, more than 2,200 died, many in rural areas._"[255]

---

[251]   *Federal Manuscript Schedule*, Population, Agricultural and Manufacturing Schedules for Waukesha County, Town of Muskego, 1860.

[252]   Photograph courtesy of Elaine Alane of Helenville, Wisconsin, e-mail to author, Apr 28, 2010.

[253]   The definition of "diphtheria" provided by Elaine Alane of Helenville, Wisconsin, in e-mail to author, Aug 12, 2010.

[254]   Elaine Alane of Helenville, Wisconsin, e-mail to author, Aug 12, 2010.

[255]   Dale E. Treleven, "One Hundred Years of Health and Healing in Rural Wisconsin." P. 135. In Numbers, Ronald L. & Judith Walzer Leavitt. WISCONSIN MEDICINE. © 1981 by the Board of Regents of the University of Wisconsin System. Reproduced courtesy of the University of Wisconsin Press, pp. 134 & 135.

IMMIGRANTS TO WISCONSIN FROM ENGLAND

Name: **William Searle**– Birthplace: **Hertfordshire County, England** (12 Feb 1814)—Spouse: **Isabel McCall**—Birthplace: **Leroy, New York** (22 Feb 1822)— Marriage: **Milwaukee County, Wisconsin Territory**-- (24 Dec 1845) --Residence in 1880: **Muskego Township, Waukesha County, Wisconsin**—Occupation: *farmer*–Children: *John* (1850), *Harriet* (1856), *Isabelle, John & Ezra*—Death: **Waukesha, Wisconsin** (17 Jan 1893) (Image and genealogy courtesy of Cathryn Larsen of Racine, Wisconsin.)[256]

Isabelle Searle (c. 1875)[257]

William Searle's birthplace:

"*Hertfordshire was the site of a number of uprisings against the Crown, particularly in the First Barons' War, the Peasants' Revolt, the Wars of the Roses and the English Civil War.* The county contains a curiously large number of abandoned settlements, which has been attributed to a mixture of poor harvests on soil hard to farm, and the Black Death which ravaged Hertfordshire starting in 1349. The Black Death or Plague was one of the most devastating pandemics in human history, resulting in the deaths of an estimated 75 to 200 million people and peaking in Europe in the years 1346–1353. *Changing economic conditions contributed to the Peasants' Revolt in 1381, in which Hertfordshire's people were deeply involved*. The 19th century was also a busy period for the military. Ten corps of Volunteer Infantry were formed in 1803. Originating in units of Rifle Volunteers formed in 1859, the regiment served in the Second Anglo-Boer War and the First and Second World Wars."[258]

Women's Clothing Styles of the 1870's:

"Isabelle is a very beautiful young lady dressed in a style suitable to the late 1860's. *Her skirt is typically full and pleated, but considering the work required of most farm women, she likely found a full hoop to be unsuitable.* Her dress is very high at the throat, with a white collar typical for everyday wear. Her dress is designed with a wide sleeve ending at the wrists. *The double striped patterning on her chest and upper arms add coloring and style to an otherwise plainly colored dress.*" **Joan Severa, "19th Century Clothing Styles"** [259]

256 *Federal Manuscript Schedule*, Population, Agricultural and Manufacturing Schedules for Waukesha County, Town of Muskego, 1880.

257 Photograph courtesy of Cathryn Larsen, of Kenosha, Wisconsin, e-mail to author, Mar 24, 2011.

258 https://en.wikipedia.org/wiki/History_of_Hertfordshire

259 Joan Severa of Madison, Wisconsin, e-mail to author, Mar 8, 2010.

IMMIGRANTS TO WISCONSIN FROM SCOTLAND

Name: --**Alexand Harris**—Birthplace: <u>**Civil Parish of Farnell, Village of Scone, City of Perth—County Angus, Scotland.**</u> (circa 1822)—Occupation: *agricultural laborer*—Spouse: **Margaret Harris**—Birthplace: <u>**Ferry-Port on Craig, Town of Forfar, County Angus, Scotland**</u> (20 Oct 1831)—married at: <u>Farnell, County Angus, Scotland</u> (15 June 1850)— Immigration: (circa: 1850's)—Residence in 1870—<u>New Berlin, Waukesha County</u>—Occupation: *farmer*—Alexand' s death: (26 Jan 1876)— Residence in 1900: <u>Muskego Township, Waukesha County</u>—Occupation: *farmer*—children: *Margaret, Emma, Jennie & Allen*—also, *August Stridier--farm laborer.* Margaret's Death: (5 May 1905)   (Image and genealogy courtesy of Libbie Nolan of Big Bend) [260]

Emma Harris (c. 1875)[261]

Alexand Harris of Scotland:

"Following the Act of Union, Perthshire returned to the House of Commons of the Parliament of the United Kingdom from 1708. *The presence of Scone two miles northeast (and the birthplace of Alexand Harris), the main royal center of the Kingdom of Alba enhanced Perth's early importance.* Perth was considered the effective 'capital' of Scotland, due to the frequent residence of the royal court."[262]

Scottish Canadians:

"A continual influx of immigrants into Canada from Scotland meant that by 1843 there were over 30,000 Scots in New Brunswick, Canada. Those immigrants who arrived in Canada after 1759 were mainly Highland farmers whom had been forced off their crofts (rented land) during the Highland and Lowland Clearances to make way for sheep grazing due to the British Agricultural Revolution.[263]   Others came because of famine. *In 1846, potato crops were blighted by the same fungal disease responsible for the Great Irish Famine, and most Highland crofters were very dependent on potatoes as a source of food. Crofters were expected to work in appalling conditions, and although some landlords worked to lessen the effects of the famine on their tenants, many landlords simply evicted*."[264]

Scottish immigration into Wisconsin:

"*Scottish immigrants to Wisconsin arrived in smaller numbers than the English, but also left behind several place names, including Caledonia, Argyle, and Scots Junction.* Many of these "English" and "Scottish" settlers came from Canada, as did many French Canadians who often found work in the fur trade and later in the lumber industry in Northern Wisconsin."[265]

[260] *Federal Manuscript Schedule*, Population, Agricultural and Manufacturing Schedules for Waukesha County, Town of Muskego, 1900.

[261] Photograph courtesy of Libbie Nolan via Pat Nolan, of Big Bend, Wisconsin, e-mail to author, Dec. 21, 2016.

[262] https://en.wikipedia.org/wiki/Perthshire

[263] https://en.wikipedia.org/wiki/Scottish_Canadians

[264] A crofter is the person who occupies and works a small landholding known as a croft. A crofter is normally the tenant of the croft, paying rent to the landlord of the croft. But many others have purchased their crofts and are owner-occupiers of their crofts." As presented in, https://de.wikipedia.org/wiki/Crofter

[265] Max Kade Institute for German-American Studies University of Wisconsin-Madison, "*Ethnic Groups in Wisconsin: Historical Background,*" the Scots. http://mki.wisc.edu/

IMMIGRANTS TO WISCONSIN FROM PRUSSIA

Name: **John B. Jermark**– Birthplace: <u>**Vernon, Waukesha County, Wisconsin.**</u> (c. 1858)— Spouse: *single* — Residence in 1870: <u>Delavan, Walworth County, Wisconsin</u>—Occupation: *farmer*–Parents: **Gottlieb Jahrmarkt** of <u>**Neumark, Brandenburg, Preußen**</u> and <u>Louisa Krueger</u> of <u>**Preußen**</u>--Residence in 1870: <u>Scottsville, Mitchell County, Kansas</u>--Occupation: *farmer*—Death: 1932.

(Image and genealogy courtesy of Judy Lynch of Manhattan, Kansas.)[266]

John B. Jermark (1877)[267]

A School for the Deaf & Dumb:

"<u>*The first woman employed as teacher at the Institute for the Deaf & Dumb at Delavan was Miss Emily Eddy In 1868, she began her experiments in speech-teaching.*</u> As early as 1861 she had observed pupils who, from disease or accident, had become deaf, and she patiently and ingeniously evolved methods of her own by which to teach these children to speak with their lips and to hear with their eyes. <u>*Later, Miss Eddy brought some improvement of teacher-method. It is said that Wisconsin and Illinois were earliest of the states of the old Northwest to adopt this branch of mute-instruction. The school year of forty weeks begins the first*</u> Wednesday of September. To the usual instruction in writing, reading, composition, arithmetic, natural science and drawing, with oral speech and lip-reading to semi-mutes and capable congenital mutes, is added training. Cabinet making began in 1860, shoe-making I 1867, printing in 1878 and baking in 1881. Girls are also taught housekeeping, baking and sewing. About 1879 began the publication of the *Deaf-Mute Press*, a home organ of the teachers and pupils." [268]

3 Jermark children attend the Institute for the Deaf & Dumb at Delavan:

"<u>*John B. Jermark was a deaf mute, as were two of his sisters. The 3 deaf/mute Jermark (Jahrmark) children (John, Matilda & Amelia) attended the school for the deaf at Delevan, Wisconsin.*</u> In fact, one of them married a teacher there who was also a deaf mute. <u>*It's a fascinating story!*</u> John Jermark never married and was very independent, living a solitary existence on his Kansas farm. In his mid-1870's he was found out near his livestock frozen to death after a severe storm. He was the brother of my great-great grandmother Augusta Jermark Wehl. <u>*Characteristics of hear impairments & muteness was passed down in the family through the years and I feel fortunate to have ended up with it.*</u>" -- *Judy Lynch*[269]

266   *Federal Manuscript Schedule*, Population, Agricultural and Manufacturing Schedules for Mitchell County, Scottsville, Kansas, 1870.

267   Photograph courtesy of Judy Lynch, of Manhattan, Kansas, e-mail to author, Oct 16, 2011.

268   Albert Clayton Beckworth. *History of Walworth County, Wisconsin*. Indianapolis: B. F. Bowen & Company, 1912, p. 164.

269   Judy Lynch, of Manhattan, Kansas, e-mail to author, Oct 16, 2011. Many deaf and hard of hearing individuals resent being told they have a disability. Passionate opposition to this idea is found in the official documents of *The National Association for the Deaf in the US*. Specific language impairment (SLI) has replaced the rigid term "muteness" as SLI has been shown to result from the combined influence of multiple genetic variations.

IMMIGRANTS TO WISCONSIN FROM PENNSYLVANIA & NEW YORK

Parents: **Chancey Baxter & Nancy Baxter**—Marriage: <u>West Burlington, Bradford, Pennsylvania</u> (1 Jan 1843)
Son: **Nathan Baxter** — Birthplace: <u>Granville Center, Bradford County, Pennsylvania</u> (2 Aug 1820)--Spouse:
Amelia Decker – Birthplace: <u>Franklin, Delaware County, New York State</u> (10 June 1827)—date of settlement
in Wisconsin (10 March 1864)—Residence in 1870: <u>Oconomowoc Township, Waukesha County, Wisconsin</u>—
Occupation: *farmer & businessman* –Children: *Eliza, George, Charles, Judson, Wilbur, Osbert, Samantha, Imogene &
Isaac.*--- moved from Wisconsin to <u>Winnebago, Faribault County, Minnesota</u> (28 March, 1887)--Nathan's Death:
(13 Oct)1908—Burial: <u>La Belle Cemetery, Oconomowoc, Waukesha County, Wisconsin.</u>
(Image and genealogy courtesy of Lola Baxter in care of Lisa Lohry of Waterville, Minnesota.)[270]

Nathan Baxter (c. 1877)[271]

From Wisconsin to Minnesota:

"*Nathan and Eliza's family moved from Waukesha County,
Wisconsin to Winnebago, Faribault County, Minnesota
on March 28, 1887*. Nathan and his sons were investors
and builders. *They loved horseracing.*" —**Lisa Lohry**[272]

Minnesota's love affair with "Dan Patch":

"Dan Patch was undefeated in open competition and
was so dominant on the racetrack that other owners
eventually refused to enter their horses against him.
Not long after buying *Dan Patch*, owner, Marion
Savage entered him in the Minneapolis Riding and
Driving Club's winter horse show held on January 29,
1903. The crowds continued to grow, reaching 40,000
in Des Moines and 50,000 in Milwaukee. *Dan Patch
made his first appearance in September of 1905 at the
Minnesota State Fair before a crowd of 98,000. Dan
Patch's achievements made him a sports celebrity, possibly the most famous athlete in America until Babe Ruth.* His name
and likeness were used to sell cigars, coffee, billiard cues and sheet music. The City of Savage, Minnesota, was
renamed for Dan Patch's owner, Marion Willis Savage, in 1904. Dan Patch Avenue on the Fairgrounds is named
for the horse."[273]

Obituary of Mrs. Nathan Baxter:

Oconomowoc: The remains of Mrs. Nathan (Decker) Baxter, who died in Winnebago City, Minn., late last
week, were brought here Tuesday for interment in La Belle cemetery. <u>Deceased was a former resident here and
had many friends.</u>
[*Waukesha Republican-Freeman* Dec. 27, 1898]

---

[270]   *Federal Manuscript Schedule*, Population, Agricultural and Manufacturing Schedules for Waukesha County, Town of Oconomowoc, 1870.

[271]   Photograph courtesy of Lisa Lohry of Waterville, Minnesota, e-mail to author, Apr 23, 2010.

[272]   Lisa Lohry of Waterville, Minnesota e-mail to author, Aug 11, 2010.

[273]   https://en.wikipedia.org/wiki/Dan_Patch

IMMIGRANTS TO WISCONSIN FROM RHINELAND/RHENISH PRUSSIA

Name: **Gerhard Reinders** – Birthplace: **Village of Qualburg, municipality of Bedburg-Hau, District of Kleve, Rheinisches/ Rheinpreußen** (10 Nov 1822)-- Spouse: **Margaretha Voss**—Birthplace: **Roemisch- Katholisch, Qualburg, Rheinisches /Rheinpreußen** (1 Jan 1827)— Married: **Roemisch-Katholisch, Riswick,** --Departure: Hamburg, Germany-- a daughter, *Helena*, died during the voyage (2 May 1854) —Port of Arrival: New York (8 May 1854)--Residence in 1860: **Oak Creek, Milwaukee, Wisconsin**—Occupation: *farmer*--Residence in 1870: **Brookfield Township, Waukesha County, Wisconsin**—occupation: *farmer*—Children: *Henry, John, Ellen, Mena, Theodore, Anton, William, Henry, John,* **John**, *Helena, Theodore, Helena, Wilhelmina (Nauertz), Henry, John, Ellen, Theodore & Bernhard*—(**John Reinders**, the young man standing at the far right (below), grew to adulthood and married **Margarethe Reitter**. The couple ran her family's general store at Elm Grove. Eventually, the business evolved into "John Reinder's General Store and Feed Mill."

(Image and genealogy courtesy of William Joynt, of Elgin Ill., in care of Peter Sjoberg of Rockford, Ill.)[274]

Gerhard Reinders' Family (c. 1877)[275]

Reinders' Family:

Back row, left to right: *William, Helena, Theodore, Wilhelmina & John.* **Front row, left to right:** *Margarethe* (mother), *Henry & Gerhard* (father).[276]

Rhenish Prussia:

"The Rhine Province, also known as Rhenish Prussia (Rheinpreußen), was the westernmost province of the Kingdom of Prussia and the Free State of Prussia, within the German Reich, beginning in 1822. *In 1815, Prussia gained control of the ecclesiastical principalities of Trier and Cologne, the free cities of Aachen and Cologne, and nearly a hundred small lordships and abbeys which would all be amalgamated into the new Prussian Rhine Province.* The left bank was predominately *Catholic*, while on the right bank about half the population was *Protestant*. The Rhine Province was the most densely populated part of Prussia."[277]

Born in Qualberg, Rhine Province.

Gerhard Reinders died at his home in Elm Grove, March 23. *He was born in Qualberg, Rhine Province, Germany, Nov. 10, 1822*; married in 1851 and came to America in 1854, settling at Oak Creek, Milwaukee County, where he resided until 1870, when he moved to Elm Grove. After the death of his wife about ten years ago, he retired from active farming, and took up his home with his son, John.   [*Waukesha Freeman* April 2, 1903]

274   *Federal Manuscript Schedule*, Population, Agricultural and Manufacturing Schedules for Waukesha County, Town of Brookfield, 1870.
275   Photograph courtesy of Peter Sjoberg of Rockford, Illinois, e-mail to author, June 27, 2010.
276   Peter Sjoberg of Rockford, Illinois, e-mail to author, June 27, 2010.
277   https://en.wikipedia.org/wiki/Rhine_Province

IMMIGRANTS TO WISCONSIN FROM BAVARIA

Name: **John Michael Stigler**– Birthplace: **Mantlach, Gross Bissendorf, Oberpfalz, Bayern** (19 June 1814) Spouse: **Mary Anna (Ostermann) Stigler**— Birthplace:— **Gross Bissendorf, Oberpfalz Bayern**—(1828-1882)— Year of immigration: (1850)--Occupation: *farmer*—Children: *Frederick* (1850-1926), *John* (1854-1936), *Mary Anna (Stigler) Salentine* (1862-1949)—Oldest son: **Frederick Stigler**—born: in village of Elm Grove (4 Dec 1850)—Spouse: *Mary Angeline (Snyder) Stigler*—birth: New Berlin: (4 Oct 1857)—married (30 Oct 1877)— occupation: *farmer*—children: *Michael, Otilia, Andrew, Frederick, John, George, Mary Ann, Joseph & Anthony.* (Image and genealogy courtesy of Mary Stigler of Brookfield, Wisconsin.) [278]

Frederik Stigler & Mary Schneider's Wedding Day (Oct. 30, 1877)[279]

The Stigler Farm in New Berlin:

"*Johan Michael Stigler and Maria Anna Ostermann immigrated to America in May or June of 1859 from their home near Gross Bissendorf, Oberpfalz, Bavaria.* The long ocean voyage across the Atlantic Ocean aboard the ship "*Alex Edmund*" ended on 15 July 1850 at the port of New York. From there they immediately took a boat up the Hudson River to Albany, then west across the state of New York via the Erie Canal to Buffalo, and into the Great Lakes to the port of Milwaukee. Upon landing in Milwaukee on the 29th of July, Mike and Mary Ann were married the same day at Old St. Mary's Catholic Church by Father Joseph Salzman. *The Stigler's initially purchased a small parcel within the Old Bavarian settlement in the village of Elm Grove, Waukesha County, Wisconsin. Mike worked as a cooper, since the small tract of land was not enough to farm productively. They lived in that village for almost six years.* During that time, three children were born--Frederick, on Christmas Eve in 1850, Otilia in October 1852 and John in September of 1854. *In 1856, Mike purchased a farm in New Berlin, heavily timbered, with a creek running through it, and a fine spring.* This farm became the basis of Stigler homestead for the next 124 years!"[280]

Women's Clothing Styles of the 1870's:

"Dark colored wedding dresses were worn centuries ago in different cultures. It was Queen Victoria who originally began the trend for white wedding gowns when she wore it to her wedding ceremony in 1840. *Mary Schneider's silhouette is the 'turkey-back' style, with the hoop being very narrow at the sides, and trailing out in a long turkey-tail. The bodice, with its long peplum, is a new style about 1870.*" — **Joan Severa, 19th Century Clothing Styles** [281]"

278 *Federal Manuscript Schedule*, Population, Agricultural and Manufacturing Schedules for Waukesha County, Town of New Berlin, 1880.

279 Photograph courtesy of Mary Stigler, of Brookfield, Wisconsin, e-mail to author, Aug 8, 2009.

280 Mary Stigler, "The History of the Stigler Farm, New Berlin, Waukesha County," In *Century Farms of Wisconsin*. (Shawnee Mission, Kansas: Inter-Collegiate Press, 1984), pp. 122 & 123.

281 Joan Severa of Madison, Wisconsin, e-mail to author, March 8, 2010.

IMMIGRANTS TO WISCONSIN FROM ENGLAND

Name: **John Lumb**--Birthplace: **Village Wrangle, Civil Parish of Kirton or "Kirton in Holland," in the Boston Borough, Lincolnshire, England.** (c. 1840). Spouse: **Emily Experience (Snyder) Lumb** – Birthplace: **Wisconsin** (1847)— John Lumb's Year of Immigration: 1852—Residence in 1910: Menomonee Falls, Waukesha County, Wisconsin—Occupation: *farmer* –Children: **Adda** (8 May 1874).
(Image and genealogy courtesy of Libbie Nolan of Big Bend, Wisconsin.)[282]

Adda S. Lumb (c. 1877)[283]

The Lumb family of Lincolnshire, England:

"*Boston is a town and small port in Lincolnshire, on the east coast of England.* It is the largest town of the wider Borough of Boston local government district. *Boston's most notable landmark is St Botolph's Church ("The Stump"), said to be the largest parish church in England, visible for miles around from the flat lands of Lincolnshire.* Edward III named it a staple port for the wool trade in 1369. In 1612 John Cotton became the Vicar of St. Botolph's and, although viewed askance by the Church of England for his non-conformist preaching, became responsible for a large increase in Church attendance. *He encouraged those who disliked the lack of religious freedom in England to join the Massachusetts Bay Company, and later helped to find the city of Boston, Massachusetts.* Around the same time, the decline of the local guilds and shift towards domestic weaving of English wool led to a near-complete collapse of the town's foreign trade. This, in turn, revolutionized the Christian beliefs and practices of many Bostonians and residents of the neighboring shires of England. In 1620, several Bostonians were among the group who moved to New England on the Mayflower. Boston remained a hotbed of religious unrest."[284]

Children's Clothing Styles of the 1870's:

"*Little Adda Lumb is adorable with her fringed patterned sown dress.* The most basic difference between girls' and women's dresses was that the children's dresses were shorter, gradually lengthening to floor length by the mid-teen years. *All girls wore long full-length pantaloons beneath these skirts with glimpses of lace white frill peeping beneath hemlines.* I would estimate that Adda's dress is from the late 1870's or early 1880's, but it's not quite typical." —*Joan Severa, 19th Century Clothing Styles*[285]

---

282 *Federal Manuscript Schedule*, Population, Agricultural and Manufacturing Schedules for Waukesha County, Town of Menomonee, 1910.

283 Photograph courtesy of Libbie Nolan via Pat Nolan, of Big Bend, Wisconsin, e-mail to author, Dec. 21, 2016.

284 https://en.wikipedia.org/wiki/Boston,_Lincolnshire

285 Joan Severa, Madison, Wisconsin, e-mail to author, Mar 8, 2010.

Immigrants to Wisconsin from England

Name: **Ephraim Beaumont**—Birthplace: **Huddersfield, Yorkshire, England** (19 Feb 1894)— Spouse: **Deborah A. Wood**—Birthplace: **Wisconsin** (c. 1848)— Residence in 1850: Merton Township, Waukesha County — Occupation: *farmer*—Children: *Saxie, Richard, Hattie, Charles, William, Bessie & Edith.*

(Image and genealogy courtesy of Jeanne Pedriana of Elm Grove, Wisconsin)[286]

Ephraim Beaumont (c. 1878)[287]

Huddersfield, Yorkshire County, England:

"There has been a settlement in Huddersfield for over 4,000 years. The remains of a Roman fort were unearthed in the mid-18th century at west of the town. Huddersfield has been a market town since Anglo-Saxon times. During the ownership, by William Ramsden, of Huddersfield Manor, the family supported the development of the town, building the Huddersfield Cloth Hall in 1766, (designed to display and sell textiles) the Sir John Ramsden's Canal in 1780, and supporting the arrival of the railway arrived in the 1840s. During this same period, Huddersfield was, also, a center of civil unrest during the Industrial Revolution (1760-1850). In a period where Europe was experiencing frequent wars, where trade had slumped, and the crops had failed, many local weavers faced losing their livelihood due to the introduction of machinery in factories. *The accumulation of many of these factors led to massive emigration from Huddersfield as well as other communities in the county of Yorkshire. Luddites[288] began destroying mills and machinery in response to poor working conditions as well as the reputation of cruelty by many mill owners."*[289]

An ever-growing interest in political pursuits:

"*Ephraim Beaumont was an American farmer, businessman, and politician. Born in 1834, near Huddersfield in Yorkshire, England, Beaumont emigrated to the United States and settled in Waukesha County, Wisconsin in 1851.* In 1854, Beaumont took part in the *California Gold Rush* and in 1862 returned to Wisconsin. *Beaumont lived in the town of Merton, Wisconsin, and was a farmer and a summer hotel keeper.* Beaumont was president of the Wisconsin State Agricultural Society. He served on the *Waukesha County Board of Supervisors* and was *Chairman of the County Board.* Beaumont also served as *Waukesha County Treasurer.* In 1875 and 1876, Beaumont served as *Waukesha County sheriff* and was a Republican. In 1889, Beaumont served in the *Wisconsin State Assembly.* Mr. Beaumont died at his home in Merton, Wisconsin, in 1918."[290]

---

[286] *Federal Manuscript Schedule*, Population, Agricultural and Manufacturing Schedules for Waukesha County, Town of Merton, 1850.

[287] Photograph courtesy of Jean Pedriana of Elm Grove, Wisconsin, e-mail to author, Apr 23, 2010.

[288] "The Luddites were a group of English textile workers and weavers in the 19th century who destroyed weaving machinery as a form of protest." https://en.wikipedia.org/wiki/Luddit

[289] *https://en.wikipedia.org/wiki/Huddersfield*

[290] https://en.wikipedia.org/wiki/Ephraim_Beaumont

SETTLERS TO WISCONSIN FROM NEW YORK

Parents: **Abraham Vanderpool** born—<u>New York State</u> (1832) & **Rebecca Vanderpool** born--**England** (1838)
Daughter: **Mary L. Vanderpool** ——Mary's birthplace: **Wisconsin** (c. 1862) Spouse: **Louis S. Winton**—
Birthplace: <u>New York State</u> (c. 1818)——Family Residence in 1870: **New Berlin Township, Waukesha County,**
Wisconsin—Occupation: *farmer* –Children: *Emma, Elmer, Mary & Nelly*. Also residing in this residence: *Janette*
Hoag, of <u>Scotland</u>-- *servant.*　　　　　(Image and genealogy courtesy of Libbie Nolan of Big Bend, Wisconsin)[291]

Mary Winton (c. 1878) [292]

Dutch families settle on lower Manhattan Island:

"*New Amsterdam (Dutch: Nieuw Amsterdam)* *was a 17ᵗʰ-century Dutch settlement established* *at the southern tip of Manhattan Island that* *served as the seat of the colonial government* *in New Netherland.* The *factorij* became a settlement outside *Fort Amsterdam*. The fort was situated on the strategic *southern* *tip* of the island of Manhattan and was meant to defend the fur trade operations of the *Dutch West India Company* in the North River (Hudson River). *In 1624, it* *became a provincial extension of the Dutch* *Republic and was designated as the capital of* *the province in 1625.*"[293]

The Dutch Vanderpool family immigrate to Wisconsin:

"*Wynant Gerritse Vanderpool, born in Meppel,* *Drenthe, Netherlands on July 25, 1699, settled* *in New Amsterdam in 1647.* The spelling of the name Vanderpool spelling evolved into '*Vanderpool.*"[294] "By 1655, the population of New Netherland had grown to 2,000 people, with 1,500 living in New Amsterdam. *On September 8, 1864, the* *armada of the Duke of York captured New Amsterdam for England, and, in his name, the settlement was renamed* *New York. A surprising number of immigrants from the old Dutch colony in New Amsterdam immigrated west with* *many settling in Wisconsin.*"[295] "A Vanderpool descendant, *Mary Ellen*, born in 1838, married *Louis S. Winton* and raised a family in New Berlin, Waukesha County."[296]

[291]　*Federal Manuscript Schedule*, Population, Agricultural and Manufacturing Schedules for Waukesha County, Town of New Berlin, 1850.

[292]　Photograph courtesy of Libbie Nolan via Pat Nolan, of Big Bend, Wisconsin, e-mail to author, Dec. 21, 2016.

[293]　https://en.wikipedia.org/wiki/New_Amsterdam

[294]　. https://www.wikitree.com/genealogy/VANDERPOOL

[295]　https://en.wikipedia.org/wiki/New_Amsterdam

[296]　Author visit with Libbie Nolan, Jan. 15, 2010.

IMMIGRANTS TO WISCONSIN FROM SCOTLAND AND ENGLAND

Name: **Thomas Steele**– Birthplace: **Inverkeithing, Fife, Scotland** (1809)—Spouse: **Katharine Freeman**—Birthplace: **England** (c. 1821)—Residence in 1860: **Genesee Township, Waukesha County, Wisconsin**—Occupation: *farmer*–Children: *James, Annie, Lillias, Thomas, Kate & John.*
(Image and genealogy courtesy of Waukesha County Historical Society and Museum.)[297]

Dr. Thomas & Katherine Steel (c. 1878)[298]

The home of the Steele family in Fife, Scotland:

"(*Thomas Steele was born in Fife, Scotland on November 6, 1809.) Inverkeithing is a royal burgh, in the shire of Fife, Scotland. The port town is in the Scottish Lowlands. King James VI of Scotland described Fife as a "beggar's mantle fringed wi gowd",* the golden fringe being the coast and its chain of little ports with their thriving fishing fleets and rich trading links with the Low Countries. *Wool, linen, coal and salt were all traded. Numerous Lowland Scots immigrated directly to Wisconsin during the 1840s.*"[299]

"Cures the Disease Slick Off:"

"One of the best-trained regular physicians in the territory of Wisconsin was Dr. Thomas Steel, whose career reveals much about the practice of frontier medicine at mid-century. *Born into a middle-class Scottish family in 1809, he began his education at the University of London and received his M.D. from the University of Glasgow in 1833.* Steel emigrated from Scotland to Wisconsin in 1843, settling in Mukwonago, Waukesha County. Steel traveled great distance on foot. *'I wish you could see me setting out on my professional visits,'* he wrote on December 13, 1843, *'with my big boots made of cow hide coming up to my knee over my trousers. You would admit that I am Yankyfied fast.'* The disease Steel treated most frequently was *malaria*. Steel was so fortunate in his treatments that *he 'got the name of the doctor who cures the disease slick off,'* he wrote home proudly on November 13, 1843. *'This character I mainly deserve from the circumstances of my having brought with me from London good Sulfate of Quinine, a medicine not to be procured genuine in this part of the country.'* During his early years in Wisconsin, Steel begged his father to send such articles as quinine, morphine, smallpox vaccine, as well as medical books, lancets and other instruments. In lieu of cash for his service and medicines, Steel frequently accepted produce, animals, or farm labor from the families of his patients."[300]

---

[297] *Federal Manuscript Schedule*, Population, Agricultural and Manufacturing Schedules for Waukesha County, Town of Genesee, 1860.

[298] Dr. Thomas & Katherine Steel (c. 1878), People S-T Box 7:8, Photography Collection, Research Center Library & Archive, Waukesha County Historical Society & Museum, Waukesha, Wisconsin.

[299] https://en.wikipedia.org/wiki/Fife#History

[300] Peter T. Harstad. "Frontier Medicine in the Territory of Wisconsin," pp. 17-19. In Numbers, Ronald L. & Judith Walzer Leavitt. WISCONSIN MEDICINE. © 1981 by the Board of Regents of the University of Wisconsin System. Reproduced courtesy of the University of Wisconsin Press, pp. 134 & 135.

IMMIGRANTS TO WISCONSIN FROM WÜRTTEMBERG

Name: **August Shaefle**– birthplace: **Ludwigsburg, Württemberg** (c. 1834) — Spouse: **Catherine**—Birthplace: **Württemberg** (1846) Children: *Sophia, John, Gusta, Kate & Emma*. Residence in 1880: Brookfield Township, Waukesha County–occupation: *physician*.
(Image and genealogy courtesy of Williams family of Oconomowoc, Wisconsin)[301]

Dr. August Schaefle (c. 1878)[302]

The German "Forty-Eighters:"

"*In the German states, the Forty-Eighters favored unification of the German people, a more democratic government, and guarantees of human rights*. Disappointed at the failure of the revolution to bring about the reform they gave up their old lives to try again abroad. Large numbers of 48er's emigrated to the United States. *Many German Forty-Eighters settled in Milwaukee, Wisconsin, helping solidify that city's progressive political bent and cultural Deutschtum.* The *Acht-und-vierzigers* and their descendants contributed to the development of that city's long Socialist political tradition. Others settled throughout the state.[303] *The revolutionary movement of 1848 did not leave Württemberg untouched, although no associated violence took place within the kingdom*. King William had to dismiss Johannes Schlayer (1792–1860) and his other ministers, calling to power men with more liberal ideas and the exponents of the idea of a united Germany. *King William did proclaim a democratic constitution but, as soon as the movement had spent its force, he dismissed the liberal ministers. Disenchanted Württembergers, also emigrated.*"[304]

Prussia Occupies Northern Württemberg:

(*August Schaefle was born in Ludwigsburg, Württemberg in 1834*.) "Ludwigsburg is located about 12 kilometers north of Stuttgart near the Neckar River. He went on to attend Stuttgart University *where he obtained a medical degree after a five-year program in about the year 1857. "In 1866, Württemberg took up arms on behalf of Austria in the Austro-Prussian War, but three weeks after the Battle of Königgrätz on 3 July 1866, her troops suffered a comprehensive defeat at Tauberbischofsheim, and the country lay at the mercy of Prussia. The Prussians occupied the northern part of Württemberg and negotiated a peace in August 1866.*"[305] As a *surgeon*, Dr. Schaefle was likely conscripted to serve for three years of the conflict. *August Schaefle immigrated to the United States near war's end becoming a resident of the Pentwater, Oceana County, Michigan* (circa 1868)."[306]

---

[301]   *Federal Manuscript Schedule*, Population, Agricultural and Manufacturing Schedules for Waukesha County, Town of Brookfield, 1880.

[302]   Photograph courtesy of the Williams family of Oconomowoc, Wisconsin, e-mail to author, Jun 27, 2010

[303]   https://en.wikipedia.org/wiki/Forty-Eighters

[304]   https://en.wikipedia.org/wiki/Kingdom_of_Württemberg

[305]   https://en.wikipedia.org/wiki/Ludwigsburg

[306]   Sue Ellen Williams of Oconomowoc, Wisconsin, adapted from an e-mail to the author, June 27, 2010.

IMMIGRANTS TO WISCONSIN FROM HESSEN AND N.Y.

Name: **Henry Snyder**--Birthplace: **Paffenhabenheim, Hesse** (9 Sept 1844)—Spouse—**Mary Elizabeth Eiler**—Birthplace: **Troy, Rensselaer, County, New York** (3 Mar 1847-24 Mar 1922)—Married—Waukesha, Waukesha County (26 Nov 1865)—Residence in 1870: Waukesha, Waukesha County—Occupation: *shoemaker & member of the Waukesha fire department*—Children: *Martin (1866-1867)—Elizabeth Burlingame (1869-1958)—Rev. Henry Snyder (1874-1954)—Mabel Barbara Perkins (1884-1963)—Gustave (1868-1969)—Amelia Wilhemina Putz (1872-1926)* **Alvin**—*employed in his father's shoe shop (1880-1934)* and **Mabel**.

(Image and genealogy courtesy of Kenneth Eiler of Overland Park, Kansas.) [307]

Mabel & Alvin Snyder (c. 1878)[308]

Henry Snyder, a shoemaker in the Village of Waukesha:

"*The cobblers sat at their low benches* and industriously tapped-tapped-tapped or drew out the long-waxed ends from morning to night in order that our farm people might be shod. There was hardly a crossroads hamlet but had its representative of that trade, of which *St. Crispin* is the patron saint. With his short, stout *'pegging awl'* he punched a hole for each peg, set the peg in place and then drove it home with a single smart blow of his broadfaced hammer. If was necessary to strike the same peg twice, by that token he was emphatically a botch and no cobbler."[309]

Order of the Knights of St. Crispin:

"*The Order of the Knights of St. Crispin was an American labor union of shoe workers formed in Wisconsin in 1867.* It soon reached a membership of 50,000 or more, largely in the Northeast. However, it was poorly organized and faded away by 1874. *They fought encroachments of machinery and unskilled labor on the autonomy of skilled shoe workers. The first lodge of the Knights of St. Crispin was organized in 1867 in Milwaukee, Wisconsin.* As a union of shoemakers, it took its name from the Catholic Saint Crispin, the patron saint of cobblers. The Order spread throughout Wisconsin and the Northeast and even into Canada. By 1871 it claimed about 400 lodges with 50,000 to 60,000 members. Dues paying members were far fewer. *In Milwaukee the Knights owned and operated three cooperative shops*. The movement eventually failed because new machines could be operated by semi-skilled workers and produce more shoes than by traditional hand sewing."[310]

---

[307]   *Federal Manuscript Schedule*, Population, Agricultural and Manufacturing Schedules for Waukesha County, Town of Waukesha, 1870.

[308]   Photograph courtesy of Kenneth Eiler of Overland Park, Kansas, e-mail to author, Jun 27, 2010.

[309]   Jared Van Wagon Jr., *The Golden Age of Homespun*. State of New York, Department of Agriculture and Markets, Bulletin 203, (Albany, N.Y.: June 1927), pp. 77 & 78.

[310]   https://en.wikipedia.org/wiki/Order_of_the_Knights_of_St._Crispin

IMMIGRANTS TO WISCONSIN FROM SAXONY & NEW YORK

Name: **Norris Collins Potter** –Birthplace: **New York** (Jan 1859) –Spouse: **Mary Louise (Bartlett) Potter**– Birthplace: **Leipzig, Sachsen, Germany** (Oct 1864)—Residence in 1900: Ottawa Township, Waukesha County, Wisconsin—Occupation: *farmer & rural route mail delivery*– Children: *Arthur* (1882), *Mary, Jay* (1885), *Harris* (1887), *Norris* (1889), *Raymond* (1890), *Maggie* (1893), *Edna* (1895), *Elva* (1897), *Clarence, Malcom, Hazel & Mabel.* (Image, text, and genealogy courtesy of Carol Logan of Chico, California)[311]

Mary Louis Potter (c. 1880)[312]

Residents of Leipzig organize Worker's Rights movement:

"The Leipzig region was the arena of the **1813 Battle of Leipzig** between Napoleonic France and an allied coalition of Prussia, Russia, Austria and Sweden. *It was the largest battle in Europe before the First World War and the coalition victory ended Napoleon's presence in Germany and would ultimately lead to his first exile on Elba.* In addition to stimulating German nationalism, the war had a major impact in mobilizing a civic spirit in numerous volunteer activities." *(conti. below)*

Yanked her Earrings:

"Mary Louis (Bartlett) Potter at about 16-18 years of age (right). Born in Leipzig, Germany, 1863. **She was Clarence Potter's mother.** *Note cleft in her left earlobe*: Mary's stepfather, named Bartlett, yanked her earrings out of her ears and tore the lobes." --*Carol Logan*[313]

"Many volunteer militias and civic associations were formed, and collaborated with churches, and the press to support local and state armies, patriotic wartime mobilization and relief. *Leipzig became a center of the German and Saxon liberal movements. The first German labor party, the General German Workers' Association.*"[314]

Saxony absorbed by Prussia:

"The King of Saxony was taken as a Prussian prisoner to the Castle of Friedrichsfeld near Berlin. *The Congress of Vienna (1814–15) took from Saxony the greater part of its land and gave it to Prussia, namely 7,800 square miles with about 850,000 inhabitants. What Prussia had obtained, with the addition of some old Prussian districts, was formed into the Province of Saxony.* Consequently, in the War of 1866, when Prussia was successful, the independence of Saxony was once more in danger; only the intervention of the Austrian Emperor saved Saxony from being entirely absorbed by Prussia."[315]

---

[311] *Federal Manuscript Schedule*, Population, Agricultural and Manufacturing Schedules for Waukesha County, Town of Ottawa, 1900.

[312] Photograph courtesy of Carol Logan of Chico, California, e-mail to author, Jun 27, 2010.

[313] Carol Logan of Chico, California, e-mail to author, Jun 27, 2010.

[314] https://en.wikipedia.org/wiki/Leipzig

[315] https://en.wikipedia.org/wiki/History_of_Saxony

IMMIGRANTS TO WISCONSIN FROM SCOTLAND

Name: **John Small**—Birthplace: **Perthshire, Scotland** (1799)—Spouse: **Isabelle Rodgers**—Birthplace: **Perthshire, Scotland** (c. 1800)—Occupation: *weaver*—Emigration on the ship *"Peruvian"* (1841)— Residence in 1850: Lisbon Township, Waukesha County, Wisconsin—son of *John & Isabelle Small*: **William Small**– Birthplace: **Perthshire, Scotland** (5 Oct 1824) —Emigrated to the United States (circa 1842) --Spouse: **Margaret Marshall**—Birthplace— **Fifeshire, Scotland** (23 Oct 1819)—married: (27 Nov 1856) --Residence in 1880: Lisbon Township, Waukesha County, Wisconsin--Occupation: *farmer*--member of the *State Assembly 1880* -- Children: *John, Isabella & William.* (Image and genealogy courtesy of Waukesha County Historical Society and Museum.)[316]

William Small (c. 1880) [317]

Large Scottish Emigration during The mid-19th Century:

"19th Century Scottish emigration was due to a lack of sufficient work to match a rapid population growth. The population of Scotland grew steadily in the 19th century, from 1,608,000 in the census of 1801 to 2,889,000 in 1851. Even with the development of industry there were insufficient good jobs; as a result, during the period 1841-1931, about 2 million Scots migrated to North America and Australia, and another 750,000 Scots relocated to England. This not only limited Scotland's population increase but meant that almost every family lost members due to emigration."[318] "Among these emigrants were Scottish Americans. Scottish Americans are Americans whose family's emigrated wholly or partly in Scotland. *Most Scotch-Irish Americans originally came from Lowland Scotland.*" [319] (*The John Small family emigrated to Wisconsin, and the town of Lisbon, from the Scottish Lowlands of Perth.*)[320]

Worked his father's farm:

"*The Small family made it as far west as Buffalo, where John Small, a weaver by trade, worked a short time as a laborer before moving to Wisconsin*. Young William remained in Buffalo while his parents and sisters settled on a quarter-section of unimproved land in the Town of Lisbon. *Eight of the ten dollars the family had when they arrived in Milwaukee was spent for a cow, and John Small soon built a modest cabin on his claim.* William arrived from the east on the 4th of July 1842, and helped his father work the farm . . ." —**Douglas T. Hennig**[321]

316 *Federal Manuscript Schedule*, Population, Agricultural and Manufacturing Schedules for Waukesha County, Town of Lisbon, 1880.

317 William Small photograph c. 1880, People S-T Box 7:8, Photography Collection, Research Center Library & Archive, Waukesha County Historical Society & Museum, Waukesha, Wisconsin.

318 https://en.wikipedia.org/wiki/History_of_Scotland

319 https://en.wikipedia.org/wiki/Scottish_Americans

320 Douglas T. Hennig, "Town of Lisbon Pioneers - Part IV, The Small Family," *Landmark*, v. 28, n. 1 & 2. (Spring-Summer Double Issue, 1985), pgs. 12 & 13.

321 Henning, "Town of Lisbon Pioneers - Part IV, The Small Family," *Landmark*, p. 12.

IMMIGRANTS TO WISCONSIN FROM SAXONY

Name: **August Thomas Caesar**–Birthplace: **Donndorf, Sachsen, Germany** (1820) — Spouse: **Christina Reinhardt** —Birthplace—**Sachsen, Germany** (1822) —Port of emigration: Bremen, Germany--Ship name: "*E. J. Wichelhausen*"-- Residence in 1880: Muskego Township, Waukesha County, Wisconsin—Occupation: *farmer*–Children: *Melinda, Herman, Fredrick, Louis, Anna & William.*

(Image and genealogy courtesy of Elaine Alane of Helenville, Wisconsin)[322]

Anna Caesar (c. 1880)[323]

Caesar family faced with Prussian aggression:

"In 1756, Saxony joined the coalition of Austria, France and Russia against Prussia. Frederick II of Prussia chose to attack preemptively and invaded Saxony in August 1756, precipitating the Seven Years' War. The Prussians quickly defeated Saxony and incorporated the Saxon army into the Prussian army. They made the mistake of keeping their units intact rather than mixing them up. Whole Saxon units deserted. At the end of the Seven Years' War, Saxony once again became an independent state. *In the War of 1866, when Prussia was successful, the independence of Saxony was once more in danger; only the intervention of the Austrian Emperor saved Saxony from being entirely absorbed by Prussia.* The kingdom, however, was obliged to join the North German Confederation of which Prussia was the head. In 1871 Saxony became one of the states of the newly founded German Empire."[324]

A pioneer family in Muskego Township:

"*August Caesar and his wife Christine pioneered to Muskego Township in 1859. They came from Saxony to the USA in 1850 and lived in Milwaukee before purchasing the property on Big Muskego Lake in Muskego Township.* There was a log cabin and probably a small barn on the property when they purchased it. It wouldn't be until 1877 that they constructed a large barn of their own. The five-bedroom cream city brick farmhouse was not started until 1880 and it was built in two phases. They had six children: *Pauline* born in Saxony. *Herman & Fredrich* were born in Milwaukee. *Luis, Anna & William* were born on the farm in Muskego."[325]

[322] *Federal Manuscript Schedule*, Population, Agricultural and Manufacturing Schedules for Waukesha County, Town of Muskego, 1880.

[323] Photograph courtesy of Elaine Alane of Helenville, Wisconsin, e-mail to author, July 10, 2010

[324] https://en.wikipedia.org/wiki/List_of_Germanic_deities

[325] Elaine Alane e-mail to author, Oct 22, 2017 *The August Caesar Family*, by Elaine Alan as presented in: *Portrait of Muskego Farmers - 1836-1980*, by the Muskego Historical Society, 1980. The 105 page, spiral bound, illustrated, booklet combines 42 stories of early immigrant families to Muskego, Wisconsin. Courtesy of Elaine Alan and the Muskego Historical Society.

IMMIGRANTS TO WISCONSIN FROM NEW YORK STATE

Name: **William Crossett Dockstader**— Birthplace: <u>New York</u> (2 Nov 1856) -- attends "<u>Philadelphia College of Pharmacy</u>" (1874-1878) --Marriage: Jan 15, 1889--<u>St. Paul, Minnesota</u>--**Mabel (George)** (age: 18) --Birthplace: <u>New York</u> (11 June 1866)—Residence in 1900: <u>Sioux Falls City, Minnehaha, South Dakota</u>--Occupation: *commercial traveler drugs; later house painter; later unemployed*—Children: *Margaret* (Gould), *Dorothy, Eliza & Dorothy*—also residing in this residence: **Dr. Egbert George**—Death of Dr. Egbert George & William Dockstader: (10 Nov 1903) - <u>Sioux Falls, Minnehaha, South Dakota</u>—Residence of Mabel Dockstader (age: 38)--1905 <u>Waukesha, Waukesha, Wisconsin</u>—Occupation: *operates lodging house.*
(Image and genealogy courtesy of Waukesha County Historical Society and Museum.) [326]

Mabel (George) Dockstader (c. 1880) [327]

The Philadelphia College of Pharmacy:

"*The Philadelphia College of Pharmacy (PCP), modeled—at least in concept—after the Collége de pharmacie in Paris, was aided by European talent in its early, formative years.* Elias Durand, who had served as "pharmacien of the Grand Army of Napoleon I," set up shop in Philadelphia in 1825, and "...in connection with the Philadelphia College of Pharmacy, exerted a strong influence on American pharmacy."[328]

William Dockstader the student:

William Crossett Dockstader attends Philadelphia College of Pharmacy (1874-1878): "The following articles appear in two Philadelphia College of Pharmaceutical Research Journals: <u>Pharmaceutical O. Thesis</u> "Chemical Affinity in Compound Medicine," by William Crossett Dockstader; <u>Pharmaceutical O. Thesis</u>, "Anamirta Cocculus," by *William Crossett Dockstader.***"[329]**

POINTS TO DOUBLE SUICIDE.
SIOUX FALLS, S.D.,

Nov. 10. — (Special Telegram.)—<u>Dr. Egbert George was found dead in bed here this morning with the door of his room closed and the gas jet wide open.</u> Very shortly afterward, in the basement of the same house, was found the body of Dr. George's son-in-law, W. C. Dockstader, formerly a traveling man and very well known throughout the state. <u>Evidently Mr. Dockstader committed suicide with a revolver and apparently Dr. George's death was suicidal also.</u> Dr. George was first to die, and it is believed that Dockstader, upon discovering what his aged father-in-law had done, decided to pursue a similar course and rid himself of the distress that has appeared to prey upon his mind during the recent months.
[*The Omaha Daily Bee*, Nov. 11, 1903]

---

[326] *Federal Manuscript Schedule*, Population, Agricultural and Manufacturing Schedules for Minnehaha, Sioux Falls City, South Dakota, 1900.

[327] Mabel Dockstader photograph c. 1880, People C-D-E Box 2:8, Photography Collection, Research Center Library & Archive, Waukesha County Historical Society & Museum, Waukesha, Wisconsin.

[328] http://www.wikiwand.com/en/History_of_pharmacy_in_the_United_States. What circumstances led the 2 men to suicide is not known. After the deaths of her husband & father, Mabel Docksteader moved to Waukesha opening a lodging house. Within 3 years she moved back to Sioux Falls for several years before relocating in Chicago.

[329] Joseph Winters & Kramer, John Eicholtz. *The First Century of the Philadelphia College of Pharmacy, 1821-1921* (England: Philadelphia College of Pharmacy: 1922), p. 501.

IMMIGRANTS TO WISCONSIN FROM ENGLAND

Name: **John Redford**– Birthplace: **Charing Cross, London, England** (Sep 1755) ---Emigration (circa 1877)—Marriage: **Sarah (född Goodwin) Redford**--(3 Feb 1786) in **New York State**--Birthplace: **London, England** (c. 1765) --Children: *Henry, James, Moses, Martha, Richard, William, Arthur, Peter, Lewis & Sarah*--Residence—Sparta, Ontario County, New York (1800)—Residence—Leicester, Genesee County, New York (1810)—John Redford's death-- Fort Harrison Prairie, Terra Haute, Indiana (12 July 1816)—Grandson: **Thomas Spencer Redford** residence in 1850: Lisbon Township, Waukesha County, Wisconsin—Occupation: *carpenter & farmer*.

(Image and genealogy courtesy of Sussex-Lisbon Area Historical Society.)[330]

Thomas Spencer Redford holding daughter Maplet (c. 1880)[331]

Running a Man-of-War:

"Men-of-War in the British navy during the 1750's were run very strictly. No seaman was allowed alcohol or spirits apart from the usual daily ration of grog. *Any disrespect given verbally or physically was generally punished by flogging on the back with a whip of cat o' nine tails.* The captain and his officers were to dine in the cabin or the gunroom, while the midshipmen and seamen dined on the gundecks. During longer voyages, a biscuit called **hardtack**[332] was eaten. *Many of the seamen serving on men-of-war were generally pressed into the service, so mutiny was a very apparent threat.*"[333]

First Settler in the Town of Lisbon:

"*There is a Redford family story that their ancestor, John Redford, born about 1755 in Charing Cross, London, was on a family errand with horse and chaise, when he was kidnapped and taken aboard an English man of war ship to fight in the Revolutionary War against the American colonies.* Was sent to America, landing in New York, and promptly escaped. As a wanted fugitive, he fled to the wild western area of *New York Colony*, to *Cattaraugus, Livingston and Genesee Counties* and later joined the American army. *Thomas Spencer Redford (John Redford's grandson) was Lisbon's first settler.* John, with his wife, four of their sons and a daughter, were among the first groups to make the pioneer run to Fort Harrison in Indiana. Thomas's father Arthur stayed in New York State, fought in the War of 1812, participating in the Battle of Niagara. *It was Feb. 28,1836 when Thomas Redford started walking west to the newly opened Wisconsin Territory. And it was April 15 when he arrived in the muddy little Milwaukee village. After staking his Lisbon claim in May 1836, he built the towns first log house.* Once he planted a small crop to hold his claim to the land, he returned to Milwaukee for the winter and plied his carpenter's trade." *–Fred Keller*[334]

---

[330] *Federal Manuscript Schedule*, Population, Agricultural and Manufacturing Schedules for Lisbon Township, Waukesha County, 1850.

[331] Photograph courtesy of the Sussex-Lisbon Area Historical Society, Mike Reilly, Website Editor, e-mail to author, Jan 1, 2017.

[332] "Hardtack (or hard tack) is a simple type of biscuit or cracker, made from flour, water, and sometimes salt. Hardtack is inexpensive and long-lasting. It is used for sustenance in the absence of perishable foods, commonly during long sea voyages, land migrations, and military campaigns." From: en.wikipedia.org/wiki/Hardtack

[333] http://pirates.wikia.com/wiki/Man-of-war

[334] Fred Keller, "Thomas Spencer Redford—The Lisbon-Sussex Sesquicentennial," *Landmark*, v. 29, n. 1 (Spring, 1986), pp. 6 & 7.

IMMIGRANTS TO WISCONSIN FROM ENGLAND & NEW YORK

Name: **Alfred Russell**—Birthplace: **England** (1816)—Year of immigration: (circa: 1848)—Residence: 1860- 1st D 9th Ward, New York, New York: Occupation: *clerk*—Marriage: **Mary Elizabeth Thomas** (circa 1850) --birthplace: **New York** (1826)— immigrated to Wisconsin in 1860—Residence in 1860: Germantown, Washington County, Wisconsin—children: **Adda** age 9, **Isaac** age 6 and **Eva** age 3. Soon after the death of the children Alfred & Mary divorced. Mary later married William Bradley— (age: 70) in 1880--of Eagle, Waukesha County.

(Image and genealogy courtesy of Libbie Nolan of Big Bend, Wisconsin.) [335]

William Bradley (c. 1880) [336]

Three of Alfred and Mary Russell's children die of diphtheria in 1868:

"Mary Elizabeth Thomas married Alfred Russell. *Their three teenage children: Adda, 17, Isaac, 15, and Eva, 13, all died of black diphtheria within a week of the birth of their baby brother, William Thomas.* Soon after, Mary and Alfred Russell divorced. Mary Elizabeth married again to *William Bradley*." [337]

High diphtheria death rates in 19th Century Milwaukee:

"Contemporary 19th Milwaukee observers noted the effects of overcrowding on people's health. Medical practitioners felt overwhelmed in their attempt to stem the tide of disaster with epidemics spread through densely populated wards. Not only was isolation impossible, but adequate ventilation, cleanliness, and proper diets remained beyond the reach of most families. [338] "*As late as 1893 one physician discussed the futility of treating diphtheria in the poorer sections of the city*: "We might as well confess it right straight off, that we just have to give up. We must give up because of the local surroundings. High death rates among children indicated the extent of the problem. A health officer in Milwaukee lamented the fact that children under five years of age accounted for 61 percent of the deaths in the city. "*This slaughter of innocents,*" he noted in 1872, "*is found, chiefly, in crowded part of the city, where families are massed together, in filthy, dark, ill ventilated tenements, surrounded by dirty yards and alleys, foul privy's, and imperfect drainage. In such an atmosphere, the child inhales a deadly miasmatic poison in every breath it draws.*"[339]

---

[335] *Federal Manuscript Schedule*, Population, Agricultural and Manufacturing Schedules for the Township of Germantown, Washington County, Wisconsin, 1860.

[336] Photograph Courtesy of Libbie Nolan via Pat Nolan, Big Bend, Wisconsin, e-mail to author, Dec. 21, 2016.

[337] Author visit with Libbie Nolan, Jan. 15, 2010.

[338] "Diphtheria produces a gray lining over the membranes of the nose and throat, or the area of the tonsils. This membrane may also be greenish or blueish, or even cause 'black diphtheria' if there has been bleeding." Taken from: https://www.thefreedictionary.com/Diptheria

[339] Judith Wallzer Leavitt "Health in Urban Wisconsin: From Bad to Better Frontier," p. 156. In Numbers, Ronald L. & Judith Walzer Leavitt. WISCONSIN MEDICINE. © 1981 by the Board of Regents of the University of Wisconsin System. Reproduced courtesy of the University of Wisconsin Press, pp. 134 & 135.

IMMIGRANTS TO WISCONSIN FROM NORWAY

Name: **J. Rolfson**– birthplace: <u>**Norge**</u> (1819) — Spouse: <u>Billy</u>—Birthplace: <u>**Norge**</u> (1821) — Children: *Robert* (b. 1844 in <u>**Norge**</u>), *Louis* (b. 1847 in <u>**Norge**</u>), *Andrew* (b. 1849 in <u>**Norge**</u>), Year of immigration: (c. 1850) --*Brady* (b. 1851 in <u>**Wisconsin**</u>), *Martin* (b. 1855 in <u>**Wisconsin**</u>) & *Edward* (b. Apr 1860 in <u>**Muskego**</u>)—Residence in 1860: <u>Muskego Township, Waukesha County, Wisconsin</u>–occupation: *farmer*—also residing in this residence: *Helick Olson (farm laborer)*. (Image and genealogy courtesy of Muskego Historical Society.)[340]

Norwegians at Muskego:

"<u>The Muskego Settlement was one of the first Norwegian-American settlements in the United States. John Nielsen Luraas (1813–1890) first led the colony which was founded in 1839, primarily by immigrants from the Norwegian county of Telemark.</u>"[342] *"What was called the Norwegian settlement began in the south part of the town (of Muskego) in 1839, and grew rapidly until some of the newly arriving immigrants brought the cholera[343] in 1849. Terrible and indescribable scenes followed the breaking out of this fearful scourge.* <u>A hospital was established on the shores of Big Muskego Lake, in a large barn, where scores of the poor people died. This plague broke out here again in 1851 and raged with frightful violence and fatality. Graves were dug and kept open for expected corpses. The plague carried such terror into the community that all but a few of the surviving Norwegian families left.</u>" —**Frank A. Flower**[344]

J. Rolfson Family of Norway (1880)

<u>Left to right back row:</u> Louis, Andrew, Martin, Edward, & Robert.
<u>Left to right sitting:</u> J. (father), Billy (mother), Brady[341]

When the Cholera broke out at Milwaukee:

"<u>*During the summer of 1849, the cholera broke out in Milwaukee. The death like stillness was appalling; nothing was seen but the death carts rolling round the streets gathering the recent dead. There seemed to be no traffic in the whole city; all seemed so sad.*</u> There were fifty deaths from cholera that day. This was in 1849. The cholera returned to <u>Milwaukee</u> in 1850, more terrible than the year before. People literally died as they walked along the streets. Those who watched corpses being hauled away would themselves be victims the next day. Official reports put the toll at over 300; some felt the number was more than double that with the bodies secretly buried to avoid reporting to authorities." --*Laura Grover*[345]

---

340   *Federal Manuscript Schedule*, Population, Agricultural and Manufacturing Schedules for Muskego Township, Waukesha County, 1860.

341   Courtesy of Muskego Historical Society, Meeting of the Board of Directors, June 2009.

342   https://en.wikipedia.org/wiki/Muskego_Settlement,_Wisconsin

343   "People usually get cholera by eating food or drinking water that is unclean. The most common symptom is large amounts of watery diarrhea. In the worst cases, diarrhea can be so bad that people can die in a few hours from dehydration." From: https://simple.wikipedia.org/wiki/Cholera

344   Frank A. Flower, *History of Milwaukee, Wisconsin*. (Milwaukee: Western Historical Company, 1881), p. 40.

345   Mrs. H. C. Carpenter (Laura Grover), *Waukesha Freeman* May 9, 1923.

IMMIGRANTS TO WISCONSIN FROM BAVARIA

Name: **John George Woelfel**– Birthplace: **Rollhofen, Bayern, Germany** (1835)—Spouse: **Regina Haberman**—Birthplace: **Bayern, Germany** (1835)—Residence in 1870: **Brookfield Township, Waukesha County, Wisconsin**—Occupation: *farmer*–Children: John Jr., George, Katherine, Frank, **Simon**, George, Mary Katherina, Frederick, Regina, Anna, Minnie, Helen, Margaret & Frederick. *Frederick Woelfel was a cousin to this family and immigrated to Wisconsin several years after the John Woelfel family.* (Image courtesy of Roger & Marian Woelfel of New Berlin, WI.; Genealogy courtesy of James A. Woelfel of Holt, MI.) [346]

Simon Woelfel (c. 1880) [347]

An immigrant family in dire straits:

"Feb. 26, 1886, Milwaukee, Wis.

To: the Kraus family,

Germersberg, Lauf, Bayern,

Hello and God be with you. I am writing to you of my children and all relatives. I want everybody to know we have a situation which is impossible to live with. It looks like to us you have not received any of my letters because we have not received any answers. Between me and my husband [Frederick] certain things have happened. *He has died, and I did my duty to give him a decent burial. It cost me $40 for the funeral and took the whole summer to pay for it. This would not be mentioned. I am not healthy for six months with a liver ailment.* For a while I was little better but now, I am paralyzed, so it is impossible to work at all. I am so thin but skin and bones. I know I look completely different now. I have taken my children and put them in an orphanage. I have tried everything, so they would be taken care of should I die. Now, I am better and work a little bit. So, my duty is to support my children again. George is 12 and Tilla is 7. *My son always says, 'why don't you write to grandfather, my father has told me so many stories about him. He says when he is grown up; 'I will go to Germany to see my relatives and get to know them'.'' My son can give information on the situation in America and how bad it is.* With God's help I hope my few lines will turn out for the best. Hoping everything is better in Germany than here. I wish you could help me as my life is worth nothing anymore. If it were not for my children, my life has no meaning. I beg you to write back real soon as possible.

Highest respects for you,

Mrs. Karoline Woelfel & children,

46 Martin St., Milwaukee, Wis." [348]

Immigrant American Working Conditions during the 1880's:

"Though most immigrants were successful in finding jobs in America, *working conditions were extremely dangerous.* Work accidents were common in factories. The injured workers were usually not fully compensated as well. *Along with this, there was very little security for their low paying, dangerous jobs. They could lose them anytime.*" [349]

---

[346] Federal Manuscript Schedule, Population, Agricultural and Manufacturing Schedules for Brookfield Township, Waukesha County, 1870.

[347] Roger & Marion Woelfel of New Berlin, Wisconsin. Permission provided over the course of numerous home visits.

[348] "Mrs. Caroline Woelfel letter to the Kraus family, of Germersberg, Bavaria (1886)," mailed to author by Louis Wasserman of Germersberg, Bavaria, Dec. 5, 1986.

[349] https://herndonapush.wikispaces.com/Immigrants%3B+Working+Conditions+and+Pay+%28post+1860%29

IMMIGRANTS TO WISCONSIN FROM BAVARIA

Name: **_Daniel Schley Sr._**– Birthplace: **_Oberpfalz, Bayern_** (25 Feb 1817)—Spouse: **_Emma Barbara Specht_** —Birthplace: **_Oberfalz, Bayern_** (1819)—Residence in 1860: <u>New Berlin, Waukesha County, Wisconsin</u>— Occupation: _farmer_–Children: Elizabeth, Daniel, Henry, George, Phillip, Catharine, Barbary, Julia & Catharine. Daniel's Death: <u>Waukesha, Waukesha, Wisconsin</u> (17 Jan 1887)

(Image and genealogy courtesy of Tricia Dingwall Thompson and extended family of Bozeman, Montana)[350]

Daniel & Barbara Schley (c. 1881)[351]

Wisconsin refugees from the Palatinate in northern Bavaria:

"The title Palatinate means the Ruler of the of the Principality. The palace of the Caesars was situated on the Palatine Hill. _The German Palatines were early 18th century emigrants from the Middle Rhine region of the Holy Roman Empire, including a minority from the Palatinate which gave its name to the entire group._ The Palatinate[352] consisted of two small regions in southern Germany near the Rhine River. The Palatinate (Pfalz), in German history, are the lands of the count palatine, a title held by a leading secular prince of the Holy Roman Empire. Geographically, the Palatinate was divided between two small territorial clusters: the Rhenish, or Lower Palatinate and the Upper Palatinate."[353]

The Daniel Schley Sr. family of the Upper Palatinate:

"Frederick V's acceptance of the Bohemian crown in 1619 contributed to the beginning of the Thirty Years' War, a war that proved disastrous to the Palatinate."[354] "_During the Thirty Years War (1618–48), the Palatine country and other parts of Germany suffered from the horrors of fire and sword as well as from pillage and plunder by the French armies_. This war was based upon both politics and religious hatreds, as the Roman Catholic armies sought to crush the religious freedom of a politically-divided Protestantism. _During the War of the Grand Alliance (1689-97), the troops of the French monarch Louis XIV ravaged the Rhenish Palatinate, causing many Germans to emigrate._" _(Many early German settlers to America were refugees from the Palatinate including the Daniel Schley family who immigrated to Wisconsin from the Oberfaltz region of northern Bavaria.)_ [355]

350   _Federal Manuscript Schedule_, Population, Agricultural and Manufacturing Schedules for New Berlin Township, Waukesha County, 1860.

351   Photograph courtesy of Tricia Dingwall Thompson of Bozeman, Montana, e-mail to author, Jun 27, 2010.

352   "The Palatinate (German: die Pfalz, Pfälzer dialect: Palz), historically also Rhenish Palatinate (German: Rheinpfalz), is a region in southwestern Germany. It occupies roughly the southernmost quarter of the German federal state of Rhineland-Palatinate (Rheinland-Pfalz), Its residents are known as Palatines." From: https://en.wikipedia.org/wiki/Palatinate_(region)

353   https://en.wikipedia.org/wiki/Palatinate

354   The Palatines - for United Empire Loyalists' Association of Canada George Anderson, "The Palatines UE 1," June 2006. WorldGenWeb The WorldGenWeb is a non-profit volunteer organization that is dedicated to the free use and access of public domain genealogical information. Copyright © 2018 WorldGenWeb Project.

355   https://en.wikipedia.org/wiki/Palatinate

IMMIGRANTS TO WISCONSIN FROM PRUSSIA

Father: **Christoph Boness**—Birthplace: **Simötzel, Kolberg-Körlin, Pomerania, Preußen,** (8 Oct 1806)—Mother: **Christine (Thurow)**—Birthplace: **Pinnow, Brandenburg, Preußen** (14 June 1802). Son: **August Boness** – Birthplace, **Preußen** (20 Aug 1836)— Spouse: **Caroline "Lena" (Neumann)**—Birthplace: **Preußen** (1845) —Occupation: *farmer*--Children: *Charles* (b.1868), *Amanda* (b.1871), *Ida* (b.1875) & *Robert* (b.1877)—family residence in 1876: Oconomowoc, Town of Oconomowoc, Waukesha County, Wisconsin— family residence in 1880: Fountain Prairie, Columbia County, Wisconsin.

(Image and genealogy courtesy of Erin Rajek of Schofield, Wisconsin)[356]

Robert R. Boness (c. 1881)[357]

Tricycles come into popularity in North America:

"*In 1789, two French inventors developed a three-wheeled vehicle, powered by pedals; They called it the tricycle.* By 1879, there were "twenty types of tricycles and multi-wheel cycles produced in Coventry, England, and by 1884, there were over 120 different models produced by 20 manufacturers" worldwide."[358]

Christoph Boness: of Simötzel, Kolberg-Körlin, Pomerania, Preußen:

"*Saint Stanislaus Kostka (Polish) church in Simötzel, Kolberg-Körlin Pomerania, Preußen, on the Baltic Sea (birthplace of Christoph Boness) was in Landkreis (county) in the Prussian Province of Pomerania between 1872 and 1945. Most of Kolberg–Körlin's other municipalities have records dating back to the 13th Century.* It belonged to the government region Köslin in the Prussian province of Pomerania, and comprised rural regions as well as the towns of Colberg and Körlin. The county seat was in Kolberg."[359]

Christine Thurow: of Pinnow, Brandenburg, Preußen:

"*Pinnow is a municipality in the Uckermark district, in Brandenburg, Germany. Uckermark became part of Brandenburg-Prussia in 1618, but was ravaged during the Thirty Years' War.* Frederick William, the Great Elector, invited large numbers of French Huguenots[360] to resettle the Uckermark and his other territories by announcing the Edict of Potsdam. The Huguenots helped to develop the economy and culture of the Uckermark. In 1815 after the Napoleonic Wars, the Uckermark became part of the Prussian Province of Brandenburg." [361]

356   *Federal Manuscript Schedule*, Population, Agricultural and Manufacturing Schedules for Oconomowoc Township, Waukesha County, 1870.
357   Photograph courtesy of Erin (Boness) Rajek of Schofield, Wisconsin, e-mail to author, Apr 23, 2010.
358   https://en.wikipedia.org/wiki/Tricycle
359   https://en.wikipedia.org/wiki/Landkreis_Kolberg-K%C3%B6rlin
360   "The term Huguenots has its origin in early 16th century France. It was frequently used in reference to those of the Reformed Church of France from the time of the Protestant Reformation. Huguenots were French Protestants who held to the Reformed tradition of Protestantism, while the populations of Alsace, Moselle and Montbéliard were mainly German Lutherans." From: https://en.wikipedia.org/wiki/Huguenots
361   https://en.wikipedia.org/wiki/Uckermar

IMMIGRANTS TO WISCONSIN FROM VERMONT

Name: **_Jesse Smith_**—Birthplace: **Andover, Windsor County, Vermont** (31 July1804)—Spouse: **Sylvia Barton**—Birthplace: **Andover, Windsor County, Vermont** (22 July 1805)—married: (18 Jan 1828) --Residence in 1860: Dodge's Corners, Vernon Township, Waukesha County, Wisconsin—Occupation: _farmer, tavernkeeper & boarder_—Children: Samuel, Carlo, Horace, Leonean, Josephine, Isaac & Mary.
(Image and genealogy courtesy of Waukesha County Historical Society and Museum.)[362]

Jesse Smith (c. 1882)[363]

Disparity in wealth caused many Vermonters to immigrate:

"_What pushed so many Vermonters west? In 1811 William Jarvis introduced Merino sheep into Vermont, leading to a rapid change in farming practices: Many farms were consolidated as it became more profitable to raise sheep on a larger scale. By 1837 there were over one million sheep in Vermont providing wool to the large textile mills in Massachusetts and over 100 smaller mills in Vermont._ Windsor County was one of four in the state that counted 200 sheep per square mile. From 1829 to 1835, the average flock size throughout New Hampshire was 500-1,000 head. _The booming wool industry created disparities in wealth as the demand for larger acreage increased land prices. Not everyone could afford a farm and the 1830s saw many young would-be northern New England farmers heading west._"[364]

Jesse Smith _continues to raise Marino Sheep:_

"_Jesse Smith, with the brothers Aaron and Amos Putnam, Col. Orien Haseltine and John Thomas, all from the state of Vermont, in 1841, came to Vernon Township_; A frame house where he used to lodge many a weary traveler over the then new road; well-remembered by the teamsters and farmers of 'Plank-road days;' the generous old dining-room, fifty feet in length, was often crowded, and it was not unusual for him to lodge 100 persons over night; and for a month or more, each fall twenty-five or thirty teams per night was not strange. _300 to 400 teams per day passed here, many from the lead mines of Southwestern Wisconsin, it was a common thing for men to order breakfast at 4 in the morning, the noted springs refreshed many a 'wayfaring' man and team._ Situated on the hill back of the house was furnished with wooden piping in 1842, and (the same year) built a very large two-and-half -story stone house (still standing in 2018 and still very beautiful) _No better representative of the good old Vermont stock can be found in the West than is found in 'Uncle Jesse Smith,' known as the genial old landlord. He now has a 350-acre homestead with over 400 Merino sheep_"[365]

---

[362] _Federal Manuscript Schedule_, Population, Agricultural and Manufacturing Schedules for Vernon Township, Waukesha County, 1860.

[363] Jesse Smith (c. 1882), People S-T Box 7:8, Photography Collection, Research Center Library & Archive, Waukesha County Historical Society & Museum, Waukesha, Wisconsin.

[364] "Migration from Vermont," from "_Flow of History Gathering and Interactions of Peoples, Cultures, and Ideas_," c/o Southeast Vermont Community Learning Collaborative, courtesy of flow@learningcollaborative.org.

[365] _The History of Waukesha County_, 1880, pp. 1000 & 1001.

IMMIGRANTS TO WISCONSIN FROM PRUSSIA & BAVARIA

Parents: **Friedrich Woelfel**—Birthplace: <u>**Rollhofen, Bayern, Germany**</u> (1816)—*Friedrich's* 3rd spouse: **Maria Anna Ostermann**—Birthplace: <u>**Batzhausen, Oberpfalz, Bayern, Germany**</u> (1828)--Name: <u>Martin Jewert</u>—Birthplace <u>**Preußen, Germany**</u> (c 1844)— Spouse: **Anna Woelfel**--Birthplace: <u>**Milwaukee, Wisconsin**</u> (15 Aug 1854)— Marriage: (1 Oct 1872)-- Martin & Anna's residence in 1890: <u>Elm Grove, Brookfield Township, Waukesha County, Wisconsin</u>–Occupation: *blacksmith* —Children: Joseph, Francis, Edward, Michael, George, & Mary Ann—Martin Jewert's death: (1895).   (Image courtesy of Roger & Marion Woelfel of New Berlin, WI.; Genealogy courtesy of Mary Stigler of Brookfield, WI.)[366]

Anna Woelfel (c. 1882)[367]

Martin Jewert's blacksmith shop:

"When *Roy Aitken* was a young boy, during the 1890's, his family lived at Goerke's Corners, in Brookfield Township. On his way home from school, he often stepped inside the local blacksmith shop and observed the work of shoeing horses going on, which he describes below. *(At the same time, just down the road, in the village of Elm Grove, the very same work was going on inside the shop of Martin Jewert).* Roy Aitken wrote: *'Shaping shoes was an art form.'* **(conti- below)**

The Woelfel family left amid civil unrest:

"*Martin Jewert's wife*, *Anna Woelfel*, was a daughter of Fredrich & Maria Anna (Ostermann) Woelfel, both of Bavaria. Fredrich served for a short time in the Bavarian army under Ludwig I, King of Bavaria, who faced demonstrations and protests preceding the Revolutions of 1848. In 1846 *Fredrich Woelfel deserted* and immigrated to Wisconsin. He settled in the town Brookfield, near the village of Elm Grove, where several brothers, along with their father, Ulrich, had already purchased neighboring parcels. The Woelfel and Jewert families were devote Catholics, and attended Sunday mass in a small log church, measuring 24 X 34 feet, consecrated to St. Ambrose, on a parcel donated by the Woelfel family along the east side of today's Highland Dr, in Elm Grove." [368]

The smithy stoked up the fire, keeping it alive by a long handle attached to the bellows, which blew air up and under the fire. *While the shoe was red hot, he lifted the shoe with long iron tongs, and dashed it into a wooden tub of cold water; then hammered it to the shape on the anvil.* The odor of the hot shoe pressed to the hoof, the noise of the shaping of the shoe on the anvil was enough to frighten any horse—except the older ones who had been shod many times. A young horse generally had to have two or three men to calm him down, one to hold the head, the smithy stroking his legs, and another helping where he could. *I could never figure out how the sharp nails being driven into the hoof didn't hurt.*"[369]

Blacksmith Shop to Cool Its Fires.

<u>*Martin Jewert's blacksmith shop was a log cabin on the east side of Elm Grove Rd. Mr. Jewert put up his building in 1883.*</u> When Jewert died, John Sanders moved the log cabin across the road and, for a time, used it as a wagon shop as part of his own blacksmith shop operation.   [*Milwaukee Journal*, June 1969]

---

[366]   *Federal Manuscript Schedule*, Population, Agricultural and Manufacturing Schedules for Brookfield Township, Waukesha County, 1890.

[367]   Photograph courtesy of Roger & Marion Woelfel of New Berlin, Wisconsin. Permission provided over the course of numerous home visits.

[368]   Author, *Brookfield: A Fine and Fertile Land*, vol. 1, p. 22.

[369]   Roy Aitkin, *"Shaping a Shoe,"* Landmark, v. 13, n. 1, (Winter, 1970), pp. 16 & 17.

IMMIGRANTS TO WISCONSIN FROM ENGLAND

Name: **William Chapman**—Birthplace: **Lincolnshire, England** (1 Jan 1822)—Spouse: **Caroline M. Horne**—Birthplace: **England** (28 Dec 1832)—Residence in 1860: Pewaukee Township, Waukesha County, Wisconsin—Occupation: *farmer*—Children: *William, George, Susan, Esther, Charles, Nettie, Fidelia & Wesley.*
(Image and genealogy courtesy of Libbie Nolan of Big Bend, Wisconsin)[370]

Elsie Chapman (c. 1882)[371]

William Chapman's farm in the town of Lisbon:

"William Chapman, farmer, Sec. 23; P.O., Waukesha; was born in Lincolnshire, England, January 1, 1822. In 1850 he crossed the Atlantic, came to Wisconsin and located in the town of Pewaukee, Waukesha County, September 1, 1853. Mr. Chapman and his wife resided in Pewaukee since their marriage. His farm finely improved and well located, possessing many natural advantages." [372]

Women's Clothing Styles of the 1880's:

"Elsie Chapman's dress style is somewhat difficult to identify as the image shows her only from the shoulders up. *However, a lot can be deduced from what is visible. Elsie's hair is swept up to the top of her head, very indicative of the mid-1880s.* She wears a high-necked day dress. Skirts were almost always layered and draped, often with an apron front and a trained back. The 1880s was, also, a decade of tight and restrictive corsetry worn under dresses with long boned bodices, tight sleeves and, again, high necks. *The pleating visible below her neckline would likely be found throughout in her skirt construction and trimming*." **—Joan Severa, 19th Century Clothing Styles** [373]

The Chapman boys likely worked at Pewaukee Lake during the ice harvest:

"*Ice harvesting was a major industry in Waukesha County before the days of automatic refrigeration.* It provided employment for farmers, tradesmen in their slack season, and transients… Probably the best known were the five huge ice houses beside Pewaukee Lake from 1890- to 1920. Workers came in flat bed sleighs from nearby towns. Armour, operator of the largest icehouse, hired and boarded 600 men."[374]

PEWAUKEE. --Savoy and Sons of Pewaukee are now prepared to supply the public with a fine quality of ice. [*Waukesha Freeman*] Jan. 4, 1894]

370   *Federal Manuscript Schedule*, Population, Agricultural and Manufacturing Schedules for Pewaukee Township, Waukesha County, 1890.
371   Photograph courtesy of Libbie Nolan, via Pat Nolan, of Big Bend, Wisconsin, e-mail to author, Dec. 21, 2016.
372   *The History of Waukesha County, 1880*, p. 933.
373   Joan Severa, of Madison, Wisconsin, e-mail to author, Feb 7, 2010.
374   Libbie Nolan, "Early Waukesha Manufacturing," *Landmark*, (autumn-winter, 1975), vol. 18, no. 4, p. 12.

IMMIGRANTS TO WISCONSIN FROM THE GRAND DUCHY OF HESSE AND N.Y.

Name: **Henry Snyder**--Birthplace: <u>Paffenhabenheim, Hessen, Germany</u> (9 Sept 1844)—Spouse—**Mary Elizabeth Eiler**—Birthplace: <u>Troy, Rensselaer, County, New York</u> (3 Mar 1847-24 Mar 1922)—Married—<u>Waukesha, Waukesha County</u> (26 Nov 1865)—Residence in 1870: <u>Waukesha, Waukesha County</u>—Occupation: *shoemaker*—Children: *Martin (1866-1867)—Elizabeth Burlingame (1869-1958)—Rev. Henry Snyder (1874-1954)—Mabel Barbara Perkins (1884-1963)—Gustave (1868-1969)—Amelia Wilhemina Putz (1872-1926) & Alvin* —employed in his father's: *shoe shop (1880-1934).*

(Image and genealogy courtesy of Kenneth Eiler of Overland Park, Kansas.)[375]

Henry Snyder (c. 1883)[376]

Grand Duchy of Hesse:

"*The Grand Duchy of between 1806 and 1816, was an independent country and member state of the Confederation of the Rhine as of 1806, when the Landgraviate of Hesse-Darmstadt was elevated to a Grand Duchy which it remained until 1918, when the monarchy was overthrown*. Before 1866, its northern neighbor was its former sister Landgraviate, since 1803 an Electorate of Hesse-Kassel – for this reason, this state was sometimes colloquially known as Hesse-Darmstadt."[377]

Boots and Shoes

Henry Snyder Manufacturer of all kinds of Boots and Shoes. <u>*Ladies' and Gents' Fine Sewed Work a specialty.*</u> Repairing done with neatness and dispatch. Opera House Block, Broadway, Waukesha, Wis. [*Daily Freeman and Republican, Waukesha, Wisconsin*, June 20, 1890]

Death of Henry Snyder

On Saturday morning, last Henry Snyder, a resident of Waukesha for many years, died suddenly at his home, of heart disease, aged 65 years. <u>*Deceased was a Civil war veteran and had been a member of the local fire department for 33 years. He was a shoemaker by trade and carried on his business to the day of his death.*</u> Mr. Snyder was a *member of the M. W. lodge of the W. B. Cushing Post G.A.R.* and in the latter organization especially he took great interest and was very popular with the old soldiers. He was but 14 years of age when he enlisted and went to the war despite the opposition of his parents.

[*Waukesha Freeman* May 13, 1909]

---

[375] *Federal Manuscript Schedule,* Population, Agricultural and Manufacturing Schedules for Waukesha County, City of Waukesha, 1870.

[376] Photograph courtesy of Kenneth Eiler of Overland Park, Kansas, e-mail to author, Jun 27, 201o.

[377] https://en.wikipedia.org/wiki/Grand_Duchy_of_Hesse

IMMIGRANTS FROM BAVARIA & ALSACE

Parents: **John Michael Stigler** & **Mary Anna Ostermann** immigrated from near <u>Gross Bissedorf, Oberpfalz, Bayern</u> to Wisconsin in 1850--Son: **Frederick Stigler**—Birthplace: <u>Elm Grove, Waukesha County</u> (c. 1842)—Spouse: **Mary Angeline Schneider**—Birthplace: <u>New Berlin, Waukesha County</u>—Mary Angeline's parents: **Andrew Schneider**—Birthplace: <u>Mulhausen, Bas-Rhine, Elsass, France</u> (7 Jan. 1811)—and **Catherine Casper**—Birthplace: <u>Elsass, France</u> (15 Oct 1811)—Residence in 1880<u>: New Berlin Township, Waukesha County, Wisconsin</u>—Occupation: *farmer*—Children: ***Michael**, **Otilia**, **Andrew***, John, George, Mary Anna, Joseph & Anthony. (Image and genealogy courtesy of Mary Stigler of Brookfield, Wisconsin.)[378]

Michael, Andrew & Otilia Stigler (c. 1883)[379]

Children's Clothing Styles of the 1880's:

This photograph of the three oldest Stigler children was taken in the early 1880's. *Otilia's dress is very typical of a child's dress from this period with its pleated trim, long fitted jacket, and crocheted collar.* Both boys wear knickers, fitted, coming just below their knees, and buttoned plackets. *Their coats are both single and double breasted, buttoned tight at the neck. Both boys are wearing Bavarian style Lederhosen.*" —*Joan Severa, 19th Century Clothing Styles*[380]

Stigler children marry into local area families:

"<u>Johann Michael (Mike) Stigler</u> (1814 - 1900) and fiancée, <u>Maria Anna Ostermann</u> (1828 - 1902) both arrived in July 1850 to Milwaukee, Wisconsin from Bavaria. They were married July 1850 in Milwaukee, and immediately moved to the Village of Elm Grove, Brookfield Township, Waukesha County, Wisconsin, where 3 children were born. The family bought land in New Berlin Township in 1856, where 4 more children born. They were *Frederick Stigler*--married **Mary Angeline Schneider** (1877) in New Berlin; *Otilia Stigler*--married **Johann Meyer** (1882). Following the death of Johann Meyer, *Otilia* married **Joseph Phillips**, both in New Berlin; *Mary Stigler*—married **Philip Salentine** (1879), in New Berlin. *Mary Ann Stigler* married **Christian Salentine** (1885) in New Berlin; *Michael & Joseph Stigler* were twin boys who died young and are buried at <u>Holy Apostles Cemetery</u>, in New Berlin."[381]

---

378 *Federal Manuscript Schedule*, Population, Agricultural and Manufacturing Schedules for New Berlin Township, Waukesha County, 1880.

379 Photograph courtesy of Mary Stigler, of Brookfield, Wisconsin, e-mail to author, Aug 8, 2009.

380 Joan Severa, of Madison, Wisconsin., e-mail to author, Feb 27, 2010.

381 Posted in "New Berlin ancestry message board," courtesy of Mary Stigler & the New Berlin Historical Society, 12 Jan 2002.

IMMIGRANTS TO WISCONSIN FROM ENGLAND

Name: **Matthew Beaumont**—Birthplace: **Huddersfield, Yorkshire, England** (c. 1811)—Spouse: **France Radcliffe**— Birthplace: **Almondburry, Agbrigg, Yorkshire, England** (c. 1816) — Residence in 1850: Merton Township, Waukesha County, Wisconsin —Occupation: *farmer*—Children: *Ephraim, Esaw & Zelpah.*
(Image and genealogy courtesy of Jeanne Pedriana of Elm Grove, Wisconsin.)[382]

Matthew and Frances Beaumont (c. 1883)[383]

Whitley Beaumont Estate:

"In around 1200 the lord of Pontefract castle, Roger de Laci presented William Bellomonte, ancestor of the Beaumonts of Whitley, 24 bovates of land in Huddersfield, half meadow and half wood and four marks rent on the mill in the same place. *Although there were probably houses built on the site in the interim, the first Hall was built by Sir Richard Beaumont in the early 17th century. The house was then rebuilt in the 18th century in an imposing Georgian style.*" [384]

The British Co-Operative Movement:

"The origins of modern co-operatives owe their beginnings not simply to the extreme poverty faced by many in the 18th and 19th centuries, but also to the rapid social changes of urbanization, and the rising food prices *The Co-operative Wholesale Society was launched in Manchester by 300 individual co-operatives in Yorkshire during 1863, along with significant branches in, Bristol, Nottingham and Huddersfield.*"[385]

Woolen Firm of "Beaumont & Stock":

"In 1810 Matthew Beaumont was born in Huddersfield, England, on land his family held since the Norman Conquest in 1066. He was had a career as an engineer with the woolen firm of Beaumont & Stock. In 1833 he married Francis Radcliffe, an accomplished musician and vocalist. They had 3 sons and 3 daughters who reached maturity. He was part of a group who put money into a fund to finance a new settlement in America called the Netherton Co-operative. In 1850, her came to Wisconsin to find a place to settle, then he brought his family over. They left from "Netherton Fold."— *Jean Pedriana.* [386]

---

[382] *Federal Manuscript Schedule*, Population, Agricultural and Manufacturing Schedules for Merton Township, Waukesha County, 1850.

[383] Photograph courtesy of Jean Pedriana of Elm Grove, Wisconsin, e-mail to author, Apr 23, 2010.

[384] https://en.wikipedia.org/wiki/Whitley_Beaumont

[385] https://en.wikipedia.org/wiki/British_co-operative_movement

[386] "Woolen Firm of "Beaumont & Stock" — by *Jean Pedriana*, e-mail to author, Apr 23, 2010.

IMMIGRANTS TO WISCONSIN FROM BAVARIA

Name: **John Woelfel**—Birthplace: <u>**Rollhofen, Bayern, Germany**</u> (1820—Spouse: **Marianne Ramstöck**—Birthplace: <u>**Germersberg, Bayern, Germany**</u> (1823)—Port of Departure: Bremerhaven—Ship: *"Bark Charleston"*--Arrival: New York: 19 Oct. 1844—Residence in 1860: <u>Brookfield Township, Waukesha County, Wisconsin</u>—Occupation: *farmer*—Children: *Cornelia,* **Simon,** *& John.*   (Image courtesy of Roger & Marion Woelfel of New Berlin, WI; Genealogy courtesy of James Woelfel of Holt, Michigan.)[387]

Rev. Simon Woelfel (c. 1883)[388]

Father Simon Woelfel:

On December 25th, 1844, **Johann Woelfel** married **Marianna Ramstöck**. Johann & Marianna had three children—**John Jr., Simon & Cunnigunda.** At age 16, Simon attended *St. Francis Seminary* in Milwaukee where he was ordained into the priesthood 19 December 1868. Father Simon Woelfel became the first native born ordained Catholic priest from Waukesha County.[389]

Leaving their small Bavarian village:

"<u>On the morning of 1 August 1845, Ulrich Woelfel awoke his 5 adult children--Konrad, Johann, Johann Georg, Georg and Katharina for the last time in their home in the small Bavarian village of Rollhofen.</u> They were about to start a long journey encompassing well over 3,000 miles, to join a younger brother, Johann, who had emigrated the previous year to Wisconsin."[390]

A long journey from Rollhofen to the sea; across a large ocean; up through a wide river; along a remarkable canal; then steaming up through the lakes & finally, their arrival at a new home; 2 ½ months on water in all. For, during the early 1840s, the highways were the waterways. "Three Woelfel children died young, while their mother, Cunigunda Ramstöck, died 19 July 1842. <u>The remainder of the family would now begin their journey on foot, six miles, to the nearby village of Germersberg, to the home of Ulrich's brother-in-law, Johann Ramstöck. From Germersberg, on 14 August 1845, the family travelled by wagon along the Weser River to the city of Bremen on the North Sea. At Bremen they travelled aboard a small boat for a two-day trip to Bremerhaven, the port city at the mouth of the Weser River. There, on 24 August 1845, they took passage on the "Bark Louis" bound for New York City.</u> The ship's manifest shows 8 October 1845 as their arrival date at the port of New York. Here, they boarded a steamer, on the Hudson River, which powered them up to Albany. They then took a shallow canal boat, for a one-week journey, via the Erie Canal to Buffalo, New York. At Buffalo, they travelled aboard a large Great Lakes steamer where they disembarked on 25 October 1845 at a pier, at the foot of Huron Street, in Milwaukee. The following day an uncle came with a span of oxen to take them to his home in Brookfield, Waukesha County. The family stayed with their brother, Johann Woelfel, who, during the past year, had constructed a log house measuring 18X20."—*James A. Woelfel*[391]

387 *Federal Manuscript Schedule*, Population, Agricultural and Manufacturing Schedules for Brookfield Township, Waukesha County, 1860.

388 Photograph Courtesy of Roger & Marion Woelfel of New Berlin, WI, e-mail to author, Apr 10, 2010.

389 Genevieve Barbian Preslik, "Woelfel-Barbian Farm," from *Century Farms of Wisconsin, v.1.* (Inter-Collegiate Press, Shawnee Mission, Kansas), 1983, p. 413.

390 James Woelfel, *The Ulrich Woelfel Family History* (self-published, 1995), pp. xv-xvi.

391 James Woelfel, *The Ulrich Woelfel Family History*, pp. xv-xvi.

IMMIGRANTS TO WISCONSIN FROM BAVARIA

Name: **George Gebhardt**—Birthplace: **Munich, Bayern, Germany** (1817)—Spouse: **Magdalena Maria Brandmiller**—Birthplace: **Traunstein, Bayern, Germany** (1820)—Year of immigration: 1840—Occupation: *farmer*—Residence in 1860: **Brookfield Township, Waukesha County, Wisconsin**—Children: *John, Mary Anna, Conrad, John, Frederick, Matthias and George. Matthias & Mary Katherine Woelfel were married in 1887 and resided on a farm in the town of Brookfield.* (Image & genealogy courtesy of Roger & Marion Woelfel of New Berlin, WI. & James Woelfel of Holt, MI.)[392]

George & Magdalena Gebhardt's adult children & spouses (1884)[393]

The Gebhardt family:

"The photograph at the left may have been organized by the Gebhardt brothers to celebrate the upcoming wedding of their sister, **Mary Anna**, (sitting near center and wearing a large white bow & ribbon) to **Nicolaus (Nick) Nauretz** on April 29, 1884. Back row-likely: (l-r): **Fred Gebhardt, Conrad Gebhardt & John Gebhardt**--Sitting (l-r): **Mary Woelfel. Mary Rossbach, Mary (Gebhardt) Nauretz & Susan Nauretz**; Sitting on floor: **George & Mathias (Matt) Gebhardt.**"[394]

SAD ACCIDENT AT BROOKFIELD.

A sad accident occurred on Saturday last at Brookfield, Waukesha County. A boy about ten years of age, son of **George Gebhardt**, had his leg torn to pieces by the tumbling rod of a threshing machine. The job of threshing was being finished up, and the boy had taken one of the teams by the bits to check the speed, when in some way his foot slipped, and his leg was caught by the tumbling rod, completely crushing it to pieces and almost tearing it from his body. The boy was attended by Dr. Bevier, who did all that medical service could do.

[*Milwaukee Sentinel* Sept. 25, 1861]

A smallpox outbreak terrorizes the county:

When *Fred Gebhardt* (appearing in the upper left in photograph) died in the Gebhardt home, in 1885, of the dreaded Black Smallpox[395], his brothers buried him in **St. Ambrosius Cemetery**. At night the family wrapped his body in a blanket and hurriedly buried him in the small cemetery near the church where *many other graves remained unmarked*.

[*Brookfield News* Aug. 16, 1956] [396]

---

[392] *Federal Manuscript Schedule*, Population, Agricultural and Manufacturing Schedules for Brookfield Township, Waukesha County, 1860.

[393] Photograph courtesy of Kathleen Nauertz Husz, Milwaukee, Wisconsin, e-mail message to author, Sep 22, 2010

[394] Kathleen Nauertz Husz, Milwaukee, WI., e-mail message to author, Sep 22, 2010.

[395] "Smallpox was an infectious disease caused by one of two virus variants, variola major and variola minor. Hemorrhagic or what is known as "black smallpox" is an even more serious type of smallpox and the patient often died. The last naturally occurring case was diagnosed in October 1977 and the World Health Organization certified the global eradication of the disease in 1980." From: https://en.wikipedia.org/wiki/Smallpox#Hemorrhagic

[396] Courtesy of the Brookfield Public Library

IMMIGRANTS TO WISCONSIN FROM HESSE & RHINELAND/RHENISH PRUSSIA

Name: **Pancratgus Duckgeischel**—Birthplace: **Hessen**—Spouse: **Catherine Kirsh**—Birthplace: **Preußen** (Jan 1833)—Son-- *__Joseph Duckgeischel__*—Birthplace: **Hessen, Germany** (15 Feb1823)—Spouse: ***Catharina Kirsch***—Birthplace: **Irrhausen, Prum, Rheinisches/ Rheinpreußen** (c. 1834)—Year of immigration: c.1850—Marriage: Buffalo, Erie County, New York (15 Dec 1851)--Residence in 1860: Delafield Township, Waukesha County, Wisconsin—Occupation: *farmer*—Children: *Barbara, Anna Marie, Catharina, Elizabeth, Frank, George, Josephine, Matthew & Margaret*—Joseph's death: Delafield, Wisconsin (25 July 1910).

(Image and genealogy of Leanne Bennett of Waukesha, Wisconsin.)[397]

Joseph and Catharina Duckgeischel (c. 1884)[398]

The Kirsh's family home in Rhein Preußen:

(Catharina Kirsch's home of) "Irrhausen, Prüm, Rheinprovinz, lies on the river Prüm at the southeastern end of the Schneifel, a range of low mountains in the western part of the Eifel mountain range in western Germany and eastern Belgium."[399] "Joseph and Catharina immigrated to America in 1850, stayed for some time in Buffalo New York, where they were married. *They then moved west were Joseph Duckgeischel purchased a 49-acre farm in the far northeast corner of Delafield Township, Waukesha County, two miles east of the Bark River.*"[400]

Growing a variety of crops:

(*Joseph Duckgeischel's* farming practices were typical of most new German immigrants in Wisconsin.) "Early Yankee farmers to Wisconsin depended almost solely on *'King wheat,'* a very profitable cash crop. *German immigrant farmers in Wisconsin, on the other hand, tended to grow a little of everything—wheat rye, corn, oats barley, potatoes, root.* They prospered not dramatically, like some of the more successful Yankee farmers, but by little and little they saved money, bought better stock and built better homes."[401]

Among the Best-Known German Residents:

Mrs. Joseph Duckgeischel a resident of this section for many years died very suddenly at her home two and one-half miles east of the village at 6:30 o'clock Thursday morning. *Mrs. Duckgeisichel was 73 years of age and was numbered among the best-known German residents of this vicinity.* She is survived by her husband and eight children, George, Frank and Matthew and the Misses Josephine and Elizabeth; Mrs. Charles Deck of Waukesha; Mrs. Matt. Weber and Mrs. Jacob Brandt of Merton.

[*Hartland News* Nov. 11, 1905][402]

397   *Federal Manuscript Schedule*, Population, Agricultural and Manufacturing Schedules for the town of Delafield, Waukesha County, 1860.

398   Photograph courtesy of Leanne Bennett of Waukesha, Wisconsin, e-mail to author, Jun 24, 2010.

399   *1907 Memoirs of Waukesha County*, p. 347

400   https://en.wikipedia.org/wiki/Prüm

401   Joseph Schafer, "The Yankee and the Teuton in Wisconsin," *Wisconsin Magazine of History*, 6-7 (December 1922-December 1923), 6: pp. 276-277.

402   Courtesy of the Hartland Historical Society.

IMMIGRANTS TO WISCONSIN FROM ENGLAND

Name: **George H. Parsons**—Birthplace: **Cornwall, England** (1 Jan 1823)—occupation: *preacher*--spouse: **Agnes Hicks**— Birthplace: **Cornwall, England**--married (1 Jan 1846)—immigrated to Wisconsin: (1850)—Children— *James, Mary, Mrs. H.C. Melcher, John, 2 children died in infancy, George*—George Parsons: joined *the Wisconsin Conference of the Methodist Episcopal Church* (1868)—preached for 57 years at 11 separate ministry locations. George & Agnes' 4th Child: **John H. Parsons** – Birthplace: Elkhorn, Walworth County, Wisconsin (27 Aug 1859)—Spouse: **Clara Seabold**—Birthplace: Menomonee Falls, Waukesha County--Children: *Milo, Marian Earl & Ethel*—Clara died: January 1887—John Parsons (2nd marriage) **Jennie Fleming**—Birthplace: Prospect Hill, New Berlin, Waukesha County—occupation: *teacher*—children: **Mary** & George-- -- Residence in 1910: Menomonee Township, Waukesha County, Wisconsin— John Parson's occupation: dairy farmer—location: Menomonee Falls, Waukesha County—Children: *Earl, Ethel, George & Walter.*

(Image and genealogy courtesy of Libbie Nolan of Big Bend, Wisconsin.)[403]

Jennie Parsons and daughter Mary. (c. 1885)[404]

"Baby Mary only lived a few months"

Worked in the tin mines:

"At its height in the 19th century the Cornish tin mining industry had around 600 steam engines working to pump out the mines. During this period the population doubled. However, by the middle and late 19th century, Cornish mining was in decline, and many Cornish miners immigrated to developing mining districts overseas, where their skills were in demand: In the first 6 months of 1875 over 10,000 miners left Cornwall to find work overseas. *Many Cornish men and women immigrated to the mining frontiers of North America. They settled in Pennsylvania, Michigan, Wisconsin, Illinois and Montana.* On the wall outside of one mine a graffitied wall read: '*Cornish lads are fishermen and Cornish lads are miners too. / But when the fish and tin are gone, what are the Cornish boys to do?*'"[405]

The Parson's Large Dairy Herd:

Parsons, J. H. --Wife: Jennie--3 children --farmer --owns farm--100 acres—6 horses --**25 Holstein dairy cows**--Menomonee Falls—Town of Menomonee--**independent telephone.**[406]

"Cow County, USA:"

"*Out on the farms, pasture animals had changed to dairy cows with all five breeds: Holstein, Guernsey, Jersey, Ayrshire and Brown Swiss gaining national recognition.* In the first decades of this century Waukesha became the hub of "COW COUNTY, USA" because they said this little 24-square had invested more in the purer bread cattle per square mile than any other in the country. *In fact, there were more cows than people!* Five grand champions out of a possible six were won by Waukesha County dairy breeders in the 1920 National Dairy Show." --**Libbie Nolan**[407]

---

[403] *Federal Manuscript Schedule*, Population, Agricultural and Manufacturing Schedules for the town of Menomonee, Waukesha County, 1910.

[404] Photograph courtesy of Libbie Nolan via Pat Nolan, of Big Bend, Wisconsin, e-mail to author, Dec. 21, 2016.

[405] https://en.wikipedia.org/wiki/Mining_in_Cornwall_and_Devon

[406] *The Farm Journal Illustrated Rural Directory of Waukesha County, Wisconsin* (Philadelphia: Wilmer Atkinson Company, 1918), p. 119.

[407] Libbie Nolan, "Cow Country USA." *Landmark*. v. 15, n. 4, Autumn, 1972.

IMMIGRANTS TO WISCONSIN FROM SAXONY & PRUSSIA

Name: **Charles Gottfried Kreig**—Birthplace: <u>Sachsen</u> (8 Apr 1837)—Spouse: **Anna Rosia Glickman**—Birthplace: <u>Preußen, Germany</u>—Year of immigration: 1856—Ship: *"Panama"*—Residence in 1870: <u>Town of Brookfield, Waukesha County</u>—Occupation: *farmer*—Children: *Bertha, Gustave, William, Anna Wilhelmina & Herbert.* Intermarriages occurred between Kreig children & individuals from other families residing in the town: Herman Krueger married ***Bertha Ritt***; Herbert Kreig married ***Mary Ritt***; Ivy Leadley married ***John Ritt***; Harriet Ritt married ***August Schildt***; Anna August Kreig married ***August Dieman*** --Charles Kreig's death: <u>Pewaukee, Waukesha County</u> (9 Mar 1916).   (Image and genealogy courtesy of Jerry Hartwell of Bowling Green, Ohio)[408]

Charles Kreig Family (c. 1885)[409]

DIES IN A BARN

Waukesha, Wis., *Coroner Hill* is investigating the death of ***Chris Gasser***, age 69, whose dead body was found in the barn of ***Charles Kreig***, in the town of Brookfield. <u>Gasser had arranged to go to work for Kreig and drove home with him from Elm Grove. He had been drinking, and on his arrival at the Kreig farm he slept in the barn two nights.</u> His body was found in the hay on Wednesday.
[The Milwaukee Journal 11, 1907]

3 Generations of Kreigs:

A beautifully <u>quarried stone</u> fronts the <u>Kreig home</u>--Partial description of family photograph: Front Center Sitting: <u>Herman & Bertha Krueger</u>--Bertha's sister: <u>Anna (Kreig) Dieman</u> is at her right. Front Right: <u>Anna & August Dieman</u>. <u>Center 2nd Row</u>: standing between the posts, are the parents: <u>Anna & Charles Kreig</u>. <u>Back Row</u>: The little boy standing at the front door is likely <u>Herbert Krueger</u>, son of <u>Bertha & Herman Krueger</u>. [410]

BROOKFIELD. A remarkable accident occurred to ***John Ritt***, a farmer of this town, while assisting in gathering oats for Mr. Moll. <u>He was on a partly loaded wagon, when a whirlwind struck the vehicle, lifted the rack and contents from the wagon, carried it 200 feet and overturned it with Ritt underneath.</u> The horses ran away but were recaptured, and in the meantime another gust of wind righted the rack and Ritt was released without injury. The greatest loss was that of time in readjusting the matters.   [*Waukesha Freeman* Aug 3, 1911]

408   *Federal Manuscript Schedule*, Population, Agricultural and Manufacturing Schedules for the town of Brookfield, Waukesha County, 1870.

409   Photograph courtesy of Jerry Hartwell of Bowling Green, Ohio

410   Kenneth Eiler of Overland Park, Kansas, e-mail message to author, Jun 27, 2010.

IMMIGRANTS TO WISCONSIN FROM CONNECTICUT

Name: **Andrew Alexander Akin**—Birthplace: <u>Norwalk, Fairfield County, Connecticut</u> (4 Nov 1811)—Spouses: 1wife: **Jane Hyatt** of <u>Connecticut</u>; 2nd wife **Harriet Hayes** of <u>Connecticut</u>; 3rd wife; Abigail Squires—Birthplace: <u>Bridgeport, Connecticut</u> (11 Aug 1822)—Year of Immigration: 1840's—Marriage to **Abigail Squires**--of <u>Waukesha County</u>, (1842) --Residence in 1870: <u>Delafield Township, Waukesha County</u>—Occupation: *farmer* & proprietor of ***Burr Oak Hotel*** in <u>Hartland</u>--Children: *George, Mary (Akin) Granger, Matilde (Akin) Herning, Clara (Aiken) Raber, William, Nelly & Charles.* Andrew Akin's death: Waukesha County (28 Dec 1899).
(Image and genealogy courtesy of Leanne Bennett of Waukesha, Wisconsin)[411]

Andrew Aikin (c. 1885)[412]

A Barefoot Host:

"While there were many innkeepers in Waukesha County, the most memorable seem to be the <u>*Akins'*</u>, <u>*known to clientele (of the Burr Oak tavern) as Ma and Pa. Memoirs of early Hartland residents recall 'Pa' as the barefoot host and 'Ma' as the pipe-smoking hostess and Cook*</u>."[413]

Mr. Aikin's place of birth:

"<u>Norwalk</u> was settled in 1649, incorporated September 1651, and named after the *Algonquin*." <u>*Norwalk has a nickname, 'Oyster Town,' due to its prominent oyster fisheries providing a large source of income to the city since the early 19th century.*</u> Norwalk Harbor's islands and proximity to New York City make it profitable for oyster harvesting."[414]

Proprietor of Burr Oak tavern:

"Andrew Alexander Aiken, farmer, sec. 1; P.O. Pewaukee; was born in, Norwalk, Fairfield Co., Conn, Nov. 4, 1811. <u>*In 1841, he came to Wisconsin, settled in New Berlin, where he remained until 1866, in which year he moved to the town of Pewaukee; lived there two years, then moved to Delafield, which has been his home since.*</u> While residing in Delafield, he purchased the Burr Oak tavern in in Hartland, built in 1853, (6 miles distance from Delafield). Of his children, *Jane Ann Aikin*, was the wife of *Peter Kunz*, Sheboygan Co., Wis.; he was a soldier in the 28th Wisconsin Volunteer Infantry during the war of the rebellion."[415]

---

[411]   *Federal Manuscript Schedule*, Population, Agricultural and Manufacturing Schedules for Waukesha County, Town of Delafield, 1870.

[412]   Photograph courtesy of Leanne Bennett of Waukesha, Wisconsin, e-mail to author, Apr 23, 2010

[413]   Courtesy of the Hartland Historical Society, e-mail to author, Aug 12, 2010.

[414]   https://en.wikipedia.org/wiki/Norwalk,_Connecticut

[415]   *1880 History of Waukesha County*, p. 456.

IMMIGRANTS TO WISCONSIN FROM ENGLAND

John Hodgson & **Elizabeth (Brown) Hodgson** from <u>Yorkshire, England</u> immigrated to Wisconsin in 1855—Son: **William Hodgson**—birth: Sept. 1845, **Marrick, Yorkshire, England**—immigrated with his parents--*William*, age 23, siblings: *Thomas*, 20, *Robert B.*, 15, *James Albert*, 11 & sisters *Mary Ella*, 5, and *Jane Anne*, 3—were living in <u>Pewaukee, Waukesha, Wisconsin</u> (1870)—Occupation: *farming--**William Hodgson** & **Emma Redford*** were married in <u>Lisbon Township</u> (1875)—daughter—***Emily***.

(Image and genealogy courtesy of Catheryn Larsen of Kenosha, Wisconsin.)[416]

(l-r): Emily (daughter) and Emma (mother) Hodgson (circa 1885)[417]

St. Mary's, Kansas:

"*By 1880, William and Emma Hodgson were no longer residing in Lisbon Township, but had moved west to St. Mary's, Pottawatomie County, Kansas.* In 1898, "the town had a doctor, dentist, lawyer, newspaper, 2 banks, 2 drug stores, veterinarian/undertaker, 2 drug stores, 2 clothing stores, a bakery with candy kitchen, restaurant, lunch counter, boarding house, livery stable, lumber yard, grain elevator, shoe cobbler, shoe store, creamery, grocery store, and a bowling alley."[418]

Fruit orchards are planted:

"By 1900, the Hodgson family again moved. This time, farther west to Fruitland, California. Fruitland is located Humboldt County, California. *The first settlers of Fruitland were a colony of immigrants from the Netherlands who planted fruit orchards.* However, the isolation of this colony in a time when there was little adequate long-distance transportation ultimately led to the dissolution of the colony's fruit market."[419]

The Hodgsons' in Los Angeles:

"William Hodgson died between 1900-10 while the family resided in Huntington Park, in southeastern Los Angeles, California. *Emily then moved, with her adult children, to San Antonio Township (1895—1910), Los Angeles, California, where Roy (24), works as a water pump engineer, Erwin (29), works as a florist and Emily (17).*"[420]

Likes California.

William Hodgson of Huntington Park, Cal., who has been spending some weeks with relatives and old-time friends in the county, left, Saturday, for the west. *While here he was the guest of his brothers, Geo. Hodgson, of Pewaukee, Dr. A. J. Hodgson, of this city (Waukesha), Thomas Hodgson, and his sisters.* Mr. Hodgson is now manager of the "***Gail Borden Ranch***" of Huntington Park, California.   [*Waukesha Freeman* July 16, 1908]

---

416   *Federal Manuscript Schedule*, Population, Agricultural and Manufacturing Schedules for Waukesha County, Town of Pewaukee, 1870.

417   Photograph courtesy of Cathryn Larsen of Kenosha, Wisconsin. e-mail to author, Mar 24, 2011.

418   William G. Cutler, *History of the State of Kansas*. Chicago, A.T. Andreas, 1883, Part 5: St. Mary's.

419   https://en.wikipedia.org/wiki/Fruitland,_California

420   Death of William Hodgson," courtesy of the Sussex-Lisbon Historical Society.

SETTLERS TO WISCONSIN FROM NEW YORK

George Palmer's grandparents brought their family from <u>New York</u> to Wisconsin (c.1850.) **George Palmer**—Birthplace: <u>Lisbon Township, Waukesha County</u> (c. 1852)—Spouse: **Bertha E. Wardrobe**—Birthplace: <u>Wisconsin</u> (c. 1870)—Residence in 1920: <u>Waukesha Ward 5, Waukesha County, Wisconsin</u>—Occupation: *retired army officer*—Children: none at home.

(Image and genealogy courtesy of the Waukesha County Historical Society and Museum)[421]

General George Palmer (c 1886)[422]

IN SEARCH OF RELATIVES.

A Mrs. Shelby, an English lady, the widow of a soldier in the regular army, who was killed by the Indians recently, about three hundred miles west of Sioux city, arrived in this city the other day, in an extremely destitute condition, in search of some relative. She states that she has an aunt living near *Elm Grove* named Green, and anxious to hear from her. *Her husband, four children, sister and sister's husband, were all murdered by the Indians about two months since, and Mrs. Green is the only relative she now has in this country.* Any information as to where whereabouts may be sent to Mayor O'Neal of this city.[*Milwaukee Sentinel* July 12, 1867]

West Point Military Academy:

"George Palmer graduated from West Point in the class of 1876 and was immediately sent to his Regiment, *the 9th United States Infantry, at the time operating against hostile Indians who had, a few days prior to his graduation, annihilated General Custer and his command.* Until 1887, he was occupied in various Indian campaigns and the establishment off frontier posts."[423]

The 9th U.S. Infantry Regiment in the west:

"In May 1876, Companies C, G and H became a part of the Big Horn and Yellowstone Expedition under command of Brigadier General Crook and were in the field until late in October taking part in the engagement with the Indians at Tongue River, Montana, 9 June, the Battle of the Rosebud, and the Battle of Slim Buttes. In the early part of September, the entire command was without rations for a number of days and subsisted on horse flesh and a small quantity of dried meat and fruit captured at Slim Buttes. In October, 1876, the Powder River Expedition was organized and Companies A, B, D, F, I and K formed a part of it. They remained in the field until January 1877, during the most severe part of the winter, and practically brought to a termination the Great Sioux War of 1876."[424]

[421] *Federal Manuscript Schedule*, Population, Agricultural and Manufacturing Schedules for Waukesha County, Town of Lisbon, 1860.

[422] Major George Palmer (c.1886), People P-Q-R Box 6:8, Photography Collection, Research Center Library & Archive, Waukesha County Historical Society & Museum, Waukesha, Wisconsin.

[423] The Association of the Graduates of the United States Military Academy Digital Library. http://digital-library.usma.edu/cdm/ref/collection/p16919coll1/id/5

[424] https://en.wikipedia.org/wiki/9th_Infantry_Regiment_%28United_States%29

IMMIGRANTS FROM NEW YORK, IRELAND & ENGLAND

(First Generation): Name: **Thomas Faulkner**—born: **Lissan, Londonderry, Ireland** (28 Apr 1793)—Spouse: **Nancy King**—born: **New York** (22 Oct 1799)— two sisters and six brothers (Second Generation): Name: **Thomas Faulkner Jr.**—born: **Mumford, New York** (12 July 1822)—Spouse: **Nancy Moorer**—Born: **Wheatland, Monroe County, New York** (15 Dec 1820)—marriage: (28 May 1846)—Children-- *Eldern, Clara, Lorinena & Viola*— Name: The oldest son: *Elderon (Lee) Faulkner*—born: **Wisconsin** (c.1857)—spouse: *Harriet Searle*—born: **Wisconsin** (c. 1856)—Residence in 1900: New Berlin, Waukesha County, Wisconsin—Children: *Lee Elden, Lora Belle & Ethel.*   (Image and genealogy courtesy of Cathryn Larsen of Kenosha, Wisconsin)[425]

Lee Elden (baby) Rufus and Harriet Faulkner (1886)[426]

The Faulkner family of Parish Lissan, Londonderry, Ireland:

"*Lissan is a civil and Anglican and Roman Catholic ecclesiastical parish that spans parts of County Londonderry and County Tyrone, (Northern) Ireland.*"[427] "In 1604, Derrie was granted its first royal charter as a city by James I of England. The settlement was destroyed in 1608 by Cahir O'Doherty, Irish chieftain of Irishwomen. *During the Plantation of Ulster by English and Scottish settlers, a new walled city was built across the River Foyle from the old site by the Irish Society.* The 1613 charter stated, "that the said city or town of Derry, hereafter be and shall be named and called the city of Londonderry."[428]

Fabricated Doors & Blinds.

Sunday morning Thomas Faulkner died of a severe attack of the grippe (Influenza). He was 81 years of age and leaves a son and a daughter, Elden Faulkner and Miss Clara Faulkner. *They moved into the village of Waukesha, where Mr. Faulkner was engaged in the manufacture of doors and blinds for several years.*   [Waukesha Freeman Feb. 25, 1904]

Victorian style of drapery:

"As the late nineteenth century rolled in, shade design was strongly influenced by a Victorian style imported from England. *These shades that had once stood on their own in beauty, literally became buried among heavy draperies, and yards and yards of swaging fabric and trim.*"[429]

425   *Federal Manuscript Schedule*, Population, Agricultural and Manufacturing Schedules for Waukesha County, Town of New Berlin, 1890.

426   Photograph courtesy of Cathryn Larsen of Kenosha, Wisconsin. e-mail to author, Mar 24, 2011

427   "The partition of Ireland (Irish : críochdheighilt na hÉireann) was the division of the island of Ireland into two distinct jurisdictions, Northern Ireland and Southern Ireland. It took place on 3 May 1921 under the Government of Ireland Act 1920." From: en.wikipedia. org/wiki/Partition_of_Ireland

428   https://en.wikipedia.org/wiki/Derry/Londonderry_name_dispute

429   http://www.hausershade.com/a-brief-history-on-the-origins-of-window-roller-shades/

IMMIGRANTS TO WISCONSIN FROM BAVARIA

Name: **George Gebhardt**—Birthplace: **Munich, Bayern** (1819)—Spouse: **Magdalena Maria Brandmiller**—Birthplace: **Traunstein, Bayern** (1820)—Year of immigration: 1840—Occupation: *farmer*—Residence in 1860: Brookfield Township, Waukesha County—Children: *Kohn, Mary Ann, Conrad, John, Frederick,* **Mathias** *& George.* **Mathias (Matt)** & **Mary Katharina Woelfel** were married in 1887--farmed in the town of Brookfield. (Image courtesy of Roger & Marion Woelfel of New Berlin; Genealogy courtesy of James Woelfel of Holt, MI.)[430]

Mathias Gebhardt & Mary Katharina Woelfel Wedding Day (Nov. 8, 1887)[431]

The Matt Gebhardt farm:

"In preparation for his marriage, which occurred on Oct. 9, 1888, Mathew Gebhardt purchased the farm of 120 acres where he now lives and to which he later added 40 acres adjoining. *On this property Mr. Gebhardt has built a handsome brick house, 46 by 56 feet, a fine barn, and has set out, an orchard of apple, cherry, plum and pear trees, all of which are bearing.* The farm supports a dairy herd, also some other live-stock, such as hogs, coarse-wool sheep, etc. The milk from the dairy is shipped to Milwaukee. *Mr. Gebhardt has operated a thresher every season for thirty-three years.* Mrs. Gebhardt, nee Mary *Woelfel,* is a native of Brookfield township, born April 2, 1866. Ten children have been born into the Gebhardt family, of whom nine are living, including: *Frank, Joseph, Regina, Alexander, Simon, Mattie, Marie, Cecelia & Laurine.*"[432]

Threshing Operation (1902):

MATHEW GEBHARDT: age 61 in 1902—is a Brookfield born farmer--he is the proprietor of **"Iron Springs Farm"** Brookfield (section 22)—advertises **"Clover & Grain Threshing."** [433]

Threshing on the Aitken's farm:

"*When (Matt Gebhardt's) stream engine came slowly up the Bluemound Road to our Brookfield [sections 30 & 31] farm, pulling the separator, followed by the water wagon being pulled by a team of horses, it was almost as exciting as going to town to see the circus parade some fifty years ago.* We would follow the slow-moving outfit with yells and our barking dog. The hired man and hired girl with apron rolled up were there. Even the horses and colts grazing in the fields came to the fences to watch the parade. *The whistle of the engine* was a signal to the neighboring farms to prepare for threshers during the next few days. We recalled how the sacks of oats and barley had to be carefully placed so that the separator would fit in between the stacks."[434]

[430] *Federal Manuscript Schedule,* Population, Agricultural and Manufacturing Schedules for Waukesha County, Town of Brookfield, 1860.

[431] Photograph courtesy of Roger & Marian Woelfel of New Berlin, Wisconsin, home visit by the author, Apr 10, 2010.

[432] Haight *Memoirs of Waukesha County,* 1907, p. 447.

[433] Author, *Brookfield: A Fine and Fertile Land—vol.* 2, p. 336.

[434] Roy Aitken & Chester Wilson, "Bringing in the Sheaves," *Landmark.* v. 10, n. 4, p. 19.

WISCONSIN FROM BAVARIA AND WÜRTTEMBERG

Name: **John Konrad Meidenbauer**—Birthplace: **Prehasusan, Bayern** (1818)—Spouse: **Catherine Schmer**—Birthplace: **Riglashof, Bayern** (1806)—year of immigration:1848—Residence in 1880: New Berlin, Waukesha County—Occupation: farmer—Children: *baby stillborn* in 1850--Nephew: **John Michael Meidenbauer**—Birthplace: **Pruhasusen, Bayern Germany** (11 May1853)—Spouse: **Anna Caroline Schoenwalder**—Birthplace: **Kreis Waldenburg, Württemberg, Germany** (c. 1865)— Year of immigration 1876—Residence in 1880: New Berlin Township, Waukesha County—Occupation: *farmer*—Children: *John, Elizabeth, William, Edward, Sabel, Anna, Emma, Josephine, Harry, Walter, Arthur & Viola.*
(Image and genealogy courtesy of Roy Meidenbauer of New Berlin, Wisconsin.)[435]

John Michael Meidenbauer (c.1888)[436]

J.K. Meidenbauer's nephew arrives:

"*J.K. Meidenbaur's* plea in his 1874 letter to his nephew *John Michael Meidenbaurer*, then serving in the Bavarian army, to come to Wisconsin, came to fruition as two years later, *John & his wife, Anna,* immigrated to Wisconsin to support his uncle on his New Berlin farm."[437]

Meidenbauer Farm (1923):

"**J.M. MEIDENBAUER:** proprietor of: **'Echo Farms'**-- (wife: **Anna**) -- 11 children-- occupation: **farming & dairying**-- owns 90 acres --3 horses--8 dairy cows--Rural Route (Waukesha County) northwest New Berlin --Bell telephone." [438]

Farmers depended on brute strength:

When J.K. Meidenbauer purchased his first acreage in the town of New Berlin in 1848, a tall task lay ahead of him. "*His first major task was clearing the forested trees on his land. This was done using a powerful yoke of oxen, an axe, picks, wedges, a bar iron and the use of heavy chains use to pull roots up out of the ground.* They typically would have had a couple of good butchering hogs. The first couple of seasons, Mr. Meidenbauer would have planted small parcels of wheat, oats, corn and potatoes, and purchased a ***scythe and cradle*** to do his threshing, while Catherine would have tended a good-sized ***vegetable garden*** from which she could pick her precious garden goods in a ***cold root cellar*** to provide nourishment during the winter months."[439]

Steam Threshing Machines.

The farmer is getting the advantages of the inventive faculty of our present age. *Steam threshing machines are displacing the old method of threshing buy horsepower. These steam engines and the Self Binding Reaper makes the farmer practically independent of hired help, for a crop of 100 acres of small grain can be sown, reaped and threshed as easy as 20 acres could be by the old method.* [*Waukesha Freeman* Nov. 30, 1882]

[435] *Federal Manuscript Schedule*, Population, Agricultural and Manufacturing Schedules for Waukesha County, Town of New Berlin, 1880.

[436] Photograph courtesy of Roy Meidenbauer, of New Berlin, Wisconsin, e-mail to author, Aug 8, 2009.

[437] Roy Meidenbauer, of New Berlin, Wisconsin, e-mail to author, Aug 9, 2009; *Federal Manuscript Schedule*, Population, Agricultural and Manufacturing Schedules for Waukesha County, Town of New Berlin, 1850 & 1880.

[438] *The Farm Journal Illustrated Rural Directory of Waukesha County, Wisconsin 1918-1923* (Philadelphia: Wilmer Atkinson Company, 1923.

[439] Author, *Brookfield: A Fine and Fertile Land*, vol. 1, pp. 29, 31, & 207.

IMMIGRANTS TO WISCONSIN FROM NORWAY

Name: **Peter Torgerson Wesley**—born: **Østre (eastern) Gausdal, Oppland County, Norge** (10 June 1804)—married: **Anne Wesley Solberg Jognannesdatter** (4 Apr 1829, **Norge**)—Residence in 1829: **Østre (eastern) Gausdal, Oppland County, Norge**--Children: *Anne, Marit, Margit, Torgher, Ingebor, Johannes, Kari, Ole, Amund, Anne & Amund*— Emigration: from Norway to Wisconsin (1848) --Residence (1849) Lebanon Township, Dodge County—Occupation: *farmer*-- 2nd. Wife: **Anne Pedersdatter Knappen**--Residence: St. Lawrence Township, Waupaca County (29 Nov 1858)—Residence: St. Lawrence Township, Waupaca Co. (1860)—Children: *John, Anton, Anne, Ole J. & Ole P.*

(Image, narrative and genealogy courtesy of Susan Goodman of Chevy Chase, Maryland.)[440]

Otto and Caspara Rasmussen wedding day (1888)[441]

Tosten Thorstein's Rasmussen Immigration story:

"Tosten Thorstein Rasmussen emigrated aboard the *brig Præciosa* departing on about (4 July1845) from the port of Kragerø (The small Norwegian port of Kragerø is located in a bay on the eastern side of Norway on the North Sea) and landed in New York on August 21, 1845, 45 days after leaving Norway. The ship carried 94 steerage passengers. Once at New York, Tosten travelled to Wisconsin via the Erie Canal and Great Lakes water routes to the port of Milwaukee. From the village of Milwaukee, the party likely travelled along the Watertown Road to Dodge County, Wisconsin, where it was a short hike into Lebanon Township."[442]

Peter Torgerson Wesley Immigration story:

"In 1848, Peter and Anne Wesley immigrated to Wisconsin along with their first seven children: aboard the '*Erek Boreson*' with his brother and families to New York City, travelled the same water routes as Tosten Rasmussen had taken, three year earlier, to the port of Milwaukee. In the fall of 1848. Peter & Anne Wesley and their children: Anne, Marit, Torgher, Ingebor, Johannes, Kari, Ole, Amund, Anne and Amund, were soon residing in the log cabin of Tosten Rasmussen (approximately 16'x 14") with a loft, along his father, mother, and siblings in Lebanon, Dodge County, Wisconsin. Quite a large number for a small cabin, but not unusual for this period. The following spring the Wesley family had moved from Lebanon Township to St. Lawrence Township, Waupaca County, where Peter Wesley purchased his own farm. Meanwhile, during the short time they had together, love must have been in the air, as Tosten Rasmussen married Peter and Anne Wesley's daughter, Marit Margit Wesley, in 1850, and soon set up their own residence in Rock River, Jefferson County (1851)."[443]

[440] *Federal Manuscript Schedule*, Population, Agricultural and Manufacturing Schedules for Waupaca County, Town of St. Lawrence, 1860.

[441] Photograph courtesy of Susan Goodman of Chevy Chase, Maryland, e-mail to author, Oct 11, 2011.

[442] Susan Goodman of Chevy Chase, Maryland e-mail to author, Oct 11, 2011.

[443] Susan Goodman of Chevy Chase, Maryland, paraphrased e-mail by the author, Oct 11, 2011.

IMMIGRANTS TO WISCONSIN FROM MECKLENBURG - SCHWERIN

Name: **Henry Bliemeister**—Birth: <u>Mecklenburg-Schwerin</u> (circa: 1855)—Religion: <u>Evangelical Lutheran</u>—year of immigration (1872)—Residence: (1890) <u>Brookfield Township, Waukesha County</u>—Occupation: *general farmer--*Spouse: **Rosa (Kueper)**—birth (Apr 1853) **Wisconsin**—Children: *Harry,* John, Arthur & Agnes—in 1914, Henry Bliemeister owns an 18-acre (section 32) *farm* at <u>Goerke's Corners, in Brookfield.</u>
(Image and genealogy courtesy from John Schoenknecht of Wauwatosa, Wisconsin.) [444]

Harry Bliemeister (1888)[445]

A Milwaukee Photo Studio:

"<u>At the age of two, Harry Bliemeister, the first child of Henry and Rosa Bliemeister of Brookfield, had his photograph taken at a Milwaukee studio</u>. Dressing young boys in *skirts* and allowing their hair to *grow long* were common practices on Wisconsin farms during the 19th century. Boys were not typically dressed in pants until the age of four or five."[446]

Henry Bliemeister determines to emigrate:

"Mass emigration, a phenomenon, that formed the grand duchy Mecklenburg - Schwerin substantially. Between 1820 and 1890 about 250,000 people left their homes in Mecklenburg in several waves. People especially went to the USA. *One of the reasons were the medieval home- and poor-man-laws*[447] *in this region, as well as the guild regulations in the cities or the hard working and living conditions of the rural people.* But one thing was of a much greater importance. Almost every peasant or farmer hoped to one day live on and cultivate his own piece of land and that would have been almost impossible to achieve in their home country. *Due to this fact a lot of people from Mecklenburg were attracted to the fertile regions of North America. The government did not support this movement at any time. The landowners on the opposite did.* They used all kinds of methods to get rid of their workers and their families. Some landowners harassed some of their day laborers until they finally left. Others lent money or paid for the crossing to the US. In some cases, the landowner even bought land in North America to make people want to emigrate."[448]

BLODGETT.

Henry Bliemeister and Mr. Lingelbach have bought De Laval Baby *cream separators* and are well pleased with their investments.
[*Waukesha Freeman* June 18, 1896]

---

[444] *Federal Manuscript Schedule*, Population, Agricultural and Manufacturing Schedules for Waukesha County, Town of Brookfield, 1900.

[445] Photograph courtesy of John Schoenknecht of Wauwatosa, Wisconsin, e-mail to author on Jan 21, 2010.

[446] Author, *Images of America: Brookfield and Elm Grove*, p. 26.

[447] "The Poor Law Amendment Act (1834) stated that no able-bodied person was to receive money or other help from the Poor Law authorities except in a workhouse. Conditions in workhouses were to be made harsh to discourage people from claiming. Workhouses were to be built in every parish." From: https://en.wikipedia.org/wiki/Poor_Law_Amendment_Act_1834

[448] Reno Stutz, article, "Mecklenburg Magazine" 1990/13; translation: Daniela Garling.

IMMIGRANTS TO WISCONSIN FROM PRUSSIA

Name: **Ernst Fredrich August Buetow**—Birthplace: village of <u>Falkenberg, city of Naugard, Pomerania, Prussia, Germany</u> (18 Mar1824)—spouse: **Wilhelmine F. Bold**--Birthplace: <u>Voigtshagen, Pomerania, Prussia</u> (1 June 1826)—married: in <u>Pomerania</u> (May 3 1848)--family emigrated from Hamburg, Germany and <u>Le Havre, France</u> to <u>New York & Wisconsin</u> (1871)--Residence in 1880: <u>Menomonee Township, Waukesha County, Wisconsin</u>—Occupation: <u>*farmer*</u>—Children: *Louise, Wilhelmine, Albertine, Dorothea Louise, Charles, Emilie Ulricke Wilhelmine, August, Ulricke Auguste & Bertha Maria Louise*—(youngest child) **Bertha Maria Buetow**—Birthplace: **Bernhagen, Naugard, Pomerania, Prussia** (10 Sep 1866)—marriage to: **Gustav Adolph Sylvester** (5 Apr 1888).

(Image and genealogy courtesy of Jane Sylvester of Madison, Wisconsin)[449]

Bertha Buetow's wedding day, April 5, 1888[450]

Women's Clothing Styles of the 1880's:

"Bertha's wedding dress is very European. <u>*Notice she is wearing a dark dress retreating folded back silk lying across the front and a tight flowered collar.*</u> She has a white veil with a *flowered chord* draped over the front. Dates to late 1880's—early 1890's. A very beautiful look for the young bride." --***Joan Severa, "19th Century Clothing & Fashion.***[451]

Pomeranians from the Baltic Sea immigrate to Wisconsin:

"During the early 14th century, Slavic narrow Pomerania became increasingly German-settled area; <u>*the remaining Polish people, often known as Kashubians, continued to settle within Eastern Pomerania along the Baltic Sea.*</u> While the German population in the Duchy of Pomerania adopted the Protestant reformation in 1534, the Polish (along with Kashubian) population remained with the *Roman Catholic* Church. The Kashubs are grouped with the Slovincians as Pomeranians. <u>*Under the German rule, the Kashubs suffered discrimination and oppressive measures aimed at eradicating its culture.*</u>"[452]

"These factors may have led to many Kashubian to immigrate to America. <u>*Many coming to Wisconsin where they settled on Jones Island along the harbor entrance to Milwaukee beginning in 1870. The Catholic Kashubian history on Jones is both colorful and fascinating. The 2nd largest settlement of immigrant Kashubians in the United States where those located at Milwaukee.*</u>"[453]

[449] *Federal Manuscript Schedule*, Population, Agricultural and Manufacturing Schedules for Waukesha County, Town of Menomonee, 1880.

[450] Photograph courtesy of Jane Sylvester of Madison, Wisconsin, e-mail to author, Nov 10, 2009.

[451] Joan Severa e-mail to author, Mar 10, 2010.

[452] https://en.wikipedia.org/wiki/Pomerania

[453] https://en.wikipedia.org/wiki/Jones_Island,_Milwaukee. For an excellent account of the Kashubians on Jones island read: Ruth Kriehn, *The Fisherfolk of Jones Island*, (Milwaukee: Milwaukee County Historical Society, 1988.)

IMMIGRANTS TO WISCONSIN FROM NORWAY

Name: **Ole Olson**—Birthplace: on <u>Saetret (small farm) in District Luksefjell, Township Gjerpen, Norge</u> (19 June 1821)—Occupation: *tailor*—Immigration: the schooner *"Salvator"* from <u>Gjerpen</u> in 1843 with his brother, **Christopher**—Residence in 1846: <u>Town of Merton</u>—Occupation: *farm laborer*—Residence: in 1848: (section 14) <u>Town of Oconomowoc</u>--Occupation: *farmer*--Spouse: **Ingeborg Johnson**--Birthplace: **Bestul in Luksefjell, Norge** (27 Jan 1827)— married by <u>Rev. Dietrichson at Pine Lake</u>--Children: ***Ole Jr.***, *Karen, Gunhild & Lizzie*. In 1891, <u>Ole Olson Jr.</u> owned an 84-acre (section 1) <u>Oconomowoc Township, Waukesha County</u> farm. Occupation: *dairy farmer*, just northwest of <u>Mapleton</u>.

(Image and genealogy courtesy of Waukesha County Historical Society and Museum.)[454]

Ole Olson Jr. (c. 1888)[455]

The home of Ole Olson in Norway:

"*Gjerpen (the birthplace of Ole Olson) is a former township which is now part of the municipality of Skien, in Telemark County, Norway.* The parish of Gjerpen was established as a municipality January 1, 1838, according to the 1835 census the municipality had a population of 4,381. *Gjerpen* was located east of the city of *Skien*. It encompassed district of *Luksefjell. Gjerpen Church* is the main church of *Gjerpen prestegjeld (parish).* It is one of the oldest churches in Norway. It is believed the church was consecrated 28 May 1153."[456]

Crop failures moved many Norwegians to immigrate to 'Amerika':

"144 km south of Gjerpen, along the eastern Norwegian coast, is located the community of Bjorvatn, Mjåvatn, Norway. As told in novelistic form, *Terje Larsen* and his family experienced that *'in 1847, and again in 1848, there were devastating failures of crops in the entire parish and in many of the neighboring parishes. The storehouses were emptied of their abundance, and there were only meager harvests to replenish the storehouses. Children on many of the farms began to look gaunt and hungry.' On Sunday mornings, more and more the word 'Amerika' was heard.* A new restlessness swept over the land, and groups of people trickled past with their wagons and possessions on the road leading to Arendal (a small port city on Norway's east coast) to board a ship that would take them to the distant land of promises and plenty— 'Amerika'… It's a territory that has recently been opened up in the newly constituted state of Wisconsin"[457]

Norwegians encouraged to immigrate to Wisconsin:

"The "*Wisconsin Commission of Emigration*" actively encouraged the settlement of European immigrants in Wisconsin. Pamphlets extolling the state's virtues were published in *German, Norwegian, Dutch, and English. From Illinois, Norwegian pioneers followed the general spread of population northwestward into Wisconsin. Wisconsin remained the center of Norwegian American activity up until the American Civil War.*"[458]

---

[454] *Federal Manuscript Schedule*, Population, Agricultural and Manufacturing Schedules for Waukesha County, Town of Oconomowoc, 1850.

[455] Ole Olson, c. 1888, People M-N-O Box 5:8, Photography Collection, Research Library & Archive, Waukesha County Historical Society & Museum, Waukesha, Wisconsin.

[456] https://en.wikipedia.org/wiki/Gjerpen Gjerpen

[457] Neil T. Eckstein, *Norton's Folly: Norwegian Immigrants and Yankee Neighbors on the Wisconsin Frontier, 1849-1857* (Grandview Books: Larsen, WI., 1997), p. 9.

[458] https://en.wikipedia.org/wiki/Norwegian_Americans

IMMIGRANTS TO WISCONSIN FROM BAVARIA

Name: **Johann Ramstöck** — Birthplace: **Germersberg, of the Landgericht Lauf, Bayern**, (28 Apr <u>1794</u>)— Spouse: #1 wife: **Anna Kunigunda Pfister**—(marriage:<u>1821</u>) --Anna's death: (29 Aug, <u>1834</u>)—2nd wife: **Katharina Rohrer**--Birthplace: **Lowenfels, Bavaria** (17 Dec <u>1803</u>)—Marriage: (circa <u>1838</u>)—Immigration: departed from port of <u>Bremerhaven</u> (Sept/Oct <u>1844</u>) aboard the bark: *"Charlesbon"*—**John Wölfel**, **Philipp Ramstöck** & **Lorenz Pfister** families immigrated together (John Wölfel joined them from a neighboring village of **Rollhofen**) all bound for <u>Wisconsin</u>-- arrived at the port of <u>New York</u> (19 Oct, <u>1844</u>)--Residence in <u>1860</u>: <u>Brookfield Township</u>, <u>Waukesha County</u>—Occupation: *farmer & butcher* –Children: *Maria Anna* (12 April 1823); *Johann George* (7 Jan, 1825); *Anna Kunigunda* (7 Feb 1827)—*Simon George* (26 Oct 1830) *Georg* (23 Nov, 1838); *Franz* (15 Nov 1840); *Johann* (11 April,1844). A son: **George Ramstöck** (born 1838) married **Anna Marie Brendel** born: (circa 1842) in **Bayern**. Death of the father-- Johann Ramstöck (1852).

(Image & genealogy provided by Hayley Ramstack of Manawa, Wisconsin)[459]

George Ramstöck (c. 1889) [460]

Brookfield's Bavarians were ethnically 'Franconian':

"Franconia is a relatively large region in the northwest of Bavaria. Ethnically, Franconians are not truly Bavarian. *There is a considerable ethnological difference between the two ethnic groups. Historically, the intellectual input of Franconians to Germany has been significant. Their language (which several families brought to Wisconsin) is very different from the Bavarian dialect.* Over time, Franconians' have been forced to become subjects of the Bavarian kings. Though Franconia is politically connected to Bavaria, the Franconians, in Bavaria, are predominately Protestant. The much wealthier Franconian Protestants resided in the areas of Nürnberg, Fürth, Hersbruck & Lauf." [461]

Protestants dominate politically and religiously in Franconian, Bavaria:

"Franconian Catholics, reside in approximately 40 relatively small villages, attached to the diocese of Bamberg and parish of Neunkirchen. *This religious disconnects from the predominance of the Protestants, was certainly one of the primary reasons for the mass-immigration of so many Catholic Bavarian families to Wisconsin beginning in the 1840's.* Among these Catholic emigrants, were the **Brandmüller** and **Wölfel** families of Rollhofen; the **Enes** family of Eschenau; the **Ramstöck & Pfister** families of Germersberg, the **Brendel** family of Rabenshof; along with the **Schlenk** & **Betzold** families of Siegersdorf. Each of these Bavarian villages were located in close proximity to each other. In turn, these same Bavarian immigrant families settled in Brookfield Township during the 1840's, and generally purchased adjoining parcels. In 1851, the colony constructed a log church measuring 24X34 consecrated to **St. Ambrose**." [462]

[459] *Federal Manuscript Schedule*, Population, Agricultural and Manufacturing Schedules for Waukesha County, Town of Brookfield, 1850.

[460] Photograph courtesy of Hayley Ramstack of Manawa, Wisconsin via Facebook posting by Molly Ramstack of Milwaukee, Wisconsin. April 7, 2019.

[461] Dr. Helmut Treis of Aachen, Rheinland, Nordrhein-Westfalen, Germany, letter to author, Sept 21, 1989.

[462] Dr. Helmut Treis of Aachen, Rheinland, Nordrhein-Westfalen, Germany, letter to author, Sept 21, 1989.

SETTLERS TO WISCONSIN FROM VERMONT

1<u>st</u> Generation: Name: **Jonathon Putnam**—Birthplace: <u>Wilton, Hillsborough, New Hampshire</u> (29 July 1770)—Spouse: **Abigail Burton**—Birthplace: <u>Wilton, Hillsboro, New Hampshire</u> (12 Nov 1772)—Children: *Prucius, Jonathan, Nathaniel, Aaron & Amos*—2<u>nd</u> Generation: Name: ***Prucious Wallace Putnam***—Birthplace: <u>**Andover Township, Windsor County, Vermont**</u> (1814) married: **Rachel Emmeline Haseltine**—Birthplace: <u>**Andover Township, Windsor County, Vermont**</u> (c. 1819)—immigrated to <u>Vernon Township, Waukesha County</u> in 1836—Prucious Putnam & Rachel Haseltine were married in <u>Vernon Township</u> (Jan. 1839)—Occupation: *retail store & post office*--Children: *Prucious, Burton, Hulda, Burton, Wilton & Leslie.*
(Image and genealogy courtesy of Waukesha County Historical Society & Museum) [463]

Prucius Putnam (c. 1889) [464]

Organizing Vernon Township:

"The first actual settlers to what would become Vernon Township were *John Dodge, Prucius Putnam* and the brothers *Curtis B. and Orien Haseltine.* These four men, along with Prucius Putnam's father, Jonathan, travelled by wagon from Vermont to Wisconsin in 1836. Jonathan Putman was taken sick on the road, with diarrhea, and died in a few days after his arrival in the town. *These men, along with their wives came from Andover Township, Windsor County, Vermont and went into the then undisturbed wilderness of Vernon, in November of that year, and made claims on sections 27 and 34 and built a log cabin at this time 15X16 feet.* The Town of Vernon was set apart and organized into the town of Vernon by an act of the Legislature, passed March 8, 1839. Before that it had been part of Muskego."[465]

Vernon town name adapted from the state of Vermont:

"*All four were Vermonters, as were many of those who came in subsequently. **The first syllable of their native State being incorporated into the new name.*** The population of Vernon Township was about equally divided between the Americans, Scotch and Germans, with a few Irish, English and Norwegians. *Prucius Putman* was *Postmaster* for a time. *Mr. Dodge* held the office of *Postmaster* until 1855. A *retail store* started there in 1846, by Prucius Putnam, was the first in the town. When Curtis Haseltine first began breaking the soil, he had a little child which had to be cared for. *To get along and loose no more time than necessary, Hazeltine prepared a sack, Indian fashion, and, putting the baby into it, strapped it to his back, and went on with the plowing undismayed and unhindered by the little squealer.*"[466]

---

[463]   *Federal Manuscript Schedule*, Population, Agricultural and Manufacturing Schedules for Waukesha County, Town of Vernon, 1860.

[464]   Prucius Putnam (c.1889), People P-Q-R Box, Photography Collection, Research Center Library & Archive, Waukesha County Historical Society & Museum, Waukesha, Wisconsin.

[465]   *1880 History of Waukesha County*, pp. 789-791.

[466]   *1880 History of Waukesha County*, pp. 792-793.

SETTLERS TO WISCONSIN FROM SAXONY & PRUSSIA

<u>Parents:</u> **Chrétien Krieg** born <u>**Brandenburg, Preußen**</u> (c. 1815) & **Charlotte Krummbach** born <u>**Brandenburg, Preußen**</u> (c. 1817)--Son: **Charles Gottfried Krieg**—Birthplace: <u>**Sachsen**</u> (8 Apr 1837)—Charles Krieg's occupation (1860): *brass finisher*—Immigration to Wisconsin (c. 1865)—Spouse: **Anna Rosina Glickman**—Birthplace: <u>**Preußen**</u> (23 Jan 1843)—married in Wisconsin (c. 1865)--Residence (June 1, 1870): <u>Brookfield Township, Waukesha County</u>--Occupation: farmer—Children: *Bertha, William & Anna Wilhelmina.*

(Image and Genealogy courtesy of Jerry Hartwell of Bowling, Ohio.)[467]

Charles Krieg c. 1890[468]

Charles Krieg in Brookfield:

"In 1873, Charles Krieg and his family resided on a 57-acre (section 19) Brookfield farm, producing a good crop of wheat, corn, oats, barley, rye & potatoes. Mr. Krieg was surrounded by several German neighbors with names such as—Deck, Benecke, Bolster, Haberland, Cunderman, Kope, Beheim, Myers & others. <u>*During the decade of the 1870's, the large influx of German immigrants into the town created significant animosity among their Yankee neighbors.*</u>"[469]

Young Grant Showerman hears talk:

"*Mrs. Putney* deals the cards inside her son's, Clate Putney's, *Brookfield Junction store.* Uncle Anthony says: "No-o, times ain't what they was, not by a good deal. One thing is, they' s gittin' to be so many foreigners." Grandpa Tyler says: "<u>*By godfrey, don't it beat all, the way there're a-comin in an' buyin' everybody out? I declare I don't see what the country's a-comin' to. They's getting to be many Dutch (referring to Germans) around't ye can't sleep nights fer hearin' their wooden shoes clatter… They laugh.!!*</u>"[470]

Charles Krieg's final years:

"By 1898, Charles and *Anna Krieg's* children included: *Harriet* and *Herbert. Anna* died January 7, 1900 in Waukesha, Wisconsin. In 1900 Charles (age: 63) maintains ownership of his farm (now 124 acres). His 17-year-old son, Herbert, supports his father on the farm. <u>*By 1910, Charles (age: 73) sells his farm to Louis Moll & boards with the Moll family.*</u> Why he did not choose to reside with one of his children's family's is unclear. He died March 9, 1916 in Pewaukee, Wisconsin."[471]

467 *Federal Manuscript Schedule*, Population, Agricultural and Manufacturing Schedules for Waukesha County, Town of Brookfield, 1870.

468 Photograph courtesy of Jerry Hartwell of Bowling, Ohio, e-mail to author, Nov 30, 2011.

469 Jerry Hartwell of Bowling, Ohio, e-mail to author, Dec 1, 2011; *Federal Manuscript Schedule*, Population, Agricultural and Manufacturing Schedules for Waukesha County, Town of Brookfield, 1870.

470 Grant Showerman, *A Country Chronicle*, pp. 54-55.

471 Jerry Hartwell of Bowling, Ohio, e-mail to author, Dec 1, 2011; *Federal Manuscript Schedule,* Population, Agriculture and Manufacturing Schedules for Waukesha County, Town of Brookfield, 1900.

IMMIGRANTS TO WISCONSIN FROM MECKLENBURG-SCHWERIN & BERLIN

Name: **David Brunkow**—Birthplace: **Dölitz, Gnoien, Güstrow, Duchy of Mecklenburg-Schwerin** (1831)—Religion: *Evangelische Kirch*--Spouse: **Dorthea Stresemann**—Birthplace: **Berlin, Germany** (1831) --Year of emigration: 1855—Residence in 1860: Oconomowoc, Waukesha County, Wisconsin—Occupation: *farmer*—The family soon relocated to Alma, Wisconsin--Residence in 1880 Nelson, Buffalo, Wisconsin-- David Brunkow died in Nelson, Buffalo County, Wisconsin (22 Apr 1896)—David & Dorthea Brunkow's Son: **Ferdinand William Brunkow**—born: **Oconomowoc, Wisconsin** (12 Apr 1861). Married: **Julia Ursula Haisch**, of **Dubuque, Dubuque County, Iowa** (25 Oct 1888)—Residence: Dubuque, Dubuque County, Iowa (1925)—Occupation: *house carpenter* (1910) --Ferdinand Brunkow died in Oak Park, Cook County, Illinois (26 Jul 1944).

(Image and Genealogy courtesy of Richard LaVerne of Sarasota, Florida)[472]

Ferdinand William Brunkow (c. 1890)[473]

A long history of struggles in Gnoien, Mecklenburg-Schwerin:

David Brunkow was born in "Dölitz in the municipality of Gnoien. "It is a small and beautiful agricultural town in the heart of Mecklenburg-Shwerin. A castle located in the northeast of Gnoien has been documented to 1331. The Gothic church of St. Marian was built in the 13th and 14th centuries. There were also, several craft guilds in the settlement. Dölitz landowners were *Eggert von Levezow* (1423) and his family (until 1634), then the families of *Lehsten.* The Thirty Years War severally damaged the city of Gnoien including the district of Dölitz. Plague was present somewhere in Europe in every year between 1346 and 1671. Plagues and cholera devastated the region surrounding Gnoien for many years. From the mid-1850's, German immigration to the U.S. was significantly large. *A high proportion of emigrants from Mecklenburg-Schwerin came as immigrants and took up homes and farms in the Midwest and the Great Lakes states including Wisconsin."*[473]

David & Dorthea Brunkow, of Dölitz, emigrated from Mecklenburg-Schwerin to Wisconsin in 1855.[475]

A leading building contractor in Dubuque:

"Ferdinand W. Brunkow, senior partner of the contracting firm of F.W. Brunkow & Sons Company, was born in Waukesha County, Wisconsin and attended high school in Wabasha, Minnesota, working at the carpenter trade in the summer months. *In 1892, he came to the City of Dubuque and has been prominently identified with the contracting and building interests of the country. He erected the Lincoln Public School and many of the best residences of which the city boasts.* Mr. Brunkow is general agent for the German-American Equation Premium Life Association, acting as such since 1907, and is an ex-president of the Local Contractor's Association. David and Julia (Hassch) Brunkow are the parents of eleven children."[476]

472   *Federal Manuscript Schedule*, Population, Agricultural and Manufacturing Schedules for Waukesha County, Town of Oconomowoc, 1870.

473   Photograph courtesy of Richard LaVerne of Sarasota, Florida, e-mail to author, Jun 15, 2010.

474   https://en.wikipedia.org/wiki/Gnoien

475   Richard LaVerne of Sarasota, Florida, e-mail to author, Jun 15, 2010.

476   Franklin T. Oldt. *History of Dubuque County, Iowa, vol. 2* (Chicago: Goodspeed Historical Association, 1911), p. 83

IMMIGRANTS TO WISCONSIN FROM BAVARIA

Name **John Konrad Meidenbauer**—Birthplace: **Preuhasusen, Landgericht Sulzbach, Oberpfalz, Bayern** (31 Mar 1818)—Fiancé: **Catherine Schmer**—Birthplace: **Riglashof, Bayern, Germany** (1806)—John & Catherine--year of immigration: 1848—Arrival: <u>New York</u>: Ship: *"Belinda"*—Marriage: John & Catherine were married in <u>Milwaukee</u> (3 Sep 1848)-- Residence in 1880—<u>New Berlin, Waukesha County</u>—Occupation: *farmer*.
(Image and genealogy courtesy of Roy Meidenbauer of New Berlin, Wisconsin)[477]

John K. Meidenbauer (c. 1890)[478]

The German Revolution:

"The middle-class elements were committed to liberal principles, while the working class sought radical improvements to their working and living conditions. *As the middle class and working-class components of the Revolution split, the conservative aristocracy defeated it. Liberals were forced into exile to escape political persecution,* where they became known as *Forty-Eighters*. Emigration began to the United States, where a large number of Forty-Eighters settling in <u>Wisconsin</u>."[479]

Coming to America:

"John K. Meidenbauer, is a native of Pruehausen, Landgericht Sulzbach, Oberpfalz, Bavaria, Germany, born March 31, 1818, and sailed from Bremen to New York, with his wife, Catherine, in 1848, where they arrived forty- two days later, having crossed the ocean in the *"Belinda,"* a vessel of American build. *Landing on Manhattan Island, they at once secured passage on a steamer going up the Hudson River to Albany; there they boarded a canal boat for Buffalo, thence went on the old steamer "Wisconsin" to Milwaukee, where they arrived in July of that year.* Mr. Meidenbauer purchased eighty acres of timber land in (section 19), of <u>New Berlin Township</u>."[480]

John Konrad Meidenbauer letter to his parents in Sulzback, Bavaria:

"To John & Anna Meidenbauer, Sulzback, Bavaria…. I am writing you from my own property, although somewhat later than I had promised to do. When I settled on my land there was work in plenty. The grain was ripe--the barley, wheat and oats… *The day after our arrival in Milwaukee we looked up Gredler, because his father-in-law in New York suggested this (John Gredler had settled in Brookfield—section 32, in 1844). They gladly took us in, with joy and kindness. He told us that we might stay with him as long as we liked.* He served us with bread, milk, eggs, butter, etc. and such hospitality is extended by all the Germans of this region…" *--J.K. Meidenbauer, New Berlin, Aug. 1848*[481]

[477] *Federal Manuscript Schedule*, Population, Agricultural and Manufacturing Schedules for Waukesha County, Town of New Berlin, 1870.

[478] Photograph courtesy of Roy Meidenbauer of New Berlin, Wisconsin, e-mail to author, Aug 8, 2009.

[479] https://en.wikipedia.org/wiki/German_revolutions_of_1848-49.

[480] *Portrait and Biographical Record of Waukesha County*, 1894, pp. 691-6.

[481] Introduction by Edward C. Wicklein, "Letter Home to Germany Reflects Religious and other Aspects of Life in New Berlin in 1848," *Landmark*. v. 20, n. 1, Spring, 1977, p. 15.

IMMIGRANTS TO WISCONSIN FROM RHINELAND AND PENNSYLVANIA

Name: **John Augustus Putz**—Birthplace: **Elberfeld, Rhineland** —spouse: **Matilda Esslinger**—Birthplace: **Berks County, Pennsylvania** (15 Feb 1834)—married: (15 Feb 1854) Milwaukee, Milwaukee County—Children: *John* (1854-1855), *Ida Amanda Huggins Swan* (1855-1923), *George* (1856-1930), *Monroe* (1859-1864), *Idda* (1860—1932), **Oscar** (1864-1911), *George* (1868-1940), *Frank* (1872-1946)*Lily* (1868-1942), *Charles* (1870 -1955), *Edward* (1874-1948),—John & Matilda's Son: --**Oscar C. Putz**—Birthplace: **Chillicothe, Ross County, Ohio** (Aug 1864)—spouse: **Amelia Wilhelmina Putz (born Snyder)**—Birthplace: **Waukesha, Waukesha County** (4 Oct 1872)—1st husband: **Charles H. Fairbanks**—2nd husband: **Oscar C. Putz**—Married: Waukesha, Waukesha County (28 May 1891)—Children: *Mark Putz*: Occupation: *apprentice—Soo Line--railroad shop*, *Irene M Mohlke (born Putz), Arthur Henry Putz, Doris Mathilde Christoph (born Putz) & Fairbanks*—Residence 1900—Fond du Lac, Ward 2, south side--Oscar Lac Putz (age: 47): Occupation 1910: *fireman for the Soo Line Railroad Chicago, Cook County, Illinois.* Death of Oscar Putz (age:47) Chicago, Cook, County, Illinois (20 Nov 1911).

(Image and genealogy courtesy of Kenneth Eiler of Overland, Kansas).[482]

Amelia (Snyder) Putz (c. 1891)[483]

"A Macabre Dance of Death":

"*The risk of injury or death for individual employed as car couplers, conductors, or brakemen for the railroad during the 19th Century was especially high.*"[484] Though Oscar Putz's death may not have been directly related to his work as a railroad fireman, his death did increase by one, the number of men killed while employed by the railroads.

A Fireman on the Soo Line.

Word has been received here of the death of Oscar Putz aged 48, a former resident of this city for over twelve years. *He was a fireman on the Soo line and while entering Chicago about noon Monday he fell from his seat in the cab and died instantly of heart trouble.* His widow was formally the Miss Amelia Snyder, daughter of the late Henry Snyder of this city. Besides his widow, he leaves four children.

[*Waukesha Freeman* Nov. 23, 1911]

Women's Clothing Styles of the 1890's:

"Amelia, a very beautiful young lady, her image dates close to 1890. *Her flowing hair is combed back as was the custom along with a layered fabric wrapped tightly around the neck, likely tide and left hanging at the back.* --Please note: no bangs were worn by children or women before the 1880s!" **—Joan Severa, 19th Century Clothing Styles**[485]

---

482 *Federal Manuscript Schedule*, Population, Agricultural and Manufacturing Schedules for Waukesha County, Town of Waukesha, 1870.

483 Photograph courtesy of Kenneth Eiler of Overland Park, Kansas, e-mail to author, Jun 27, 2010.

484 *Brookfield: A Fine and Fertile Land, vol. 1*, p. 145.

485 Joan Severa, Madison, Wisconsin., e-mail to author, Jan 31, 2010.

IMMIGRANTS TO WISCONSIN FROM PRUSSIA

Name: **John Frederick Dryer**—Birthplace **Brackel District in the town of Westfalen, Preußen** (29 Apr 1811) –Spouse: **Elizabeth Dech**—Birthplace: **Hesse Darmstadt** (c. 1825)—Year of immigration: (c.1842)—Married: (circa 1842)—Residence in 1870: <u>Ottawa Township, Waukesha County, Wisconsin</u>—Occupation: *farmer*—Children: *Caroline, Julia, Margaret, Clara, John & Fred—also residing with this family is Elizabeth Dech* (age: 84—mother-in-law). (Image and genealogy courtesy of Waukesha County Historical Society and Museum)[486]

John Frederick Dreyer (c. 1892)[487]

The District of Brackel:

"Brackel is a district (and birthplace <u>of John Dryer)</u> <u>of the Westphalian city of Dortmund.</u> *Brackel is characterized by its location on the 5000-year-old Hellweg, a connecting and trading route from the pre-Roman-Germanic period.* Brackel developed as a farming village. The larger, eastern part belonged to the king as Reichsgut, the smaller western part to the Count of Dortmund."[488]

Westphalan Immigration to America:

"The uncertainty about land ownership was one of the causes of rural riots in Westphalan at the beginning of the March Revolution in 1848. In addition, agricultural reforms led to growing dissatisfaction among several rural groups. *Several poor crops in the 1840s caused food prices to rise, especially in the cities. Between 1845 and 1854, about 30,000 people emigrated, mainly to America, and almost half came from the crisis Dyrka lin.*[489]"[490]

The Dryer farm in Ottawa Township:

In 1873, Fred Dryer owned a well-developed 160-acre (sections 12 & 13) town of Ottawa farm with a spring running water through a creek, which ran next to the family home.[491] *During the early 1870's, the region produced crops of wheat, corn, oats, barley and potatoes; with livestock, including horses, neat cattle, sheep and swine.* "The blow that ended Wisconsin's wheat era was struck by a tiny, evil smelling relative of the bedbug, called the 'chinch bug.' The chinch bug held sway in the fields of Wisconsin through most of the decade of the 1870's."[492]

---

[486] *Federal Manuscript Schedule*, Population, Agricultural and Manufacturing Schedules for Waukesha County, Town of Ottawa, 1870.

[487] John Frederick Dryer (c.1892), People C-D-E Box 2:8, Photography Collection, Research Center Library & Archive, Waukesha County Historical Society & Museum, Waukesha, Wisconsin.

[488] https://de.wikipedia.org/wiki/Brackel_(Dortmund)

[489] "Dyrka lin (Linum usitatissimum) refers to flax seed and the spread of the Black Plague throughout northern Europe during this period. Fleas carried by ground rodents (i.e. rats) invaded the flax seed trade. It spread east through Germany and Scandinavia from 1348 to 1350. It was introduced in Norway in 1349 when a ship landed at Askøy, then spread to Bjørgvi (modern Bergen) and Iceland." From: https://en.wikipedia.org/wiki/Black_Death

[490] https://no.wikipedia.org/wiki/Provinsen_Westfalen

[491] *Federal Manuscript Schedule*, Population, Agricultural and Manufacturing Schedules for Waukesha County, Town of Ottawa, 1870.

[492] Austin, H. Russell. *The Wisconsin Story: The Building of a Vanguard State*--1st Edition (Milwaukee, Wisconsin, for the *Milwaukee Journal*, 1948), p. 225.

IMMIGRANTS TO WISCONSIN FROM SAXONY

Name: **August Thomas Caesar**—Birthplace: <u>Sachsen</u> (14 Mar 1811) –Spouse: **Christine Caesar (born Reinhardt)** —Birthplace: <u>Preußische Sachsen</u> (16 Oct 1822)— Married (circa 1846)--Emigration: From <u>Bremen, Germany</u> (1850)—Arrival: <u>New York</u> (18 May 1850)—Residence in 1870: <u>Muskego Township, Waukesha County, Wisconsin</u>—Occupation: *farmer*—Children: *Victor, Herman, Louis William, Melinda, Frederick & Anna.*
(Image and genealogy courtesy of Elaine Alane of Helenville, Wisconsin.)[493]

William Caesar & Margaret Veenendaal Wedding (July 27, 1892)[494]

1849 Revolution in Saxony:

"During the 1848–49 constitutionalist revolutions in Germany, Saxony became a hotbed of revolutionaries, with anarchists taking part in the May Uprising in Dresden in 1849."[495]

The Caesar Family & the canal:

"August Caesar and his wife, Christine, emigrated from Saxony to the port of Milwaukee in 1850. August Caesar purchased a 60-acre (section 33) Town of Muskego farm at the southern base of Big Muskego Lake in 1859. There was a log cabin, about 20' X 20' existing on the property at the time of the purchase and likely a barn. *The main barn was built before the farmhouse in 1877.* The 5-bedroom cream city brick home, which still stands today, was constructed in 1880. *August and Christine's 4th son, William, married Margaret Veenendaal, daughter of Albert Veenendaal, who had immigrated to Wisconsin from Holland and purchased a 60-acre Muskego (section 25) farm at Durham Hill along the town line.*"[496] "In April 1891, a canal was dredged from Big Muskego Lake through the *J. Curran farm*, just to the east of the *August Caesar farm*, south to Wind Lake in Racine County. A dam was also built on the *Caesar* farm, to control water flow from Big Muskego Lake onto farmland south of the lake."[497]

Albert and Meta continue operation of the Caesar farm:

"William and Margaret (Veenendaal) Caesar continued to farm the property for many years. *Margaret* died October 12, 1923. *When their son Albert married Meta Arndt, August 30, 1924, they moved in with William and helped him work the farm.* *Albert & Meta* had 3 children: *Billy, Robert & Lois.* The farm was, again, divided when *William Caesar* died in February of 1953."[498]

493 *Federal Manuscript Schedule*, Population, Agricultural and Manufacturing Schedules for Waukesha County, Town of Ottawa, 1870.

494 Photograph courtesy of Elaine Alane of Helenville, Wisconsin, e-mail to author, Apr 28, 2010

495 https://en.wikipedia.org/wiki/Saxony

496 Amended Caesar family history as presented by Elaine Alane of Helenville, Wisconsin, in e-mail to author, Apr 28, 2010. Portions taken from *Portrait of Muskego Farmers 1836-1980*, courtesy of the Muskego Historical Society.

497 E.A. Birge and C. Juday, "The Inland Lakes of Wisconsin, 1. The Dissolved Gases and their Biological Significance," *Bulletin of the Wisconsin Geological and Natural History Survey, Volume 22, 1911*, pp.22-23.

498 Elaine Alane of Helenville, Wisconsin, e-mail to author, Apr 28, 2010.

IMMIGRANTS TO WISCONSIN FROM ENGLAND

Name: **Edward Sears**—Birthplace: **England** (c. 1813)—Spouse: **Ann Sears**—Birthplace: **England** (c. 1825)—Year of Emigration: (c. 1850)—Residence in 1860: <u>Oconomowoc Township, Waukesha County</u> —Occupation: *farm laborer*—Children: *Charlotte, William, Harry, Ellen & John*.

(Image and genealogy courtesy of Libbie Nolan of Big Bend, Wisconsin)[499]

Martie and Ellen Sears (Feb 13, 1892)[500]

WEALTH AND POVERTY.

A few years since a man resided in England of sober and industrious habits, -- yet so poor that the oversees of the parish—the parish officers fearing that they should have him and is family to support, very humanly (as the result has shown—though no thanks to them that they did not starve in this country), assisted him to remove to the United States. He found his way at length to Wisconsin, and a few days since I had the pleasure of viewing his cultivated and beautiful farm, where I saw a large field of excellent wheat *of luxurious growth and abundant crops of grain.* He has 310 acres of good land and as well cultivated as can be found in this fertile and beautiful Territory [of Wisconsin], with sheep, cattle and horses—in short, his property is worth over $5,000, and besides all this he is a temperate moral man, a good neighbor, and a good citizen…

[*Milwaukee Sentinel* Aug. 28, 1846]

Women's Clothing Styles of the 1890's:

"A beautiful portrait of two sisters. **Martie** (on the left) wears her hair in a pre-1890's style, flattened down at the center and tightly gathered together at the back. Around her shoulder is a waterproof shawl, often stiff and uncomfortable to wear. The standard for identifying neck styles to the 1890s, as worn by both sisters, are collars worn high and tight to the neck. **Martie's** collar is draped by a thin layer of lace. **Ellen** wears her hair quite differently than her sister. Her curly hair is neatly brushed back, cut and pulled back from her temples. Her sleeves, starting at the shoulder are wide and puffy. **Ellen's** bodice and collar are hand stitched. Both wear pins though their collars." -- ***Joan Severa, 19th Century Clothing Styles.***[501]

---

[499]   *Federal Manuscript Schedule*, Population, Agricultural and Manufacturing Schedules for Waukesha County, Town of Oconomowoc, 1860.

[500]   Photograph courtesy of Libbie Nolan, via Pat Nolan of Big Bend, Wisconsin, Jan. 15, 2010.

[501]   Joan Severa, Madison, Wisconsin, e-mail message to author, Jan 23, 2010.

IMMIGRANTS TO WISCONSIN FROM IRELAND

(1ˢᵗ Generation): Name: **Thomas Faulkner Sr.**—Birthplace: <u>Tyrone County, Ireland</u> (28 Apr. 1793)-Spouse **Harriet (Searle) Faulkner**—Birthplace: <u>Ireland</u>—occupation: *farmer*—Emigration from <u>Ireland</u> (circa: 1820)--Children: *Thomas Les & Ethel*—(2ⁿᵈ Generation): Name: **Thomas Faulkner Jr.** —Birthplace: **Mumford, Town of Wheatland, Monroe County, NY.** (12 Jul 1822)—Spouse: **Nancy (Moorer/Cheney) Faulkner**—Birthplace: **Monroe, County, New York State** (15 Dec 1821)—Residence: <u>Prospect Hill, New Berlin, Waukesha County, Wisconsin</u> (1870)—Occupation: *farmer, surveyor, teacher & cabinet maker*--Children: *Nancy, Viola, Clara & Elden*—also residing in this household is Thomas' mother-in law: *Lydia Cheney.*—(3ʳᵈ Generation): Name: ***Rufus Elden Faulkner***—Birthplace: <u>Prospect Hill, New Berlin, Waukesha County, Wisconsin</u> (4 Sep 1857)—Spouse: **Harriet (Searle) Faulkner**—Married at: <u>Rochester, Racine County</u> (6 Mar 1883)[502]—In 1873, J. Faulkner owned a 49 ¾ acre farm (section 32) along the south slope of <u>Prospect Hill</u>, on the east side of the road leading to <u>Muskego</u>.--Residence 1900: <u>New Berlin, Waukesha County, Wisconsin</u>—Occupation: *farmer*—Children: *Lee Aldus & Ethel.*   (Imagine & genealogy courtesy of Catheryn Larsen of Racine, WI.)[503]

Rufus Elden Faulkner (c. 1892)[504]

17ᵗʰ Century Tyrone County, Ireland:

"*County Tyron (the birthplace of Thomas Faulkner) was the traditional stronghold of the various O'Neill clans and families, the strongest of the Gaelic Irish families in Ulster, surviving into the seventeenth century.* In 1608 during O'Doherty's Rebellion areas of the country were plundered and burnt by the forces of Sir Cahir O'Doherty following his destruction of Derry."[505]

The Thomas Faulkner Family initially farmed in Wheatland, Monroe County, N.Y.:

"The first settlers to Wheatland, Monroe County arrived circa 1789. In those days, the growing of wheat and the manufacture of flour were the county's primary economic activity, and the Wheatland area figured prominently in this trade. *The US Census of 1850 notes that the counties of Monroe and Livingston led the entire United States in wheat production. As the vast agricultural expanses of the American Midwest opened up, the local wheat industry went into decline, beginning in the decade prior to the Civil War.*"[506]

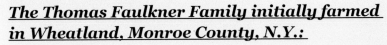

PROSPECT.

An extremely enjoyable event was the celebration on last Thursday of the golden wedding anniversary of Mr. and Mrs. Thomas Faulkner. The festivities were arranged by Miss *Clara Faulkner* assisted by friends and were an entire surprise to *Mr. and Mrs. Faulkner. Mr. and Mrs. Faulkner* were presented with a handsome set of silver spoons. *Mr. and Mrs. Faulkner are both of New York birth and have lived in Waukesha County since 1846. Mrs. Faulkner's maiden names was Harriet Searle. Mr. Faulkner was a teacher in his youth, later became a farmer.*   [*Waukesha Freeman* June 4, 1896]

---

502   *Atlas of Waukesha Co. Wisconsin, 1873,* Town of New Berlin.

503   *Federal Manuscript Schedule*, Population, Agricultural and Manufacturing Schedules for Waukesha County, Town of Oconomowoc, 1860.

504   Photograph courtesy of Cathryn Larsen of Kenosha, Wisconsin. e-mail to author, Mar 24, 2011

505   https://en.wikipedia.org/wiki/County_Tyrone

506   https://en.wikipedia.org/wiki/Mumford,_New_York

IMMIGRANTS TO WISCONSIN FROM CANADA

Name: **William Sherman**: Birthplace: **Dundas, Wentworth, Ontario, Canada** (6 Apr 1809)— Occupation: *a sailor between New York And Liverpool, England* –Residence: **Jericho**, near the village of <u>Eagle, Waukesha County</u> (1836)—married: **Louisa Parsons** at **Ripley, Chautauqua County, New York** (5 Feb 1835)—Occupation: *farmer*—children: *George, William, Job, Adelia, Charles, Lewis, Mary & Alice*—William's death: <u>Lake Geneva, Walworth County, Wisconsin</u> (26 Mar 1908)—***William & Louisa*** *are buried in the little cemetery at* **Jericho,** along with their daughter ***Mary*** (5 Jan 1863).

(Image and genealogy courtesy of Waukesha County Historical Society & Museum.) [507]

William Sherman, Josephine and Dwight Allen Jr., (c. 1892)[508]

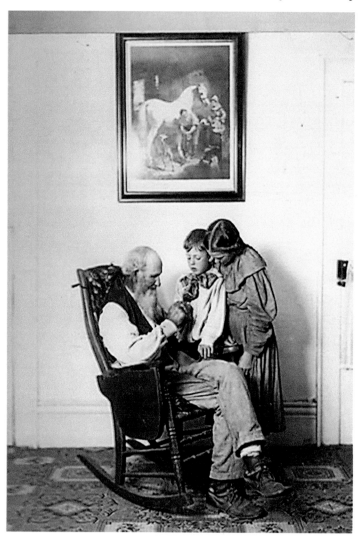

Heading West.

Mr. Sherman was the oldest man in this section, being born April 26, 1809, in the village of Dundas, near Hamilton, Canada. In early life Mr. Sherman learned the tanner's trade near Dansville, N.Y. Mr. Sherman started west with two yoke of oxen and two cows. It took 37 days to make the trip. *At Milwaukee, he headed west passing through the Indian villages of Waukesha and Mukwonago and located a claim of 160 acres at* Jericho and built a log cabin. Mr. Sherman farmed at Mukwonago, Eagle & Whitewater until 1876, when he bought a farm in the town of Linn, Walworth County, where he lived for five years, before moving to this city (Lake Geneva), which has since been his home. Mrs. Sherman died April 2, 1900. Burial was by the side of his beloved wife in the little cemetery at Jericho, near Eagle, in Waukesha County.

[*Eagle Quill*, April 10, 1908]

An Artist from Chicago:

"Photograph of Mr. William Sherman, with his grandchildren: *Josephine & Dwight Allen Jr.*, of Lake Geneva. William Sherman settled in Jericho, Waukesha Co. in 1836. *The photograph was taken about 1892 (near Lake Geneva) by Leo D. Weil, an artist from Chicago.* He came to the home and asked permission to photograph them."[509]

---

[507] *Federal Manuscript Schedule*, Population, Agricultural and Manufacturing Schedules for Waukesha County, Town of Mukwonago, 1850.

[508] William Sherman photograph c. 1892, People S-T Box 7:8, Photography Collection, Research Center Library & Archive, Waukesha County Historical Society & Museum, Waukesha, Wisconsin.

[509] *Photograph Descriptor*, William Sherman (back side of photograph card), Photography Collection, Research Center Library & Archive, Waukesha County Historical Society & Museum, Waukesha, Wisconsin.

IMMIGRANTS TO WISCONSIN FROM BAVARIA AND WALDENBURG

Name: **John Michael Meidenbauer**—Birthplace: **Pruhasusen, Bayern Germany** (1854)—Spouse: **Anna Caroline Schoenwalder**—Birthplace: **Woeste Gucresdorf Kreis, Waldenburg, Württemberg, Germany** (c. 1765)—Year of immigration: 1848—Residence in 1880: **New Berlin Township, Waukesha County**—Occupation: *farmer*—Children: *John, Elizabeth, William, Edward, Sabel, Anna, Emma, Josephine, Harry, Walter, Arthur & Viola.*
(Image and genealogy courtesy of Roy Meidenbauer of New Berlin, Wisconsin.)[510]

John M. and Anna Meidenbauer (1902)[511]

John and Anna Meidenbauer enjoyed the festivities at the Jarmarkt:

"*Located on Grove (South 5th) Street and National Avenue in 1902, there is something for everyone at the German Jarmarkt (festival).* For the hungry there is a host of food booths with all kinds of Teutonic goodies like kuchen, pretzels, and pfeffernuss, many of them made on the spot. For the adventurous there is a Ferris wheel; passenger carrying balloon ascensions. The Venetian gondola; a beautiful $50,000-dollar carousel; a snake pit; and the crystal maze. For the curious there is Electra, the flying woman; Chiquita, the world's smallest woman; the streets of old Cairo display; and from Toronto, the Bostock exhibit of lions. *For the thirsty, the beer in Dorf Bierburg flow like water as 'Erin Prosit' is drunk over and over to the 'oom-pah-pah' of the German bands.*" [512]

BROOKFIELD.

There were more people at the *Burns* barn dance Saturday evening, seemingly than at the **Jahrmakt** last fall.

[*Waukesha Freeman* June 30, 1904]

The Jarmarkt comes to an end:

The *"Jarmarkt"* on Grove Street (South Fifth) gave shopping a festive air. *By 1905, the neighborhood was becoming more Polish than German. But everybody in Milwaukee knew what the "Wilkommen" sign meant.*[513]

510 *Federal Manuscript Schedule*, Population, Agricultural and Manufacturing Schedules for Waukesha County, Town of New Berlin, 1880.

511 Photograph courtesy of Roy Meidenbauer, of New Berlin, Wisconsin, e-mail to author, Aug 9, 2009.

512 John Utzat & Ruth Ruege, eds., *Southside in the Sun*. This book contains a compilation of articles from the *Southside Urban News*, published between 1977 & 1981.

513 Robert W. Wells, *Yesterday's Milwaukee* (Miami, Florida: E.A. Seeman Publishing, Inc., 1976), p. 77.

IMMIGRANTS TO WISCONSIN FROM ALSACE, FRANCE

(1<u>st</u> Generation): Name: **John H. Phillips**—Birthplace: *Elsass, France* (7 Aug 1818) —Spouse: **Catherine Casper**-- Birthplace: *Stundweiller, Elsass, France* (12 May 1821) — Marriage: (1842)-- (During the period of large emigration from Alsace-Lorraine to Wisconsin (1840s), French was the predominant language spoken in Lorraine, though the majority of Alsatians, such as the Phillips, Casper and Schneider families, Spoke Alsatian, a combination of neighboring Germanic dialects, and clung to their Catholic religion, during the era they left Europe and immigrated into the town of New Berlin, Waukesha County.)[514] Year of the Phillips family immigration: 1842 Residence (1860): <u>New Berlin, Waukesha County</u>—Occupation: *farmer*—owns an 87 acre New Berlin (section 27) farm in 1873--Children: *Joseph* (age: 22), *Barney* (age: 20) & *Helen* (age: 17)—John H. Phillips Death: (7 Dec 1885)-- Cemetery: *Holy Apostles Cemetery*-- Catherine (Casper) Phillips Death (8 May 1891)--Cemetery: *Holy Apostles Cemetery.* --(<u>2nd</u> generation): Name: **Bernard (Barney) Phillips**—Birthplace: <u>New Berlin</u> (25 Oct 1858)—Spouse: **Mary Kau**—Birthplace: <u>New Berlin</u> (19 Aug 1869)—married *Holy Apostles Catholic Church* (25 Nov 1890)—Residence: <u>Muskego Township, Waukesha County</u>—Occupation: *farmer*--owns an <u>35.86 acre</u> town of <u>Muskego</u> farm bordering the town of <u>New Berlin</u>--Children: *Helen* (born: 19 Oct 1891), *William* (born: 26 Jan 1893), *Amanda* & *Caroline* (born: 12 June 1897)—in (1918) Barney & Mary Phillips—owns <u>40 acres with 3 horses, 8 cattle, rural route 11—mail at Calhoun & Bell telephone service.</u>[515]   (Image & genealogy courtesy of Lois (Phillips) Alton of Hartland, Wisconsin; Genealogy courtesy of Mary Stigler of Brookfield, Wisconsin.)[516]

Catherine (Casper) Phillips (c. 1888)[517]

Large Emigration from Alsace:

"The combination of economic and demographic factors led to hunger, housing shortages and a lack of work for young people. Thus, it is not surprising that people left Alsace. Many Alsatians also began to sail to the United States, settling in many areas from 1820 to 1850. *In 1843 and 1844, sailing ships bringing immigrant families from Alsace arrived at the port of New York*."[518]

New Berlin families from Alsace:

"John H. Phillips born in *Alsace, France*, his wife, <u>Catherine Casper</u>, born <u>in Stundweiller, Alsace, France</u> along with <u>Bernard Casper</u>, also of *Stundweiller*, and <u>Thomas Andrew Schneider</u> of *Wahlbach, Kries Mulhausen, Haut-Rhine, Alsace, France* where the among the organizers of the first Catholic church in New Berlin, which they named for **St. Valerius, of Ellelum (Ehl) in Alsace**. Today, *St. Valerius* is known as *Holy Apostles Catholic Church*." [519]

Valerius of Trèves:

"*According to an ancient legend, St. Valerius was a follower of Saint Eucharius, the first bishop of Trier*. Eucharius was sent to Gaul by *Saint Peter* as bishop, together with the deacon Valerius and the sub deacon Maternus, to preach the Gospel. *They came to the Rhine and to **Ellelum (Ehl) in Alsace**, where Maternus died*. His two companions hastened back to *St. Peter* and begged him to restore the dead man to life. St. Peter gave his pastoral staff to Eucharius, and, upon being touched with it, Maternus, who had been in his grave for forty days, returned to life."[520]

---

[514]   https://en.wikipedia.org/wiki/Alsatian_dialect

[515]   *The Farm Journal Illustrated Rural Directory of Waukesha County*, 1918, p. 122.

[516]   *Federal Manuscript Schedule*, Population, Agricultural and Manufacturing Schedules for Waukesha County, Town of New Berlin, 1860.

[517]   Photograph courtesy of Lois (Phillips) Alton of Hartland, Wisconsin, e-mail to author, Dec. 29, 2016

[518]   https://en.wikipedia.org/wiki/History_of_Alsace

[519]   From the genealogy of "The Phillips Family of Muskego," 2017, by the author, unpublished

[520]   https://en.wikipedia.org/wiki/Valerius_of_Trève

IMMIGRANTS TO WISCONSIN FROM VERMONT & NEW YORK

Name: **Walter R. Sawyer**—Birthplace: **Vermont** (c.1847)—Spouse: **Nellie Williams**—Birthplace: **New York** (1850)—Marriage: (21 May 1872) -- Residence in <u>1910</u>: <u>Waukesha Ward 5, Waukesha County, Wisconsin</u>—Occupation: *Bank President*—Children: *Maude & Mary,* <u>twins, died in infancy</u>; *Carl* (concrete worker), *Percy* (concrete worker), *Julia* (teacher), *Eleanor* & ***Howell*** (foreman-- steel worker).
(Image and genealogy courtesy of Waukesha County Historical Society and Museum.)[521]

Howell Sawyer c. 1893 [522]

A major early banker arrives in Waukesha from Vermont:

"*Silas S, Sawyer* was reared and educated in his *Chester, Vermont,* and on reaching manhood was married, in the spring of 1842, to Miss *Julia S, Sargeant,* Mrs. Sawyer was also born in *Chester, Vermont,* in 1821. In the autumn of 1853 Mr. Sawyer's came with his family to Waukesha. <u>He had already accumulated considerable property and was interested first in mercantile business and shortly after in banking, being one of the incorporators of the first bank of Waukesha, the Waukesha County Bank, which began business in 1855.</u>"[523]

The Sawyer Family:

Mr. and Mrs. Sawyer had a family of three sons: *George, Walter & Charles.* Walter P. Sawyer attended Carroll College. His elder brother *George* enlisted, during the Civil War, at the age of eighteen, as a member of *Company A, 28th Wisconsin infantry,* on Aug. 13, 1862, and served through the entire conflict, being mustered out with his regiment, Aug. 23, 1865. <u>On May 21, 1872, Mr. Sawyer was married to Miss Nellie Williams, daughter of William Howell and Anne (James) Williams, both natives of Wales, and residents of Freedom, N. Y.</u> Six children have been born to Mr. and Mrs. Sawyer: *Maud and Mary,* (twins, died in infancy), *Carl, Walter Percy, Julia & Howell.* In 1882, he assisted in organizing the **National Exchange Bank of Waukesha**, which has from the first been one of the strong financial institutions of the county. Both Mr. and Mrs. Sawyer are members of the Baptist Church." [524]

Miss Sawyer Engaged as Teacher

Miss Julia Sawyer has engaged as assistant teacher in the primary department of the Union School and began her work Monday. Miss *Sawyer* takes her place as Miss *Clinton's* assistant. Miss Sawyer is the only daughter of Mr. and Mrs. *W. P. Sawyer.* <u>She graduated last year from the state university, having before graduated from the local high school and been for several years at Milwaukee-Downer College.</u> She will be a valuable addition to the teaching corps of the city.   [*Waukesha Freeman* April 16, 1903]

521 *Federal Manuscript Schedule,* Population, Agricultural and Manufacturing Schedules for Waukesha County, City of Waukesha, 1910.
522 Howell Sawyer (c.1893), People S-T Box, Photography Collection, Research Center Library & Archive, Waukesha County Historical Society & Museum, Waukesha, Wisconsin.
523 *Memoirs of Waukesha County,* 1907, pp. 616.
524 *Memoirs of Waukesha County,* 1907, pp. 616-617.

IMMIGRANTS TO WISCONSIN FROM BAVARIA TO WISCONSIN

Parents: **John Michael Stigler** & **Mary Anna Ostermann--** immigrated from near **Gross Bissedorf, Oberpfalz, Bayern** to Wisconsin in 1850--Son: **Frederick Stigler**—Birthplace: **Village of Elm Grove, Wisconsin** (24 Dec 1850) — Spouse: **Mary Angeline Schneider**—— Birthplace: **Wisconsin** (c. 1857) --In 1918, Fred & Mary Stigler had 7 children; owned a 143 acre (Sections 9 & 10) New Berlin; Occupation: *dairy farmer*; including 4 horses & 25 dairy cows; Rural Mail Route #11, Calhoun Station; Bell telephone service—Children: *Michael, Otilia, Andrew, Frederick, John, George, Mary Anna, Joseph & Anthony.* [525]

(Image and genealogy courtesy of Mary Stigler of Brookfield, Wisconsin.)[526]

Fred & Mary Stigler Family (c. 1893)[527]

Back row (L-R): John Killian, Michael, Andrew, Frederick Xavior & Otilia,
Front row (L-R): Mary Ann, George & Joseph (on Ottilia's lap.)

THROWN INTO AIR

NARROW ESCAPE OF MEN IN EXPOSION.

Threshing Machine Engine Blows Up Near Waukesha One Man Badly Hurt Escape of Several More is Miraculous--Boy Blown Through Roof of Covered Wagon.

WAUKESHA, Wis., Oct. 10—The explosion of a threshing engine yesterday in the town of New Berlin, caused a destructive blaze, and the serious injury of Fred Stigler, the engineer. A work on the farm, which is occupied by Henry Gasser, and Stigler was running the engine. Suddenly there was a threshing crew was at terrible explosion, and Stigler was hurled about three rods. He was picked up bleeding and burned, and Drs. Ward and Philler of this city, and Tibbits, of Prospect, hastily summoned. *It was found that he had sustained a compound fracture of the arm and numerous cuts, burns and bruises.*

Cause Is Unknown.

What caused the explosion is unknown, but the force was tremendous. *Instead of bursting into pieces the engine was blown over sixty feet, alighting upside down and burrowing into the ground.* Chris. & James Salentine, Will Metz, John Becker, Henry Gasser and John Stigler, members of the threshing crew, who were working on the stack at the time were hurled some distance, and their escape from death seems marvelous, as wood and iron were hurled in all directions.

Blown Through Wagon Top.

John Gasser, a small boy, was sitting in a covered wagon nearby, and was blown straight through the top and landed some feet away, escaping without a scratch. The horse was badly burned and cut. Three large grain stacks were entirely destroyed by fire, but the threshing crew, by the hardest kind of work, managed to save the barns. The explosion was heard several miles away.

[*The Milwaukee Journal* October 7, 1902]

---

[525] *The Farm Journal Illustrated Rural Directory of Waukesha County, Wisconsin,* 1918, p. 154.

[526] *Federal Manuscript Schedule,* Population, Agricultural and Manufacturing Schedules for Waukesha County, Town of Brookfield, 1900.

[527] Photograph of courtesy of Mary Stigler of Brookfield, Wisconsin, e-mail to author, Aug 22, 2009.

IMMIGRANTS TO WISCONSIN FROM PRUSSIA & RHENISH PRUSSIA

Name: **Jacob Franz Brandt**—Birthplace: **Nörvenich, Rheinland, Preußen** (1851)—Christening: **Nörvenich, Rheinpreußen**—Emigration from Germany: (1852)--Occupation: *farmer*—married: **Anna Marie Duckgeischel** at Waukesha (30 Jan 1877)—Birthplace: **Wisconsin** (25 Sep 1854)—Residence in 1880: **Pewaukee Township, Waukesha County**—Residence in 1910: **Lisbon Township, Waukesha County, Wisconsin**—Occupation: *farmer*-- Children: **_Agnes_**, *John, Peter, Francis, Barbara, Joseph. Margaret K., Anna, Margaret, Katherine, Elizabeth, Florence, Estelle & John.*   (Image and genealogy courtesy of Leanne Bennett of Waukesha, Wisconsin) [528]

Jacob Franz Brandt Family (c. 1893)[529]

17ᵗʰ Century defense of Nörvenich:

"Nörvenich, (the birthplace of Jacob Franz Brandt) was accessible via a truncheon (a corduroy road constructed with round timber or planks) paved path which preceded the gates. Here was an attacker's strongest resistance. _The gates were likely destroyed a during the siege of Nörvenich and the subsequent capture and pillaging by the troops of the French general, Marshal of Luxembourg, in 1678._ Surrounding Nörvenich was the wild, "The Hague." The word Hag comes from the Old High German Hiac and meaning brambles, bushes, fencing, but especially the dark and gloomy ones. In order to fend off preying opponents, young trees were cut and bent. Blackberry and thorn bushes were planted between the young shoots which grew out in large numbers. Thus, these hedges formed fortifications through which one could not walk nor see."[530]

The Brandt farm in Pewaukee, 1873:

"_In 1873, the Brandts owned an 86 acre (section 13 farm) in the town of Pewaukee, near Duplainville._ The Catholic Church and cemetery were built on a small parcel along the road fronting their farm, the Brandt's may have leased or donated land for the church's use."[531]

Social and Personal.

The wedding of Miss Agnes Brandt, daughter of John Brandt was celebrated Tuesday morning, August 8, at seven o'clock at St. Mary's Catholic church. The ceremony at the church was followed by a wedding breakfast at Zaun's hotel.
[*Waukesha Freeman* August 10, 1914]

---

528 *Federal Manuscript Schedule*, Population, Agricultural and Manufacturing Schedules for Waukesha County, Town of Lisbon, 1910.
529 Photograph courtesy of Leanne Bennett of Waukesha, Wisconsin, e-mail to author, Jun 24, 2010.
530 https://de.wikipedia.org/wiki/ Nörvenich
531 *Standard Atlas of Waukesha County, Wisconsin, 1914,* Town of Pewaukee.

IMMIGRANTS TO WISCONSIN FROM LOWER SAXONY

1st Generation: Name: **August Heinrich Vogel**—Birthplace: **Lower Sachsen (Niedersachsen), Germany** (1795)—Spouse: **Dorothy (Hartung) Vogel**—Immigration to Wisconsin: (1847)-August & Dorothy's 3 sons: *Karl (1825-1909)*, *Henry William (1833-1896)* & *Christian (1825-1909)*— 2nd Generation: **Christian Vogel**—born: (25 Apr 1825)—**Hanover, Landkreis Hannover, Lower Sachsen (Niedersachsen), Germany**--located in the Town of Brookfield, Waukesha County— Spouse: **Caroline Dorothy Garvens**, born: (2 Feb 1827) in **Hanover, Landkreis Hannover, Lower Sachsen (Niedersachsen), Germany**—Married: (April 10, 1853). In 1859, **August Vogel** owned a 60-acre (section 36) Town of Brookfield farm—Children: *Caroline Wilhelmine Louise, August Frederick, Theresa Maria, Louise Anna Carolina, Albert George, Otto, Otto C. & Charles.*[532] By 1873, **Christian Vogel** purchased a 59 acre (section 2) Town of New Berlin farm—they have Bell Telephone service; there are 2 houses located on the property 3rd Generation: Christian's son **Otto Vogel**-- spouse: **Sophia Schwenn**—Otto & Sophia had 6 children: *Lena, August, Theresa, Louisa, Albert & Otto*[533]--By 1923, **August F. & Frances Vogel** own a 120 acre farm--Rural Mail Route 14, Town of Wauwatosa farm-they have 3 children, along with 4 horses & 35 cattle—**Karl & Catherine Vogel** own a 59-acre , Town of New Berlin farm, Rural Mail Route 6—**Gottlieb Vogel** owns a 59-acre Town of New Berlin farm, with 6 children, 3 horses, 5 cows, Rural Mail Route 6 –**Otto & Sophia "Emma" (Schwenn) Vogel** own a 60 acre Town of New Berlin farm, with 3 horses & 16 cattle, Rural Mail Route 12—and Bell Telephone Service.[534]   (Image and genealogy courtesy of Terry Haslam-Jones of Rossendale, England)

Vogel Brothers: (l-r) Karl (Charles), William & Christian. (circa: 1893)[535]

"The Woodburning Monster:"

August Vogel was killed Dec. 12, 1861 in Wauwatosa, Wisconsin. He was 66. An account of his death is provided by *William B. Vogel* with his uncle, *Oswald Vogel*, the last surviving son of *Charles Vogel*. Based on how Oswald described it, <u>August was killed at the Village of Wauwatosa rail crossing at what today is known as W. State St. and W. Harwood Ave. The horses he was driving were frightened by the train, called "the woodburning monster." The horses shied, reared and turned over the wagon. August was thrown violently to the ground, suffering a broken neck, and died almost instantly.</u>[536]

Before We had Electric Lights:

"In middle-class homes during the 1880s and 1890s, first in urban areas and later in the country, kerosene lamps began to give way to gas and electric lighting. <u>If the homeowner could afford it and lived close to a gas supply, despite its **dangers**, gas lights offered a welcome alternative to the dirt and odor of the kerosene lamp</u>."[537]

Elm Grove.

A number of people of this vicinity visited the **gas explosion** at *August & Frances Vogel's* home at Wauwatosa, Last Sunday.   [*Waukesha Freeman* May 11, 1911]

---

532   *1860 Federal Manuscript Schedule*, Population, Agricultural and Manufacturing Schedules for Waukesha County, Town of Brookfield.

533   *Atlas of Waukesha County, Wisconsin, 1873*. Town of Brookfield.

534   *The Farm Journal Illustrated Rural Directory of Waukesha County, Wisconsin, 1923*. Town of New Berlin.

535   Photograph courtesy of Terry Haslam-Jones of Rossendale, England, e-mail to author, Jul 4, 2018.

536   David M. Vogel "letter," *The Garvens Newsletter, Volume XI (1991)*. Excerpt provided courtesy of Terry Haslam-Jones of Rossendale, England; a relative of the Garvins/Vogel families of Wisconsin and contributor of the "Garvins Newsletter."

537   *Tompkins, American Eras: 1878-1899*, p. 303.

IMMIGRANTS TO WISCONSIN FROM PRUSSIA

"Name: **John Christian Dieman**— born: **Neve, Preußen, Germany** (23 May1823) –spouse: **Pauline Suter**—born: **Preußen, Germany** (9 Dec 1826) —Immigration year: 1845—John & Pauline marriage: (circa: 1850) --Residence in 1860: <u>Town of Pewaukee, Waukesha County, Wisconsin</u>—Occupation: *farmer*— John Dieman owned a 55-acre (sections 3 & 10) --Children: *Pauline, Charles, August & Art.*

(Image and genealogy courtesy of Jerry Hartwell of Bowling Green, Ohio)[538]

John Christian Dieman (February 1, 1894)[539]

Cannon Fodder:

"Family tradition says about John Christian Dieman, that he emigrated to the United States because he did not wish to be required to serve in the army of the Prussian King of the German Empire, King William IV. *There is speculation that John had a difference of opinion about becoming cannon fodder in the Prussian king's war of aggression in Europe which went against his own personal philosophy of thinking about life.*"[540]

The Dieman Family arrive in Wisconsin:

"<u>Between March 2nd and September 5th, 1840, about fourteen thousand Germans had arrived in New York, the majority of whom were on their way to settle in the West. Many of these may came to Wisconsin.</u> By 1846 a number of individuals began to advertise Wisconsin in Germany. The clause in the new Constitution of the State permitting an alien to vote after a year's residence, the Revolution of 1848 in Europe, together with religious disturbances within Germany, were incentives for these people to seek homes in Wisconsin."[541]

The Diemans settle at Duplainville:

The small burg of Duplainville, in Pewaukee Township, was at one-time, home of the Duplainville Tavern building, which held a small grocery store and the post office. Threshing time was generally looked forward to with excitement and anticipation. Neighborhood farmers helped each other, providing a large enough crew to get the job done in the least time. *Fields of corn, grain, hay, garden produce, fruits, poultry and other animals were raised.* The way of life in the early 1900's and late 1800's was so completely different that it is hard to imagine.[542]

---

538 *Federal Manuscript Schedule*, Population, Agricultural and Manufacturing Schedules for Waukesha County, Town of Pewaukee, 1860.

539 Jerry Hartwell of Bowling Green, Ohio, e-mail to author, Nov 30, 2011.

540 Jerry L. Hartwell, "A Family History of the Descendants of John Christian Dieman—August Dieman Branch", 2006.

541 "The Movement of American Settlers into Wisconsin and Minnesota," *The Iowa Journal of History & Politics, Vol. 17, No. 3, Jul. 1919,* p, 426.

542 Mildred E. Wiedeman, "The Green Road and Duplainville Area," September 1992. Courtesy of the Pewaukee Area Historical Society.

IMMIGRANTS TO WISCONSIN FROM FRANCE & SWITZERLAND

(1st Generation): Name: **Jacob Sanner**– birthplace: **Elsass, France** (c. 1819) — Spouse: **Mary E. (Schleuraff)**—Birthplace: **Schweiz** (c. 1822)— occupation: *tailor* —year of immigration (circa 1848)—Residence in 1850: Erie, Pennsylvania—Residence in 1856: Village of Waukesha, Waukesha County--Children: *Harriet, Justus, William, Ada, Brian, John, Alice, Grace & Jacob*—(2nd Generation): Son: ***William Sanner***—birthplace: **Erie, Pennsylvania** (2 July 1852)—Spouse: **Esther (King)**-- Birthplace: **Troy, N. Y.**--married in Milwaukee (26 April 1877) --Children: Roy, Edith & Louise—Occupation: *Drug Store*—Location: No. 414 Main Street, Waukesha—Residence: No. 605 Barstow Street, Waukesha (1884)[543]

(Image and genealogy courtesy of Waukesha County Historical Society and Museum.)[544]

William Sanner (c. 1895)[545]

Fancy Goods.

Sanner Bros. are selling all <u>toys and fancy goods</u> cheap in their Waukesha Store.
[Waukesha Freeman Jan. 11, 1877]

Sanner's Drug Store on Main Street:

"William Leroy Sanner, proprietor of one of the leading drug stores of Waukesha, is a native of Erie, Pa. His father, Jacob Sanner, came to the United States, locating at Erie, Pa., where he learned the tailor's trade. In 1856, the family, consisting of parents and three children, emigrated to Waukesha. The father had visited Wisconsin before, and worked a short time at his trade in Racine. When he arrived in Waukesha Jacob Sanner had only $5 left. *When eighteen years of age, William Sanner entered the store of I. M. White to learn the drug business, continuing with that gentleman for some five years.* The succeeding four years he spent in the office of J. E. Patton Co., wholesale dealers in oils and paints in Milwaukee. In 1884 he again came to Waukesha and engaged in the drug business, which he has conducted continuously since. Mr. Sanner has a well selected and tastily arranged stock. Close attention to every detail of his business, and courteous and fair treatment of his customers are the secrets of his prosperity." [546]

Waukesha. --*Clarence M. Allen had a bicycle stolen in front of W. L. Sanner's drug store last evening.* Up to this morning no trace of the thief had been found.   [*Milwaukee Journal* July 9, 1895]

[543] *Portrait and Biographical Record of Waukesha County*, 1894, p. 800.

[544] *Federal Manuscript Schedule*, Population, Agricultural and Manufacturing Schedules Waukesha County, Village of Waukesha, 1860.

[545] William Sanner photograph (c. 1895), People S-T Box 7:8, Photography Collection, Research Center Library & Archive, Waukesha County Historical Society & Museum, Waukesha, Wisconsin.

[546] *Portrait and Biographical Record of Waukesha County*, 1894, p. 800.

IMMIGRANTS TO WISCONSIN FROM ENGLAND

Name: **John Foster**–Birthplace: **England** (c. 1819) — Spouse: **Elizabeth White (Harwood) Foster** —Birthplace: **England** (c. 1815)–Residence in 1880: Town of Waukesha (section 20), Waukesha County, Wisconsin—Occupation: *farmer*—"**Broad Ripple Farms**"–Children: *Edward, Eliza, Thomas & Winthrop*--John Foster deceased--(circa: 1870's)--John & Elizabeth's oldest son: **Edward Foster**—Birthplace: **England** (circa 1851)— Spouse: **Elizabeth Foster** —Edward's occupation: *farmer-- raising sheep along with grain crops*—Residence in 1880: inherited his father's (J. H. Foster) 327 acre (section 20) *Town of Waukesha farm*—the **Fox River** runs through the farm. Edward & Elizabeth Foster's children: *Elizabeth* (single—born in Canada), **Edward** (son-in-law—keeps drug store), *Mary* (married)—also residing on this farm are: *Charley Porter* (farm laborer), *John Kimpull* (farm laborer), *Leonard Hill* (farm laborer), *Eliza Groff* (house servant), *John Westerdale* (nephew—carpenter)—in 1895, Edward Foster's widow, **Elizabeth**, resides at *East Ave. and Cook St. in the city of Waukesha*.[547]

(Image and genealogy courtesy of Waukesha County Historical Society and Museum.)[548]

Elizabeth Foster (c. 1895) [549]

Another Waukesha Druggist:

"During the 1870's, *Edward Foster* engaged in the drug business village of Waukesha. His place of business being on the corner of Main and Clinton Streets. *For eight years he was one of the leading druggists of that village.* Mr. Foster simultaneously began accumulating valuable real estate property in the village of Waukesha. On the 14th of January 1878, Edward Foster married Miss Mary E. Porter, daughter of Edward Porter, one of the pioneers of Waukesha."[550] "*Edward Foster, under the tutallidge of his farther-in law, Edward Porter, began accumulating much wealth in the wool industry.*"[551]

Edward Porter's Wool Storehouse:

"In 1876, *Edward 'Porter'* erected a large wool and grain storehouse, near the Fox River. *He had purchased from the farmers, adjacent to the town of Waukesha, over ten-year period, upwards of 1,225,000 pounds of wool, for which he has paid Eastern prices, less transportation.* He made his shipment principally to the cities of Philadelphia, Boston, Syracuse, and North Adams, Massachusetts."[552]

Edward Foster's Wool Storehouse:
"*Edward 'Foster'*, the well-known wool buyer of Waukesha, was a native of the town of Lisbon, his birth occurring on the 13th of February 1851. His parents John H. and Elizabeth White (Harwood) Foster, had six children, Edward being the third in order of birth. Full of enterprise and push he had been most successful. Along with his drug business, and the purchase of Waukesha real estate, Edward Porter also devoted his time and attention to the wool business, having dealt in that commodity for most of the decade of the 1880s. *During the year of 1894, his purchases reached to one hundred and seventy-five thousand pounds.*"[553]

[547] Photograph Descriptor, Elizabeth Foster (back side of photograph card), Photography Collection, Research Center Library & Archive, Waukesha County Historical Society & Museum, Waukesha, Wisconsin.

[548] *Federal Manuscript Schedule*, Population, Agricultural and Manufacturing Schedules for Waukesha County, Town of Waukesha, 1880.

[549] Elizabeth Foster photograph c. 1895, People F-G-H, Photography Collection, Research Center Library & Archive, Waukesha County Historical Society & Museum, Waukesha, Wisconsin.

[550] *Portrait and Biographical Record of Waukesha County, Wisconsin, 1894,* pp. 888-889.

[551] *1880 History of Waukesha County,* p. 509

[552] *Portrait and Biographical Record of Waukesha County, Wisconsin, 1894,* pp. 888.

[553] *1880 History of Waukesha County,* p. 509

IMMIGRANTS TO WISCONSIN FROM CANADA AND ENGLAND

Name: **Morris D. Cutler**– Birthplace: **Canada** (13 June 1810)—during the 1830s, Morris & Alonzo Cutler laid claims to land running along the Fox River at Prairieville (Waukesha)-- Spouse: **Morris D, Cutler** married **Ruth Head** of **Preston, Lancastershire, England** (8 April 1845) at Waukesha—Morris & Ruth had no children. Ruth (Head) Cutler passed away (20 Feb 1863)--In 1873, Morris Cutler—Occupation: *purchased, owned and developed property*--(Section K) *Cutler's addition*; (Section L) *Cutler's 2nd addition*, along with (Section Q) *Cutler's & Dakin's addition*, all in the developing city of Waukesha-- Death of Morris Cutler (22 Jan 1897)-[554]-In 1914, Cutler's heirs inherited large parcels of Waukesha city lots initially purchased by Morris Cutler including: *"Cutler's 1st Addition"* which now included <u>18 city lots;</u> *"Cutler 2nd addition"* which included <u>30 city lots.</u> *Waukesha High School, Middle School* as well as the *public library* where all located on these lots; along with *"Cutler & Dakin's Addition,"* which included a vast number smaller lots, including *the entire original block of Carroll College.*[555]

(Image and genealogy courtesy of Waukesha County Historical Society and Museum.)[556]

Morris D. Cutler (c. 1895)[557]

Immigrating to the West:

"Morris D. Cutler was born in Canada on the 13th of June 1810, though his parents, Leonard and Mercy Cutler, were from Bennington, Vermont. Not long after the birth of their son Morris D. they returned to Vermont, but soon removed with their family to White Pigeon, Mich., and subsequently to La Porte, Ind. in 1834. Soon thereafter, Morris and his brother, Alonzo R., left their family home for the west. On reaching Prairieville about the 7th of May 1834, *they found a few log cabins without floors, windows or doors."* *"<u>Delighted with the country the Cutler brothers at once blazed out claims on the banks of the Fox River, one of which embraced the water power; in fact, the rapids at this place was one of the chief inducements in selecting Waukesha as a location.</u> It is said that during the first years of his residence in Waukesha he went bare-footed and bare-headed in summer, and frequently in winter had no boots, cloth moccasins made by himself served both as shoes and stockings."*[558]

Laying claims to prime real estate leads to prosperity:

Morris Cutler's shanty soon gave way to a comfortable frame house which now stands in the center of a fine park in the heart of Waukesha." "<u>Cutler's original holdings consisted of 160 acres and over the years he gave generously to educational and religious institutions including the land that Carroll University now stands on.</u> He passed away on January 22, 1897, and in 1902, the city of Waukesha paid $30,000 to his heirs for nine acres for a park with the stipulation that it would be named after him and would always remain a public park. <u>The present location of the Waukesha Public Library and Cutler Park is included in those nine acres."</u>[559]

[554] *Federal Manuscript Schedule*, Population, Agricultural and Manufacturing Schedules for Waukesha County, Village of Waukesha, 1880.

[555] *Atlas of Waukesha Co. Wisconsin, 1873*. Hartland, Waukesha, Sussex.

[556] *Standard Atlas of Waukesha County, Wisconsin, 1914*, City of Waukesha, south & west sides.

[557] Morris D, Cutler photograph c. 1895, People C-D-E Box 2:8, Photography Collection, Research Center Library & Archive, Waukesha County Historical Society & Museum, Waukesha, Wisconsin.

[558] *1880 History of Waukesha County*, p. 666.

[559] Morris D Cutler. *"Historical Marker Project,"* Cutler Park. Courtesy of the Waukesha County Historical Society and Museum.

IMMIGRANTS TO WISCONSIN FROM PRUSSIA

Name: **William Gumm** – Birthplace: **Preußen** (1 Mar 1838)— Spouse: **Whilhelena "Minna" Schultz**— Birthplace: **Preußen** (c. 1839)—Year of immigration: (1867)—Residence: in 1870: Town of Richfield, Washington County—Occupation: *farm laborer*--Children: Amelia (age: 4), Emma (age: 2), **Herman** (age: 2), *William* (age: 2/12), born after 1870: **Mary**, *Annie, Clara & Charles* . Family residence in 1880: Lisbon Township, Waukesha County, Wisconsin--Occupation: *farmer*--in 1900: *Charles Gumm*, (age 20), is *a Section Laborer with the RR.* (Image and genealogy courtesy of Andrew Dent Pierce of Eugene Lane, Oregon.) [560]

Mary Gumm (c. 1895)[561]

The Gumm family arrive at Castle Garden:

"In the first half of the 19th century, most immigrants arriving in New York City landed at docks on the east side of the tip of Manhattan, around South Street. *On August 1, 1855, Castle Garden became the Emigrant Landing Depot, functioning as the New York State immigrant processing center (the nation's first such entity). It was operated by the state until April 18, 1890.* After many unnecessary deaths, and scandals over immigration workers cheating and stealing from immigrants, immigration processing, soon moving the center to the larger, more isolated Ellis Island facility on January 2, 1892. *The new facility was needed because immigrants were known to carry diseases, which led to epidemics of cholera & smallpox.*"[562]

BLODGETT. *Tom Steiner* has been ill 3 months with *typhoid fever.* [*Waukesha Freeman* Jan. 10, 1901]

   --**ELM GROVE.** *Dr. H. A. Mount* of this place makes daily visits on the *Daniel Keuper* family, who are all ill with *typhoid fever.* [*Waukesha Freeman* Sept. 25, 1902] --**SUSSEX: *Herman Gumm*** *is still very low with typhoid pneumonia.* [*Waukesha Freeman* Nov. 3, 1904]

Causes of Typhoid Fever:

"Many wells that suppled water to Milwaukee's dinner tables were polluted by the 20,000 privy vaults still in use. *Typhoid fever was contracted by persons who drank contaminated milk or ate infected food.* In 1891, 166 cases of typhoid fever were reported in Milwaukee, and 77 cases of them proved fatal. The years after, 220 cases broke out, with 81 deaths."[563]

Immigrants suffered from numerous illnesses:

"Settlers in the immediate post-Civil War period found littler that resembled the healthful paradise they expected after reading the glowing immigration reports. The new arrivals soon enough learned that sickness and disease regularly passed political boundaries and wrought havoc among those in the hinterland as well as the cities. *Typhoid fever, typhus, diphtheria, and smallpox, along with pneumonia, measles, scarlet fever, mumps and other diseases appeared with appalling frequency.*"[564]

560   *Federal Manuscript Schedule*, Population, Agricultural and Manufacturing Schedules for Waukesha County, Town of Lisbon, 1880.

561   Photograph courtesy of Andrew Dent Pierce of Eugene Lane, Oregon, e-mail by a relative to author, Nov 8, 2011.

562   https://en.wikipedia.org/wiki/Castle_Clinton

563   W.E. Morton, *The Wisconsin Centennial Story of Disasters and Other Unfortunate Events, 1848-1948.* (Wisconsin State Centennial Committee, 1948).

564   Treleven, "One Hundred Years of Health and Healing in Rural Wisconsin," pp. 134 & 135.

IMMIGRANTS TO WISCONSIN FROM ENGLAND

Name: **George Boyce** (age: 20)—Birthplace: **England** (1831)—Spouse: **Elizabeth "Eliza" Porter** (age: 24)—Birthplace: **Chatteris, Fenland District, Cambridge, England** (1835)—Residence in 1860: **Merton Township, Waukesha County, Wiscosnin**--Occupation: *farm laborer*—Children: *Robert, John & **Jarvey***.
(Image and genealogy courtesy of Debra Woidyla Barham of Clearfield, Utah) [565]

Jarvis Porter Boyce (c. 1895) [566]

The Mining Institute of Scotland:

(George Boyce likely attended The Scottish Mining Institute of Scotland located in Bothwellhaugh, North Lanarkshire. The distance between Bothwellhaugh and Edinburg, Scotland is approximately 32 miles.) "Until recently, the membership of the Institute has kept pace with the development of the coal industry. *When a boy of twelve years enters a coal pit, he is attached to his father and becomes what is known technically as a "quarter-man."* [567]

W. C. CONDUCTOR NOW MINING ENGINEER.

Mr. George Boyce drifted towards railroading upon landing in this country. Twenty-four years ago, however, in Sept. 1891, *George W. Boyce* turned in his keys as a *conductor* on the Wisconsin Central Railway and headed for the mining sections of the west. *He had been educated as a mining engineer in Edinburg, Scotland, and Mr. Boyce is now handling mining properties in Colorado for his companies and has headquarters in Leadville.*
[*Waukesha Freeman* May 13, 1915]

Rich minerals found in Colorado Rockies:

Apparently, not finding life as a railroad conductor to be "his cup of tea," moved to the mountains of Colorado where he might find employment in the field of his education in Scotland. "By 1880, Leadville was one of the world's largest and richest silver camps, with a population of more than 15,000. Income from more *than thirty mines and ten large smelting works producing gold, silver, and lead amounting to $15,000,000 annually."* [568]

---

[565]   *Federal Manuscript Schedule*, Population, Agricultural and Manufacturing Schedules for Waukesha County, Town of Merton, 1860.

[566]   Photograph courtesy of Debra Woidyla Barham of Clearfield, Utah, e-mail to author, Apr 23, 2010.

[567]   Taken from an article in "Tait's Edinburgh Magazine," c. 1840.

[568]   https://en.wikipedia.org/wiki/Leadville,_Colorado

IMMIGRANTS TO WISCONSIN FROM THE NETHERLANDS

Name: **Albert Veenendall**—Birthplace: **De Bilt, Netherlands** (6 July 1835)—year of immigration: (1846)—Spouse: **Maria Kommers**—Birthplace—**Scoondijke, Zind., Netherlands** (16 Jan 1844) married: <u>Milwaukee, Wisconsin</u> (13 Sep 1865)—residence in 1860—<u>Town of Franklin, Milwaukee, Wiscosnin</u>—In 1873, Albert Veenendall owned a 60—acre <u>Muskego Township farm</u> on the eastern town line at <u>Durham Hill</u>—Occupation: farmer—Children: *Elizabeth, Margaret, Jennie, Magdalena & Isaac*—Albert & <u>Margaret Veenendaal both died at Durham Hill, Muskego Township. Waukesha County & are buried at the</u> **Dutch Reformed Church Cemetery** at Franklin, Milwaukee County. (Image and genealogy courtesy of Elaine Alane of Helenville, Wisconsin.)[569]

Albert Veenendaal holding Eddie Krause (c. 1895)[570]

Dutch emigration:

"The Dutch economy of the 1840s was stagnant and much of the motivation to emigrate was economic rather than political or religious. *There were also political pressures at the time that favored mass emigration of Catholics in the face of the more politically influential Dutch Reformed Chueddalrch in Holland*."[571]

The Dutch Reformed Church:

"The Dutch brought with them to the New World a strong loyalty to the Dutch Reformed Church, which had its roots in the Reformation of the sixteenth century. In 1792, the Dutch Reformed Church in the United States became an independent denomination, the Reformed Protestant Dutch Church. *Doctrinal differences within the newly independent church in North America continued to influence the speed and degree of Dutch assimilation into mainstream American culture*."[572]

DeBilt, Province of Utericht, Holland:

(Albert Veenendall was a member of the Dutch Reformed Church, in De Bilt, Utrecht, Netherlands.) "*Before the demise of the Dutch Republic in 1795, the Dutch Reformed Church enjoyed the status of 'public' or 'privileged' church. Consequently, the Church had close relations with the Dutch government.*"[573]

---

[569] *Federal Manuscript Schedule*, Population, Agricultural and Manufacturing Schedules for Waukesha County, Durham Hill, Town of Muskego, 1870.

[570] Photograph courtesy of Elaine Alane of Helenville, Wisconsin, e-mail to author, Apr 28, 2010

[571] https://en.wikipedia.org/wiki/Dutch_Americans.

[572] http://immigrationtounitedstates.org/468-dutch-immigrants.html

[573] https://en.wikipedia.org/wiki/Dutch_Reformed_Church

IMMIGRANTS TO WISCONSIN FROM VERMONT & NEW YORK

Name: **William Sharp**--Birthplace: **Vermont** (c. 1834) — Spouse—**Katherine**—Birthplace: **New York** — Residence in 1890: Vernon Township, Waukesha County, Wisconsin—Occupation: *farmer*–Children: *Frank, Florence, Rachel & William.*

(Image and genealogy courtesy of Waukesha County Historical Society and Museum.[574]

Katherine Sharpe (c. 1896)[575]

Working a farm in Vernon Township:

"In 1873, *William Sharpe* owned an 80-acre (section 16) Town of Vernon farm. The Sharpe farm was situated within walking distance from Vernon Center where there was located a blacksmith shop, a shoe shop, a general store and the *school*."[576] "Vernon is justly noted for its fine timber, fertile soil, large supply of water-courses, and many curious mounds and embankments. The soil here is lighter, warmer and more arable, being of rather a sandy loam quality, and highly productive where properly cultivated. The first Postmaster was Asa A. Flint, who had the office in his log house, which was long ago demolished, and which stood on the spot where **Mr. William Sharp** now lives."[577]

The Merino sheep craze in Vermont:

"By 1837 there were over one million sheep in Vermont. Changes in tariff laws created economic booms and busts for Merino sheep owners. Wool prices dropped from 57 cents per pound in 1835 to 25 cents per pound in the late 1840s. Vermont sheep farmers were also suffering from competition from farmers out West. *The average annual cost of keeping a sheep in New England was $1.00-2.00 a head, while farmers further west were spending 25 cents a head.* Many Vermont sheep farmers suffered great financial loss during this period and headed west."[578]

Marino Sheep are now grazing on Vernon Township farms:

As Merino sheep breeding became unprofitable in Vermont, many Vermonters moved west to Wisconsin. *A number of those same former Vermont sheep breeders, purchasing grazing land in Vernon Township, Waukesha County, to start new flocks of Merinos.* Like Jesse Smith, another former Vermont sheep breeder, who settled in Vernon Township, now maintaining a flock of over 400 Merinos. William Sharp carried over the same tradition of raising Merinos on his Vernon Township farm.[579]

[574] *Federal Manuscript Schedule*, Population, Agricultural and Manufacturing Schedules for Waukesha County, Town of Vernon, 1890.

[575] Katherine Sharpe photograph c. 1896, People S-T Box, Photography Collection, Research Center Library & Archive, Waukesha County Historical Society & Museum, Waukesha, Wisconsin.

[576] *1873 Atlas of Waukesha County*, Town of Vernon.

[577] Haight, *Memoirs of Waukesha County, 1907*, pp. 790, 792 & 293.

[578] "William Jarvis & the Merino Sheep Craze." vermonthistory.org/educate/online-resources/an-era-of-great-change/work-changing-markets/william-jarvis-s-merino-sheep

[579] *"The History of Waukesha County, 1880.* "Biography of Jesse Smith, Vernon, Township," pp. 1000 & 1001.

IMMIGRANTS TO WISCONSIN FROM WÜRTTEMBERG AND NEW YORK

(1ˢᵗ Generation): **Dr. August Schaeffel's**--birthplace: **Balgheim, Tuttlingen, Württemberg** (c. 1848) –Residence: 1860: <u>Menomonee Township, Waukesha County</u>—occupation: *physician*--Marriage: **Katherine Hengstler**- (27 Apr 1874)—Religious association: *German Evangelical Church, Brookfield, Waukesha, Wisconsin*—Residence: 1880: <u>Brookfield, Waukesha, Wisconsin</u>-- (2ⁿᵈ Generation): **John Schaeffel**– birthplace: **Town of Menomonee, Waukesha, Wisconsin** (2 July 1869) — Marriage: **Mary Orilla Harris** (1896)—Birthplace: **New York** (1879) —Residence in 1910: Ward 1, <u>Waukesha, Waukesha County, Wisconsin</u>— Occupation: (1910) *laborers at motor works*—(1920) *shipping clerk/iron factory*—(1930) *city coroner*—(1940) *janitor*--John & Maria's Children: *Dale, Katherine, John, Charlotte & Emma*—Other residents: *George Cook* (brother-in-law to John Schaeffel)—*Emma (Schaeffel) Cook*—occupation: *laborer.*

(Image and genealogy courtesy of the Williams family of Oconomowoc, Wisconsin and other locations.)[580]

John Schaeffel Family (c. 1897)[581]

(L-R): John R. (father)—Emma (baby), standing—Mary O. Harris (mother), John's sister— Emma, holding her niece—Charlotte.

Balgheim, Tuttlingen Württemberg:

(August Schaeffel's birthplace of <u>Balgheim is a municipality in the district of Tuttlingen, Württemberg, in Germany.</u>)"It was first mentioned in writing in 1113. after which its rule changed often until it became part of Württemberg in 1806."[582] "The town of **Tuttlingen** lies in the valley of the **Upper Danube**."[583]

The German Evangelical Church:

"<u>*The unsuccessful revolutionary movement of 1848 caused many people to emigrate from Württemberg. (The August Schaeffel family was likely one of those families.)*</u> Upon their arrival in Wisconsin, they continued to maintain their association with the **German Evangelical Church**. The *Schaeffel* family began attending Sunday services at the *Zion Evangelical Church of Brookfield* (section 26) after their arrival in <u>Menomonee Township</u> in the 1850s. Like the Schaeffel family, "the congregation was organized entirely by immigrants from Württemberg who settled in Brookfield beginning in 1842. *Jacob Keebler* and *Charles Sheets, Sr.* from Sulzbach on the Murr River, were the first immigrants **Württemberg** to settle in Brookfield."[584] "Trinity United Methodist Church of Milwaukee, indicates that the congregation was organized in 1847 a year in which many Waukesha County churches were being organized, They erected an 18 x 20 log church on what is now Highland Drive north of Watertown Plank Road at what is still the church cemetery in 1848-50, in today's village of Elm Grove."[585]

---

[580]   *Federal Manuscript Schedule*, Population, Agricultural and Manufacturing Schedules for Waukesha County, Town of Menomonee, 1860.

[581]   Photograph courtesy of Sue Ellen Williams of Oconomowoc, Wisconsin, e-mail to author, Jul 8, 2010.

[582]   en.wikipedia.org/wiki/Balgheim

[583]   en.wikipedia.org/wiki/Tuttlingen_(district)

[584]   J.H.A. Lacher, "German Pioneers of Brookfield," *Wisconsin Domesday Book—Town Studies, vol. 1* (Madison: Wisconsin Historical Society, 1924), p. 32.

[585]   Edward C. Wicklein, "Two Churches Named Zion," *Landmark*. v. 20, n. 1 (Spring 1977), pp.10-14.

IMMIGRANTS TO WISCONSIN FROM SAXONY

Name: **Frederick Dunkel**– Birthplace: **Dinkelsbühl, Sachsen** (27 Oct 1812) — Spouse: **Christina Bogel**— Birthplace: **Sachsen** (9 Aug 1813) —Marriage: (circa 1838)—Residence in 1860—**Wauwatosa, Milwaukee County, Wisconsin**—Residence in 1870: Town of Rubicon, Dodge County, Wisconsin--Residence in 1890: **Brookfield Township** (sections 26 &35) **Waukesha County, Wisconsin**— Occupation: *farmer*--Children: *Henrich, Carl, William & Herman.* (Image and genealogy courtesy of Elmbrook Historical Society.)[586]

Christina Dunkel(c. 1898)[587]

Dates to Medieval times:

Dinkelsbühl (The birthplace of Frederick Dunkel) is an historic city in Central Franconia. "Franconia (as discussed earlier) is a region in Germany, characterized by its culture and language, and may be roughly associated with the areas in which the East Franconian dialect group, locally referred to as fränkisch,[588] is spoken in a region of Germany that is now part of the state of Bavaria, in southern Germany." [589]

Expansion of the Prussian Empire:

"At the Battle of Leipzig (16–18 October 1813), when Napoleon was completely defeated, the greater part of the Saxon troops deserted to the allied forces. The King of Saxony was taken as a Prussian prisoner to the Castle of Friedrichsfeld near Berlin. —The Congress of Vienna (1814–15) took from Saxony the greater part of its land and gave it to Prussia. (Both Frederick Dunkel and Christina Boyd were born just before Saxony's takeover by Prussia). In the War of 1866, when Prussia was successful, the independence of *Saxony was once more in danger*, only the intervention of the Austrian Emperor saved Saxony from being entirely absorbed by Prussia. (In various census, *Frederick Dunkel* and *Christina Boyd* are listed as born in Saxony while others give their locations of birth as Prussia.) It was this relentless diminishing of Saxony's territory which caused many Saxons to emigrate (1840s-1860s.)"[590]

---

[586] *Federal Manuscript Schedule*, Population, Agricultural and Manufacturing Schedules for Waukesha County, Town of Brookfield, 1890.

[587] Photograph courtesy of the Elmbrook Historical Society.

[588] "The West Germanic languages and dialects are known as Franconian languages , which were spoken by the Franks at the time their ethnogenesis of the Frankish Empire (5th 9th century). The large spreading area of Franconian dialects shows the importance of Bavaria in Germany for the formation of a common German language. The medieval German State emerged under the rule of the Franks, firm - and balancing languages between the different tribal territories were created." From: https://de.wikipedia.org/wiki/Fr%C3%A4nkische_Sprachen

[589] https://en.wikipedia.org/wiki/Franconia

[590] https://en.wikipedia.org/wiki/History_of_Saxony

BASEBALL

The 1870s were prolific years for baseball in Wisconsin. By the late 1870s, most Wisconsin towns had organized at least one club. Waukesha County boys, too, were enthralled with the game. *Their enthusiasm remained strong despite occasional lopsided and demoralizing losses to much stronger teams from* **Milwaukee** *and* **Waukesha**."[591] "Newspaper accounts not only reported on the popularity of town baseball clubs but also reported on youth baseball teams established before the turn of the 19th century in Southeastern Wisconsin."[592]

(Image courtesy of Craig Black of Brookfield, Wisconsin)

Elm Grove Youth Baseball (c. 1898)[593]

BASE BALL AND QUOIT CLUB. —A movement is on foot to organize a *Base Ball* and *Quoit Club*,[594] and to set apart a convenient spot on the route of the Horse Rail for the use of the party to have two games a week. [*Milwaukee Sentinel* June 9, 1862]

WAUKESHA.

In a game of baseball Saturday between the (Waukesha) village boys and a Brookfield club, the former succeeded in scoring **66** to the latter's **9**. [*Waukesha Freeman* May 9,1877]

Brookfield.

This town has the baseball fever bad. It can now boast no less than four clubs, either one of which will, in a short time, be prepared to play for the championship of the United States that of Brookfield. It matters but little which. [*Waukesha Freeman* June 28, 1877]

Baseball. --The Clippers, a *juvenile baseball club* of this town [Milwaukee], will engage in combat with the *Brookfield Muffers*[595] on Thursday.

[*Milwaukee Sentinel* Aug. 6, 1877]

MILWAUKEE CLUB NEAR THE END OF THE RACE FOR THE PENNANT.

Milwaukee's season of baseball will wind up with the three St. Paul games. The first of which will be played tomorrow. These games are the last of the season.
[Milwaukee Daily Journal Sept. 19, 1887]

---

591 Author, *Brookfield: A Fine and Fertile Land vol. 1*, footnote, p. 159.

592 Quote from, Martin "Marty" Perkins, during author visit at "Old World Wisconsin," 15 June 2008.

593 Photograph courtesy of Craig Black of Brookfield, Wisconsin, e-mail to author, Jul 19, 2011.

594 "Quoits (koits, kwoits, kwaits) is a traditional game which involves the throwing of metal, rope or rubber rings over a set distance, usually to land over or near a spike (sometimes called a hob, mott or pin)." From: https://en.wikipedia.org/wiki/Quoits

595 The Milwaukee boys were apparently having some fun with our Brookfield boys by referring to them as MUFFERS. In a definition submitted by David Wachsman - 30/08/2012, to Collins Dictionary, a muffer is: "One who muffs a ball, who fails to hold on a ball when attempting a catch. One that does something stupidly or clumsily."

IMMIGRANTS TO WISCONSIN FROM PRUSSIA

Father: **Wilhelm Gottlieb Bartz**—born: (1 Apr 1832)--Place of birth: <u>**Ruedke, Provence of Pösen, Preußen**</u>— Spouse: <u>**Augusta Brandt**</u>—born (29 Sep 1843) <u>**Preußen**</u>—Emigrated--from <u>**Stettin, Pomerania**</u> (on the Oder River)-- ship: *"Franklin"*—arrived at New York (21 Apr 1873)—Residence: (1880) <u>Pewaukee Township, Waukesha County</u>—Occupation: *farmer*--Children: *Minnie, Emily Bertha, Julius, Auguste Mathilde & Herman.*
(Image and genealogy courtesy of Jan Pace of Waukesha, Wisconsin.)[596]

Augusta (Bartz) & August Gehrt Wedding, (March 11, 1899)[597]

Served in the Franco-Prussian War:

"Wilhelm Gottlieb Bartz along with his wife, *Augusta* came to America in 1873 and located in Milwaukee. Before his immigration he was a soldier in the German army and took part in the Franco-Prussian war of 1870. After living in Milwaukee, a year, the family moved to Wauwatosa township, where the *Gottlieb* bought 24 acres of land, working at the same time in a lime-kiln. After four years they removed to Pewaukee township."[598]

Pösen became part of the newly unified Germany in 1871:

(The Wilhelm Gottlieb Bartz family resided in Ruedke, Provence of Pösen, well within the Polish region of Prussia.) "Among the German-speaking population of the province as well as in the Prussian capital, anti-Polish sentiments arose. While the local Pösen Parliament voted 26 to 17 votes against joining German Confederation, on 3 April 1848, the Frankfurt Parliament ignored the vote, forcing status change to a common Prussian province and its integration in the German Confederation."[599]

Poles faced discrimination at the hands of the "German Confederation":

"The Province of Pösen became part of the German Empire. *Bismarck's hostility towards the Poles was already well known, as in 1861 had written in a letter to his sister:* "Hit the Poles so hard that they despair of their life; I have full sympathy for their condition, but if we want to survive, we can only exterminate them." Poles suffered from discrimination by the Prussian state; numerous oppressive measures were implemented to eradicate the Polish community's identity and culture. The Polish inhabitants of Pösen, who faced discrimination and even forced Germanization, favored the French side during the Franco-Prussian War. France and Napoleon III were known for their support and *sympathy for the Poles under Prussian rule.* Demonstrations at news of Prussian-German victories manifested Polish independence feelings and calls were also made for *Polish recruits to desert from the Prussian Army.* Failure to secure independence from the newly unified Germany in 1871, many Poles from the province of Pösen chose to emigrate."[600]

---

[596] *Federal Manuscript Schedule*, Population, Agricultural and Manufacturing Schedules for Waukesha County, Town of Pewaukee, 1880.

[597] Photograph courtesy of Jan Pace of Waukesha, Wisconsin, e-mail to author, Feb. 9, 2016.

[598] Haight, *Memoirs of Waukesha County, 1907*, p. 357.

[599] https://en.wikipedia.org/wiki/Province_of_Posen

[600] https://en.wikipedia.org/wiki/Province_of_Posen

IMMIGRANTS TO WISCONSIN FROM POMERANIA, PRUSSIA

(1st Generation): Name: **Frederick Schrubbe**– Birthplace: **Pommern, Preußen** (3 Jan 1835)—Spouse: **Johanna (Hanna) Harp**—Birthplace: **Ramelow, Pommern, Preußen**. (23 May 1842)—year of immigration: (1864) –Marriage of Frederick & Joanna: (1865) -- Residence in 1870: Milwaukee Ward 9, Milwaukee, Wisconsin —Frederick's Occupation: *laborer*--Children: *Henry, Frank, Ernest, Anna &* ***Albert.*** (1910)--Residence: Wauwatosa, Milwaukee, Wisconsin--*Frederick* (age: 75) & *Johanna's* (age: 68) -- Occupation: *General Farming*--Frederick Schrubbe's death--11 Sep 1912. (2nd Generation): **Albert** (born: 1867) & **Christina (Pegler) Schrubbe**—Marriage: Milwaukee, Wisconsin (13 Jan 1900)—Albert's death--circa: (1914-1919)--Occupation: *general farming*--(1920) Residence: Elm Grove, Brookfield Township, Waukesha County (section 24)—**Christina Schrubbe**— Occupation: *farmer*: including--94 acres--4 horses—9 cattle—Bell Telephone Service-- Children: *Erna, Albert Jr. & Otto.* Also resides in the household *Hattie Ohm, a nurse.* [601]

(Image and genealogy courtesy of Betty Ann Kramer of Clovis, California.)[602]

Albert & Christiana (Pegler) Schrubbe's Wedding—Jan. 13, 1900 [603]

Emigration from Pomerania:

"Pomerania is a historical region on the southern shore of the Baltic Sea in Central Europe, split between Germany and Poland. The name derives from the Slavic 'po' more, meaning *'by the sea'*."[604] " "There were laws starting in 1730 *prohibiting emigration* without permission. In 1827, families looking for land moved from Kreis east into West Prussia and Posen. *Between 1844 and 1871 an estimated 91,279 people emigrated from Pomerania, with many going to the United States.* The Old Lutheran emigration lasted from 1835 to 1854. The largest number of these came from Pomerania, with 2,567 going to America."[605]

"The Farmhouse at Elm Grove":

"The house was infected with bedbugs and (Christi-) Anna had a problem *ridding the house of the bugs. She used kerosene to paint the walls, floors and furniture, and finally succeeded. There was a cornfield surrounding the house and Anna was kept quite busy watching the twins, so they would not get lost; and as there were many grass snakes, Anna feared for the twins.* While working the land, the family found many arrowheads, and a large 1868 penny."[606]

---

[601] *The Farm Journal Illustrated Rural Directory of Waukesha County 1918-1923*, p. 142.

[602] *Federal Manuscript Schedule*, Population, Agricultural and Manufacturing Schedules for Waukesha County, Town of Brookfield, 1920.

[603] Photograph courtesy of Betty Ann Kramer of Clovis, California, e-mail to author, Jul 27, 2011.

[604] "Pomerania" https://en.wikipedia.org/wiki/Pomerania

[605] "Emigration from Pomerania," https://en.wikipedia.org/wiki/Pomerania

[606] Betty Ann Kramer of Clovis, California, e-mail to author, Jul 27, 2011.

IMMIGRANTS TO WISCONSIN FROM PRUSSIA

(First Generation): Name: **Nicholas Bettendorf**—Birthplace: **Niedermenning, Rheinland, Preußen** (9 Oct 1812)—Spouse: **Catherine Thielen**—Birthplace: **Preußen** (July 1830)—Year of Immigration: 1852—Residence in 1860: New Berlin Township, Waukesha County, Wisconsin— Occupation: *farmer*–1860 census records: "Nicholas Battendorf… 40 yr. *farmer*, born in **Prussia**, "can't read or write"--Children: *Henry, Eva, **Frank**, Peter, Margaret, Susanna, Nicholas, Katharine & Margaret.*—In 1873, Nicholas Bettendorf owned a 40 acre (section 33) New Berlin farm on the New Berlin/ Muskego town line. Nicholas Bettendorf 's death: New Berlin (18 May 1890)—Burial: ***Holy Apostles Cemetery***, New Berlin, Waukesha, Wisconsin--(Second Generation): Name: **Frank Berst** (born: 1848)—wife **Margaret Bettendorf** (born: 1862)—married: (1882)—Frank & Margaret Berst headed west to **Nebraska** in hopes of finding new farmland--Residence (1900): **Logan & Spring Creek Precincts, Howard County, Nebraska** --Occupation: *farmer*—Children: *Anna, Joseph, Mary, Margaret, Laura, Lotte, Frank & Charlie.* (Image and genealogy courtesy of Jessica Schmus of Oak Creek, Wisconsin.)[607]

Frank Berst Family (c. 1900)[608]

(L-R):Frank, Mary, Margaret, Loretta, Frank, Charlie (the baby), Margaret (Bettendorf) Berst (mother), and Lottie. This photograph was taken after the Bettendorf family had moved from New Berlin, Wisconsin to St. Paul, Howard County, Nebraska.[609]

The Rhineland:

"A 'Rhineland' conceptualization did not evolve until the 19th century after the War of the First Coalition, when a short-lived Republic was established on territory conquered by French troops. The term covered the whole occupied zone west of the Rhine. After the collapse of the French dominated West Bank in the early 19th century, the regions of Lower Rhine were annexed to the Kingdom of Prussia. In 1822 the Prussian administration reorganized the territory as the Rhine Province. (also known as Rhenish Prussia). [610]

The Bettendorf family of Neidermenning:

(Niedermenning, the birthplace of Nicholas Bettendorf is located near the western border of Rheinland with Alsace-Lorraine, then controlled by France.) "France took direct control of the Rhineland and radically and permanently liberalized the government, society and economy. The Coalition of France's enemies made repeated efforts to retake the region, but France repelled all the attempts. The population was about 1.6 million in numerous small states. The most important impact came from the abolition of all feudal privileges and historic taxes."[611]

---

[607]   *Federal Manuscript Schedule*, Population, Agricultural and Manufacturing Schedules for Waukesha County, Town of New Berlin, 1860. *Federal Manuscript Schedule*, Population, Agricultural and Manufacturing Schedules for Spring Creek Precincts, Howard County, Nebraska, 1900.

[608]   Photograph courtesy of Jessica Schmus of Oak Creek, Wisconsin, e-mail to author on Apr 24, 2010.

[609]   Jessica Schmus of Oak Creek, Wisconsin, e-mail to author on Apr 24, 2010.

[610]   https://en.wikipedia.org/wiki/Rhine_Province

[611]   https://en.wikipedia.org/wiki/Rhineland

IMMIGRANTS TO WISCONSIN FROM HESSE

Name: **John Best**—Birthplace: **Großherzogtum, Hessen** (1863)—Year of Immigration: 1867— Spouse: **Elizabeth Katherine Schmidt**--Residence in 1880: Summit Township, Waukesha County, Wisconsin— Occupation: *farmer*–Children: **Elva Marie, Irene,** *Arthur, Norman & Eleanor.* In 1918, John & Elizabeth Best resided in Summit Township—*Occupation: poultry man* in the Village of Dousman, town of Ottawa, Waukesha County.[612]
(Image and genealogy courtesy of Fred C. Smyth of Whidbey Island, Washington.)[613]

Best children (c. 1900)[614]

(L-R): Irene, Elva, Arthur, and Norman

Dutchy of Hesse:

"During the Austro-Prussian War of 1866, the greater territories of Hesse had supported the defeated Austrian monarchy and had consequently lost large regions to the victorious Prussians. In 1867, the northern half of the Grand Duchy *Hessen-Darmstadt* (Upper Hesse) became a part of the "North German Confederation," while the half of the Grand Duchy south of the Main Starkenburg and Rhenish Hesse remained outside."[615] The continued expansion of the Prussian empire, along with the breakup of the Grand Duchy likely sparked the Best family's decision to immigrate to Wisconsin in 1867.

Town of Summit. --One study belonging to **Irene Best** was lost in some unaccountable way, although she passed along with Ethel Kelley, Lone Waite, **Elva Best**, Lulu Quintus and Frank McGovern.
[*Waukesha Freeman* May 21, 1908]

A Poultry Farmers Practical Guide, 1911:

"This little book is intended to help farmers and villagers conduct the poultry business with pleasure and profit. Few people have an adequate idea of the importance of the poultry business in this country. It is estimated that there are in the United States over three hundred million chickens. There are produced in one year nearly one billion dozen eggs of an average worth of ten cents per dozen, making the annual value of the total egg product one hundred million dollars. If in addition to this the yearly product of poultry meat is considered, the importance of this branch of rural economy will be more fully appreciated."[616]

[612] *The Farm Journal Illustrated Rural Directory of Waukesha County 1918-1923*, p. 27.
[613] *Federal Manuscript Schedule*, Population, Agricultural and Manufacturing Schedules for Waukesha County, Town of Summit, 1880.
[614] Photograph courtesy of Fred C. Smyth of Whidbey Island, Washington, e-mail to author, Apr 25, 2010.
[615] en.wikipedia.org/wiki/Grand_Duchy_of_Hesse
[616] Jacob Biggle, *Biggle Poultry Book: A Concise and Practical Treatise on the Management of Farm Poultry*, (Wilmer Atkinson Co., Philadelphia, 1911. 8th Edition), p. 8 & 9.

IMMIGRANTS TO WISCONSIN FROM PRUSSIA

2 Related Families: (1ˢᵗ. Generation):--Name: **Charles (Carl) Behrend**-- (age: 36) -- Görlitz, Brandenburg Province, Preußen— Spouse: **Minnie**-- Age: (age: 36)—Birthplace: **Preußen**--Residence in 1880—City of Oconomowoc, Waukesha County, Wisconsin—Occupation: *farmer*—Children: *Herman*—(age: 12) (born in Preußen), *Annie*—(age: 9) (born in Preußen), *Paul*—(age: 8), *Charles*—(age: 7), *Louis*—(age: 5), *Ida*—(age: 3), & *George*—(age: 1). (2ⁿᵈ. Generation): Name: **Charles Behrend**— Residence in 1900--City of Oconomowoc, Waukesha County, Wisconsin--Birthplace: **City of Oconomowoc, Waukesha County, Wisconsin**—age: (28)— Spouse: **Emma**--Birthplace: **Wisconsin** (Oct 1875—age: (24) -- Marriage: (circa 1898)——Charles' Occupation: *tailor*--Children: *Ida Holbrook* (step-daughter)—(age: 6), *Grace* (age: 2) & *Leone* (age 7/12). (*the 2ⁿᵈ Related Family*):--Name: — **Carl F. Meuler**–Birthplace: **"Germany"** (Oct 1868)—Year of immigration: (1887)---ship: *"Main"*—arrival: Baltimore, Maryland--Spouse: **Anna Behrend**–(Anna is the daughter of Carl & Minnie Behrend)—Minnie's occupation: *dressmaker* -- Birthplace: **Görlitz, Brandenburg Province, Preußen, "Germany"** — married: (circa 1892)---Residence in 1900—*Carl* (age: 32) & *Anna* (age: 29) *Mueler's* residence:--Oconomowoc Township, Waukesha County, Wisconsin—Occupation: *foreman at resort*–Children: *Arthur & Dorothy*.
(Image and genealogy courtesy of Jonathan Brumfield of Huntsville, Alabama)[617]

Behrend Sisters (c. 1900)[618]

Demonstrating seamstress skills:

Seamstress workers (several are Behrend sisters) demonstrate their skills at a photography studio. They likely work out of the home of Charles Behrend who is a tailor in Oconomowoc. Such homebased "tailor shops" were not unusual in Wisconsin during the late-1800's.[619]

A family from Brandenburg:

"Before immigrating to Wisconsin during the 1870s, the (Carl) Behrend family resided in Görlitz, an historical region in northeastern Germany a municipality in the far north of the district Uckermark in Brandenburg."[620] "Though Prussia continued its expansionist policies into neighboring German states during the 19ᵗʰ century, many young men from the Province of Brandenburg, in Prussia, became tired of the continues fighting causing many families from the province to emigrate in lieu of war. The 6ᵗʰ Division of the Prussian army, itself, was recruited in the Province of Brandenburg."[621]

Oconomowoc. --Charles F. Behrend of this city has recently been granted a patent for a garment folder and has already received several very good offers from Eastern parties for the right to manufacture the same. He is a son of Carl Behrend, an old resident of this place.
[*Waukesha Freeman* March 5, 1896]

---

[617] *Federal Manuscript Schedule*, Population, Agricultural and Manufacturing Schedules for Waukesha County, Town of Oconomowoc, 1880.

[618] Photograph courtesy of Jonathan Brumfield of Huntsville, Alabama, via Dorothy Meuler, e-mail to author, Aug 24, 2010.

[619] *Federal Manuscript Schedule*, Population, Agricultural and Manufacturing Schedules for Waukesha County, City of Oconomowoc, 1900.

[620] https://en.wikipedia.org/wiki/Göritz.

[621] https://en.wikipedia.org/wiki/6th_Division_(German_Empire)

IMMIGRANTS TO WISCONSIN FROM PENNSYLVANIA AND VERMONT

Name: **Dr. Caleb C. Harris**– Birthplace: **Erie County, Pennsylvania** (22 Sept 1834) — Spouse: **Josephine E. (Chubb)** —Birthplace— **Windsor, Vermont** (23 Nov 1833)—Marriage date: (11 Feb. 1869)--Residence in 1880: Ottawa Township, Waukesha County, Wisconsin—Occupation: *physician*–Children: *Bertram, Silas, Helen & Winnifred.*—in 1891, Dr. Harris ran a 200-acre Town of Ottawa (section 14) dairy farm near the town hall at the center of the town.[622]

(Image and genealogy courtesy of Waukesha County Historical Society and Museum.)[623]

Dr. Caleb C. Harris (c. 1900)[624]

A practicing physician in Ottawa Township:

"Caleb C. Harris, M.D., has been a practicing physician and surgeon in this county for twenty-seven years, and is therefore well known to its citizens. In 1867 he came to Ottawa Township, and about two years later located on the farm where he now lives. The Doctor gives considerable attention to the dairy business, having a fine herd of thoroughbred Holstein cows, the only one in the township. In 1878 he attended the Chicago Eclectic Medical College, from which he received a diploma. At the same time, he pursued a special course of study on the eye and ear in the Chicago School of Ophthalmology, and Otology from which he also has a diploma. He is a member of the State Eclectic Medical Society, [625] and among his professional brethren is recognized as a practitioner of great skill and ability."[626]

In Wisconsin, 19th Century "Eclectic" physicians learned useful in medicinal treatments from local Native tribes:

OJIBWE MEDICINAL PLANTS—"*The Flambeau Ojibwe* boil the bark of the red maple to obtain a tea with which to wash and cure sore eyes. *Winterberry* has been employed by eclectic practitioners as a tonic and astringent. Flambeau Ojibwe used all parts of the *Smooth Sumac* are suitable for medicine, *the root bark, trunk bark, twig bark, leaves, flowers and fruit. Indian Turnip*--Small doses of the partially dried root have been used by the white man in the treatment of chronic bronchitis, asthma, flatulent colic and rheumatism, certainly widely different maladies. The Ojibwe are probably the best informed and the *strictest observers of the medicine lodge ceremonies* in the country. *Their knowledge of plants both in their own environment and far away is probably the best of any group of Indians.* There is an agreement in names of Lac du Flambeau and Leech Lake Ojibwe, that well checks information received. Much of the knowledge of white men originated from studying the Indian plant uses, in the early days. Eclectic practitioners sought the Indian *herbs* and observed what parts of the plant were used."[627]

622 *Plat Book of Waukesha County Wisconsin,* Minneapolis: C.M. Foote & Co., 1891, Town of Ottawa.

623 *Federal Manuscript Schedule,* Population, Agricultural and Manufacturing Schedules for Waukesha County, Town of Ottawa, 1880.

624 Dr. Caleb C. Harris photograph c. 1900, People F-G-H Box, Photography Collection, Research Center Library & Archive, Waukesha County Historical Society & Museum, Waukesha, Wisconsin.

625 "Eclectic medicine was a branch of American medicine which made use of botanical remedies along with other substances and physical therapy practices, popular in the latter half of the 19th and first half of the 20th centuries." From: https://en.wikipedia.org/wiki/Eclectic_medicine

626 *Portrait and Biographical Record of Waukesha County, Wisconsin,* 1894, pp. 319 & 320.

627 Huron H. Smith, "Ethnobiology of the Ojibwe Indians," *Bulletin of the Milwaukee Public Museum of the City of Milwaukee* (Milwaukee: Aetna Press, vol. 4, no. 3, May 2, 1932), pp. 348, 353-358.

IMMIGRANTS TO WISCONSIN FROM PRUSSIA

Name: **Carl F. Meuler**–Birthplace: **"Germany"** (1868)-- Spouse: ***Anna Behrend***—Birthplace: **Göritz, Brandenburg Province, Preußen** (1871)——Residence in 1900: <u>Oconomowoc Township, Waukesha County</u>—Occupation: farmer–Children: *Arthur,* ***Ida*** *& Dorothy*——Anna's occupation: *dressmaker.* Anna's death: (age 32) in 1903.—her husband, *Carl,* remarried.　　　Image and genealogy courtesy of Dorothy Meuler of Oconomowoc, Wisconsin)

Daughter & Mother: Ida and Anna (Behrend) Meuler (c. 1900)[628]

The Village of Göritz:

The small village of Göritz (the birthplace of Anna Behrend) was first mentioned in 1503 under the name Goricz documentary. <u>At the Congress of Vienna in 1815, after the defeat of the Kingdom of Saxony, territorial cessions were passed to the Kingdom of Prussia, which also affected Göritz.</u>"[629]

The Prussian Province of Brandenburg:

<u>Göritz was located in the Province of Brandenburg when it was established in 1815 within the Kingdom of Prussia.</u> In contrast, the rural outer regions, though *serfdom* had been officially abolished by the 1807. <u>Prussian reforms were still characterized by large–scale land holding of the Junker nobility</u>.[630]. The conditions in the countryside remained largely untouched, even during the Revolutions of 1848 that led to violent fights in the streets of Berlin. Though the large estates now had to deal with low soil quality and the lack of natural resources.[631]

<u>Anna (Behrend) Meuler was employed as a seamstress in her husbands' "tailor" shop:</u>

"<u>By the 1850s, **Isaac Singer** developed the first sewing machines that could operate quickly and accurately and surpass the productivity of a seamstress or tailor sewing by hand</u>. While much clothing was still produced at home by female members of the family, more and more ready-made clothes for the middle classes were being produced with sewing machines. (Anna Behrend, by 1900, as a *dressmaker,* most likely had her own sewing machine to work on her sewing patterns)"[632]

---

[628]　Photograph courtesy of Dorothy Mueler, via Jonathan Brumfield of Huntsville, Alabama, e-mail to author, Aug. 24, 2010.

[629]　https://en.wikipedia.org/wiki/Göritz

[630]　"The Junkers were members of the landed nobility in Prussia. They owned great estates that were maintained and worked by peasants with few rights. These estates often stood in the countryside outside of major cities or towns. They were an important factor in Prussia and, after 1871, in German military, political and diplomatic leadership." from: https://en.wikipedia.org/wiki/Junker_(Prussia)

[631]　https://en.wikipedia.org/wiki/Province_of_Brandenburg

[632]　https://en.wikipedia.org/wiki/Sewing

IMMIGRANTS TO WISCONSIN FROM BAVARIA

Name: *Herman Grundmann*– Birthplace: **"Germany"** (16 Oct 1866) — Spouse: **Amelia Badziong** — Birthplace— **Gatlinburg, Bayern** (c. 1866)—Year of immigration: 1891—Immigrant Ship: *"Friesland"*— Port of Departure: Antwerp, Belgium—Port of Arrival: New York—Residence in 1895: Pewaukee Township, Waukesha County, Wisconsin—Herman Grundmann's (age: 53) --Occupation: *home carpenter*–Children: *Karl, Herman, Anna, Emma, Helen, Rose, Paul, Walter & Richard.* –Residence—1900: Waukesha Ward 2, Waukesha, Wisconsin. (Image and genealogy courtesy of Erica Crom of Rantoul, Illinois)[633]

Herman Grundmann Family (c. 1901)[634]

L-R): Anna, Emilia (mother), Rose, Carl, Anna, Herman (father) & Ann

Southern Europeans:

"After 1880 larger steam-powered oceangoing ships replaced sailing ships, which resulted in lower fares and greater immigrant mobility. Meanwhile, farming improvements in Southern Europe created surplus labor. Young people between the ages of 15 to 30 were predominant among newcomers. *This wave of migration may be better referred to as a flood of immigrants, as nearly 25 million Europeans made the long trip*."[635]

A building boom in the city of Waukesha:

Herman Grundman may have used his carpentry skills in the building of Victorian style homes in the city of Waukesha, during which may have been the city's most exciting home construction era. "Victorian architecture generally describes styles that were most popular between 1860 and 1900. Though Victorian architecture is generally considered to have ended in about 1900, various forms of Victorian construction continued in the United States through at least the first decade of the 20th Century. A list of these styles most commonly includes *Second Empire* (1855–85), *Stick-Eastlake* (1860–ca. 1890), *Folk Victorian* (1870-1910), *Queen Anne* (1880–1910), *Richardsonian Romanesque* (1880–1900), and *Shingle* (1880–1900)." *In the city of Waukesha, perhaps the best-preserved collection of Victorian-era architecture existing today, include homes standing in the Carroll University neighborhood, particularly along College Avenue.*[636]

Waukesha.

Mr. and Mrs. Paul Badziong of Erfurt, Bavaria, Germany, arrived in this city Thursday to make their home. They are now guests of their relatives, Mr. and Mrs. **Herman Grundman**. [*Waukesha Freeman* May 8, 1913]

633 Federal Manuscript Schedule, Population, Agricultural and Manufacturing Schedules Waukesha County, City of Waukesha, 1900.

634 Photograph courtesy of Erica Crom, of Rantoul, Illinois, e-mail to author, Oct 26, 2010.

635 https://en.wikipedia.org/wiki/European_emigration

636 https://en.wikipedia.org/wiki/Victorian_architecture

Immigrants to Wisconsin from Bavaria

Name: **Franz Schäfer**–Birthplace: **Oppau, Bayern, Germany** (15 April 1817) –Spouse: *Katharine Fuhr*—Birthplace: **Bayern** (26 October 1823) –Residence located near the River Rhine, Bayerische Pfalz, Germany—Married at: **Speyer, Bayern** on the River Rhine (16 July 1846) year of immigration: (1847)—Port of departure: Le Havre, France—spent thirty-two days on the ocean—Arrival: Port of New York--Residence in 1850: <u>Muskego Township (section 13), Waukesha County, Wisconsin</u>—Occupation: *farmer*—in 1873 Franz Schäfer owns a (63 acre) town of Muskego farm bordering the northern tip of Big Muskego Lake[637]--Children: *9 births/6 survived to adulthood--Henry, Adam, Elizabeth, Magdalena, John & Frank.*[638]

(Image and genealogy courtesy of Waukesha County Historical Society and Museum.)[639]

Katherina Fuhr (c. 1901)[640]

Speyer, Bayern:

Speyer (the town in which Franz & Katharine were married.) is a town in the Rhineland-Palatinate, Germany, located beside the river Rhine. Founded by the Romans, it is one of Germany's oldest cities. Speyer is dominated by the Speyer Cathedral, a number of churches and the Altpörtel (old gate). The city is famous for the 1529 Protestation at Speyer. Speyer was eventually annexed to Bavaria. In 1816, Speyer becomes the seat of administration of the Palatinate and of the government of the Rhine District of Bavaria (later called the Bavarian Palatinate). *Devastating economic situation caused large Palatine emigration during the 19th century, especially to North America.*"[641]

An undaunted persistence:

The Franz Schäfer family were among the earliest German immigrant families to settle in the town of Muskego during the 1850s. Beginning a Wisconsin farmstead, during this period, took enormous effort and perhaps even greater good fortune. Wisconsin historian, Robert Gard wrote, "Wisconsin immigrant farmers had religion faith, and awareness that they were engaged in hazardous occupation, for who could predict what a year would bring, what disasters upon crops from weather or insects, or what sickness might befall. 'NEXT YEAR' was the term they understood, for next year would be, must be, better, with more land under plow, with more confidence, with more faith, and the optimistic expectation of a bumper crop. <u>In the early days Wisconsin was the greatest 'next year country on earth!</u>"[642]

---

[637] *Atlas of Waukesha County, Wisconsin, 1873.* Town of Muskego.

[638] *Portrait and Biographical Record of Waukesha County, 1894,* p. 848.

[639] *Federal Manuscript Schedule,* Population, Agricultural and Manufacturing Schedules Waukesha County, Town of Muskego, 1850.

[640] Katharina Fuhr photograph (c. 1901), People F-G-H Box, Photography Collection, Research Center Library & Archive, Waukesha County Historical Society & Museum, Waukesha, Wisconsin.

[641] https://en.wikipedia.org/wiki/Speyer

[642] Robert & Milo Gard, *My Land, My Home, My Wisconsin, 1978,* p. 29.

IMMIGRANTS TO WISCONSIN FROM IRELAND

Name: **William Caldwell**–year of immigration (1835) at age (22)--Spouse: **Johanna (Cronin)**-Birthplace: **Ireland**—William & Johanna emigrated separately—they met & were married in New Haven, Connecticut— they moved west to Pewaukee, Waukesha County (1843)—occupation: *farmer*—Children: *John, Alexander & Margaret.*—with William's passing in 1868, son **Alexander** took over the farm & owned 2 separate 53.35 acre Pewaukee Township (section 4) parcels in 1873[643]—daughter, *Margaret Caldwell's* residence in 1900: Waukesha, Waukesha County, Wisconsin—Occupation: *physician*–household servant: *Carrie Gilbertson*— Birthplace: Norway. (Image and genealogy courtesy of Waukesha County Historical Society and Museum.)[644]

Dr. Margaret Caldwell (c. 1902)[645]

Waukesha's First female physician:

"Women studying to become physicians was almost unheard of in the 1870's. Yet, despite all odds, William & Johanna Caldwell's daughter, Margaret, was determined to pursue a career practicing medicine. In the early 1870s, Margaret enrolled and was accepted into the **Woman's Hospital Medical College of Chicago**. The Woman's Hospital Medical College of Chicago was founded in 1870 in order to provide equal education opportunities for female medical students. *(conti. below)*

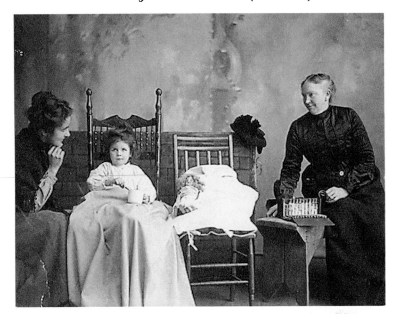

Not allowed to serve on staff:

"Many of her first patients were wives, widows, and children of Union soldiers. Because only one of Chicago's two existing hospitals admitted women patients, and neither allowed women to serve on staff, Dr. Mary Thompson founded the Chicago Hospital for Women and Children in 1865, serving as its head physician and surgeon. During its first year, there were 17 matriculates, and the session was considered a real success."[646] Completing her training, "Dr. Margaret Caldwell was a well-known doctor in Waukesha County at the turn of the nineteenth century. She graduated from the Chicago's Women's Medical College in 1876. She was physician to Bethesda Spring's Summer House. Dr. Caldwell was well respected and much liked by patients throughout her many years in practice. She was a popular physician and has a large practice. As a country doctor in a pioneer town, Dr. Margaret Caldwell (1846-1938) was an important part of life in Waukesha."[647]

[643]   *Atlas of Waukesha County, Wisconsin, 1873*, Town of Pewaukee.

[644]   *Federal Manuscript Schedule*, Population, Agricultural and Manufacturing Schedules Waukesha County, Town of Pewaukee, 1870.

[645]   Dr. Margaret Caldwell photograph (c. 1902), People C-D-E Box, Photography Collection, Research Center Library & Archive, Waukesha County Historical Society & Museum, Waukesha, Wisconsin.

[646]   Courtesy of Philadelphia Digitized material of Medicine, Legacy Center of Medicine, Legacy Center, Archives and Special Collections on Women in Medicine and Homeopathy. Chicago Women's Medical College/Northwestern University Women's Medical School Records, (1870-1924).

[647]   Haight, *Memoirs of Waukesha County. Chicago, Western Historical Association, 1907*, p. 386

IMMIGRANTS TO WISCONSIN FROM NEW YORK

Name: <u>William M. Frazier</u>– Birthplace: <u>Homer, New York</u> (Sept 1816) — Spouse: <u>**Martha (Thompson)**</u> — Birthplace: <u>**Lodi Plains, New York**</u> (c. 1826) —Occupation: *farmer* --In 1873: William Frazier owns a 480-acre (sections 24 & 25) <u>Mukwonago Township, farm</u>.[648] The **Fox River** runs through his large farm. His acreage borders <u>Vernon Township</u> on its east.– Children: *Martha & Lillian.*

(Image and genealogy courtesy of Waukesha County Historical Society and Museum.)[649]

William Melvin Frazier (c. 1902)[650]

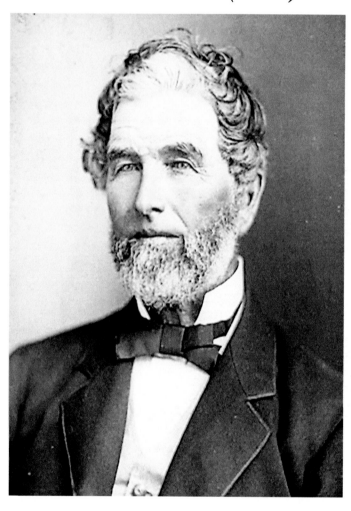

An energetic and successful farmer:

"William Frazier, of Scotch ancestry, settled on his farm of over 500 acres in Mukwonago Township, June 1845. <u>In early days he saw the Janesville and Milwaukee road thronged with teams loaded with wheat passing his farm to market.</u> His many farm structures include a log house, built forty-four years ago, later he built his present frame farm house, which was replaced in 1858; his first barn, built with a basement, was 30x40 ft., and since, he has built two sheep barns, one 20x120 ft. and one 18x36 ft., into which he maintains a large flock of sheep, a horse barn 24x48 ft., a corn house 18x24 ft., a tool-house 16x40 ft., a granary and a colt stable. Mr. Frazier was always open to new and improved farm technology as they came on the market."[651]

A GREAT DAYS WORK.--Thursday last week was one of the busiest days ever known in our city [Milwaukee]. <u>From early morning till late in the evening the streets where crowded with wheat teams.</u> The actual receipts at the different mills and warehouses were 20,980 bushels. Allowing 40 bushels to load, there must have been seven hundred teams, with wheat alone, in our city that day.

[*Milwaukee Sentinel* Sept. 29, 1849]

A NEW BINDER.--Rial Rolf was one of 21 farmers to endorse the **'Burson's American Grain Binder,'** after witnessing a trial of it on B. Hardell's farm, in <u>Summit</u>, August 15th. The farmers concluded it could do the work of three men.[*Waukesha Freeman* Sept. 12, 1865]

---

[648] Atlas of Waukesha County, Wisconsin, 1873. Town of Mukwonago.

[649] *Federal Manuscript Schedule*, Population, Agricultural and Manufacturing Schedules Waukesha County, Town of Mukwonago, 1870.

[650] William Melvin Frazier photograph (c. 1902), People F-G-H Box 3:8, Photography Collection, Research Center Library & Archive, Waukesha County Historical Society & Museum, Waukesha, Wisconsin.

[651] *The History of Waukesha County, Wisconsin, 1880*, p. 968.

IMMIGRANTS TO WISCONSIN FROM BAVARIA

Parents, **John Michael Stigler** & **Mary Anna Ostermann** immigrated from near **Gross Bissedorf, Oberpfalz, Bayern**, to Wisconsin in 1850--One Son: **Frederick Stigler**– Birthplace: **Village of Elm Grove, Town of Brookfield** (c. 1842)— Frederick's spouse: **Mary Angeline Schneider**—— Birthplace: Wisconsin (c. 1857) —Residence in 1910: New Berlin, Waukesha County, Wisconsin—Occupation: *farmer*—Children: *Michael, Otilia,* ***Andrew****, Frederick, John, George, Mary Anna, Joseph & Anthony.*

(Image and genealogy courtesy of Mary Stigler of Brookfield, Wisconsin.)[652]

Andrew Stigler (c. 1902) [653]

Hose Company Officer for the **City** *of Waukesha Fire Department*

A History of the City of Waukesha Fire Department --*(in part)*

Courtesy of Chief Steve Howard

Reliance Hook & Ladder Company # 1:

"The City of Waukesha Fire Department has a proud history dating back to July 21, **1852**. On this date, the *Reliance Hook and Ladder Company Number 1* was formed with a complement of **28 volunteers**. The cost for this undertaking was somewhere in the neighborhood of $100 ($70 for a hook and ladder wagon, $14 for 5 ladders, and the rest for 3 pike poles, 4 axes, 20 pails and 100 feet of hose)."

Bucket Brigade:

"These were truly the days of the old **'bucket brigade'** in that a local ordinance stated that 'every householder and every person occupying any mechanic shop, manufactory, store, or mill, within alarm of fire, *shall furnish one suitable pail or bucket at the place of such fire for the purpose of extinguishing the same, under penalty of one dollar for each and every default*'."

Reorganization:

"In 1869, the department was reorganized and re-equipped. *The Village purchased 2 hand pumpers and constructed a frame engine house on South Street for $295*. Soon after, the department was reorganized by the Village and a Fire Chief was appointed. George C. Pratt, 58 years old at the time, was appointed as the Village's first Fire Chief from December of 1869 to May 1872."

First Firehouse:

"By 1867, the department consisted of 51 men. On August 11, 1884, the cornerstone of the Village's first firehouse (on Clinton Street) was laid. (This building was used until 1957.) The first horse drawn piece of fire equipment, a hose wagon, was purchased in early 1896 by the Village Board for $487." [654]

652   *Federal Manuscript Schedule*, Population, Agricultural and Manufacturing Schedules Waukesha County, Town of New Berlin, 1910.

653   Photograph courtesy of Mary Stigler of Brookfield, Wisconsin, e-mail to author, Aug 8, 2009

654   "A History of the City of Waukesha Fire Department," courtesy of then Assistant Chief Steve Howard, City of Waukesha Fire Dept., e-mail to author, March 30, 2012.

"Immigrants to Wisconsin from Scotland

(1st Generation): Name: **Maxwell Frame**– Birthplace: **Ayrshire, Scotland** (1808) — Spouse: **Jane (Aitken)** — Birthplace: **Ayrshire, Scotland** (c. 1800)—Year of immigration: (c. 1836)–Initial resided in: Fowlerville, N. Y.—Occupation: *blacksmith*—Relocated to Waukesha, Wisconsin (circa 1840)--Children: *Hen*ry (born: 22 June 1842) & **Andrew** (born: 19 Feb 1844) —(2nd Generation): Son-- **Andrew Frame** married **Emma J. (Richardson)** in (1869); they resided in the city of Waukesha, Waukesha County, Wisconsin—Children: *Harvey, Walter, William & Esther* & **Mabel**. Occupation: **President of the Waukesha National Bank** (1890)
(Image and genealogy courtesy of Waukesha County Historical Society and Museum.)[655]

Mable Foster and Emma J. Richardson (1903)[656]

A 1903 Northern Runabout:

"The 1903 Northern was a runabout model. It could seat 2 passengers and sold for US $750. *The flat-mounted water-cooled single-cylinder engine, situated at the center of the car, produced 6 hp (4.5 kW). A 2-speed transmission was fitted. The tubular-framed car weighed 950 lb. and used Concord springs*. In 1903 the company produced 300 examples of the runabout." [657] "This is **Mable Frame** driving her mother **Emma** on Wisconsin Avenue, Waukesha in 1903. This *"Northern"* one-cylinder auto was purchased by her father, **A. J. Frame**, June 13, 1903. The camera was facing east toward the Baptist Church on the corner of Wisconsin and Grand Avenues." [658]

President of the Waukesha National Bank:

"Andrew J. Frame entered the bank as an office boy, and successfully worked his way up until in 1866 he was elected cashier of the bank, which was then in bad shape. Mr. Frame, though only twenty-two years of age, went to work to establish the institution on a firm financial footing, and the present condition of the bank shows how well he accomplished his purpose. The bank was organized in 1855 as the Waukesha County bank, with a capital of $25,000. On Jan. 1, 1856, it carried deposits of $53,000. In 1904 the capital stock, including surplus, amounted to $250,000 and on Jan. 1, 1907, the deposits had reached the sum of $2,300,000. The bank has weathered three great panics—1857, 1873, and 1893—meeting every demand promptly and emerging from each crisis in a way that shows the practical management of the bank does not belie its motto: "Stronger than ever." In 1880, at the age of thirty-six, he became president of it, which responsible position he has held continuously ever since."[659]

[655] *Federal Manuscript Schedule*, Population, Agricultural and Manufacturing Schedules Waukesha County, Village of Waukesha, 1870.

[656] Mabel Foster and Emma J. Richardson photograph (c. 1903), People P-Q-R Box 6:8, Photography Collection, Research Center Library & Archive, Waukesha County Historical Society & Museum, Waukesha, Wisconsin.

[657] https://en.wikipedia.org/wiki/Northern_(automobile)

[658] *Photograph Descriptor*, recorded on the back of Mabel Foster and Emma J. Richardson photograph, Photography Collection, Research Center Library & Archive, Waukesha County Historical Society & Museum, Waukesha, Wisconsin.

[659] Haight, *Memoirs of Waukesha County, 1907*, pp. 440 & 441.

IMMIGRANTS TO WISCONSIN FROM BAVARIA

Name: **John Michael Stigler & Mary Anna Ostermann** immigrated from near **Gross Bissedorf, Oberpfalz, Bayern, "Germany"** to Wisconsin in 1850. Children: *Michael, Otilia, Andrew,* **Frederick***, John, George, Mary Anna, Joseph & Anthony.* **Frederick Stigler**– Birthplace: **Village of Elm Grove, Brookfield Township** (c. 1842)— Residence in 1920: <u>New Berlin, Waukesha County, Wisconsin</u>—Occupation: *farmer*—In 1920, Fred & Mary Stigler have 7 children at home; they own a 143-acre (sections 9 & 10) town of <u>New Berlin</u> farm; they have 4 horses; 25 dairy cows & Bell Telephone Service.[660]

(Image and genealogy courtesy of Mary Stigler of Brookfield, Wisconsin.)[661]

George Stigler (c 1903)[662]

The Bicycle:

"Safety bicycles with uniform wheels, chain drive, and pneumatic tires came appeared in the mid-eighties and caught on with a rush. By the early 1890's, there was a bicycle craze." [663]

Bicycle racing clubs were all the rage:

"*In 1892, the Milwaukee Wheelmen (1892) were the largest club in the city, with a membership of 250.* W.C. Sanger, the champion racer of Wisconsin, is a member of the club. With six of the Milwaukee wheelmen as escorts next morning, including a mute rider from Chicago (William A. Amory), we all started for Waukesha. The country now becomes slightly rolling. Following a good road, past, past Wauwatosa and through Elm Grove, we reached Waukesha for dinner. Here all but the mute rider turned back. *He and I visited the famous springs which abound hereabouts. This watering place has a well-earned reputation. Its waters are shipped to Chicago and Milwaukee extensively. He was rather quiet company to me, riding side of by side with me for mile after mile without a word to exchange.* Sometimes we would rest by the roadside, then he would bring forth pencil and paper and we would hold written conversations. Parting with him at Oconomowoc, I pushed on towards Watertown."[664]

BLODGETT. Sunday seemed to be the advent of Spring, as the bicycle went into active business again. *There were more riders from the city tasting the delights of their silent steeds than we have flies in summertime.*

[*Waukesha Freeman* April 23, 1896]

---

[660] *The Farm Journal Illustrated Rural Directory of Waukesha County, Wisconsin, 1918-1923.* p. 154.

[661] *Federal Manuscript Schedule*, Population, Agricultural and Manufacturing Schedules Waukesha County, Town of New Berlin, 1920.

[662] Photograph courtesy of Mary Stigler of Brookfield, Wisconsin, e-mail to author, Aug 8, 2009

[663] Robert Nesbit, *History of Wisconsin* v. 3, *Urbanization and Industrialization, 1873-1893.* Madison: Wisconsin Historical Society, 1985, p. 145.

[664] Frank G. Lenz, "Around the World with Wheel and Canvas," (Outing, *An Illustrated Monthly Magazine of Recreation*, Nov. 1892), p. 149-150.

IMMIGRANTS TO WISCONSIN FROM ENGLAND

(1ˢᵗ Generation): **Richard and Elizabeth (Bray) Parsons**—birthplace: **England**— Residence (1840): **Cornwall, England**—(2ⁿᵈ Generation): **George Parsons**—birthplace: **Cornwall, England**--Marriage: **Agnes Hicks** (1 Jan 1846) in **England**-- Children: *James (born in England)*--Year of emigration: (1850)—*Richard Parsons died at sea--* **Elizabeth** settled in **Sugar Creek, Walworth County**— *George & Agnes Parson's* Residence: Jericho, Waukesha County, WI. (1850)—Children born in Wisconsin: *George, Agnes Mary, John & two who died in infancy*—George joined the ***Wisconsin Conference of the Methodist Episcopal Church*** (1868)—*Rev. George Parsons retired from the active work, after 53 years of preaching, built a home in Menomonee Falls and remained there for the remainder of his life*—(3ʳᵈ Generation): **John Parsons**--birthplace: Elkhorn, Walworth County, Wis., (27 Aug. 27 1859)— Residence (1886): Menomonee Township, Waukesha County—Marriage: **Clara Seabold**—occupation: *farmer*— Children—*Milo, Earl, Ethel & Marian—Death of Clara (Seabold) Parsons: (1895)—John Parson's 2ⁿᵈ wife:* **Jennie Fleming**—previous residence: Prospect Hill, New Berlin Township, Waukesha County—John & Jennie's church affiliation: members of the ***Methodist Episcopal Church*** of Menomonee Falls--her occupation: *teacher*—children: *Mary & George.* (Image and genealogy courtesy of Libbie Nolan of Big Bend, Wisconsin.)[665]

George Parsons (c. 1904)[666]

Rev. George Parsons of Cornwell served Methodist Episcopalians in Wisconsin:

"From the early nineteenth to the mid-twentieth century Methodism was the leading form of Christianity in Cornwall, England. *With large immigration of and spread of English Methodism into the U.S. during the 19ᵗʰ century, the Methodist Episcopal Church became the largest and most widespread denomination in the United States.* In the Antebellum era, new generation of leaders, upwardly mobile preachers and laity, would lead the Methodist Episcopal Church toward social respectability and inclusion within America's Protestant establishment."[667]

Dairy farming on the Parson's Farm:

"*In 1914, John Parsons ran a (section 9) 100-acre dairy farm in Menomonee Township largely devoted to dairying.* The farm is one of the best in the vicinity, having excellent buildings and other improvements."[668]

How Wisconsin Became the Dairy State:

In the 1870s, leaders of the Wisconsin cheese industry organized several professional organizations. One of the most famous organizations was the **Wisconsin Dairyman's Association**, founded in Watertown in 1872. *Wisconsin's German and Scandinavian immigrant families also helped grow the dairy industry. They adapted to dairying quickly and created European style cheeses inspired by their home countries. Wisconsin was soon famous for its Swiss cheese.* Wisconsin became the leading dairy state in 1915, producing more butter and cheese than any other.[669]

---

[665] *Federal Manuscript Schedule*, Population, Agricultural and Manufacturing Schedules for Waukesha County, Town of Menomonee, 1880.

[666] Photograph courtesy of Libbie Nolan, via Pat Nolan of Big Bend, Wisconsin, e-mail to author, Dec. 21, 2016.

[667] https://en.wikipedia.org/wiki/Methodist_Episcopal_Church

[668] Haight. *Memoirs of Waukesha County, 1907*, p. 577

[669] https://www.wisconsinhistory.org/Records/Article/CS411

IMMIGRANTS TO WISCONSIN FROM NEW YORK

(First Generation): Name: **Thomas Faulkner**—Birthplace: **New York** (born: *1822*)—Spouse: **Nancy (Moorer) Faulkner**--Birthplace: **New York**--Year of immigration to Wisconsin: (c. *1856*). Residence in *1860*: Prospect Hill, New Berlin Township, Wisconsin —Occupation: *farmer & surveyor* –Children: *Viola, Clara, Rufus & Frank*. (Second Generation): Father: **Rufus E Faulkner** (b. *1856*) place of birth: **New Berlin, Waukesha County**— Spouse: **Harriet (Searle) Faulkner** (b. 1856)--place of birth: **Wisconsin**--Marriage: (*6 Mar 1883*)--Occupation: *farmer*--by 1914, Rufus & Harriet Faulkner own a 39-acre New Berlin (section 32) *farm on the south slope of Prospect Hill*—Children: *Lee Eldon & Ethel Elmira*–(Third Generation): **Lee & Eva May (Russell) Faulkner**—Eva's birthplace: **Leroy, New York** (c. *1896*)—married (circa: *1917*) They have one child *Elizabeth*; they own a 40-acre *Waukesha County farm; a telephone; 2 horses; 5 cows*[670]--Residence: *1930*: Vernon Township, Waukesha County— Occupation: *farmer*—Children: *Elizabeth, Virginia & Margaret*--Residence: *1940* - State Highway 15, Vernon Township, Waukesha County—Occupation: *farmer*--Wife: *Eva's*—Occupation: *restaurant waitress*.
(Image and genealogy courtesy of Cathryn Larsen of Kenosha, Wisconsin.)[671]

Lee Elden Faulkner (c. 1904)[672]

The Freewill Baptist Church:

"*Its bell was not cracked, nor its pulpit Bible even touched after arsonists set fire to Wisconsin's oldest Freewill Baptist Church, at Prospect Hill, this past April (1985).* Its 1860 pulpit Bible is inscribed by *Great Grandfather Thomas Faulkner* as congregational clerk. *Rev. Rufus Cheney* had come to the Wisconsin Territory from Antrim, N.H., in 1837. Here he settled, contributing land for what is now **Sunnyside Cemetery**. The year *the Prospect Ladies' Aid* was organized, April 13, 1886, tells of its early growing congregation. *It was the early Aid women who held socials and oyster suppers, fancy work and apron sales to buy the church bell, pew hymnals, pulpit chairs, and an organ for the church.* Somehow it seems that there must be a Higher reason why the bell fell the way down from the belfry onto the floor in the roaring inferno and didn't crack… and how did the loosely wrapped Bible escape the flames?"[673]

Another burial at Sunnyside Cemetery:

Eva May Faulkner (1896-1947) was killed by lighting when closing a window during a violent thunderstorm. Her husband, *Lee Elden Faulkner*, is said to have died a few years later from *a broken heart*. They were the parents of our local historian, author and artist, *Libbie Faulkner Nolan*.[674]

Death of Mrs. Adda S. Russell.

Funeral services were held yesterday afternoon for *Mrs. Adda S. Russell*, 75. Mrs. Russell was the only child of *John* and *Emily Lumb*. *After her husband died, she lived with her only daughter, Mrs. Lee Faulkner, who was killed by lightning three years ago.* Mrs. Faulkner is survived by her son-in-law, Lee Faulkner, of Mukwonago.   [*Waukesha Daily Freeman* August 10, 1949]

[670]   *The Farm Journal Illustrated Rural Directory of Waukesha County 1918-1923*, p. 27.

[671]   *Federal Manuscript Schedule*, Population, Agricultural and Manufacturing Schedules for Waukesha County, Town of New Berlin, 1860, 1930 & 1940.

[672]   Photograph courtesy of Cathryn Larsen, Kenosha, WI., LinkedIn, e-mail to author, Mar 25, 2011

[673]   Libbie Nolan, "A Burned Building, Its Bible and Bell," *Landmark.* v. 28, Nos. 1 & 2, Spring & Summer, 1985, pp. 11 & 14.

[674]   Libbie Faulkner Nolan, "Sunnyside Cemetery Brochure" 2008, *New Berlin Almanack, Vol. XI.*

IMMIGRANTS TO WISCONSIN FROM NEW YORK STATE

(1ˢᵗ Generation): Name: **Warren Spaulding**—Birthplace: **Pawling, Dutchess County, NY.** (1811)—Spouse: **Mary Van Wyke (Field) Spaulding**—Birthplace: **Putnam County, N. Y.** (2/12/1813)—married (4/1/1835)—Residence: Bethel & later Danbury, Connecticut—Warren's Occupation: *hat maker & Harlem Railroad Company*—1856: family arrives in *Milwaukee*—1857: family moved to *Waukesha County*—Warren purchases 149-acre (section 29) *Oconomowoc farm bordering the east side of Lake La Belle*—Children: *(3 children die in infancy), Edward, Sarah, Arthur, Emma, Frances & Willis*—(2ⁿᵈ Generation): **Willis Spaulding**—Occupation-- *retained 80-acres of his father's original Lake LaBelle dairy farm and proprietor of summer resorts*—(married): **Julia E. Kellogg** (1876)—*Julia's death* (1892)—*Willis* (remarries): **Mable M, Burdick** (28 Nov. 1894)—children: *Willis Warren & Clarence*—Willis & Mable **(divorce)**: (14 Sept 1904)--*Willis Spaulding's* (third marriage): **Genise Van Brunt** (March 1905)—children: *Leona & Genise*—Residence in 1905: *Oconomowoc, Waukesha County, Wisconsin* —*Willis Spaulding's* occupation: *proprietor of hotel, summer resorts & dairy farm*—Residence of Leona & Genise—at *La Belle Villa (Oconomowoc):* *Clarence (son), Lucy Burdick: hired hand, August Schombeck: farm laborer, Carl Netehost: boarder, H.W. Waterman: boarder, Albert Brunweger: boarder & William Sanderson: boarder.*[675]

(Image and genealogy courtesy of Waukesha County Historical Society and Museum.)[676]

Spaulding Wagon Accident (1905)[677]

Hit by an automobile

"This is an early auto & buggy accident, July 26, 1905. They were hit by a drunk summer resident. *The horse is 'Old Joe' & the man is Willis Spaulding. The woman in the front seat is his wife, Genis (Van Brunt) Spaulding. The young lady in the back seat is Hattie Tulmer."*[678]

Quite an entrepreneur:

"Willis H. Spaulding became one of the most enterprising and progressive men in the community of Oconomowoc. *About 1891, Willis built **La Belle Villa**, a summer hotel, which he has been opened for about fifteen seasons.* He has sold considerable portions of the farm but still retains about 80 acres of valuable land, much of it bordering on Lac La Belle. He owns 'Sand Beach Park' *and is transforming a tract of 30 acres into an island. 'Landslee Park' is also his property and he has expended thousands of dollars in improving his Lake La Belle lake front, much of his property being desirable for summer homes.* Some of the nation's wealthiest families built stately summer homes on the lakes, and by the 1880s Oconomowoc featured several luxury resorts." [679]

---

[675] Haight, *Memoirs of Waukesha County, 1907*. pp. 644 & 645.

[676] *Federal Manuscript Schedule*, Population, Agricultural and Manufacturing Schedules for Waukesha County, Town of Oconomowoc, 1870 & 1890.

[677] Spaulding Wagon Accident (1905), Transportation, Photography Collection, Research Center Library & Archive, Waukesha County Historical Society & Museum, Waukesha, Wisconsin.

[678] Photograph Descriptor, recorded on the back of "Spaulding Wagon Accident" photograph, Photography Collection, Research Center Library & Archive, Waukesha County Historical Society & Museum, Waukesha, Wisconsin.

[679] Haight, *Memoirs of Waukesha County, 1907*. pp. 644 & 645.

IMMIGRANTS TO WISCONSIN FROM PRUSSIA

(1ˢᵗ Generation): **Christian Nauertz**– Birthplace: <u>**Wintrich, Rheinland, Preußen**</u> (Aug 8 Aug 1817)—Spouse: <u>**Susanna Marx**</u>—married: (Feb 16, 1843) in <u>**Wintrich, Rheinland, Preußen**</u> --Occupation: *farmer*—emigrated from the port of Antwerp aboard the ship *"Elisha Denizen"* with two children (*Anna Marie & Elizabeth*) landing in New York (27 May 1850)— Residence in 1860: <u>Brookfield Township</u>--Children born in Wisconsin: *Michael, Elizabeth, Christian, Susanna, Mathias & Nicholas*[680]--Residence (1870): Christian owns <u>*a 40-acre (section 35), Waukesha County farm on the Brookfield/New Berlin town line*</u>—to the north & east is the <u>**John Simon**</u> (108--acre) farm—(2ⁿᵈ Generation): **Nicholas Nauertz**--Birthplace: (5 Jan 1860) <u>**Brookfield Township, Waukesha County**</u>— Spouse—**Mary (Gebhardt)**—Occupation: *Dairy Farmer*—In 1910 Nicholas Nauertz owns a 74-acre Brookfield *(section 35) farm*--Children: *Mary, Theresa, George, Lizzie, Christian, Mathew & Teresa.*
(Image, narrative, and genealogy courtesy of Kathleen Nauertz-Husz of Milwaukee, Wisconsin.)[681]

Nauertz Family (c. 1905)[682]

The Naurertz Family:

Left to right—back row: Christian, Nick (father), Matthias—Left to right—middle row: Elizabeth, Mary (mother), and Anna Left to right—front row: Teresa, Mary and George. [683]

Wintrich, Rhineland, Preußen:

"*The municipality of Wintrich (the birthplace of Christian Nauritz) lies in the natural and cultivated landscape of the Moselle River.* Against this, however, moderate slopes covered in vineyards and in places by *woods* climb up to the Eifel Mountain Range on the other side of the river. Quite early on, Celts, Romans & Franks settled the land where Wintrich would later stand. Timber-frame houses, lanes with little nooks, bear witness to the historic tradition."[684]

A builder of barns, homes & other beamed structures:

"Some of the Simons came to Wisconsin with Christian Nauertz and his wife, Susanna Marx, and two children landing in New York on May 27, 1850. Their ship, the "Elisha Denizen," left the port of Antwerp. The area of origin is Wintrich, Rheinland, Preußen. *Further Nauertz-Marx-Simon connections are: Christian's oldest daughter Anna Nauertz married Mathias Marx and had 10 children. The 1870 Federal Census has them living on a farm adjacent to the in-laws, Christian and Susanna Nauertz.* He was a *carpenter* and was known for his barns in the Brookfield area."—*Kathie Nauertz Husz* [685]

Elm Grove--The barn dance at *Nic Nauritz's* was well attended; *over 100 tickets were sold.* The next one will be held at George Gebhardt's barn on North Avenue. These barn dances are given to benefit the new ***Catholic Church* at Elm Grove.**
[*Waukesha Freeman* June 22, 1921]

680   Kathleen Nauertz-Husz of Milwaukee, Wisconsin, e-mail to author, September 13, 2010.

681   *Federal Manuscript Schedule*, Population, Agricultural and Manufacturing Schedules for Waukesha County, Town of Brookfield, 1860 & 1910.

682   Photograph courtesy of Kathleen Nauertz-Husz of Milwaukee, Wisconsin, e-mail to author, September 22, 2010.

683   Kathleen Nauertz-Husz of Milwaukee, Wisconsin, e-mail to author, September 22, 2010

684   https://en.wikipedia.org/wiki/Wintrich

685   Kathleen Nauertz-Husz of Milwaukee, Wisconsin, e-mail to author, September 22, 2010

IMMIGRANTS TO WISCONSIN FROM ENGLAND

(1st Generation): Name: **Alfred Russell**—Birthplace: **England** (1816)—Year of immigration: (circa: 1848)—Residence: 1860- *1st D 9th Ward, New York, New York*: Occupation: *clerk*—Marriage: **Mary Elizabeth Thomas** (circa 1850) --birthplace: **New York** (1826)— 1860 residence: **Germantown, Washington County, Wisconsin**—children: *Adda age 9, Isaac age 6* and *Eva age 3*. All three of their teenage children: *Adda, 17, Isaac, 15,* and *Eva, 13 died of* **black diphtheria** *within a week of the birth of their baby brother, William.* Soon after the death of the children-- Alfred & Mary (*divorc*ed). (2nd Generation): *William Russell* (age: 1)—was born in *Germantown, Washington County, Wisconsin,* before his parent's divorce, (Feb 1869)— *William* now resides in the *Village of Menomonee Falls* in 1870 with his mother *Mary Elizabeth*—In (circa 1895) **William Russell** (age: 26)—marries: **Adda Lumb** [686]— Birthplace: **Wisconsin** (c. 1875)— Residence in 1910: *Village of Menomonee Falls, Waukesha County, Wisconsin*—Occupation: *farmer*–a Child: **Eva May**. In 1918 William & Adda Russell own a home on Fond du Lac Ave. in the village of Menomonee Falls; they have home telephone —Occupation: William works as a *mason*. There are no children at home. Rural Directory—in 1930 William (age: 61) & Adda Russell (age: 56) reside in: Menomonee Falls, Waukesha County[687]—Occupation: *contractor-cement blender*---Mary (William Russell's divorced mother) later married **William Bradley** (age: 70) in 1880--of *Eagle, Waukesha County*.

(Image and genealogy courtesy of Libbie Nolan of Big Bend, Wisconsin) [688]

Eva May Russell (c. 1905)[689]

Stonemasonry in the early 20th Century:

"When Europeans settled the Americas, they brought the stonemasonry techniques of their respective homelands with them. Settlers used what materials were available, and in some areas, stone was the material of choice. In the first waves, building mimicked that of Europe, to eventually be replaced by unique architecture later on. Prior to the end of the 19th century, most heavy work was executed by draft animals or human muscle power. In the 20th century, stonemasonry saw its most radical changes in the way the work is accomplished. Masonry was more commonly used for walls and buildings. Brick and concrete block were more most common types of masonry in use and may be either weight-bearing or a veneer. (**William Russell** was already using blocks of cinder concrete or ordinary concrete blocks in his work in the village of Menomonee Falls.) They usually are much larger than ordinary bricks and are much faster to lay for a wall of a given size." [690]

Stepping into the early 1900's:

"The early 20th century was marked by continued growth in the new Village and the establishment of modern infrastructure and transportation routes. In 1902, *the Menomonee Falls-Hubertus-Holy Hill Telephone Company* offered the *first public telephone service* in the Village, and in 1907 *a local electric plant began offering a lighting alternative to kerosene lamps for the first time. Water mains were first installed* in the 1910s, and *the first sewer lines were laid* in 1924. The combined population of the Village and the Town reached 3,303 in 1910. *The first automobiles* were sold in the Village in 1910, and by 1912, *a dozen vehicles were registered* in Menomonee Falls. *In 1916, a new Ford touring car or convertible could be purchased from Wittlin Motors for $360. Automobile use increased rapidly after concrete pavement was installed on Main Street and Fond du Lac Avenue (now Appleton Avenue) in 1919*."[691]

[686] *Standard Atlas of Waukesha County, Wisconsin,* 1914, Town of Menomonee

[687] *The Farm Journal Illustrated Rural Directory of Waukesha County 1918-1923,* p. 135.

[688] *Federal Manuscript Schedule,* Population, Agricultural and Manufacturing Schedules for Waukesha County, Village of Menomonee Falls, 1910.

[689] Photograph courtesy of Libbie Nolan via Pat Nolan both of Big Bend, Wisconsin, e-mail to author, Dec. 21, 2016.

[690] https://en.wikipedia.org/wiki/Stonemasonry

[691] *"Welcoming Modernity,"* Courtesy of the Village of Menomonee Falls, Wisconsin.

IMMIGRANTS TO WISCONSIN FROM WÜRTTEMBERG AND NEW YORK

(1ˢᵗ Generation): **Dr. August Schaeffel's**--birthplace: **Balgheim, Tuttlingen, Württemberg, Germany** (c. 1848) –Residence: 1860: *Menomonee Township, Waukesha County*—occupation: *physician*--Marriage: **Katherine Hengstler**- (27 Apr 1874)—Church Membership: *German Evangelical*, Brookfield, Waukesha, Wisconsin— Residence: 1880: *Brookfield, Waukesha, Wisconsin*-- (2ⁿᵈ Generation): **John Schaeffel**– birthplace: Town of Menomonee, Waukesha, Wisconsin (2 July 1869) — Marriage: **Mary Orilla Harris** (1896)—Birthplace: New York (1879) —Residence in *1910: Ward 1, Waukesha, Waukesha County, Wisconsin*— Occupation: (1910) *laborer at motor works*—(1920) *shipping clerk/iron factory*—(1930) *city coroner*—(1940) *janitor*--*John & Maria's* Children: *Dale, Katherine, John, Charlotte & Emma*—Other residents: **George Cook** (brother-in-law to **John Schaeffel**)— daughter, *Emma (Schaeffel) cook.*

(Image and genealogy courtesy of the Williams Family of the Oconomowoc, Wisconsin area)[692]

(l-r): George E. Cook and John R Schaeffel (c. 1905)[693]

"Mock Fisticuffs"

Waukesha Motor Works:

(John Shaaeffel was employed at Waukesha Motor Works for about 10 years beginning in 1910). "WAUKESHA MOTORS" have proved by the severe tests of hard usage to be the most efficient motors made for truck and tractor service. In the latter field, their records have been such as to commend them to the careful consideration of every tractor maker, dealer and user. The experience of many tractor users has shown Waukesha Motors to be unequalled for strength, reliability, economy and long life. 'The Waukesha' may be obtained either as a motor or unit power plant in sizes ranging from 3 1/3 x 5 ½ to 4 ¾ x 6 ¾. Write for complete data."[694]

Waukesha City Coroner:

John Schaeffel served as the Waukesha City Coroner from 1912 to 1916 and again from 1927 to 1937.[695]

Herman Tucker's Body Found in Lake

Eight-day Search Successful at Pewaukee; Victim was a Former Supervisor
The body of **Herman Tucker**, 58, former state assemblyman and former member of the Milwaukee County Board, was recovered Friday noon from Pewaukee Lake by two professional log rollers who had experience in recovering bodies from under ice. Circumstances indicated that *Tucker* had slashed himself with a razor and then jumped or fell into the lake. The body was taken to the *Larsen* undertaking rooms in Waukesha. **Coroner Schaeffel** said his verdict would be suicide. According to Schaeffel the body showed no other marks of violence except cuts on both wrists. In Tucker's pockets was $87 in bills and $3.02 in change. *Among his effects were also a set of keys, a check book showing a balance of $142.03 as of Nov. 21, and a pair of glasses. A few hours before he disappeared, Tucker had been seen in a Pewaukee restaurant, writing a note, which he placed in an enveloped. The envelope, torn open and empty was found in a pool of blood in an outbuilding near a fishing shack. It was addressed to the "sweetest girl I ever loved."* [*The Milwaukee Journal* December 4, 1936]

---

692   *Federal Manuscript Schedule*, Population, Agricultural and Manufacturing Schedules for Waukesha County, City of Waukesha, 1910.

693   Photograph courtesy of Sue Ellen Williams of Oconomowoc, Wisconsin, e-mail to author, Jul 8, 2010.

694   Waukesha Motor Works advertisement in the *Automobile Trade Journal*, 1916, volume 20, p. 14.

695   *Waukesha County Farms Directory and Plat Book* (Waukesha: Waukesha County Directory Publ. Co., 1940), p. 28.

IMMIGRANTS TO WISCONSIN FROM SWITZERLAND

(First Generation): Name: **John Hoffman**--Birthplace: **Horgenbach, Canton Thurgau, Schweiz** (7 Feb 1819)—Spouse: **Elizabeth Anna Wellauer**-- Birthplace: **Wagenhousen, Canton Thurgau, Schweiz** (29 Mar 1828) ---Marriage: **Evangelisch, Kurzdorf, Thurgau, Schweiz** (12 Apr 1849)— Residence in 1870: *Brookfield Township, Waukesha, County, Wisconsin*—Occupation: *proprietor of the "Phoenix Inn" & owns a Brookfield (section 28) farm*--Children: *Sophia, Federnaul, Caroline, Henry, Elizabeth, Caroline Mina & John.* (Second Generation): **John Hoffman (Jr.)**—born in **Brookfield** (1854)— spouse: **Harriet Hattie) Benecke** –They are the proprietor of *"Oak Lawn Farm"* in Brookfield (section 16)— they have 4 children: *Arthur, Harry, Viola & Harold.* In 1918, John & Harriet Hoffman; own a 64-acre farm; with 3 horses, 18 dairy cows; and Bell telephone service—Children: *Arthur, Harry, Viola, Harold & **Albert**.*[696]   (Image courtesy of Sally Clarin of Brookfield, Wisconsin; Genealogy courtesy of Maralyn A. Wellauer-Lenius of Winnipeg, Manitoba.) [697]

Albert Hoffman at the University of Wisconsin-Madison (1906)[698]

"Bed, Board and Blossoms:"

"Elizabeth Hoffman, a short chubby, good-natured lady was a guiding force in the public and an indispensable helpmate to her husband, John, the proprietor of the Phoenix Hotel, situated along the south side of the Watertown Plank Road in Brookfield. Her domain covered the spacious inn with its full sized second story dance hall, its many guests sleeping rooms, the huge wainscoted dining room, and even a bar-room. It covered the gardens of vegetables, the cheese room, and the picket fenced yard with its bake oven, chicken house and her flowers. Her big black cook stove steamed, brewed, or baked the old **Swiss** and **German** dishes she served travelers. *She stored cabbage, beets, carrots and turnips in the bins on the cold earth floor of her cellar; canned fruits and vegetables on the shelves along the stone walls; and sauerkraut, salt pork, brined fresh pork and pickles in tall crocks near the stairway.* Dozens of loaves of both rye and white bread steaming with yeasty fragrance came out of the stone bake oven which stood between the well and the barns. Cured meats, sides of bacon, hams, shoulders, and homemade sausages hung from the black smoke-house joists north of the kitchen door. Moist cheese pressed into bricks, came out from the cold sweet-sour smelling cheese room made from milk from their own herd."[699]

Ball at The Phoenix Hotel.

A grand ball will be given at the Phoenix Hotel, in the town of Brookfield, on the Watertown Plank Road, and the undersigned takes pleasure in respectfully inviting to this occasion all people fond of dancing. An excellent music band is engaged. Most Respectfully, JOHN HOFFMAN   [*Waukesha Plaindealer* Oct.4, 1870]

---

[696]   *The Farm Journal Illustrated Rural Directory of Waukesha County, 1918-1923*, p. 74.

[697]   *Federal Manuscript Schedule*, Population, Agricultural and Manufacturing Schedules for Waukesha County, Town of Brookfield, 1870.

[698]   Photograph courtesy of Sally Clarin of Brookfield, Wisconsin, via home visit, July 15, 2012.

[699]   Libbie Nolan, "Bed, Board and Blossoms," *Landmark*. v. 9, n. 3, (Summer, 1966), pp. 12 & 13. ("Bed, Board and Blossom's" is my personal favorite of all of Libbie's numerous articles published in *Landmark*. It's not heavy laden with facts but provides vivid imagery which opens one's imagination, along with a sense of the heavy load 19th century women often carried either on the family farm or in a family business. I do believe I could still see this old grey, clapboard landmark, standing all alone on the north side of the then relatively quiet Bluemound road back in the early 1960's.)

IMMIGRANTS TO WISCONSIN FROM SAXONY

(1ˢᵗ Generation): Name: **Frederick Dunkel**—birthplace: **Dinkelsbuhl, Sachsen** (c.1812)—Spouse; **Christina Boyd**– Birthplace: **Sachsen** (c. 1813)—Residence in 1890: **Brookfield Township, Waukesha County, Wisconsin**— Occupation: *farmer* –Children: *Heinrich, George, Sybilla, Charles, William & Herman.* (2ⁿᵈ Generation): **Charles Dunkel**—born in **Sachsen** (Nov 1843)—Spouse—**Barbara Gredler**—born born in **Sachsen** (Nov 1845)— In 1876 Charles Dunkel owned a 64.75-acre Town of Wauwatosa, Milwaukee County farm--bordering Waukesha County. *Underwood Creek* passes through the family farm, along with the *Milwaukee & St. Paul Rail*road[700] In 1887, *Charles Dunkel* (1843-1909) and his two sons, *Henry & Herman*, moved to *Brookfield* from Wauwatosa, and in the same year *purchased a 180-acre Brookfield (section 26) farm* from Charles Zimdars. *By 1918, Charles & Barbara own a 220-acre (sections 27 & 34) Brookfield farm*—Children: *Henry & Herman*-- their home was the old "Dousman Inn" dating to the early 1840's. *The Dunkel house survives today and is maintained by the Elmbrook Historical Society as the Dousman Stagecoach Inn Museum.* (Image and genealogy courtesy of the Elmbrook Historical Society.)[701]

Charles Dunkel (c. 1906)[702]

The Milwaukee County Asylum:

"Milwaukee's first mental hospital, known as **the Milwaukee County Asylum for the Chronic Insane**, opened in 1880 on the County Grounds in Wauwatosa. The state reimbursed the county $1.50 a week for every patient in its care. 'Accommodations were anything but lavish, usually two to a room, sleeping on cots and sharing a sink. '*There was no psychiatry or meaningful therapy,' said (anonymous), who worked there as an internist. 'People were basically drugged and warehoused*'."[703]

COMMUNICATIONS AND PETITIONS.

Wauwatosa, Wis., Aug. 12, 1889, To the Board of Supervisors of Milwaukee County—GENTELMEN: I have the honor herewith, as per instructions of the board of trustees of the Milwaukee County Asylum for the Chronic Insane. The mode of payment of the officers and employees of the asylum, and the appropriation of fire extinguishers. Very truly yours, G. W. Mayhew, Secretary. Committee on county farm, almshouse and water works: CONTRIBUTIONS-- **Charles Dunkel**.... $72.00 et el.   [*Milwaukee Daily Journal* August 17, 1889]

LIGHTING CONTRACT VETOED--**Mayor Rose** this afternoon affixed his signature to a veto of the resolution to award to **Charles** and **L.W. Dunkel** *a five-year contract to light the outlying districts with sixty power naphtha[704] lamps at a rate of $22.83 per light.*   [*Milwaukee Daily Journal* June 5, 1901]

700   *Milwaukee County Atlas, Wauwatosa Township*, Chicago; H. Belden & Co. 1876, pp. 46 & 47.
701   *Federal Manuscript Schedule*, Population, Agricultural and Manufacturing Schedules for Waukesha County, Town of Brookfield, 1900.
702   Courtesy of the Elmbrook Historical Society via Lynda Thayer, e-mail to author, Dec 23, 2016.
703   Milwaukee County Asylum-Asylum Projects, http://www.asylumprojects.org/index.php/Milwaukee_County_Asylum
704   " Naphtha is a flammable liquid hydrocarbon mixture. Mixtures labelled naphtha have been produced from natural gas condensates. In different industries and regions naphtha may also be a crude oil or a refined product such as kerosene, also known as paraffin or lamp oil, for producing light." From: ttps://en.wikipedia.org/wiki/Naphtha

IMMIGRANTS TO WISCONSIN FROM GERMANY

Name: **Louis Golemgeske** — Birthplace: **Ostóda, East Preußen** (19 Nov 1866)—Louis' year of Immigration: (1884)--Spouse: **Amelia Bertha Bartz**–Birthplace: **Ruedke Province, Preußen** (12 Feb 1873)—Year of emigration of the Bartz family to Wisconsin (31 Dec 1885)--Marriage of Louis & Amelia: (Nov 9, 1889) at the **Ev Lutheran Church** of Waukesha Residence in **1900**: the family resides in the City of Waukesha, Waukesha County— Occupation: *blacksmith*–Children: *Leona Anna, Louis, Walter, Hulda, Agnes, Erwin, Edwin, Alice, Elmer & Herman.*[705] In **1914**, Louis & Amelia have 10 adult children, 25 dairy cows, 4 horses, along with Bell telephone service, on a *Town of Pewaukee (Section 36) farm* just east of the Waukesha City limits.

(Image and genealogy courtesy of Jan Pace of Waukesha, Wisconsin.) [706]

Agnes "Ida" Golemgeske (c. 1907)[707]

Fought over by Poland & Prussia:

"During the Thirteen Years' War (1454–1466), Ostóda (the birthplace of Louis Golemgeske in 1866) was repeatedly captured by both the Poles and Prussian Confederation on one side and the Teutonic Knights on the other. From 1525 until 1701 Ostóda was part of Ducal Prussia, a fief of Poland, and after 1701 part of Kingdom of Prussia. *The majority of inhabitants were Protestant and the Evangelical church books date back to 17ᵗʰ century. In 1818 it became the seat of a Kreis (district) within the Kingdom of Prussia.*"[708]

Women's Clothing Styles of the early 1900's:

"A beautiful young lady. The focus is on her rounded pompadour hair. For women, during this period, Ida's pompadour was created by backcombing or ratting at the roots of the hair towards the top of the head. Then the hair is combed up and over the front up in a curl straight back, and the sides pulled back towards the center. Hats were part of everyday life, and her hair was styled accordingly to accommodate the hat. Ida's hair was a late Edwardian hair style. You can imagine those large flat cartwheel hats of the early 20ᵗʰ Century.*"--Joan Severa, early 20ᵗʰ Century Clothing Styles*[709]

'Honey and Milk' Advocate Insane

FROM THE JOURNAL'S WAUKESHA BUREAU

Waukesha, Wis.— Mrs. **Hulda Hoefs** has been committed to the state hospital at Mendota. Arriving at Mendota after the woman had been committed, **Herman** and **Walter Golemgeske**, her brothers, sought an audience with the governor. They claimed **Gov. LaFollette** told them to "come back sometime." With *Albert Hoefs*, husband of *Hulda*, they planned to do so Tuesday. Mrs. Hoefs lived with her husband on the farm of her father, Louis Golemgeske, two miles west of here in the town of Pewaukee. Seven persons made up the household. "Solid foods are possessed of the devil," she used to tell them.

[*The Milwaukee Journal* February 17, 1931]

---

[705] *Federal Manuscript Schedule*, Population, Agricultural and Manufacturing Schedules for Waukesha County, Town of Waukesha, 1900.

[706] *The Farm Journal Illustrated Rural Directory of Waukesha County, 1918-1923*, p. 61.

[707] Photograph courtesy of Jan Pace, of Waukesha, Wisconsin, e-mail to author, April 5, 2011.

[708] https://en.wikipedia.org/wiki/Ostóda

[709] Joan Severa, Madison, Wisconsin., e-mail to author, Jan 31, 2010.

IMMIGRANTS TO WISCONSIN FROM HESSE

Name: **John Best**—Birthplace: **Darmstadt-Hessen, Germany** (1863)—Year of Immigration: 1867— Spouse: **Elizabeth Katherine Schmidt**--Residence in 1880: Summit Township, Waukesha County, Wisconsin—Occupation: *farmer*–Children: *Elva Marie, Irene, Arthur, Norman & Eleanor*. In 1918, John & Elizabeth Best *reside in Summit Township*, with 5 children—Occupation: *poultry man in the village of Dousman, town of Ottawa, Road #27.*[710] John Best—Residence 1930—Village of Dousman, Summit Township (age 66)—occupation: *common laborer*—Spouse: Elizabeth—one son at home: *Norman*: (age: 27)—Norman's occupation: *electrician—house wiring*.　　　　(Image and genealogy courtesy of Fred C. Smyth of Whidbey Island, Washington.)[711]

John & Elizabeth Best Family (circa 1907) [712]

The Best Family:

(l – r): John (the father) Norman, Irene, Elizabeth (the mother) Arthur & Elva.[713]

Family Clothing Styles of the early 1900's:

"During the early 1900's a drastic change in women's clothing appeared. Women were now wearing more natural, practical and comfortable dresses. Elizabeth does maintain the style of a collared neck. The girls, Irene and Elva, wear bows in their hair very much the trend for young girls during this period; with bibbed dresses and lose chords hanging from their necks. Arthur wears a double-breasted jacket with a low hung belt. You might get the notion that Elizabeth was just happy to get her husband, John, changed into his cleanest bib overalls." *--Joan Severa, 20th Century Clothing Styles*[714]

Chronological History of Dousman, Wisconsin:

"1861 *First Presbyterian Church* of Ottawa organized—1881 *Chicago & Northwestern Railway Co.* complete railroad in area— *Griffith Thomas* built a store and became the *first* merchant and first postmaster. The post office was moved from Utica to Dousman—1882 A Mr. Steinica built *the first hotel*, it burned down within two years. The first *Dousman Coronet Band* built a Music Hall.—1883 *Herman Claus* built and operated a *harness shop*—1888 *President Grover Cleveland made a whistle-stop in Dousman*—1890 Bullfrog Station[715] settlement has 150 residents—1893 *Mary Moody* was *the first teacher at the Dousman school*, earning a $1.50 a day"[716]

---

[710]　*The Farm Journal Illustrated Rural Directory of Waukesha County, 1918-1923,* p. 27.

[711]　*Federal Manuscript Schedule,* Population, Agricultural and Manufacturing Schedules for Waukesha County, Town of Summit, 1880 & 1930.

[712]　Photograph courtesy of Fred C. Smyth of Whidbey Island, Washington, e-mail to author, Apr 23, 2010.

[713]　Fred C. Smyth of Whidbey Island, Washington, e-mail to author, Apr 23, 2010.

[714]　Joan Severa of Madison, Wisconsnin, e-mail to author, Apr 10, 2010.

[715]　"The Village of Dousman was at one time called "Bullfrog Station" because of the numerous bullfrogs in the area. The local baseball team is still called the Dousman Frogs and an annual frog jumping competition takes place during Dousman's Derby Days." From: ttps://en.wikipedia.org/wiki/Dousman,_Wisconsin

[716]　*"Chronological History of the Dousman Area, Waukesha County, Wisconsin,"* Courtesy of the Dousman Historical Society.

IMMIGRANTS TO WISCONSIN FROM WALES

Family #1, (1ˢᵗ Generation): Father-in-law: **Thomas D. Jones**—birthplace: <u>Wales</u> (Nov 1834)— year of immigration: (1840)--spouse: **Margaret**—birthplace: <u>Wales</u> (May 1835)--year of immigration: (1842)--marriage: (c. 1862)—*In 1914 Thomas D. Jones owns an 81-acre Village of Wales (sections 9 & 16) farm—a spring flows through the farm.* [717] (Family #1, 2ⁿᵈ Generation): Son-in-law: **Samuel D. James**– birthplace: <u>Wisconsin</u> (June 1863) —Parents place of birth: <u>Wales</u>--Spouse: <u>Ann Jones</u>—Birthplace: <u>Wisconsin</u> (Jan 1865) —Children: *Mamie, Mary, Maurice, Sarah, & Sadie*— Residence in 1910: *Genesee Township, Waukesha County*[718]–occupation: *retail merchant—general merchandize.* In 1923, *Thomas D. Jones* is retired— *maintains ownership of his an 81-acre farm with independent telephone.*[719] (Family #2, First Generation): Father: **William H. Elias**– birthplace: <u>Genesee Township, Waukesha County</u> (c. 1861)— Spouse: **Mary K.**—Birthplace: <u>Wisconsin</u> (c. 1861) — Children: *William, Mary & Elizabeth. Both of William Elias' parents were born in* <u>Wales</u> *and immigrated to Wisconsin during the 1850's—In 1860, William H. Elias's* father, **W. H. Elias**, was **the President of the Wales Bank, Wales**. In 1914 *William H. Elias* <u>owned a 42.75-acre Town of Wales (section 4) farm just to the west of the Village of Wales—The Chicago & Northwestern Railroad ran through his far</u>m[720]--Residence in 1920: *Genesee Township, Waukesha County*—occupation: *farmer. In 1873 Elizabeth Elias inherited 160-acre of his father's (section 4) Town of Genesee farm.* [721]   (Image and genealogy courtesy of Wales Village Hall, Wales, Wisconsin.)

Sadie James & Elizabeth Elias (1908)[722]

Welshmen Hoped for a Better Life Here

By CHARLIE HOUSE

John Hughes and their six children who arrived here from **Carmarthenshire** in 1840. *The hilly country of Waukesha County might seem like the Hughes' Welsh homeland, a place of rocky Paleozoic hills and long, deep green valleys.* **Hughes** bought his property in the glacial hills of the **town of Genesee** near <u>Lime brook</u>, calling his farm **Nant-y-calch**. By 1842, the <u>Welsh</u> population nearby was 99. A colony of 15 families arrived, led by **Richard Jones** of **Bronyberllan, Wales**. *Bronyberllan* became the name of the *Jones* farm, and, because of his leadership of the colonists, *Richard* became known good humoredly as **"King Jones."** An 1841 study on children in Welsh coal mines brought out such revelations as these--_**William Richards**: "I have been down (in the mines) about three years. When I first went down, I couldn't keep my eyes open. I don't fall asleep now, I smokes my pipe._" For such reasons, the **Welsh** hurried to America when they could depart.

[*The Milwaukee Journal Sunday*, November 13, 1966]

Welsh Aid Sought (1966): *(attached to the above article)*

Residents of Wisconsin and Michigan's Upper Peninsula are being asked to aid the stricken families of **Aberfan, Wales**, *where tons of coal slag descended upon the village and killed at least 150 persons, most of them children*. The state chairman of the drive, sponsored by the Gymanfa Ganu, a national Welsh organization (asked that) contributions should be mailed to Aberfan Disaster Fund, Box 4446, Milwaukee, Wis.   [*The Milwaukee Journal Sunday*, November 13, 1966][723]

717   *Standard Atlas of Waukesha County, Wisconsin.* Chicago, 1914, Town of Genesee.

718   *Federal Manuscript Schedule*, Population, Agricultural and Manufacturing Schedules for Waukesha County, Town of Genesee, 1900 & 1930.

719   *The Farm Journal Rural Directory of Waukesha County, 1918-1923*, p. 82.

720   *Standard Atlas of Waukesha County, Wisconsin.* Chicago, 1914, Town of Genesee.

721   *Atlas of Waukesha County, 1873*, Town of Genesee.

722   Photograph courtesy of Wales Village Hall, via Gail Tamez e-mail to author, Dec 21, 2016.

723   *The Milwaukee Journal Sunday*, November 13, 1966

IMMIGRANTS TO WISCONSIN FROM PRUSSIA

(1ˢᵗ Generation): Name: **Gottlieb Bartz** — Birthplace: **Preußen** (1 Apr1832)—Spouse: **August Brandt**—Year of Immigration: (1873)—Immigrant ship: *"Franklin"*—Port of arrival: New York (21 April 1873) — Residence in (1900) --Brookfield Township, Waukesha County—Occupation: *farmer.* –Children: *Amelia, Minnie & Herman* (2ⁿᵈ Generation):--Name: **Julius Bartz**—Born: (1874)--Birthplace: **Pewaukee, Township, Waukesha County**—Spouse: **Maggie Galatin**—Born: **Wisconsin** (1876)— Residence: (1900)—Brookfield Township, Waukesha County—also residing in this household-- father: Gottlieb Bartz (age: 68)---occupation: *mason*—his wife is deceased[724] --brother: *Herman*—Born: Wisconsin (1885)—*at school*—(1920) *Julius & Mary Bartz* Residence—City of Waukesha, Waukesha County—Children: *Viola, Vernie, Mabel, Arthur, Alvin, Dorothy & Edna.*[725]

(Image and genealogy courtesy of Jan Pace of Waukesha, Wisconsin.)

Gottlieb Bartz Family (1908)[726]

(l-r): Vernon, Gottlieb (grandfather), Julius (father), Art, Margaret (wife), Mabel & Viola.

Emigration:

"Julius Bartz is a native of Wauwatosa, Milwaukee county, his father having come to America in 1873 and locating in Milwaukee. *Before his immigration he was a soldier in the German army and took part in the Franco-Prussian War of 1870.* After living in Milwaukee, a year, the family moved to Wauwatosa township, where the father bought 24 acres of land & works a lime-kiln[727]."[728]

The Bartz Farm in Brookfield:

"After living there four years they removed to Pewaukee township and six years later to the farm in Brookfield where Julius now lives. The father, now seventy-five years of age (in 1907), still makes his home there, his wife having died in 1894. *Except about two and one-half years, when he was engaged in carrying milk, Julius has spent his life on the farm which he bought from his father and now devotes principally to dairying, making his own butter.* He raises some stock but only for his own use. Julius was educated in the district schools of Pewaukee and Brookfield townships and on arriving at maturity the family belongs to the **Lutheran church**, and Mr. Bartz supports the Republican party, although he has never taken a part in practical politics."[729]

---

[724] *Federal Manuscript Schedule,* Population, Agricultural and Manufacturing Schedules for Waukesha County, Town of Brookfield, 1900.

[725] *Memoirs of Waukesha County,* p. 357.

[726] Photograph courtesy of Jan Pace of Waukesha, Wisconsin, e-mail to author, Apr 5, 2011.

[727] "A lime kiln is used for the calcination of limestone to produce the form of lime called quicklime. The earliest descriptions of lime kilns differ little from those used for small-scale manufacture a century ago. Knowledge of its value in agriculture is ancient. Agricultural lime is a soil additive made from pulverized limestone or chalks which reduces soil acidity." (Several 19ᵗʰ Century lime kilns can still be seen in southeastern Wisconsin.) https://en.wikipedia.org/wiki/Lime_kiln

[728] *Memoirs of Waukesha County,* p. 357.

[729] *Memoirs of Waukesha County,* p. 358

IMMIGRANTS TO WISCONSIN FROM SAXONY & THE NETHERLANDS

Name: **William Henry Bishoff**-- Birthplace: <u>Sachsen</u> (Aug 1843) — William Bishoff's year of immigration: (c. 1850)--**Spouse: Anna Wensing** —Birthplace: **Province of Holland, Netherlands** (Oct 1854)—Year of immigration: 1856—In 1873, <u>Fred Bishoff owns a 58 ½ acre (section 14) Town of Muskego parcel bordering the north side of Big Muskego Lake</u>—Occupation: *farmer & cooper*--neighboring his farm to the east is Fred's brother **William Bishoff's** (30-acre farm)[730]-- William Bishoff's Residence in 1880: <u>Muskego Township, Waukesha County</u>— Occupation: *farmer*--William Bishoff's Residence in 1900: <u>Muskego Township, Waukesha County</u>— Occupation: *farmer*—Children: *William, Clara, George, Adolph, Rudolph & Edward.*— brother: **Fred Bischoff**-- Birthplace: <u>Sachsen</u> (Aug 1849)[731]—Spouse: **Miss Johanna "Mina" Bravier** of <u>Franklin Township</u>—the William Bischoff family's residence 1910: <u>Town of Washington, Shawano County</u>.
(Image and genealogy courtesy of Donna Hoff-Grambau of Mount Pleasant, Michigan.)[732]

William Henry Bishoff and Clara Elizabeth Rynders Wedding (June 30, 1908)[733]
Wedding held at St. Martins, Franklin Township, Milwaukee County.

Large demand for coopers:

"During the 19th Century, coopers <u>made everything that was round and drawn together with bands.</u> There was no member of the community more indispensable. He made <u>cisterns</u>, <u>meat tubs</u>, <u>churns</u> and <u>butter tubs</u>. He made the <u>milk pail</u> and the <u>water pail</u> and the <u>bucket that hung from the old well-sleep, and the pail from which the calves were fed.</u> He made <u>sap buckets</u>—hundreds of thousands of them— all from native lumber with <u>wooden hoops</u>. He made <u>flour barrels</u> and <u>cider barrels</u>. Practically speaking, he made everything which have been replaced with tin and iron."[734]

Frederick Bishoff—Cooper:

"Frederick Bishoff, *farmer*, Sec. 13; P.O. **Tess Corners**; born in 1849 in **Saxony**; his parents *Christopher and Christina B.*, emigrated in 1851; spent two years in Milwaukee County, then came to Waukesha County. *Frederick Bishoff settled on his present farm of (34--acres) in 1873; is a cooper by trade, manufacturing pork barrels for the Milwaukee houses.* He married **Miss Johanna Bravier**, of **Franklin, Milwaukee County**; they have three children—*Frederick, Edward & William*—all born on the farm."[735]

---

730   *Atlas of Waukesha County, Wisconsin, 1873*, Town of Muskego.

731   *The History of Waukesha County, 1880*, p. 904

732   . *Federal Manuscript Schedule*, Population, Agricultural and Manufacturing Schedules for Waukesha County, Town of Muskego, 1900.

733   Photograph courtesy of Donna Hoff-Grambau of Mount Pleasant, Michigan, e-mail to author, Apr 24, 2010.

734   Wagenen, "The Golden Age of Homespun." *Agricultural Bulletin, No. 203*, p. 88.

735   *The History of Waukesha County, 1880*, p. 904.

IMMIGRANTS TO WISCONSIN FROM NEW YORK

Name: **A. J. Coleman**– Birthplace: <u>New York</u> (1818) — Spouse: <u>Matilda</u> –Birthplace: <u>New York City</u> (c. 1819)— Residence in 1860: <u>Brookfield Township, Waukesha County</u>—Occupation: *farmer*—Children: *William,* ***Charles**, Hannah, Julia, Oliver & William.* (Image and genealogy courtesy of Roberta Poetsch of Rochester, Minnesota.)[736]

Charles B. Coleman (c. 1909)[737]

Horse Thieves Captured.

On Sunday morning **Mr. Charles Coleman** *et.al.,* of Brookfield, came to Waukesha and announced the fact that a horse has been stolen belonging to Mr. W. R. Blodgett, who is a member of the "Thief Detective Society." *In a few moments the officers of the Society, with Deputy Sheriff Robert (Bob) Jones, were on hand to assist them, and they soon found the horse and thieves at the American House.* It seems that two Germans so-called peddlers came along by Blodgett's[738] and took from his stable a fine young horse and left theirs by the roadside. They arrived in Waukesha about 5'oclock, got breakfast, and were about starting out when our Brookfield friends arrived. On seeing them the horse thieves took leg bail up the banks of the mill race, One was caught at the upper bridge and the other ran till he was forced to surrender or put into the mill pond but chose the latter. *After being surrounded sometime in the pond and listening to "Bob's" revolver, he concluded to "give up the job."* (conti- below)

"Anxious to drown or hang the thieves"

A majority of the crowd present were anxious to drown or hang the thieves, but they were finally conducted to jail in "good order." The thieves are two young men who travel the country disguised as peddlers, while their business is that of "petty thieves," but are not smart enough for horse thieves. "Bob" waded through the mud into the river and brought out the head thief. While we admire "Bob's" pluck, we are free to say we would much rather have shot him while defying us in the river and taken out his lifeless body. But, the best joke of the whole was played on the first one captured, While "Bob" and his crowd were following the last one, we stood guard on the Bridge Street bridge over the first one. *In the meantime, quite a crowd gathered, among whom was our old friend,* ***Russell Wheeler**; and we suggested to the crowd, that in order to save expense we hang him or drown him, when someone shouted out "drown him," and in a moment Wheeler caught him from us and threw him in over the railing of the bridge into the race, but he caught upon the timbers and was permitted to "come ashore*. The thieves gave their names as **Charley May**, 21 years of age, and **Carl Recart Luber**, 24 years of age.---They are from Milwaukee, and they say *they go for Grant for president. We thought so.*" [*Waukesha Plaindealer* Sept. 24, 1872]

---

736 *Federal Manuscript Schedule*, Population, Agricultural and Manufacturing Schedules for Waukesha County, Town of Brookfield, 1860.

737 Photograph courtesy of Roberta Poetsch of Rochester, Minnesota, e-mail to author, May 10, 2009.

738 "The settlement was originally called Storyville, after Augustus Story who settled in the area about 1837. It was later known as Blodgett for Chester Blodgett who arrived in 1843. The Watertown Plank Road between Milwaukee and Watertown was built through this area during 1848-54, and a spur to Waukesha in 1850. The current name of Goerke's Corners comes from Frederick Goerke, blacksmith, wagonmaker, and innkeeper in this area in the 1870s." From: https://en.wikipedia.org/wiki/Goerke%27s_Corners,_Wisconsin

IMMIGRANTS TO WISCONSIN FROM IRELAND

Name: **Robert Hunter** — Birthplace: **Ireland** (c 1822)— Spouse: **Mary**— Birthplace: **Ireland**--Year of "Immigration: c. 1848—Residence in 1860: Ottawa Township, Waukesha--Occupation: *farmer*--Children: *Elizabeth, James, Robert, Sarah, David & William*: In 1873, Robert Hunter owned a 397 1/2-acre (section 11) Town of Ottawa farm. On his farm are 2 rather large lakes with *Scuppernong Creek* meandering through his fields.[739] By 1914, the Hunter family has sold their farm, however, the larger lake is now named **Hunter's Lake** and bordering the west side of the lake is a small park named *Hunter's Lake Park*.[740]

(Image and genealogy courtesy of "OTTAWA HISTORIAN" Carl L. Borgstram, of Ottawa, Wisconsin.)[741]

Robert Hunter Family (c. 1910)[742]

Hunter Family:

(L-R): Robert, Gay (grandson, James—Parents: Robert & Mary—Daughter & Husband: Mary & James.[743]

"The Springtime of the People:"

"*1848 was revolutions throughout continental Europe.* In a *year of* February 1848, King Louis-Philippe of France was overthrown, and the Second Republic was proclaimed in Paris. *This revolution sent political shock waves across Europe, and revolutions broke out in Berlin, Vienna, Rome, Prague, and Budapest.* It was sometimes described as *"The Springtime of the people"*. Ireland was also still reeling from the impact of the Great Famine. Inspired by these events and the success of liberal, romantic nationalism on the European mainland, they took an uncompromising stand for a national Parliament with full legislative and executive powers. At its founding, the Confederation resolved to be based on principles of freedom, tolerance and truth. *Their goal was independence of the Irish nation and they held to use any means to achieve that which were consistent with honor, morality and reason.*" (The ultimate failure of the Young Irelander Rebellion coupled with the failed movement of the "48er's" movement throughout mainland Europe may have caused numerous Irish families, such as the Hunters, to immigrate to America.)[744]

---

[739] *Atlas of Waukesha Co. Wisconsin, 1873,* Town of Ottawa.

[740] *Standard Atlas of Waukesha County, Wisconsin, 1914,* Town of Ottawa.

[741] *Federal Manuscript Schedule,* Population, Agricultural and Manufacturing Schedules for Waukesha County, Town of Ottawa, 1860.

[742] Photograph courtesy of Carl L. Borgstram Town of Ottawa Wisconsin, author home visit, Aug 10, 2009.

[743] Carl L. Borgstram Town of Ottawa Wisconsin, author home visit, Aug 10, 2009.

[744] https://en.wikipedia.org/wiki/Young_Irelander_Rebellion_of_1848

IMMIGRANTS TO WISCONSIN FROM ENGLAND

Name: **Albert Beecroft** — Birthplace: <u>**Walsall, Staffordshire, England**</u> (1864)—Spouse: **Mary Ann Wilson** –Birthplace: <u>**England**</u>—Year of Immigration: c. 1902—Residence in 1910: <u>Waukesha, Waukesha County, Wisconsin</u>—Occupation: *farmer*–Children: *Mabel, Ethel, Dorothy & Florence.*
(Image and genealogy courtesy of Mark J. Kelly of Texas City, Texas.)[745]

Albert Beecroft Family (c. 1910)[746]

(L-R): Dorothy, Mary Ann (mother), Florence, Mabel, Albert (father) & Ethel.

Walsall, Staffordshire, England:

By the first part of the 13th century, Walsall (the birthplace of Albert Beecroft in 1864) was a small market town. *The Industrial Revolution changed Walsall from a village of 2,000 people in the 16th century to a town of over 86,000 in approximately 200 years.* The town manufactured a wide range of products including saddles, chains, and plated ware. Nearby, limestone quarrying provided the town with much prosperity.[747]

Ellis Island:

"On April 18, 1890, and Congress appropriated $75,000 to construct America's first federal immigration station on Ellis Island. Ellis Island became the gateway for over 12 million immigrants to the U.S. as the United States' busiest immigrant inspection station for over 60 years. *The first station was a three-story-tall structure with outbuildings, built of Georgia Pine. It opened with fanfare on January 1, 1892."*[748] (*the Albert Beecroft family past through Ellis Island inspection station that same year.*) Once ferried over to Manhattan, the Beercrofts likely hurried to a train which would take them from New York City all the way to Chicago and then transfer to another train going north where they departed at the Chicago & Northwestern's glamorous new train station at Milwaukee. With its stone Romanesque architecture and a clock tower reaching 234 ft., the new station became an instant source of great pride by the local citizenry.[749]

Immigrants from many lands:

"At first, the majority of immigrants arriving through Ellis Island were Northern and Western Europeans (Germany, France, Switzerland, Belgium, The Netherlands, Great Britain, and the Scandinavian countries). *Eventually, these groups of peoples slowed in the rates that they were coming in, and immigrants came in from Southern and Eastern Europe, including Jews. Many reasons these immigrants came to the United States included escaping political and economic oppression, as well as persecution, destitution, and violence.* Other groups of peoples being processed through the station were Poles, Hungarians, Czechs, Serbs, Slovaks, Greeks, Syrians, Turks, and Armenia."[750]

---

745   *Federal Manuscript Schedule*, Population, Agricultural and Manufacturing Schedules for Waukesha County, Town of Waukesha, 1910.

746   Photograph courtesy of Mark J. Kelly of Texas City, Texas, e-mail to author, Jul 12, 2010.

747   https://en.wikipedia.org/wiki/Walsall

748   ttps://en.wikipedia.org/wiki/Ellis_Island

749   https://en.wikipedia.org/wiki/Lake_Front_Depot

750   ttps://en.wikipedia.org/wiki/Ellis_Island

IMMIGRANTS TO WISCONSIN FROM BADEN & IRELAND

Name: **Thomas Michael Blessinger** – Birthplace: **Sinsheim, Baden** (1835) — Spouse: **Elizabeth Hutchinson** –Birthplace: **Ireland**– Port of Emigration: Liverpool, England— ship: *"Trumbull"*— listed occupation: *servant*—Port of Arrival: New York (18 Sept. 1851)—In 1873, Michael Blessinger owns a small 5-acre (section 35) parcel near the *Prairie du Chien Division of the Milwaukee & St. Paul Railroad* running alongside the Fox River, in Pewaukee Township—leading into the Village of Waukesha—Occupation: *laborer*–Children: *John, Helen, Margaretha, Lena, Michael & Louis.*[751] Circa 1880's: the parents—Michael & Elizabeth Blessinger relocated to Milwaukee.

(Image and genealogy courtesy of Georgia Davis Briggeman of Deer Lodge, Powell Co., Montana.)[752]

Thomas Michael Blessinger (c. 1910)[753]

A Revolution Demanding Democracy Sparked at Sinsheim:

"During the Baden Revolution in 1848 there were rebellions of Democratic citizens and craftsmen in Sinsheim (the birthplace of Michael Blessinger in 1835). Revolutionaries: took control of the Sinsheim town hall during April of 1848 and proclaimed, there, the "Democratic Republic of Baden". Afterwards they moved with 250 armed free-marchers to Heidelberg to assist revolutionaries there. [754]

"The Legacy of the Great Famine":

(Irish: An Gorta Mór or An Drochshaol, litt: The Bad Life) followed the catastrophic period of Irish history between 1845 and 1852 during which time the population of Ireland was reduced by 20 to 25 percent (*Elizabeth Hutchinson*, who immigrated from Ireland to Wisconsin near the end of the famine, was born there permanently changed the island's during the 1830s.) *The famine was a watershed in the history of Ireland.* Its effects demographic, political and cultural landscape. *For both the native Irish and those in the resulting diaspora[755], the famine entered folk memory and became a rallying point for various nationalist movements.*"[756]

The Whistling Motorman.

Michael Blessinger, 78, who was one of the first motormen between Milwaukee and Waukesha, died at his home in Milwaukee yesterday. While living here Blessinger was night watchman at the old Woolen mills. *In Milwaukee, Blessinger was mourned today by hundreds of streetcar riders who had known him as 'the whistling motorman' because of the whistle he carried.* In Milwaukee, Blessinger was mourned today by hundreds of streetcar riders who had known him as 'the whistling motorman' because of the whistle he carried. [*Waukesha Daily Freeman* December 26, 1946]

---

[751] Atlas of Waukesha County, 1873, Town of Pewaukee.

[752] *Federal Manuscript Schedule*, Population, Agricultural and Manufacturing Schedules for Waukesha County, Town of Waukesha, 1870.

[753] Photograph courtesy of Georgia Davis Briggeman of Deer Lodge, Powell Co., Montana, e-mail to author, July 8, 2010.

[754] https://sco.wikipedia.org/wiki/Sinsheim

[755] "Diaspora has come to refer to involuntary mass dispersions of a population from its indigenous territories. The term would apply to the mass exodus of one million Irishman during and after the Irish Famine." From: https://en.wikipedia.org/wiki/Diaspora

[756] https://en.wikipedia.org/wiki/Legacy_of_the_Great_Irish_Famine

IMMIGRANTS TO WISCONSIN FROM BADEN

Name: **Joseph Blessinger** & **Margareta (Deer) Blessinger** of <u>Siegelsbach, Baden</u>--emigrated from Le Havre, France, on board the *"Confederation"*--arriving in the Port of <u>New York</u> on Christmas Day of 1851, after a voyage of thirty-six days. By 1873, Joseph Blessinger owns a 100-acre (section 7) <u>Town of Muskego</u> farm—all unimproved timber land— Children: *Catherine* (widow of Valentine Plumb, resides in ***Deer Lodge County, Montana***), *Margareta, Joseph, Michael, Louis*—(wife of **Joseph Lossel**, a *hotel man* of ***Pioneer, Deer Lodge County, Montana***)-- *Louis Magdalena, Magdalena, Hannah & Phillip--the youngest of this family, was killed during a thunder shower in **Deer Lodge County, Montana*** — a son of *Joseph*, **Louis Blessinger**, married: **Margareta Sickel** (28 Apr 1867)--Children: *Katie, Josephine*—(died in childhood), *Elizabeth, Louis*—(died in childhood), *Amanda, Mary*--(died in childhood), *George & Lena*--during the early 1880's, after the death of his father—*Joseph*--***Louise Blessinger*** sold his father's farm and purchased a 100-acre (section 25) <u>Town of Muskego</u> farm at <u>Durham Hill</u>—[757] In 1889, **Louis Blessinger** purchased a 125.5 (section 19) as well as a 40-acre (section 30), <u>Town of New Berlin</u> farm—By 1914, a son of Louise, **George Blessinger**, takes ownership of the family farm--occupation: *farmer & stock breeder*. By 1923, George Blessinger is single, he owns 160-acre (sections 19 & 30) <u>Town of New Berlin dairy farm</u>, with 7 horses & 23 dairy cows; Rural Route 4 and Bell telephone service--the Blessinger family was Catholic [758] (Image and genealogy courtesy of Georgia Davis Briggeman of Deer Lodge County, Montana)[759]

Joseph Walter Kau (circa 1910)[760]

Young Kau & Blessinger dreamers from New Berlin & Muskego head to Montana, but late, as the Gold Rush had peaked decades earlier:

Caspar Kau: born on Jan. 12, 1826, in **Strassfeld, Prussia**—Spouse: **Margareta "Maggie" Blessinger** born on October 1, 1829, in **Siegelsbach, Sinsheim Co, Baden**—a son: **Joseph Kau** born: June 26, 1866-<u>New Berlin, Waukesha County</u>—ventured west to ***Butte, Montana*** (circa 1888)— He had this photo taken at Butte & purchased a *saloon* with a partner in ***Pioneer*** (at the outskirts of Butte) that same year--married **Laura Hess—age: 17** (17 Dec 1891) at ***Deer Lodge, Montana***—children: Margaret, Joseph & Clayton—all born at ***Pioneer Missoula County, Montana*** –Joseph & Laura divorced (1898)—Joseph died—Jan 26, i918 in ***Missoula***.[761]

Butte, Montana: "In 1864, the founding of the *'Asteroid Mine'* attracted prospectors from Cornwall, Ireland & Wales seeking gold and silver. *By the early 1900's, Butte became the largest producer of copper in North America*. The amount of ore produced in the city earned it the nickname "<u>The Richest Hill on Earth</u>." It built a sizable workforce with miners performing hazardous work."[762]

Deer Lodge, Montana: "*'Anaconda'*, in Deer Lodge County, Montana, was founded by Marcus Daly, one of the *'Copper Kings'* who *financed the construction of a smelter on nearby 'Warm Springs Creek' to process copper ore from the Butte mines.*"[763]

Helena, Montana: "*By 1888, about 50 millionaires lived in Helena, more per capita than in any city in the world.* They had made their fortunes from gold. About $3.6 billion (in today's dollars) of gold was taken from *"Last Chance Gulch"* over a 20-year period. *'The Last Chance Placer' is one of the most famous placer deposits[764] in the western United States.* Most of the production occurred before 1868."[765]

[757]   *Atlas of Waukesha County, 1873*, Town of Muskego.

[758]   *Standard Atlas of Waukesha County, Wisconsin, 1914*, Town of Muskego.

[759]   *Federal Manuscript Schedule*, Population, Agricultural and Manufacturing Schedules for Waukesha County, Town of Muskego, 1870.

[760]   Photograph courtesy of Lois (Phillips) Alton of Hartland, Wisconsin, e-mail to author, June 5, 2010.

[761]   Genealogy courtesy of Bryan Ramstack of San Antonio, Texas

[762]   https://en.wikipedia.org/wiki/Butte,_Montana

[763]   Georgia Davis Briggeman of Deer Lodge, Powell County, Montana, e-mail to author, Jul 9, 2017 & https://en.wikipedia.org/wiki/Deer_Lodge,_Montana

[764]   "In geology, a placer deposit or placer is an accumulation of valuable minerals formed by gravity separation from a specific source rock during sedimentary processes. The name is from the Spanish word placer, meaning " alluvial sand" Taken from: en.wikipedia.org/wiki/Placer deposit

[765]   https://en.wikipedia.org/wiki/Helena,_Montana

IMMIGRANTS TO WISCONSIN FROM MECKLENBURG SCHWERIN

(1ˢᵗ Generation): Name: **Carl Christian Friedrich Boldt** – Birthplace: <u>**Gnoien, Mecklenburg Schwerin**</u> (1824) — Year of immigration: (1846)-- Spouse: **Friedricke Louise H. Tess** —Birthplace: <u>**Nord West Mecklenburg Schwerin**</u> (March 1834)— came with her parents to America in 1854, her father, **Jacob Tess**, a native of **Mecklenburg**, being one of the first settlers at **Tess Corners**, which hamlet, <u>in the Town of Muskego</u>, was named in his honor. **Carl & Friedrich** were married at the **Lutheran Church**--(2ⁿᵈ Generation): **Henry Boldt**, born: (Aug. 18, 1848), at <u>Tess Corners, Muskego township</u>—married (Sept. 1881) **Caroline Holz**, born in <u>Muskego township</u> (18 Sept 1850)—Children: *Bertha, Ellen William Edward & Henry*--<u>Caroline died</u> (26 Dec 1891)—**Henry Boldt's** (2ⁿᵈ marriage): **Bertha (Holz)** (1892)--sister of his first wife and widow of **August Kister**—Children: *Rudolph & Adelia*—by 1914, Heinrich Bolt owns a 108. 14-acre (section 2) <u>Town of Muskego farm</u> on the northwest side of Tess Corners—a stream meanders through his farm —by 1923, Henry & Bertha have retired—6 adult children remain on the family's Muskego farm—*reduced to 47 acres; 1 horse, 1 cow; Rural Mail Route 11, at Calhoun Station; with Bell telephone service.* [766]——By 1923, Henry & Bertha have retired—6 adult children continue to reside on the family's Muskego farm—now reduced to 47 acres; 1 horse, 1 cow; Rural Mail Route 11, at Calhoun Station, along with Bell telephone service. [767]   (Image and genealogy courtesy of Crystal Keslin of Lubbock, Texas.)[768]

Heinrich Boldt Family (c. 1910)[769]

The Boldt Family:

Sitting-(l-r): Heinrich (Father), Adelia, Bertha Holz (mother) & Ellen: Standing-(l-r): —William, Rudolph, Henry, Bertha & Edward.[770]

The Boldt family of Mecklenburg:

"**Gnoien** (the birthplace of Carl Christian Friedrich Boldt) is a small town in the district of Mecklenburg. <u>The Thirty Years' War severely damaged the city.</u> Followed by periods of plague and cholera."[771]

A full life at Tess Corners, Muskego Township:

"Henry Bolt started out for himself at the age of twenty-two, purchasing a farm of 68 acres, to which he later added 40. *This farm is devoted to general agriculture and dairying, the herd numbering 30 high-bred cattle, for the milk of which the creamery at Tess Corners forms a convenient market.* As is usual in this part of the county, considerable attention is also given to the raising of hogs. The Lutheran church the religious faith of the family." [772]

---

766 *Standard Atlas of Waukesha County, Wisconsin, 1914,* Town of Muskego.

767 *The Farm Journal Rural Directory of Waukesha County, 1918-1923,* p. 29.

768 *Federal Manuscript Schedule,* Population, Agricultural and Manufacturing Schedules for Waukesha County, Tess Corners, Town of Muskego, 1870.

769 Photograph courtesy of Crystal Keslin of Lubbock, Texas, e-mail to author, May 3, 2010.

770 Crystal Keslin of Lubbock, Texas, e-mail to author, May 3, 2010.

771 https://translate.google.com/translate?hl=en&sl=de&u=https://de.wikipedia.org/wiki/Gnoien&prev=search

772 *1907 Memoirs of Waukesha County,* p. 370

IMMIGRANTS TO WISCONSIN FROM DENMARK & NORWAY

Name: **Mads Larson** -- Birthplace: **Musse, Lolland, Dänmark** (12 May1847) --Immigrated to America: (23 April 1868)— Spouse: **Lena Marie Narum**, of the **Town of Norway, Racine County**—Lena's Birthplace: **Norge** (1846)— Mads & Lena were married: 29 May 1877--Residence in 1810: <u>Delafield, Waukesha County, Wisconsin</u> --Occupation: *blacksmith*–Children: *William, Peter & Hans.*

(Image and genealogy courtesy of the Hartland Historical Society.)[773]

Mads Larson (c. 1910)[774]

Denmark's failure to maintain political ties results in crushing defeats:

"Musse, Lolland, (the birthplace of Mads Larson), is a small village on the island of Lollans, in Denmark. Denmark was brought into the Napoleonic Wars on the French side when attacked by Britain at the Battles of Copenhagen in 1801 and 1807. The eventual defeat of Napoleon led to the break-up of the Denmark-Norway union. Since the early 18th century Schleswig-Holsteins aimed for independence from Denmark. *The First Schleswig War (1848–1851) broke out after constitutional change in 1849 and ended with the status quo because of the intervention of Britain and other Great Powers. (conti. below)*

National-Liberals demanded permanent ties between Schleswig and Denmark:

Denmark faced war against both Prussia and Austria in what became known as the Second Schleswig War (1864). The war lasted from February to October 1864. *Denmark was easily beaten by Prussia and Austria and obliged to relinquish both Schleswig and Holstein. The war caused Denmark, as a nation, severe trauma, forcing large immigration to North America.* (Mads Larson immigrated to the United States through the port town of Nystad on the east coast of Denmark through the Baltic Sea in 1868.)[775]

"OLD AND PROMINENT CITIZEN PASSES AWAY"

Mads Larson Had Been Identified with Hartland's Progress for Many Years.

The death of Mr. *Mads Larson,* on Monday evening, February 19, has removed one of Hartland's most highly esteemed men, a public-spirited citizen and a resident of many years. Mr. Larson had lived in Hartland since 1868, at which time he came to this country from his home in Denmark. *Having served his apprentice as a blacksmith in Denmark, he began to work at his trade here in the shop of John Krause. On June 9, 1873, he started a shop of his own and continued in that work until September 1903.* Being of a reserved nature, he never sought preferment in public office, but he was at various times tendered public positions in the community, and also served as village president. He was a charter member of the Hartland Fire department and had served as its treasurer for twenty-four years.

[*Hartland News* February 24, 1917]

---

773 *Federal Manuscript Schedule,* Population, Agricultural and Manufacturing Schedules for Waukesha County, Town of Delafield, 1900.

774 Image courtesy of the Hartland Historical Society, e-mail to author, Aug 17, 2010.

775 https://en.wikipedia.org/wiki/Military_history_of_Denmark

IMMIGRANTS TO WISCONSIN FROM ALSACE, FRANCE & RHENISH PRUSSIA

Name: **John H. Phillips** and his spouse **Catherine Casper**—both of **Elsass, France**[776] (12 May 1821)— Son: **Barney Phillips**—and his spouse: *Mary Catherine Kau* —Birthplace: **New Berlin, Waukesha County** (1870) —Mary's parents: **Caspar Kau** of **Strassfeld, Kreis Rheinbach, Bezirk Cöln, Rheinisches/ Rheinpreußen** and **Margaretha Blessinger** of **Heidelberg, Baden**. **Barney & Mary Phillips** residence in 1900: **Muskego Township, Waukesha County**[777]—Occupation: *farmer*– In 1914, Barney & Mary (Kau) Phillips run a 35.86-acre (section 3) farm in **Muskego, Township**[778]--Children: *Helen*—(employed at the Milwaukee County Home for Dependent Children on the County Grounds in Wauwatosa --1912-1915), *William*—WWI Veteran, *Clara (Caroline) & Amanda*. By 1923 Barney & Mary Phillips-owns a 40-acre town of Muskego farm, they have 4 adult children, along with 3 horses, 8 cattle; Rural Mail Route 11 (Calhoun Station) and Bell Telephone service.[779]   (Image courtesy of a Lois (Phillips) Alton of Hartland, Wisconsin; Genealogy courtesy of Mary Stigler of Brookfield, Wisconsin.)[780]

Mary Phillips' oldest daughter--Helen (circa 1910)[781]

Mary (Kau) Phillip's Cookbook:

"The cookbook was probably written sometime around 1900 and would have been added to throughout *Grandma Mary Phillips'* life. It was created from recipes shared among her Muskego & New Berlin friends and neighbors. *Cooking was an art; there was nothing scientific about it.* Woodburning stoves did not typically have temperature gauges. The cook learned by trial and error how much and what kind of wood to add to the firebox. *Little girls learned the "art" at Mama's knee—watching, listening, and finally attempting "receipts" for themselves.* Everyday recipes were not written down. It would have only been the special cakes and cookies or pickles and preserves not often made that would have gone into those handwritten treasures." *--Mary Meier-Ramstack* [782]

Neighbor's names along with their recipe "names" found inside Mary Phillips' recipe book:

MRS. N. RAUSCH--Hot Water Sponge Cake, Spice Fruit Cake, Lemon Pie==**MRS. HANSON**—Graham Cake, Graham Bread==**MRS. ELGER:** Baking Powder Biscuit, Potato Dumpling, Apple Sauce Cake, Oatmeal Cookies, Drop Cookies-- **IRMA** --Loaf Fig Cake, Date Cake, Potato Cake=**MRS. M.A. KLEINHENS**—Fruit Cake, Sunshine Cake, Fried Cakes, Fog Frosting, Marble Cake, Cornstarch Cake, German Coffee Cake, Eggless Cake, Expensive Sponge Cake, Johnny Cake, Bunt Sugar Cake, Brine for Cucumber Pickles, Dandelion Wine=**MRS. FRED BURBACK**—Baking Powder Biscuit, Mincemeat. Potato Dumpling, Dutch Peach Cake, Jelly Roll Cake, Two Egg Cake, Hot Water Sponge Cake==**MAMIE CASPER**—French Cucumbers, Sweet Sour Green Tomatoes, Spiced Beets, Lazy Wife Pickles, Jumbles, Mahogany Cake, Feather Cake, Breas Pudding==**MRS. GOETZ**—Blitz Torte, Graham Cake, Rye Bread, Tea Rolls, Parker House Rolls, Potato Pancakes, Good Cookies, Caned Pie plant, Mustard Pickles, Canned Beans, Grape Wine.[783]

[776] "The Imperial Territory of Alsace-Lorraine (German: Elsass-Lothringen) was a territory created by the German Empire in 1871, after it annexed most of Alsace and the Moselle department of Lorraine following its victory in the Franco-Prussian War." From: https://en.wikipedia.org/wiki/Alsace-Lorraine. It's important to keep in mind that the great majority of the families who immigrated to Wisconsin from Alsace Lorraine, France, did so before their annexation into the German Empire in 1871.

[777] *Federal Manuscript Schedule*, Population, Agricultural and Manufacturing Schedules for Waukesha County, Town of New Berlin, 1873; Town of Muskego, 1900.

[778] *Standard Atlas of Waukesha County, Wisconsin, 1914.* Muskego Township.

[779] *The Farm Journal Rural Directory of Waukesha County*, 1918, p. 122.

[780] *Federal Manuscript Schedule*, Population, Agricultural and Manufacturing Schedules for Waukesha County, Town of Muskego, 1900.

[781] Photograph courtesy of a Lois Alton of Hartland, Wisconsin, e-mail to author, Dec.16, 2016. (Helen (Phillips) Ramstack was the author's and, oh yes, my 9 sibling's grandmother.

[782] "From Mary (Kau) Phillip's Cookbook," by Mary Meier-Ramstack, Dec. 1997.

[783] Great-Grandmother "Mary Kau Phillips' recipe book," from author's collection.

IMMIGRANTS FROM ALSACE, FRANCE & CANADA

(1ˢᵗ generation): Name: **Joseph Casper**—birthplace: **Elsass, France** (circa: 1786)—Spouse: **Katherine Detinger**—birthplace: **Elsass, France** (29 June 1824--(2ⁿᵈ generation): Son: **Bernard Casper**--Birthplace: **Als Elsass, France** (29 June 1824)—Immigrated to U.S. (1845)—Residence in 1845: **Rochester New York**—Occupation: *cooper*--Spouse: **Catherine Lehman**—married: (14 Aug 1848) in **Preston, Ontario, Canada**—Residence in 1851: <u>New Berlin Township, Waukesha County</u>—Occupation: *saloon owner & farmer*--(Served for 12 years as Town of New Berlin Supervisor)—Children: *George, Bernard, Alois, Joseph* (1854-1860), *Joseph* (1860-1861), *Catherina, Andreas, Elizabeth, Valentine, Charles, John Vincent & William*--(3ʳᵈ generation): Name: **John Vincent Casper**--place of birth: <u>New Berlin Township, Waukesha County</u> (1864)—Spouse: **Maria Magdalena**--Occupation: *tavern keeper, farmer & Assistant Postmaster*—Children—*Valentine, Rosalia "Rosie," Andrew & Veronica.* In 1914, John Casper owns, along with a *tavern*, a 56.5-acre (sections 15 & 22) *Town of New Berlin farm*--By 1923, John Vincent owns a <u>*56-acre farm*</u>, with <u>*one adult child*</u> at home—including: *2 horses, 10 cows; Rural Route 11, mail posted from Calhoun.* (Image courtesy of Lois Alton of Hartland, Wiscosnin; Genealogy courtesy of Mary Stigler of Brookfield, Wisconsin.)[784]

John and son, Valentine, in front of the John Casper "Central Hotel" (1912)[785]

Bernard Casper's famous sidewalk:

THE TAVERN: *The original Bernard Casper's, "New Berlin Central Hotel." building still stands today, located on W. National Ave just to the west of Holy Apostles Catholic Church.* Casper's was a popular gathering place for local farmers beginning in 1858. At the turn of the century, Bernard Casper's son, John, advertised "Independent Milwaukee Lager Beer."

THE CHURCH: *St. Valerius (present day Holy Apostles) was New Berlin's oldest church, organized in 1844 by immigrants from Alsace, France.* A two-story brick church with a 134-foot steeple was replaced, in 1967, by its present structure. (conti, b<u>elow)</u>

CONNECTING THE TWO: *Bernard Casper built a sidewalk, from his tavern east a few hundred feet to St. Valerius Catholic Church for his daughter's wedding.* It is the only known 19ᵗʰ Century sidewalk designed specifically to connect a ***church*** and a ***saloon*** in Waukesha County."[786]

Gas Kills Him: Bernard Casper of New Berlin--Meets Death in Milwaukee.

Bernard Casper, aged 70, postmaster at New Berlin, and an old resident of the town, was found dead in his bed at the residence of Frank Laner, a Milwaukee south side saloon keeper, Tuesday morning. He stayed at Laner's Monday and in turning off the gas partly turned it back on again. *The gas escaped so slowly that Casper did not notice it before going to sleep.* Mr. Casper married Miss Catharine Lehman of Canada. Mr. Casper was a prominent member of St. Valerius (Catholic) Church and held a number of offices. He leaves a large family of grown children.
[*Waukesha Freeman* March 26, 1896]

---

[784] *Federal Manuscript Schedule*, Population, Agricultural and Manufacturing Schedules for Waukesha County, Town of New Berlin, 1860.

[785] Photograph courtesy of Lois Phillips of Hartland, Wisconsin, e-mail to author, Dec.16, 2016.

[786] *New Berlin Landmarks Commission* CHAPTER 4: "Cultural & Historical Resources." Revisions approved by Council on 6/14/2016 via Ordinance #2568, New Berlin 2020, Comprehensive Plan 4:20

IMMIGRANTS TO WISCONSIN FROM PRUSSIA

(1st Generation): Name: **Gottlieb Bartz** (1908) — Birthplace: **Preußen** (1832)—Spouse: *widowed*—Year of Immigration: 1873—immigrant ship: *"Golden Light"*—Port of arrival: Quebec— Residence in 1900: Brookfield Township, Waukesha County--(2nd Generation)--Name: **Julius Bartz**—Spouse: **Margaret**--In 1914, Julius owns a (section 29) 59-acre Town of Brookfield farm--Children: *Viola, Mabel, Vernon & Arthur*——-Occupation: *farmer. Poplar Creek meanders through the Bartz farm.* --In 1918, *Julius & Margaret Bartz* own 3 horses & 12 cows; Rural Mail Route 7; with Bell telephone service.[787]   (Image and genealogy courtesy of Jan Pace of Waukesha, Wisconsin.)[788]

Bartz Family (c. 1912)[789]

Bartz Family

Left to right:
Gottlieb (the grandfather)— wearing wooden clogs, Viola, Albert, (Julius' brother), Arthur (the youngest), Mabel, Vernon, Margaret (mother) and Julius (father).[790]

Clothing Styles of the early 1900's:

"The Bartz family photograph is marvelous—those bib overalls are so good to get in an image. The girls wear long plain work dresses reaching below the knees. *Gottlieb, standing to the left, wears a pair of **wooden clogs**, not at all unusual footwear for immigrant farmers in Wisconsin.* They were regarded as barn shoes were a farmer might stomp through mud or cow manure out in the barn. They could, then, be easily changed into a clean pair as they stepped back into the house."***--Joan Severa.***[791]

The Julius Bartz farm:

Gottlieb Bartz came to American in 1873 and locating in Milwaukee. Previous to his immigration he was a soldier in the German army and took part in the Franco-Prussian war of 1870. *A son, Julius Bartz, has spent his life on the Brookfield farm which he bought from his father and now devotes principally to dairying, making his own butter.* He raises some stock but only for his own use. The family belongs to the *Lutheran Church.*[792]

787   *The Farm Journal Rural Directory of Waukesha County, 1918*, p. 23.

788   *Federal Manuscript Schedule*, Population, Agricultural and Manufacturing Schedules for Waukesha County, Town of Brookfield, 1900.

789   Photograph courtesy of Jan Pace of Waukesha, Wisconsin, e-mail to author, Apr 5, 2011.

790   Jan Pace of Waukesha, Wisconsin, e-mail to author, Apr 5, 2011.

791   Joan Severa, e-mail to author, Mar 8, 2010.

792   Haight. Memoirs of Waukesha *County, 1907*. pp. 357 & 358.

IMMIGRANTS TO WISCONSIN FROM BAVARIA

Name: **Ulrich Woelfel**—born: **Rollhofen, Bayern** (24 Nov 1793)—Spouse: **Kunigunda Ramstöck**—born: **Germersberg, Bayern** (25 Sep 1796)—married: St. Walburga Catholic Church in Kirchröttenbach, Bayern--Children: *Friedrich, Conrad, Johann, Anna Cunigunda, Johann, Johann Georg, Georg, Friederich, George & Katharina*—*Kunigunda, the mother, died* (19 July 1842)—The remainder of the family emigrated from **Rollhofen** (1 Aug 1845) to **Wisconsin**, aboard the *"Bark Louis"*—arrived at the port of New York (8 Oct 1845)—Occupation: *farmer*—by 1850, Ulrich Woelfel owns a Brookfield (section 23) farm.

(Image & genealogy courtesy of Louise Wasserman of Germersberg, Bavaria.)[793]

The Ulrich Woelfel Home (1913)[794]

When this photograph was taken in 1913, it was the home of thr Heinrich Britting Family.

The Woelfel Family immigration story:

They travelled from Rollhofen to Bremen by wagon. *The trip took two days and from Bremen it was a two-day boat trip on the Weser River to the port of Bremerhaven before they could board the sailboat which brought them to New York, a voyage which lasted 46 days.* They then took a small steamboat to Albany, then went via the Lake Erie, Huron and Michigan to Milwaukee where they docked on October 25th. An uncle came with a span of oxen to take them to his home in Brookfield. The seven visitors stayed with this family temporarily until Ulrich Woelfel bought 80-acres of forest for $365. They then set out to clear the land of brush and stone and built a house. The sister-in-law assisted them by doing their washing, and baked bread of wheat and corn. *To help them with their work they bought a yoke of oxen for $55. Made a drag with 11 prongs and bought a plow for $7. They also bought a cow for $13. When they harvested their winter wheat, they had 164 bushels for which they paid 60 cents per bushel in Milwaukee.*

[*Chilton Times* September 6, 1913]

The Bavarian Catholic Church of Brookfield:

"In March 1851 Ulrich Woelfel donated two acres of land for a *Catholic church* and cemetery. *In that same year a log church measuring 24 X 35 feet was built and consecrated to St. Ambrose.*[795] A stone fence was built surrounding the church and cemetery. Mass was celebrated here by priests from Old St. Mary's in Milwaukee, as this was the only, until 1872 that the old log church was razed. By 1900 the grave markers had for the most part disappeared, though traces of the stone fence remained until as late as 1938."[796]

---

[793] *Federal Manuscript Schedule*, Population, Agricultural and Manufacturing Schedules for Waukesha County, Town of Brookfield, 1850.

[794] Photograph courtesy of Louise Wasserman of Germersberg, Bavaria, via letter, dated Dec. 15, 1986.

[795] "Saint Ambrose, also known as Aurelius Ambrosius, is one of the four original doctors of the Church. He was the Bishop of Milan and became one of the most important theological figure of the 4th century. Ambrose was born around 340 AD to a Roman Christian family. He grew up with his siblings, Satyrus and Marcellina, in Trier, Belgic Gaul (present-day Germany)." From: en.wikipedia.org/wiki/Ambrose

[796] La Vies, John G., and Johnson, Peter Leo. Early Catholic Church Property in the Archdiocese of Milwaukee Wisconsin. (Archdiocese of Milwaukee), 1941.

IMMIGRANTS TO WISCONSIN FROM ILLINOIS

Name: **Edward J. George**– Birthplace: <u>Wisconsin</u> (1855) — Spouse: ***Florence (Harding) George***—Birthplace— <u>**Sterling, Illinois**</u> (31 Oct 1865) ——Residence in 1890: <u>Pewaukee Township, Waukesha County, Wisconsin</u>— Occupation: *Davol Rubber Company Salesman*–Children: none.
(Image and genealogy courtesy of Waukesha County Historical Society and Museum.)[797]

Florence George (c. 1915)[798]

"Flogged to Exhaustion"

"In the 1870's it was the pedestrian who was terrified. *The engine of city mayhem was the horse, underfed and nervous, this vital brute was often flogged to exhaustion by pitiless drivers, who exulted in pushing ahead 'with utmost fury, defying law and delighting in destruction.'* Runaways were common. The havoc killed thousands of people."[799]

19th *Century Horse Owners often Abused their animals:*

"American documents relate several cases of horse exploitation leading to abuse, notably in bus and tram companies. These horse-drawn vehicles were often overloaded, and the horses pulling them were beaten and subject to hard labor. The first definitions of horse maltreatment centered on the withholding of food and care, and the act of hitting them. *The courts of New York were pioneers in this area, publishing a law that punished those who kill or deliberately tortured animals in 1829.* In 1860, Pennsylvania fined those who beat horses $200, double that charged to mothers who beat their children under 7 years old. [800]

Waukesha's First Humane Society:

"**Florence George** began Waukesha County's first humane society, chartered by *Secretary of State Donald* on May 10, 1915. Mrs. George's early list of humane cases ranged from dog poisoning to child neglect. <u>Once she found a man whipping an old horse. Fierce in her anger, she grabbed the whip away from him and walloped him with it</u>. A priest complained against a Pewaukee resident for wife beating. Mrs. George went to talk to the wife. Not finding the woman in the house she looked in the basement and discovered several barrels of home brew."[801]

[797] *Federal Manuscript Schedule*, Population, Agricultural and Manufacturing Schedules for Waukesha County, Town of Pewaukee, 1890.

[798] Florence George c. 1915, People F-G-H Box 3:8, Photography Collection, Research Center Library & Archive, Waukesha County Historical Society & Museum, Waukesha, Wisconsin.

[799] Otto L. Bettmann, *The Good Old Days—They Were Terrible.* (New York: Penguin Random House, 1974), pp. 22 & 23.

[800] https://en.wikipedia.org/wiki/Horses_in_the_United_States

[801] Charles R. Phillips, "Waukesha's Carrie's Nation," *Landmark,* v. 12, Nos. 2 & 3 (Spring & Summer, 1969), p. 2.

IMMIGRANTS TO WISCONSIN FROM SAXONY

Name: **August Thomas Caesar**– Birthplace: **Danzig, Sachsen, Germany** (1820) — Spouse: **Christina Reinhardt** — Birthplace— **Sachsen, Germany** (1822)–Immigrated to Wisconsin: 1850. Residence in 1880: Muskego Township, Waukesha County, Wisconsin—Occupation: *farmer*–Children: *Fredrick, Louis, Anna, William & Andrew.* (Image and genealogy courtesy of Elaine Alane of Helenville, Wisconsin.)[802]

Andrew Caesar c. 1915 [803]

A dance at Hiram Showerman's place in Brookfield (1880's):

"Lon goes on with his tune and the calling off. He is playing *The Wrecker's Daughter*. Old Mr. Ledly calls it *The Wreckard's Daughter*. Lon plays *Saint Patrick's Day* next, and then *Fisher's Hornpipe* for the last figure. *I know almost all of Lon's tunes by heart. There is Soldier's Joy, The Devil's Dream, and Washing Day, and Flowers of Edinburgh, and Captain Jinks and Irish Washerwoman, and others.*" (conti. below)

Dancing to the sound of the fiddle:

"August Caesar played the fiddle. We have kept his fiddle in our family. His brother Andrew would come out to the Caesar farm in Muskego from time to time. *When he did, they would move all the furniture in the dining room out of the way and they would both play. Neighbors, farm workers and family would all dance to their music.*"
— **Memories of Elaine Alane**[804]

Hiram's son, Grant, replays in his mind, the delightful sounds of the fiddler:

"My father and brother can play Lon's tunes on the fiddle, too. *I am so used to them that when I am going anywhere alone, I whistle and hum them and keep step. When my brother Harry is turning the fanning mill, or churning, or when the old mares are trotting along to Town, I can always here Lon's tunes.* Mrs. Purdy says: 'Folks don't dance as much as what they used to when the country was first settled. When we first come, back in the early forties, they used to be a dance somewhere every Sat'day night, jest as sure as Sat'day night come' round'."[805]

Garret Veenendaal's place at Union Church:

"If I recall correctly, **Garret Veenendaal** was a postmaster at Union Church[806] for some time. *They would occasionally have dances at his place, too!* Garret was **Albert Veenendaal's** brother – Albert was postmaster at <u>Durham Hill</u> for many years."[807]

802   *Federal Manuscript Schedule*, Population, Agricultural and Manufacturing Schedules for Waukesha County, Town of Muskego, 1860.

803   Photograph courtesy of Elaine Alane of Helenville, Wisconsin, e-mail to author, Apr 30, 2010.

804   Elaine Alane of Helenville, Wiscosnin, e-mail to author, Apr 30, 2010.

805   Showerman, *A Country Chronicle*. pp. 45, 50 & 54.

806   Union Church is an unincorporated community located in the towns of Norway and Raymond, Racine County. From: https://en.wikipedia.org/wiki/Union_Church,_Wisconsin

807   Elaine Alane of Helenville, Wiscosnin, e-mail to author, Apr 30, 2010.

IMMIGRANTS TO WISCONSIN FROM SWITZERLAND

Name: **John Hoffman**: an immigrant *farmer & hotel keeper* from **Horgenbach, Canton Thurgau, Schweiz**—By 1860, he is the proprietor of the *Phoenix Hotel* located within Brookfield's **Swiss settlement** on the north side of the Watertown Plank Road in Brookfield (section 28)—his wife is **Elizabeth**—they have 5 children—*Sophia, John, Henry, Elizabeth & Caroline.*   (Genealogy & photograph courtesy of Sally Clarin of Brookfield, Wisconsin)[808]

Horgenbach, Canton Thurgau, Switzerland (c. 1917)[809]

This young lady, of Horgenbach, was a niece of the John Hoffman family who immigrated from Horgenbach, Canton Thurgau, Switzerland to Brookfield, Wisconsin in 1849.

Swiss families settle in the town of Brookfield:

BENJAMIN GESSER: an immigrant boot & shoemaker from **Switzerland**—settled in (**section 28**)—single.

HENRY GROB: an immigrant farmer from **Rossan, Canton Zurich, Switzerland**—located in (**section 28**)—his wife is Fanny—they have 4 children.

JOHN HOFFMAN: an immigrant farmer & hotel keeper from **Horgenbach, Canton Thurgau, Switzerland**—proprietor of the "Phoenix Inn"—they settled in (**section 28**)—his wife is Elizabeth—they have 5 children.

HENRY KUHN: an immigrant boot & shoemaker from **Switzerland**—they settled in (**section 29**)—his wife is Solamie—they have 2 children.

NICHLAS MAURER: an immigrant farmer from **Canton Bern, Switzerland**—they settled in (**section 33**)—Mr. Maurer operates a Swiss cheese factory.

CHRISTIAN OCHSNER: an immigrant farmer from **Horgenbach, Canton Thurgau, Switzerland**—they settled in (**section 28**)--his wife is Elizabeth—they had 3 children.

GOTTFRIED RIES: an immigrant farmer from **Burgdorf, Canton Bern, Switzerland**—they settled in (**section 16**)—his wife is Mesina---they have 4 children.

CHRISTIAN SCHMUTZ: an immigrant farmer from **Interlaken, Canton Bern, Switzerland**—they settled in (**section 28**)—his wife is Rosina—they have 5 children.

JOHN SCHMUTZ: an immigrant farmer from **Interlaken, Canton Bern, Switzerland**—they settled in (**section 28**)— Mr. Schmutz operates a cheese factory.

JACOB STREIFF: an immigrant shoemaker & farmer from **Oberhaven, Canton Bern, Switzerland**—they settled in (**section 28**)—his wife is Elizabeth—they have no children.

HENRY WELLAUER: an immigrant farmer from **Wagenhausen, Canton Thurgau, Switzerland**—they settled in (**section 36**)—his wife is Anna—they had 4 children.

CHRISTIAN WELLAUER: an immigrant farmer from **Canton Bern, Switzerland**—they settled in (**section 32**)—his wife is Susan—they have 2 children.

CHRISTIAN WINZENREID JR.: an immigrant farmer from **Canton Bern, Switzerland**—they settled in (**section 32**)—his wife is Anna—they have 4 children.[810]

808   *Federal Manuscript Schedule,* Population, Agricultural and Manufacturing Schedules for Waukesha County, Town of Brookfield, 1860.
809   Photograph courtesy of Sally Clarin of Brookfield, Wisconsin, home visit, June 10, 2010.
810   Author, *Brookfield: A Fine and Fertile Land,* vol.1, pp. 25 & 26.

IMMIGRANTS TO WISCONSIN FROM PRUSSIA

Name: *Joachim Barton* — Birthplace: **"Germany"** (c 1833)—Spouse: Katherine Casper (1821) — Birthplace: **Elsass France** —Year of Immigration: 1850's—Residence in 1910: New Berlin Township, Waukesha County—lives with son's family: **George Barton**—Birthplace: **Wisconsin** (c. 1860)—Spouse: **Bertha**— Birthplace: **Wisconsin** (c. 1868) —Occupation: *farmer*--Children: *John, **Edward,** Edna, Viola & Mabel.* In 1873, Joachim Barton owns a *120-acre (section 35),* Town of New Berlin *farm on the town's southern border with the Town Of Muskego[811]*; By 1914, son, George Barton *owns a (section 34) 160-acre Town of New Berlin farm—there are 2 streams running through the farm*—The 1914 "Waukesha County Patrons Directory" states that *"George Barton is a farmer & stockbreeder—Post Office: Calhoun—farm purchased in 1873"*[812]   (Image and genealogy courtesy of Lois Alton of Hartland, Wisconsin.)[813]

Edward Barton's Threshing Crew (c.1917)[814]

Wheat & Oats threshing crew on the Ed Barton farm in New Berlin

Threshing Machines:

"In 1869 Case offered an improved thresher called the ***Eclipse***." *(conti- below:)*

*When steam engines powered threshing **machines:***

"To the right, is a turn of the century threshing machine. Pulled by a steam engine. When it was time to thresh oats, a long belt was connected from a pulley on the steam engine to a pulley on the threshing machine. Power from the steam engine powered the threshing machine." *--Courtesy of Denny Sullivan of Plainview, Minnesota.* [815]

The Eclipse thresher:

"It had an advanced system for moving both and grain kernels through the machine. By 1876 steam traction engines—began appearing. These ponderous beasts, with steel wheels and a cast-iron frame, could be driven down the road toting a threshing machine behind. By 1886 J. I. Case, of Racine, Wisconsin, was the world's premier manufacturer of steam engines."[816]

Steam Threshing Machines

Steam threshing machines are slowly but surely displacing the OLD METHOD of threshing by horsepower. These steam threshers combined with the improved machinery for putting the grain into the ground in the spring (we refer to the Screw Pulverizer) and the Self-Binding Reaper, For a crop of 100 acres of small grain can be sown, reaped and threshed as easy as 20 acres could be by the old methods"   [*Waukesha Freeman*, Nov. 30, 1882]

---

[811]   *Atlas of Waukesha County, Wisconsin, 1873*, Town of New Berlin.

[812]   *Standard Atlas of Waukesha County, Wiscosnin, 1914*. Town of New Berlin.

[813]   *Federal Manuscript Schedule*, Population, Agricultural and Manufacturing Schedules for Waukesha County, Town of New Berlin, 1860.

[814]   Photo courtesy of Lois Alton of Hartland, Wisconsin, e-mail to author, Dec.16, 2016.

[815]   "When steam engines powered threshing machines," courtesy of Denny Sullivan, of Plainview, Minnesota.

[816]   Jerry Apps, *Horse-Drawn Days: A Century of Farming in Wisconsin* (Madison: Wisconsin Historical Society Press, 2010), pp.149 & 150.

IMMIGRANTS TO WISCONSIN FROM RHENISH PRUSSIA & BADEN

Kau Family: (1st Generation) Name: **Johann Gerhardis Kau**--Born (24 Mar 1771) in Rhineland/Rhenish Prussia —Spouse: **Catherine (Lammersmith)** Children: *Mathias & Caper Kau* (2nd Generation) Son: **Casper Kau**-born (17 March 1784) – **Strassfeld, Kreis Rheinbach, Bzirk Cöln, Rheinisches/ Rheinpreußen** (12 Jan 1826)—Spouse: Margaretha "Maggie" Blessinger-- born: (1 Oct 1829) in **Siegelsbach, Kreis Sinsheim, Bezirk: Heidelberg, Baden, Germany**." Children: *Joseph Kau*—born: (26 June 1866), New Berlin, Waukesha County— married to **Laura Hess**—born: (Nov 1874 Nov), **Drummond, Deer Lodge County, Montana**—Children: *1.) Mathias Kau* was baptized (29 July 1866) at *St. Valerius Catholic Church* in New Berlin—*died in childhood, 2.) Mathies Kau*—born: (1871); *3.)* **Maria "Agnus" Kau**—born: (10 May 1868), New Berlin, Waukesha County--married to: **John Bergmann** (22 Nov 1887), in **Helena, Montana**--died: (29 Sep 1955), **Missoula, Missoula County, Montana**; *4.) Mary Catherine Kau*—Birthplace: New Berlin, Waukesha County (28 Aug 1869)-- *Joseph Blessinger's death*: **Helgate Township, Missoula County, Montana**--(26 Jan 1918).

Phillips Family: **Barney Phillips**--Birthplace: New Berlin, Waukesha County born: (24 Oct 1859) --Spouse: **Mary Kau** —Birthplace: New Berlin, Waukesha County --born: (28 Aug 1869)—In 1874, Barney Phillips owns a 40-acre (section 34) farm in the town of Muskego-(**Coincidently—soon to be wed, Mary Catherine Kau's family's farm in New Berlin & Barney Phillips farm in Muskego where directly across the town line road from each other**). -Barny & Mary Phillips' children: *Helen, William, Clara & Amanda (twins).*[817] — (Image courtesy of Lois Alton of Hartland, Wisconsin; Genealogy courtesy of Georgia Davis Briggeman of Deer Lodge, Powell Co., Montana)[818]

Mary (Kau) Phillip--standing between her 2 daughters (1918)[819]

On the Phillips' farm: (L-R) Art Schiltz, Clara (Caroline) Phillips, Mary Catherine (Kau) Phillips (mother) & Amanda Phillips. The "Blue Star Flag" hanging in the window indicates that their son, William, is in the military, serving in the European War.

Postcard mailed from Veronica Casper, of New Berlin, to the twin daughters of Barney & Mary Phillips of Muskego:

Miss Amanda & Caroline Phillips
May 15, 1910.
Dear friends, I will write you a few lines and let you know that I am well and hope the same of you. Dear friends, would you be so kind and bring your freezer along on Sunday, because we want to make it ready for my communion. Will close. Best regards to all. Yours Truly,
Veronica Casper
R. R. 1 Calhoun [820]

Postcard mailed from Lena (Kau) Baney, of Washington State, to Mary (Kau) Phillips in Muskego:

Mrs. Mary Phillips,   October 12, 1910
Dear cousin, how are you? We are all quite well, having a fine time. How are all the little girls by this time. Can they sing yet? If I come back, I would love to hear them.
Love to all from all. *Lena L. Baney, Walla Walla, Washington*[821]

817   *Standard Atlas of Waukesha County, Wisconsin, 1914,* Town of New Berlin.

818   *Federal Manuscript Schedule,* Population, Agricultural and Manufacturing Schedules for Waukesha County, Towns of New Berlin & Muskego, 1870.

819   Photograph courtesy of Lois Phillips of Hartland, Wisconsin, e-mail to author, Dec.16, 2016

820   Postcard courtesy of Lois Phillips of Hartland, Wisconsin, e-mail to author, Dec.16, 2016

821   Postcard courtesy of Lois Phillips of Hartland, Wisconsin e-mail to author, Dec.16, 2016

IMMIGRANTS TO WISCONSIN FROM BAYERN

Name: **Peter Blattner**– Birthplace: **Bayern, Germany** (c. 1821) — Spouse: **Adelena**—Birthplace: **Bayern, Germany** (c. 1815)—year of immigration: 1851—Grandson: **Theodore Blattner**--—Spouse: **Barbara Wanasak**—Birthplace: Wisconsin— Residence in 1920: Durham Hill, Muskego Township, Waukesha County, Wisconsin—Occupation: *farmer*–Children: *Theodore*: (WWII Veteran & Korean War Veteran), *Barbara, Rose,* **Ralph**, *Henry, Leona, Marion & Eleanor.* Son: **Ralph Theodore Blattner**--Spouse: **Rose Anna Unger** (1916 - 1995)—Residence: *North Cape Road, Muskego Town, Waukesha County*--Occupation: *employed at Pressed Steel Tank Co. in West Allis*—Children: *Gary (1942-2007), Stephen (1943), Mary Ann (Blattner) Mayer (1944-2005), Rosemary Leona (Blattner) Linder (1946), Henry Peter (1949)-- Suzanne Helen (Blattner) Zefinning (1957).*
(Image and genealogy courtesy of Steve and Carol Blattner of Waukesha, Wisconsin.) [822]

Henry, Ralph, Rose, and Barbara Blattner (c. 1918)[823]

Dairy farmers upset!

Feb. 14, 1933: In the depths of the depression. "I'm hearing on the radio the famous long talked that the milk strike will start tonight. If our milk haulers won't drive, we won't be able to ship milk, and there will be no milk check. Farmers are protesting the low prices."—*From the Diaries of Wilma Gerkin*[824]

Fixed Bayonets Drive Off Pickets-- All of Durham Hill Village Gassed

The Battle of Durham Hill will go down as one of the major engagements of the milk "war." The battle Wednesday began with a skirmish about noon, when four deputy sheriffs attempted to seize a man who was making an inflammatory speech. As they reached him, fists began to fly! … The sheriff ordered the Durham Hill crowed dispersed. *He sent 60 more guards, most of them armed with bayoneted rifles and telephoned contact points to raise more reinforcements. Before the battle was over, about 150 special deputies mostly guardsmen were at Durham Hill….*The crowd had raised an American flag at the corner and massed around it. The soldiers threw bomb after bomb and the fumes broke up the crowed. The pickets scrambled for the open fields with the bayonets at their backs. Most of the crowed had surged back to the crossroads. The deputies returned there tossing bombs. *After about 40 bombs had been thrown and then fumes permeated the whole village, causing the crowd to pretty well scatter.*   [*The Milwaukee Journal* May 18, 1933]

"Pa recalled **Grampa Theodore (Teddy) Blattner** returning to the house about noon on Wednesday, in the heat of the battle. *Sweating, red faced, and fuming with adrenaline, he told how he had punched someone in the face during the midst of all the pushing, shoving and gaging gas bombs.* The family was shocked and surprised by grandpa's admission as he had always been a quiet man and rarely moved to anger." --***From the Recollections of Steve Blattner*** [825]

[822]   *Federal Manuscript Schedule*, Population, Agricultural and Manufacturing Schedules for Waukesha County, Town of Muskego, 1920.

[823]   Photograph courtesy of Steve & Carol Blattner, of Waukesha, Wisconsin, e-mail to author, Dec 5, 2016.

[824]   From the diaries of Wilma Gerkin of Sussex Township, as presented by Fred H. Keller, in "Depression Diaries," *Landmark,* v. 37, n. 1, Spring, 1994. p. 21.

[825]   "Pa recalled Grampa Theodore (Teddy) Blattner," from the Recollections of Steve Blattner

IMMIGRANTS TO WISCONSIN FROM SAXONY & NEW YORK

Name: **Norris Collins Potter** –Birthplace: <u>New York</u> (Jan 1859) –Spouse: **Mary Louise (Bartlett) Potter**–Birthplace: <u>Leipzig, Sachsen, Germany</u> (Oct 1864)—Residence in 1900: <u>Ottawa Township, Waukesha County, Wisconsin</u>—Occupation: *farmer & rural mail delivery*– Children: *Arthur* (1882), *Mary, Jay* (1885), *Harris* (1887), *Norris* (1889), *Raymond* (1890), *Maggie* (1893), *Edna* (1895), *Elva* (1897), ***Clarence***, *Malcom, Hazel & Mabel*.
(Image, text, and genealogy courtesy of Carol Logan of Chico, California)[826]

Pvt. Clarence Potter (c. 1918)[827]

Severa, "*The Red Arrow Division*":

The United States 32nd Infantry Division was formed from Army National Guard units, from Wisconsin and Michigan and fought primarily during World War I and World War II. With roots as the Iron Brigade in the American Civil War, the division's ancestral units came to be referred to as the *Iron Jaw Division. During tough combat in France in World War I, it soon acquired from the French the nickname* **Les Terribles**, *referring to its fortitude in advancing over terrain others could not.* It was the first allied division to pierce the German Hindenburg Line of defense, and the 32nd then adopted its shoulder patch; a line shot through with a red arrow, to signify its tenacity in piercing the enemy line. It then became known as the **Red Arrow Division**.[828] "*The Battle of the Argonne Forest, the final major Allied offensive of World War I stretched along the entire Western Front.* It was fought from 26 September 1918 until the Armistice of 11 November 1918. The Meuse-Argonne Offensive was the largest in United States military history, involving 1.2 million American soldiers. *The battle cost 28,000 German lives and 26,277 American lives.*"[829]

Clarence Potter, Corporal, 32nd Division, 128th Infantry, in the Battle of the Argonne Forest:

The following is an account of Clarence Potter's WWI experiences taken from recollections gathered by his granddaughter, **Carol Logan**: "*While engaged in the large spring engagement,* **Grandpa Clarence Potter** *recalled bombs blasts landing near him, propelling him high up into the air along with tons of mud and dirt. His rapid action machine gun was lethal in slaughtering hundreds of German soldiers. This massive killing of so many of the enemy greatly haunted him throughout the remainder life.*"[830] Like numerous other soldiers, on both sides of the trenches, Clarence was **mustard gassed** on several occasions. *After a heavy bombardment, his legs were laced with shrapnel. The doctors assessing his wounds, determined that complete amputation of both legs was the only approach.* Horrified by the thought of losing his legs, he talked them out of the procedure. *His jaws were so full of shrapnel that they proceeded to pull all his teeth.* For the remainder of the war, he was assigned to '**253 Ambulance Company 14**'. At wars end, Clarence received an '*Honorable Discharge' on 25/19.*"[831]

---

826 *Federal Manuscript Schedule*, Population, Agricultural and Manufacturing Schedules for Waukesha County, Town of Ottawa, 1900.

827 Photograph courtesy of Carol Logan of Chico, California, e-mail to author, Jun 27, 2010.

828 https://en.wikipedia.org/wiki/32nd_Infantry_Division_(United_States)

829 https://en.wikipedia.org/wiki/Meuse-Argonne_Offensive

830 Carol Logan of Chico, California, adapted from e-mail to author, Jun 28, 2010.

831 Carol Logan of Chico, California, adapted from e-mail to author, Jun 27, 2010; https://en.wikipedia.org/wiki/Meuse-Argonne_Offensive

IMMIGRANTS TO WISCONSIN FROM ALSACE, FRANCE

Name: **Barney Phillips**– Birthplace: New Berlin, Waukesha County (10/25/1858)—Parents**: John Phillips & Mary Casper**. **Mary Kau** —Birthplace: New Berlin, Waukesha County (8/29/1869) —Parents: **Casper Kau & Margaretha Blessinger**. Barney Phillips & Mary Kau were married at *St. Valerius Catholic Church* in New Berlin (11/25/1890). Residence in 1900: Muskego Township, Waukesha County[832]—Occupation: *farmer*– By 1914, Barney Phillips owns a 35.86-acre (section 3) farm in Muskego, Township[833]--Children: *Helen, William,* (WWI Veteran), *Clara & Amanda.* By 1923, Barney & Mary Phillips *maintain ownership of their 40-acre town of Muskego farm, they have 4 adult children— with 3 horses, 8 cattle, Rural Mail Route 11 (Calhoun) and Bell Telephone service.*[834]　　(Image courtesy of a Lois (Phillips) Alton of Hartland, Wisconsin; Genealogy courtesy of Mary Stigler of Brookfield, Wisconsin.) [835]

William Phillips (1918)[836]

Soldier's Assignment in France:

William H. Phillips, R 11, Calhoun, Waukesha, *Army Headquarters, Bordeaux Embarkation Camp, Army Service Corps,* **Private 1ˢᵗ Class, Service number: 3892971**

Postal to a fellow soldier:
Soldier's Mail
Hdqts. Co. Paillac
Port of Embarcarkation
A.P.O. 705 B. Am. E.F., France

Dear Joe,　　　　　　　Oct. 21, 1918
You are missing a very good time. We've been shot at about a dozen times since we left. We are camped out in that same hotel we stayed at when we first arrived. It's O.K. to tell the folks where we are. Hope this war ends soon!
William Phillips,
U.S. Army, Belfaux, Switzerland"[837]

Reaching an Armistice agreement:

"The Armistice of 11 November 1918 was the armistice that ended fighting on land, sea and air in World War I between the Allies and their last opponent, Germany. *It came into force at 11 a.m. Paris time on 11 November 1918 ("the eleventh hour of the eleventh day of the eleventh month") and marked a victory for the Allies and a complete defeat for Germany.*"[838]

[832]　*Federal Manuscript Schedules,* Population, Agricultural and Manufacturing Schedules for Waukesha County, Town of New Berlin, 1870; Town of Muskego, 1900.

[833]　*Standard Atlas of Waukesha County, 1914,* Muskego Township.

[834]　*The Farm Journal Rural Directory of Waukesha County, 1918, p. 122.*

[835]　*Federal Manuscript Schedule,* Population, Agricultural and Manufacturing Schedules for Waukesha County, Town of Muskego, 1900.

[836]　Photograph courtesy of Lois (Phillips) Alton of Hartland, Wisconsin, e-mail to author, Dec.16, 2016

[837]　Soldier's Mail: *William Phillips to Joseph Ramstack Sr.,* author's collection.

[838]　https://en.wikipedia.org/wiki/Armistice_Day

IMMIGRANTS TO WISCONSIN FROM PRUSSIA

(1ˢᵗ Generation): Name: **Gottlieb Bartz** — Birthplace: **Preußen** (1 Apr1832)—Spouse: **August Brandt**—Year of Immigration: (1873)—Immigrant ship: *"Franklin"*—Port of arrival: New York (21 April 1873) — Residence in 1900: Brookfield Township, Waukesha County—Occupation: *farmer* –Children: *Amelia, Minnie & Herman* (2ⁿᵈ Generation):--Name: **Julius Bartz**—Born: (1874)--Birthplace: Pewaukee, Township, Waukesha County—Spouse: **Maggie Galatin**—Born: Wisconsin (1876)— Residence: (1900)—Brookfield Township, Waukesha County—also residing in this household-- father: *Gottlieb Bartz* (age: 68)---occupation: *mason* (widower)--brother: *Herman*— Born: Wisconsin (1885)—at school[839]—By 1914, Julius Bartz was the owner of a 59 acre farm (section 29) Brookfield Township—*Poplar Creek* runs through the center of the Bartz farm[840]—By 1918, Julius & Margret retain ownership of the family farm *with 7 adult children, 3 horses, 12 dairy cows, along with Bell telephone service.* (1920) Julius & Mary Bartz Residence—City of Waukesha, Waukesha County—Adult children: *Viola, **Vernie,** Mabel, Arthur, Alvin, Dorothy & Edna.*[841]   (Image and genealogy courtesy of Jan Pace of Waukesha, Wisconsin.)

Vern Bartz Hauling ice (c. 1919)[842]

Making & Storing Ice at the turn of the century:

We who lived on farms in the 1890s, before refrigeration was available, had ice houses. Especially so if we shipped milk to Milwaukee or sour cream to Waukesha creameries. And where did we get the ice? My father Elvin Aitken built a rather large icehouse where he stored ice each winter. *We hauled ice from Poplar Creek less than a mile east of our farm. North of Goerke's Corners on what is now Barker Road.* Poplar Creek crossed the road close to the bridge which was very low at that time, the creek widened; *and each summer the Julius Bartz family, whose farm bordered the creek, would rake the weeds from the water and did away some of the dirt to make it available for swimming.* Before winter came, the stream was cleaned again for weeds and debris. They kept the stream clean and deep enough for ice to reach a foot or more thickness. I loved to go with father and the hired man and watch them used the big saws with long handless to cut and saw strips of ice. One sawyer would saw in one direction, while another would saw in the other, so as to make square chunks. This method made it easier to handle the ice after it was cut, especially so in storing it in the icehouse. To preserve the ice, the men enveloped the chunks with saw dust. --***Memories of Roy Aitken*** [843]

BLODGETT: *Julius Bartz* has finished harvesting 11,000 cakes of ice on Poplar Creek.
[*Waukesha Freeman* Jan. 30, 1902]

---

[839] *Federal Manuscript Schedule,* Population, Agricultural and Manufacturing Schedules for Waukesha County, Town of Brookfield, 1900.
[840] *Standard Atlas of Waukesha County, 1914,* Brookfield Township.
[841] *The Farm Journal Rural Directory of Waukesha County, 1918,* p. 23.
[842] Photograph courtesy of Jan Pace of Waukesha, Wisconsin, e-mail to author, Apr 5, 2011.
[843] Roy Aitken, "Summer Ice," *Landmark,* v.12, n. 1, Winter, 1969. p. 7.

IMMIGRANTS TO WISCONSIN FROM PRUSSIA & "GERMANY"

Name: **Karl Frederick Kleist**– Birthplace: **Witzmitz, Pommern, Preußen** (1840) — Spouse: **Laura W. Bonness**— Birthplace: **"Germany"** (1847) – Year of Emigration: 1867—Residence e in 1880: Oconomowoc Township, Waukesha County, Wisconsin—Occupation: *farmer*–Children: *Frederick, Henry & Charles.* By 1914, Karl (Charles) Kleist owns a 100-acre (section 19) Town of Oconomowoc farm on the north side of Lake La Belle[844]—By 1923, **Karl Kleist** and his second wife, **Clara Radtke,** maintain their now 110-acre Town of Oconomowoc farm-5 adult children live at home; occupation: farming; they have telephone service; 3 horses; 13 dairy cows; & rural mail delivery (route 26) from Oconomowoc—members of the *Lutheran Church* in Oconomowoc.[845]
(Image and genealogy courtesy of Marlene Connell of Hartford, Wisconsin.)[846]

Karl Kleist (c. 1920)[847]

The Prussian Province of Pomerania:

Witzmitz (the birthplace of Karl Kleist) is a village in the administrative West Pomerania. In 1812, French troops invaded Swedish Pomerania, and also occupied Prussian Pomerania. In March 1813, all French forces left Pomerania, except for Stettin, *which was held by the French until December 5, 1813. On October 23, Swedish Pomerania was merged into the Prussian province, both now constituting the Province of Pomerania.*[848]

Pomeranians in Wisconsin:

In Pomerania you were born into a social level where you usually stayed your entire life. It is said that if you didn't own land in Pomerania you didn't have any status. Acquiring land which gave you stability was very hard. In America they were given the chance to succeed, which most did. *By the mid-19th century, many German immigrants had settled in Wisconsin and by the latter half of the 1800s German immigrants had chosen Wisconsin over other American states as their destination.* This was due to the state's resources, available land, and the land agents. These immigrants (such as the Kleists) were referred to **"Old Lutherans."** The name was applied to Lutherans who and wanted to escape religious persecution."[849]

The Lutheran settlement at Freidstadt, Ozaukee County:

"The Wisconsin city of *Freistadt*, for example, was founded by 300 German Lutherans from Pomerania, who were escaping Prussian religious reform and persecution. *They called their colony Freistadt, or "free city", most likely to commemorate their newfound religious freedom in the Americas. Both their faith and maintenance of their East Pomeranian dialect were important to the Freistadters.*"[850]

844   *Standard Atlas of Waukesha County, 1914*, Oconomowoc Township.
845   *The Farm Journal Rural Directory of Waukesha County, 1918*, p. 88.
846   *Federal Manuscript Schedule*, Population, Agricultural and Manufacturing Schedules for Waukesha County, Town of Oconomowoc, 1880.
847   Photograph courtesy of Kelly Dennis in care of Marlene Connell of Hartford, Wisconsin, e-mail to author, Jun 29, 2010.
848   https://en.wikipedia.org/wiki/Wicimice
849   https://en.wikipedia.org/wiki/Old_Lutherans
850   https://en.wikipedia.org/wiki/Wisconsin_German

IMMIGRANTS TO WISCONSIN FROM WALES

Name: <u>**Owen Roberts**</u>– birthplace: <u>**Cornheleg, Llanfachreth-Anglesey, Wales**</u> (1851) Spouse: <u>**Margaret Sarah Morris**</u>—Birthplace: <u>**Columbus, Columbia County, Wisconsin**</u>—Children: *Henry, Sarah, Owen, Ines, Christmas, Mary & Willie.* —<u>In 1914, the descendants of Owen Roberts own a 40-acre (Section 8) farm in Genesee Township, Waukesha County, Wisconsin with the town school located on his parcel</u>—Neighboring the <u>**Roberts farm**</u>, to the east is the <u>**D. J. Roberts farm**</u> with the *Presbyterian Church* & cemetery located on his parcel[851]–
(Image and genealogy courtesy of Wales Village Hall, Waukesha County, Wisconsin.)[852]

Elwyn & Evelyn Roberts (circa 1920)[853]

Children of Pastor Kendrick Roberts of Jerusalem Church

The Roberts family immigrate to Wisconsin:

Cornhelg, Llanfachreth (the birthplace of Owen Roberts) is a settlement some three miles north-east of Dolgellau. The village name Llanfachreth is derived from the Welsh soft mutation of that saint's name. Nonconformity was an important issue in the late 18th century. *William Evans (Fedew Arian, Bala) preached the first Methodist sermon by Pwllgele Lake in Llanfachreth parish in 1783.* The traditional church so opposed to alternative ministries that this had to be held in the open air.[854]

Hard times for the working class of Wales:

"The Welsh immigrants seem to have left their native country simply because of hard times. *The condition of the working class was miserable, from eight to twelve cents a day being the farm wage in Wales, and this misery was being proclaimed from every platform in the kingdom by the Chartist orators in their vigorous campaigns for reform.* "Both the wretchedness and the agitation concerning it conspired to develop in the working man a frame of mind which demanded some sort of a change, and so when rumors came of the new world beyond the seas that was a poor man's paradise, so turning his few possessions into money, gathering his family about him and resolutely setting sail for a new continent and a new home." *The Welsh who settled in Waukesha County came mostly from Cardiganshire and Angleyshire on the west coast of Wales.*"[855]

Welsh settlement in the town of Wales:

"Mr. Hughes and family arrived in Milwaukee in August of 1840. On Lake Erie they had met **Rev. Moses Ordway** who had recommended Waukesha county, where he resided, as a desirable place for settlement, they purchased land in the town of Genesee and settled down to the life of the pioneer. '*Mr. Hughes liked the country and wrote back to his relative, Thomas Jones, in Wales, setting forth its many attractions. Jones had the letter printed in a Welsh magazine and this letter was the means of bringing many settlers to Waukesha county*.'"[856]

851   *Standard Atlas of Waukesha County, 1914*, Genesee Township.

852   *Federal Manuscript Schedule*, Population, Agricultural and Manufacturing Schedules for Waukesha County, Town of Genesee, 1900.

853   Photograph courtesy of Village of Wales, via Gail Tamez, e-mail to author, Dec 21, 2016.

854   https://en.wikipedia.org/wiki/Llanfachreth

855   Haight, Memoirs of Waukesha County, *1894*, p. 231.

856   Haight, *Memoirs of Waukesha County, 1894,* p. 230.

IMMIGRANTS TO WISCONSIN FROM BAVARIA AND WÜRTTEMBERG

Name: **John Michael Meidenbauer** – Birthplace: **Pruehausen, Landgericht Sulzbach, Oberpfalz, Bayern, Germany** (11 May 1854) — Spouse: **Anna Caroline Schoenwelder** —Birthplace— **Woeste Goersdorf Kreis, Waldenburg, Württemberg, Germany** (23 October 1865)——Residence in 1880: New Berlin, Waukesha County, Wisconsin—Occupation: *farmer*– By 1923, John & Anna Meidenbauer remained involved in farming & dairying on their 90-acre, New Berlin (section 19) *"Echo Farm"*—*They possess 3 horses, along with 8 dairy cows & they now have Bell telephone service.* Son Arthur supports his parents in farm labor & will take over operation of the farm with their passing. [857] (Image and genealogy courtesy of Roy Meidenbauer of New Berlin, Wisconsin.)[858]

John K. & Anna Meidenbauer (circa 1923)[859]

Primogeniture as a cause for emigration:

"Primogeniture is the right, by law or custom, of the paternally acknowledged, first born son to inherit his parent's entire or main estate, in preference to daughters, elder illegitimate sons, younger sons and collateral relatives. Most monarchies in Europe eventually eliminated male preference in succession: Belgium, Denmark, Netherlands, Norway, Sweden and the United Kingdom."[860]

The Origin of the Heuerling System:

"The Heuerleute system was created as an alternative source of income for those who were not inheritors of farms through the system of Primogeniture. The Heuerleute would receive from the farmer a piece of land, grazing rights on the "common land" and living quarters. The weaving of linen fabric, which could engage all family members or work in the farm fields of Holland cutting peat moss supplemented the income for many Heuerleutes. But the Heuerleutes soon suffered greatly. English-produced cotton textile items had negatively impacted linen (flax) production. This ongoing, hopeless situation of the Heuerleute was an important factor in prompting emigration to America."[861]

The Primogeniture & Huerling Systems may have been overestimated by some historians as major factors for emigration:

"These systems, generally, only occurred in small regions of Germany (in Niedersachsen along the Dutch border and in parts of Westfalen). Many Heuerleutes spent part of the year to Holland serving on ships, especially whaling or onboard slave ships. Like many other German families, the Meidenbauer were very likely not influenced by either system. More likely, poverty among all Germans was the primary influence for German emigration during the 2nd half of the 19th century.* In Bavaria, Württemberg, Rheinland-Pfalz, for example, small & inefficient farms, ongoing crop failures, and the potato blight, caused many German farms to fail. The inheritance-system provided littles advantage for these families. When one family from a small village departed, neighbors or relatives from surrounding villages, often followed. In the territory of Wisconsin, there was great demand for population growth. Those who came were, for the most part, the most willing and courageous people, determined to find a better life." [862]-- **Dr. Helmut Treis, of Aachen, Nordrhein-Westfalen, Germany**

[857] *The Farm Journal Rural Directory of Waukesha County, 1918*, p. 108.

[858] *Federal Manuscript Schedule*, Population, Agricultural and Manufacturing Schedules for Waukesha County, Town of New Berlin, 1880.

[859] Photograph courtesy of Roy Meidenbauer of New Berlin, Wisconsin, e-mail to author, Aug 8, 2009.

[860] https://en.wikipedia.org/wiki/Primogeniture

[861] Gemeindechronik Holdorf 1188 - 1988, Community History Holdorf (Kreis Vechta, Province Oldenburg)
        Publisher: Gemeinde Holdorf * Grosse Str. 19 * 49449 Holdorf, ISBN 3-88441-032-6

[862] Dr. Helmut Treis, of Aachen, Rheinland, Nordrhein-Westfalen, Germany, e-mail to author, Jul 16, 2018.

IMMIGRANTS TO WISCONSIN FROM NEW YORK & VERMONT

Name: **Sebina Danford Barney**--Birthplace: <u>**Vermont**</u> (22 July 1802)— Spouse: <u>**Polly Manderville**</u>—Birthplace: <u>**Mohawk Valley, Oneida County, New York**</u> (1 Jan 1802)—Married: 2 Feb 1824--Residence in 1860: <u>Waukesha, Waukesha County, Wisconsin</u>—Occupation: *blacksmith & farmer*–Residents: Sebina's father: **John**--Children: **George**—<u>By 1874, Sebina's son, George, has taken ownership and manages the 186-acre (section 17) Barney farm in the Town of Waukesha</u>—The Fox River runs through a small section along the eastern edge of the farm.[863] (Image and genealogy courtesy of Jennifer Doane of Clinton, Utah.)[864]

Sebina Danford Barney with baby George (c. 1925)[865]

Early years in Jefferson County, New York:

"When he was a small boy, *Sabina Barney*'s parents moved to Adams, Jefferson County, N.Y. <u>*In Adams Village, he learned the trade of blacksmithing and carried on the business for fifteen years.*</u> Sebina & Polly Barney's son, **George**, was born in the town of Adams on June 22, 1825. <u>*In 1827, Sebina Barney was accidently shot by careless boys who were shooting at a mark; it affected his health throughout his subsequent life.*</u>"[866]

Creating a successful life in Wisconsin:

"<u>*During the spring of 1837, the family, including Sebina's father, came by way of the lakes to Milwaukee, having a rough and tempestuous trip, the ice breaking the wheels from the steamer.*</u> Landing in Milwaukee in June, they reached Prairieville on the 4th of July. *Sebina Barney* bought a claim on Sec.14, at that time, and through his labor and care it was made one of the best farms in the county. In 1855, he became connected with the *Waukesha County Bank* at its organization and was one of its officers being for many years Vice President." He was a believer in *Spiritualism* as well as a *Freemason*."[867]

"Jesse's Woods"

"One of the itinerant buyers in this county was *Jesse James*, later to go down in history as a *notorious outlaw*. He was very specific as to the kind of horses he wanted. They were to be matched. <u>*The Sebina Barney farm, southwest of Waukesha, was one of his stops, and he and his traveling companies spent the night in Barney's woods. The Barney family has called it 'Jesse's Woods' from that time to this day*</u>."[868]

863 Standard Atlas of Waukesha County, Wisconsin, (Chicago, Geo. A. Ogle & Co., 1914) Plat of Waukesha Township.

864 *Federal Manuscript Schedule*, Population, Agricultural and Manufacturing Schedules for Waukesha County, Town of Waukesha, 1860.

865 Photograph courtesy of Jennifer Doane of Clinton, Utah, e-mail to author, May 14, 2010.

866 *1880 History of Waukesha County*, pp. 589 & 836.

867 *1880 History of Waukesha County*, pp. 589 & 836.

868 Celia Barney, "Old Homesteads Their Owners: Barney Home." *Landmark*. v. 5. n. 3, Spring, 1962, pp. 6 & 7.

IMMIGRANTS TO WISCONSIN FROM NEW YORK & MICHIGAN

Name: **William Howie**– Birthplace: <u>New York</u> (c. 1842)—Occupation: *presently at sea* — Spouse: **Adda**— Birthplace: <u>Michigan</u> (c. 1852)—Residence in 1880: <u>Brookfield Township, Waukesha County, Wisconsin</u>— Occupation: *farmer*–Children: *Lillie, William & Martha.*
(Image and genealogy courtesy of Waukesha County Historical Society and Museum, 1915)[869]

Adda Howie (1928)[870]

WORLD-FAMED DAIRY WOMAN IN PRESCOTT.

"*Mrs. Adda F. Howie is one of the most famous women in the United States—one about whom, more has been written and printed in this and foreign countries than about any other woman now living and who is engaged in an industrial pursuit for the benefit of the country and humanity in general*. She has won her practical experience, being known throughout the dairying world as the breeder and importer from the Jersey Islands of blue-ribbon Jersey stock. On her dairy farm, called "<u>Sunny Peak Farm</u>," near Elm Grove (section 35), Wisconsin, she has a herd of eighty-four head bred on the farm. *Her herd today, is recognized as the very finest herd in the entire country.*"
[*Prescott, Arizona, Journal-Miner*, Nov. 25, 1914]

FOREMOST DAIRYWOMAN OF COUNTY ASSISTS IN BIG GARDEN CAMPAIGN.

Mrs. Adda F. Howie, who is a visitor in Birmingham in connection with the war garden campaign of the **International Harvester Company**, is a woman of world renown, her good work being known and having been featured in both America and Europe. She is owner of <u>Sunny Peak Farm</u>, near Milwaukee, which is unique in the history of farms of our country. She holds a permit from King Edward to visit the royal dairies of England and the British Isles. *Due to the wonderful methods she has developed at Sunny Peak Farm, she has developed dairying there into a high science, and have made her probably the greatest woman dairy specialist in America.* Mrs. Howie is endowed with a charming personality, and so imbued with the spirit and truth of her work she radiates helpfulness and inspiration wherever her labors take her. [*The Birmingham News* Feb. 13, 1918]

---

[869] *Federal Manuscript Schedule*, Population, Agricultural and Manufacturing Schedules for Waukesha County, Town of Brookfield, 1880.

[870] Image courtesy of the Waukesha County Historical Society and Museum, 2009, (by Eric Vanden Heuvel, previous Archivist).

CONCLUSION

Human movement from one location to another has occurred since the peopling of our planet began. "Today, according to UN calculations there are over 7 billion humans living on our planet. For thousands of years, the population grew only slowly but in recent centuries, it has jumped dramatically. Between 1900 and 2000, the increase in world population was three times."[871]

"Historical demographers estimate that around the year 1800 the world population was only around 1 billion people."[872] This number closely corresponds with the era when hundreds of thousands western European immigrant's arrived in North America, among them were tens of thousands eastern American as well as Western European immigrates arriving in Wisconsin (1839 -1860).

"By the late 1880's, immigrants to the United States were arriving from Southern and Eastern Europe. Much like the motivations of Western Europeans before them, Southern and Eastern Europeans yearned to escape political and economic oppression, as well as persecution, destitution, and violence. Ellis Island, in Upper New York Bay, was the gateway for over 12 million immigrants to the U.S. as the United States' busiest immigrant inspection station for over 60 years. Among others, large groups of peoples being processed through the station were Poles, Hungarians, Czechs, Serbs, Slovaks, Greeks, Syrians, Turks and Armenians."[873] "The peak year of European immigration to the United States

was in 1907, when 1,285,349 persons entered the country."[874] Among this immigration group, large numbers of Poles, Italians, Serbs, Jews Croats, Greeks and Ukrainians settled in Milwaukee. Meanwhile, during this same period, numerous Hispanic and African-Americans from the south, arrived in the city.[875]

In 2019, increasing numerous of emigrants from the strife torn Middle East are attempting to seek asylum in western Europe; creating economic and social stress in those regions. While in the United States, Middle Eastern refugees along with refugees from gang controlled, violent, and poverty stricken Central American countries are currently seeking refugee statues here in the United States. Our current administration, however, has taken a hard stance towards limiting refugees seeking asylum in the United States.[876]

At the Literacy Services of Wisconsin, located in downtown Milwaukee, a number of, generally, retirement age volunteers, me included, are presently serving as a tutors, teaching English language skills among the Milwaukee area's newest immigrants. Personally, I have worked with emigrants from: Jordan, Mexico, El Salvador, Ukraine, China, South Korea, Laos, the Democratic Republic of the Congo and Iran. On the downside, the historical account which you just read, certainly suggests that

---

[871] Esteban Ortiz-Ospina and Max Roser, "World Population Growth," 2013; updated April 2017. As presented in *Our World in Data*.

[872] Esteban Ortiz-Ospina and Max Roser, "World Population Growth," 2013; updated April 2017. As presented in *Our World in Data*.

[873] https://en.wikipedia.org/wiki/Ellis_Island

[874] Esteban Ortiz-Ospina and Max Roser, "World Population Growth," 2013; updated April 2017. As presented in *Our World in Data*,

[875] John Gurda, *The Making of Milwaukee*. Milwaukee: Milwaukee County Historical Society. 1999, p. 180.

[876] https://asylumadvocacy.org/ The Asylum Seeker Advocacy Project. The (ASAP) prevents wrongful deportations by providing community support and emergency legal aid to refugee families — no matter where they are located in the United States.

animosity directed towards new immigrant groups will, likely mount, worldwide, particularly as our world population continues to reach an estimated "eight billion by 2024." [877]

These issues aside, reflecting on many of our own local ancestors with western European roots, as documented in this work, we owe these family's much gratitude for all we enjoy today. Considering the hardships they experience in mid-19th Century Europe, it certainly took great courage for so many of them to simply pack up and leave in the hopes of beginning a new life in this virtually unknown land—Wisconsin. Once here, they often faced new, more difficult and even heartbreaking challenges. We can only surmise that it was their persistence and endurance which allowed so many to thrive. So that today, we descendants, often five generations removed, reap the benefits of their sacrifices in so many ways as we enjoy incredibly advanced technologies, more creature comforts, and amazingly improved health advances. And yet we too, just like our forefathers, must stand ever on guard to preserve our nation's ongoing experiment in Democracy which, as always, remains tenuous without our constant vigilance!

---

[877] Esteban Ortiz-Ospina and Max Roser, "World Population Growth," 2013; updated April 2017. As presented in Our World in Data.

BIBLIOGRAPHY

ONLINE SOURCES PROVIDED BY WIKIPEDIA

"Alexander Randall"

"Unification of Germany"

"Medieval European Peasants"

"List of Historic States of Germany"

"Commoner"

"Anti-Catholicism"

"Beriah Brown"

"British Immigrants—Immigration
    to the United States"

"Canandaigua, New York"

"County Cork"

"Covenanters"

"Danish Americans"

"Dutch Americans"

"Dutchy of Hesse"

"Economic History of Scotland"

"18th Wisconsin Volunteer
    Infantry Regiment"

"1st Wisconsin Heavy Artillery Regiment"

"5th Wisconsin Volunteer Infantry Regiment"

"Franco Prussian War"

"Gausdal"

"Great Lakes"

"History of Education in the United States"

"History of Yorkshire"

"Irish Potato Famine"

"Murphy"

"The Murphy Clan…Clan-History"

"New Amsterdam"

"New Amsterdam, Wisconsin"

"Opposition to the War of 1812
    in the United States"

"Øyvind Holmstad"

"Paris Green"

"Peasant"

"Royal Scots"

"Shoemaking"

"Tintype"

"28th Wisconsin Volunteer
    Infantry Regiment"

"Unification of Germany"

 "Valerius of Trèves"

 "Wareham, Massachusetts"

 "Waukesha, Wisconsin"

 "Timber Framing"

 "Hessen-Philippsthal-Barchfeld"

 "History of Hertfordshire"

 "Perthshire"

 "Crofters"

 "Scottish-Canadians"

 "Dan Patch"

 "Rhine Province"

 "Boston, Lincolnshire"

 "Huddersfield"

 "Ephraim Beaumont"

 "Forty-Eighters"

 "Kingdom of Württemberg"

 "Ludwigsburg"

 "Order of the Knights of St. Crispin,"

 "Leipzig"

 "History of Saxony"

 "History of Scotland"

 "Scottish Americans"

 "List of Germanic Deities"

 "History of Pharmacy in the United States"

 "Man of War"

 "Muskego Settlement, Wisconsin"

"Immigrant Working Conditions & Pay"

 "Palatinate"

 "Prüm"

 "Tricycle,"

 "Landkreis Kolberg"

 "Uckermar"

 " Whitley Beaumont"

 "British C0-Operative Movement"

 "Mining in Cornwall and Devon"

 "Norwalk, Connecticut"

 "St. Mary's History"

 "Fruitland, California"

 "9th U.S. Infantry Regiment"

 "Parish Lissan, Londonderry, Ireland"

 "A Brief History on the Origins of Window, Roller Shades"

 "The Poor Law Amendment Act (1834)"

 "Kashubians"

 "Pomerania"

 "Jones Island, Milwaukee"

 "Gjerpen"

 "Norwegian Americans"

 "Gnoien"

 "German Revolutions of 1848-49"

 "Brackel (Dortmund)"

 "Provinsen Westfalen"

 "Black Death"

 "County Tyrone"

"Mumford, New York"

"Alsace"

"Nörvenich"

"Castle Clinton"

"Leadville, Colorado"

"Dutch Americans"

"Dutch Reformed Church"

"Balgheim"

"District of Tuttlingen"

"Franconia"

"Dinkelsbühl"

"History of Saxony"

"List of baseball parks in Milwaukee"

"Province of Posen"

"Pomerania"

"Emigration from Pomerania"

"Rhineland"

"Left Bank of the Rhine"

"Grand Dutchy of Hesse"

"Göritz"

"6th Division (German Empire)"

"Province of Brandenburg"

"Sewing"

"Victorian Architecture"

"Speyer"

"Northern (automobile)"

"Methodist Episcopal Church"

"Wintrich"

"Stonemasonry"

"Ostóda"

"Young Irelander Rebellion of 1848"

"Ellis Island"

"New York, Chicago and St. Louis Railroad"

"Walsall"

"Sinsheim"

"Legacy of the Great Irish Famine"

"Butte, Montana"

"Deer Lodge, Montana"

"Helena, Montana"

"Gnoien"

"History of Denmark"

"Cruelty to Animals"

"32nd Infantry Division (United States)"

"Meuse Argonne Offensive"

"Armistice of 11 November 1918"

"Wicimice"

"Old Lutherans"

"Wisconsin German"

"Llanfachreth"

"Primogeniture"

NEWSPAPERS

Augsburger Allgemeine, (General Newspaper), Bavaria

The Birmingham News

Brookfield News

Chilton Times

Eagle (Wisconsin) Quill

Hartland News

Living Sussex Sun

Madison Argus

Milwaukee Courier

The Milwaukee Journal

The Omaha Daily Bee

Prescott, Arizona, Journal-Miner

Rochester (N.Y.) Daily Register

Southside (Milwaukee) Urban News

Waterford Post

Waukesha Freeman

Waukesha Plaindealer

Waukesha Republican-Freeman

BOOKS

Atlas of Waukesha Co. Wisconsin. Madison. Wis.: Harrison & Warner, 1873.

Anbinder, Tyler. *Nativism & Slavery: The Northern Know Nothings & the Politics of the 1850s.* New York, Oxford University Press, 1992.

Apps, Jerry. *Horse-Drawn Days: A Century of Farming in Wisconsin:* Madison, Wisconsin Historical Press, 2010.

Austin, H. Russell. *The Wisconsin Story: The Building of a Vanguard State (1st Edition):* Milwaukee, Wisconsin, The Milwaukee Journal, 1948.

Barbian-Preslik, Genevieve, "Woelfel-Barbian Farm," Century Farms of Wisconsin, v.1. Inter-Collegiate Press, Shawnee Mission, Ks.: 1983.

Beckwith, Albert Clayton. *History of Walworth County, Wisconsin.* Indianapolis: B. F. Bowen & Company, 1912.

Bergland, Martha & Hayes Paul G., *Studying Wisconsin: The Life of Increase Lapham, Early Chronicler of Plants, Rocks, Rivers, Mounds and All Things Wisconsin.* Madison, WI.: Wisconsin Historical Society Press, 2014.

Bettmann, Otto L. *The Good Old Days—They Were Terrible.* New York: Penguin Random House, 1974.

Biggle, Jacob. *Poultry Book: A Concise and Practical Treatise on the Management of Farm Poultry,* Wilmer Atkinson Co., Philadelphia, 1911. 8th Edition.

Buenker, John D. *The History of Wisconsin, Volume 4: The Progressive Era, 1893–1914*. Madison: Wisconsin Historical Society, 1998.

Crowell, Benedict and Wilson, Robert F. *The Road to France: The Transportation of Troops and Military Supplies. 1917-1918.* New Haven, Yale University Press, 1921, Vol.1.

Current, Richard, *History of Wisconsin, v. 2. the Civil War Era, 1848-1873.* Madison: Wisconsin Historical Society, 1976.

Cutler, William G. *History of the State of Kansas.* Chicago, A.T. Andreas, 1883.

Davies, Phillips G. *Welsh in Wisconsin (Revised and Expanded Edition).* Madison: Wisconsin Historical Society Press, 2006.

Dayton Fred Erving & Lochhead. *Steamboat Days.* Newport News, VA.: The Mariners' Museum, 1948.

Eckstein, Neil T. *Norton's Folly: Norwegian Immigrants and Yankee Neighbors on the Wisconsin Frontier, 1849-1857.* Grandview Books: Larsen, WI., 1997,

The Farm Journal Illustrated Rural Directory of Waukesha County, Wisconsin 1918-1923, Philadelphia: Wilmer Atkinson Company, 1923.

Flower, Frank A. *History of Milwaukee, Wisconsin.* Milwaukee: Western Historical Company, 1881.

Gard, Robert & Milo, *My Land, My Home, My Wisconsin, The Epic Story of the Wisconsin Farm and farm Family from Settlement Days to Present.* Racine, WI., Western Publishing Co., 1978. Currently available via WorldCat

Haight, Theron Wilber, *Memoirs of Waukesha County*, Western Historical Association: Madison, Wisconsin, 1907.

Harstad, Peter T. "Frontier Medicine in the Territory of Wisconsin." In Numbers, Ronald L.& Judith Walzer Leavitt. eds. *Wisconsin Medicine—Historical Perspectives.* Madison: University of Wisconsin Press: 1981.

History of Napa Valley and lake Counties, California, comprising their geography, geology, topography, climatographic, timber… together with a full record of the Mexican Grants… also separate histories of all the townships… and sketches. San Francisco: CA.: Slocum, Bowen & Co., 1881.

History of Dane County, Wisconsin. Chicago: Western Historical Co., 1880

The History of Waukesha County. Chicago: Western Historical Co., 1880.

Johnson, Peter Leo. *Early Catholic Churches in the Archdiocese of Milwaukee*, St. Ambrose. (Milwaukee, 1941).

Lacher, J.H.A. "German Pioneers of Brookfield," *Wisconsin Domesday Book—Town Studies, vol. 1.* Madison: Wisconsin Historical Society, 1924.

La Vies, John G., and Johnson, Peter Leo. Early Catholic Church Property in the Archdiocese of Milwaukee Wisconsin. [Archdiocese of Milwaukee], 1941.

Leonard, Bill J. and Jill Y. Crenshaw. *Editors, Encyclopedia of Religious Controversies in the United States, 2nd. Edition. Volume One: A-L, ABC-CLIO*, Santa Barbara California, Denver, Colorado, Oxford, England: 2013, preview.

Love, William D. *Wisconsin in the War of the Rebellion, vol.1.* Chicago: Church & Goodman, 1866.

"Milwaukee County Atlas, Wauwatosa Township." H. Belden & Co. Chicago, 1876.

Moreno, Barry. *The Illustrated Encyclopedia of Ellis Island, New York*: Fall River Press, 2004,

Morton, W. E., *The Wisconsin Centennial Story of Disasters and Other Unfortunate Events, 1848-1948.* Wisconsin State Centennial Committee, 1948.

Nesbit, Robert. *History of Wisconsin v. 3, Urbanization and Industrialization, 1873-1893.* Madison: Wisconsin Historical Society, 1895.

Numbers, Ronald L. & Judith Walzer Leavitt. WISCONSIN MEDICINE. © 1981 by the Board of Regents of the University of Wisconsin System. Reproduced courtesy of the University of Wisconsin Press.

Oldt, Franklin T, *History of Dubuque County, Iowa.* Chicago: Goodspeed Historical Association, 1911, vol. 2.

Plat Book of Dane County, Wisconsin. Madison: Harrison & Warner, 1873.

Plat Book of Iowa County, Wisconsin. Madison: Sewyn A. Brant, 1895.

Portrait and Biographical Record of Waukesha County, Wisconsin. Chicago: Excelsior Publishing Co., 1894.

Portraits of Muskego Farmers 1836-1980, Muskego Historical Society, 1980.

Ramstack, Thomas, *Brookfield: A Fine and Fertile Land—An Early History of Brookfield Township, Waukesha County, Wisconsin.* Collierville, TN: InstantPublisher.com, 2007.

_____, *Images of America*: *Brookfield and Elm Grove*, Charleston, South Carolina: Arcadia Publishing, 2009.

Severa, Joan, *Dressed for the Photographer: Ordinary Americans & Fashion, 1840-1900*, Kent, Ohio & London, England: Kent State University Press, 1995.

Showerman, Grant, *A County Chronicle.* New York: The Century Co., 1916.

Standard Atlas of Waukesha County, Wisconsin. Chicago: Geo. A. Ogle & Co, 1914.

Stigler, Mary. *"The History of the Stigler Farm, New Berlin, Waukesha County," In Century Farms of Wisconsin.* Shawnee Mission, Kansas: Inter-Collegiate Press, 1984.

Ulvestad, Martin, Translation. *Nordmændene i Amerika.* Minneapolis, MN.: History Forlog, 1907.

Weatherford, *Doris, Foreign and Female; Immigrant Women in America, 1840-1930.* New York: Facts on File, 1995.

Wells, Robert W., *Yesterday's Milwaukee.* Miami, Florida: E.A. Seeman Publishing, Inc., 1976.

Winters, Joseph & Kramer, John Eicholtz. *The First Century of the Philadelphia College of Pharmacy, 1821-1921.* England: Philadelphia College of Pharmacy, 1922.

Woelfel, James *The Ulrich Woelfel Family History*, Holt, MI.: self-published, 1995.

Utzat, John. & Ruth Ruege, eds., *Southside in the Sun.* This book contains a compilation of articles from the "Southside Urban News," (1977 – 1981).

ONLINE IMAGES

Steamship Empire," Courtesy of Maritime History of the Great Lakes Maritime History of the Great Lakes," IMAGE, e-mail
walter@maritimehistoryofthegreatlakes.ca

"The German Confederation," MAP, Wikipedia, https://en.wikipedia.org/wiki/List_of_states_of_the_German_Confederation

"A Farm in 1794," IMAGE, Wikipedia, https://en.wikipedia.org/wiki/Peasant

"From the Old to the New World" shows German emigrants boarding a steamer in Hamburg, to New York. Harper's Weekly, (New York) November 7, 1874, IMAGE, Wikipedia," © Deutsches Reich 1, png: kgberger/Wikimedia Commons/ [http://creativecommons.org/licenses/by-sa/3.0/CC-BY-SA3.0]/[http://en.wikipedia.org/wiki/Wikipedia:Text_of_yhe_GNU_Free_Documentation_License GFDL] "

"Milwaukee (1858)," IMAGE, https://commons.wikimedia.org/w/index.php?title=File:Milwaukee_1858.jpg&oldid=210029982,

"Østre Gausdal Kirke," IMAGE, https://no.wikipedia.org/wiki/%C3%98stre_Gausdal_kirke

Pierre-Georges Jeanniot's Portrait, Depicting The Battle of Mars-la-Tour," IMAGE, wikipedia+Pierre-Georges+Jeanniot+Portrait,+Depicting+The+Battle+of+Mars-la-Tour,"&rlz=1C1CHBF_enUS815US815&source=lnms&tbm=isch&sa=X&ved=0ahUKEwif2-LpgOTdAhUIWK0KHaoOBnUQ_AUIDigB&biw=1005&bih=564,

Wallach, Miriam and Ira D. Wallach "View on the Erie Canal." Division of Art Prints and Photographs: Print Collection, The New York Public Library. The New York Public Library Digital Collections, 1829. http://digitalcollections.nypl.org/items/510d47d9-7ba7-a3d9-e040-e00a18064a99, MAP.

"Great Lakes 1913 Storm," Shipwrecks. pnghttps://en.wikipedia.org/wiki/File:Great_Lakes_1913_Storm_Shipwrecks.png, MAP

PRIMARY SOURCES

Caesar, Fredrich (1871). *"Fredrich Caesar Letter from Ormelle, France to his cousin in Wisconsin,"* courtesy of Elaine Alane of Helensville, Wisconsin.

Casper, Veronica, *"1910 postcard to Amanda & Caroline Phillips,"* from the author's collection.

_____, *"1912 postcard to Amanda & Caroline Phillips,"* from the author's collection.

Castleman, Alfred L. *"The Journal of Surgeon Alfred L. Castleman."* From Behind the Scenes--Daily Observation of the Civil War, December 19, 2012. The American Civil War, The Army of the Potomac. *Behind the Scenes--Daily Observation of the Civil War,"* January 2, 2012.

_____ *"The Journal of Surgeon Alfred L. Castleman."* From Behind the Scenes--Daily Observation of the Civil War, December 19, 2012. The American Civil War, The Army of the Potomac. Behind the Scenes--Daily Observation of the Civil War,"

Curran, Jean Alonzo, M.D., "Charles Curran letters, summer, 1868-Sept. 1868," *Curran Family History, U/P, 1970.*

Baney, Lena. *"1910 postcard to Mary Phillips,"* from the author's collection.

Hawks, Nelson Crocker. *"Boats Ran on the Great Lakes to Chicago," from* Nelson Hawks' scrapbook."

Hawks, Nelson Crocker. *"From New York State to Wisconsin,"* from Nelson Hawks' scrapbook.

Hawks, Nelson. *Nelson C. Hawks' letter to his sister Frances (Fannie).* "Grand suppers were prepared at the Delafield House"

Hawks' Nelson Crocker scrapbook. "Nelson Hawks Opens an Inn at Delafield"

Howie, Adda, "Letter to the Wisconsin Historical Society" (c. 1930)

Lenz, Frank G. "Around the World with Wheel and Canvas," Outing, An Illustrated Monthly Magazine of Recreation, Nov. 1892.

Meidenbauer, John K. "John K. *Meidenbauer letter to his nephew serving in the Bavarian army,"* courtesy of Roy Meidenbauer of New Berlin, Wisconsin.

Phillips, Helen, *"Post card to her parents in Muskego,"* from the author's collection.

Phillips, Mary (Kau), *"Recipe Book,"* (c. 1900.) from the author's collection

Spaulding, Willis (Bill) H. *"diary,"* presented to the Oconomowoc Public Library by a daughter, Leona Postell.

Woelfel Mrs. Caroline, *"Letter to the Kraus family, of Germersberg, Bavaria,"* (Feb. 26, 1886).

SECONDARY SOURCES

Alane, Elaine, *"Albert and Meta continue operation of the Caesar farm,"* e-mailed account, Apr 28, 2010.

Alane, Elaine, *"A Pioneer Family in Muskego,"* e-mailed account, Oct 22, 2017.

Alane, Elaine, *"Caesar Family History,"* e-mailed account, Apr 28, 2010.

Alane, Elaine, *"Dancing to the sound of the fiddle,"* Apr 30, 2010.

Alane, Elaine, *"Garret Veenendaal's place at Union Church,"* Apr 30, 2010.

The Association of the Graduates of the United States Military Academy Digital Library. http://digital-library.usma.edu/cdm/ref/collection/p16919coll1/id/5

Barker, Lauren. "Battle of Helena Arkansas, Saturday, July 4, 1863," *Proceedings of the 28th Wisconsin Volunteer Infantry, 31st Annual Reunion,"* Milwaukee: Houtkamp Printing Co., 1913, pp. 72-77.

_____. "Some Incidents Regarding the 28th Regiment," *Proceedings of the Society of the 28th Wisconsin Infantry, 15th Annual Reunion, Elkhorn, Wisconsin, June 26, 1902, v. 2.*

Blattner, Steve. Recollections, *"What a day it was!" Dec 5, 2016.*

Birge, E.A. and C. Juday, "The Inland Lakes of Wisconsin, 1. The Dissolved Gases and their Biological Significance," *Bulletin of the Wisconsin Geological and Natural History Survey, Volume 22, 1911.*

"Chronological History of Dousman, Wisconsin," Courtesy of Dousman Historical Society.

Curran, Jean Alonzo. *"Curran Family History" u/p, 1970.*

Cutler, Morris D., *"Historical Marker Project,"* Cutler Park. *Waukesha County Historical Society and Museum.*

Drexel University College of Medicine, Legacy Center: Archives and Special Collections on Women in Medicine and Homeopathy.

Gemeindechroni Holdorf 1188 - 1988, Community History Holdorf (Kreis Vechta, Province Oldenburg) Publisher: Gemeinde Holdorf * Grosse Str. 19 * 49449 Holdorf, ISBN 3-88441-032-6

Genz, Marilyn. https://www.ancestry.co.uk/boards/searchResults.aspx?db=mb...Genz...Genz...

Goodman, *"Tosten Thorstein Rasmussaen Immigration Story,"* e-mail to author, Oct 11, 2011.

Logan, Carol. "The Final major Allied offensive of W.W.I," e-mailed to author Jun 28, 2010.

_____ *"Clarence Potter, Corporal, 32nd Division, 128th Infantry, in the Battle of the Argonne Forest,"* Jun 27, 2010.

_____ *"Yanked her Earrings,"* e-mailed account to author, Jun 27, 2010.

Lynch, Judy. *"3 Jermark children attend the Institute for the Deaf & Dumb at Delavan."* e-mailed account, Oct 16, 2011.

content.wisconsinhistory.org/u? /wda,2268

Daniels, Megan. "Hollandsche Berg: MKE'S Dutch Settlement." *From-Following the Plank Road blog.*

Eiler, Kenneth. *"3 Generations of Kreigs,"* e-mailed account, Jun 27, 2010,

Everst, Kate A. "Early Lutheran Immigration in Wisconsin," *Wisconsin Academy of Science, Arts and Letters. Transaction 8 images.library.wisc.edu Abstract, 1892.* pp. 289 & 293 - 295.

Fuller, Margaret. *Summer on the Lakes, in 1843 .* (Boston: Charles C. Little and James Brown; New York, Charles S. Francis and Company, 1844.) Available in digital form on the Library of Congress Web site, pp.68 & 70.

Hartwell, Jerry L., *"Charles Krieg in Brookfield."*

_____ *"A Family History of the Descendants of John Christian Dieman—August Dieman Branch,"* 2006. Courtesy of Jerry R. Hartwell

Heli, Richard, *"Elsass Alsace History, With Extensive Bibliography, A Genealogy Page,"* *https://www.familysearch.org/wiki/ en/Get_Involved_in_Wiki_Projects*http:// immigrationtounitedstates. org/468-dutch-immigrants.html

Howard, Chief Steve. *"A History of the City of Waukesha Fire Department."*

Kramer, Betty Ann *"The Farmhouse at Elm Grove,"* e-mailed to author, Jul 27, 2011.

The Palatines - for United Empire Loyalists' Association of Canada George Anderson, https://www.uelac.org/Loyalist-Research/Palatines.pdf "The Palatines UE 1," June 2006. WorldGenWeb. The WorldGenWeb is a non-profit volunteer organization that is dedicated to the free use and access of public domain genealogical information. Copyright © 2018 WorldGenWeb Project.

Perkins, Martin (Marty), former Supervisor of Interpretation at Old World Wisconsin, an open-air museum located near Eagle, Waukesha County, Wisconsin. Interview with author, 15 June 2009.

Kuhm, Herbert W. "Ve Goink Milvowkee!" *Historical Messenger of the Milwaukee County Historical Society, Milwaukee.* v. 31, n. 4 Winter, 1975.

"Ethnic Groups in Wisconsin: Historical Background, British Immigrants to Wisconsin, the Scots," *Max Kade Institute for German-American Studies, University of Wisconsin-Madison.*

Meier-Ramstack, Mary, *"Mary (Kau) Phillip's Cookbook,"* Dec 1997.

Migration from Vermont," from "Flow of History Gathering and Interactions of Peoples, Cultures, and Ideas," c/o Southeast Vermont Community Learning Collaborative, flow@learningcollaborative.org.

Milwaukee County Asylum-Asylum Projects, http://www.asylumprojects.org/index. php/Milwaukee_County_Asylum

Nauertz-Husz, Kathleen & Peter Sjoberg, *"The Gebhardt Family,"* e-mailed account to the author.

New Berlin Landmarks Commission CHAPTER 4: "Cultural & Historical Resources." Revisions approved by Council on 6/14/2016 via Ordinance #2568, New Berlin 2020, Comprehensive Plan 4:20

Sullivan, Dennis, *"Modern Threshing Machines,"* 6 Aug 2018.

Nolan, Libbie Faulkner, "Sunnyside Cemetery Brochure" 2008, Find A Grave, New Berlin Almanack, Vol. X. Courtesy of the New Berlin Historical Society.

_____. *"Three of Alfred and Mary Russell's children die of diphtheria in 1868,"* e-mailed account, Jan. 15, 2010.

"Old Lutherans Leave Pomerania, 1835-1854," http://www.bafrenz. com/birds/Genealogy/

Lohry, Lisa. *"From Wisconsin to Minnesota,"* e-mailed account, Aug 11, 2010.

Smith, Huron H. *"Ethnobiology of the Ojibwe Indians,"* Bulletin of the Milwaukee Public Museum of the City of Milwaukee. Milwaukee, Aetna Press, vol. 4, no. 3, May 2, 1932.

Stutz, Reno. translation: Daniela Garling .... Article in "Mecklenburg Magazine" 1990/13,

Thayer, Linda. *"Milwaukee County Asylum,"* Dec 23, 2016.

Treis, Dr. Helmut. *"Primary factors for families such as the Meidenbauer's to emigrate,"* Jul 16, 2018.

_____. *"Nordrhein-Westfalen, Germany,"* letter to author, Sept 21, 1989.

Migration from Vermont," from *"Flow of History Gathering and Interactions of Peoples, Cultures, and Ideas,"* c/o Southeast Vermont Community Learning Collaborative, flow@learningcollaborative.org

"The Mining Institute of Scotland," *Tait's Edinburgh Magazine, c. 1840.*

"The Movement of American Settlers into Wisconsin and Minnesota," *The Iowa Journal of History & Politics, Vol. 17, No. 3, Jul. 1919.*

Pedriana Jean, *"Woolen Firm of 'Beaumont & Stock',"* e-mailed account, April 23, 2010,

Ramstack, Thomas, *"The Phillips Family of Muskego,"* unpublished, 2017.

Schafer, Joseph. *"The Yankee and the Teuton in Wisconsin,"* Wisconsin Magazine of History, 6-7 (December 1922-December 1923),

Stigler, Mary. *"New Berlin Ancestry Message Board,"* 12 Jan 2002.

James Woelfel, James," *"The Ulrich Woelfel Family History,"* Holt, MI.: self-published,1995, pp. xv-xvi.

Van Wagon Jr., Jared. "The Golden Age of Homespun." *State of New York, Department of Agriculture and Markets, Bulletin 203, Albany, N.Y.: June 1927.*

Vogel, David M. "letter," *The Garvins Newsletter Volume XI (1991).*

Waukesha Motor Company advertisement in the *Automobile Trade Journal*, 1916, volume 20.

William Jarvis & the Merino Sheep Craze." vermonthistory.org/educate/online-resources/an-era-of-great-change/work-changing-markets/william-jarvis-s-merino-sheep.

"Wisconsin's Cultural Resource Study Units," *Wisconsin Historical Society*.

"Welcoming Modernity," Courtesy of the Village of Menomonee Falls, Wisconsin.

"Welsh Immigrant Historical Scrapbook," courtesy of Wales Village Hall.

Williams, Sue Ellen. "Horse Whipped," e-mailed to author, June 27, 2010.

Williams, Sue Ellen. *"Prussia Occupies Northern Württemberg."* e-mailed to author, June 27, 2010.

Wiedeman, Mildred E. *"The Green Road and Duplainville Area,"* September 1992. Courtesy of the Pewaukee Area Historical Society.

FEDERAL CENSUS RECORDS FOR WAUKESHA COUNTY AVAILABLE ON MICROFILM AT THE WAUKESHA PUBLIC LIBRARY. IN STATE & OUT OF STATE CENSUS RECORDS AVAILABLE THROUGH INTERLIBRARY LOAN.

1840 Federal Manuscript Schedule, Population of Milwaukee County, Wisconsin Territory.

1850 Federal Manuscript Census, Manufacturing Schedules for Waukesha County, Towns of,

Brookfield Delafield, Eagle, Merton, Muskego, New Berlin, Oconomowoc, Pewaukee, Vernon & Waukesha.

1860 Federal Manuscript Schedule, Population, Agricultural and Manufacturing Schedules for Waukesha County, Towns of Brookfield, Delafield, Genesee, Menomonee, Muskego, New Berlin Oconomowoc, Ottawa, Pewaukee & Village of Waukesha.

1860 Federal Manuscript Schedule, Population, Agricultural and Manufacturing Schedules for Waupaca County, Town of St. Lawrence.

1870 Federal Manuscript Schedule, Population, Agricultural and Manufacturing Schedules for Waukesha County, Towns of: New Berlin, Village of Waukesha, Waukesha, Muskego, Pewaukee, Oconomowoc, Brookfield, Delavan, Ottawa, Mukwonago,

1870 Federal Manuscript Schedule, Population, Agricultural, fruit production, timber, and manufacturing schedules, the City of St. Helena, Napa County, California.

1880 Federal Manuscript Schedule, Population, Agricultural and Manufacturing Schedules for Waukesha County, Towns of Genesee, Lisbon, New Berlin, Muskego, Village of Waukesha, Brookfield, Pewaukee, Summit, Oconomowoc, Ottawa,

1880 Federal Manuscript Schedule, Population, Agricultural and Manufacturing Schedules for Walworth County, Town of Lafayette.

1890 Federal Manuscript Schedule, Population, Agricultural and Manufacturing Schedules for Waukesha County, Towns of Brookfield, Pewaukee, New Berlin, Vernon, Oconomowoc,

1900 Federal Manuscript Schedule, Population, Agricultural and Manufacturing Schedules for Waukesha County, Towns of Menomonee, Delafield, Oconomowoc, New Berlin, Brookfield, Muskego, Ottawa, City of Waukesha,

1900 Federal Manuscript Schedule, Population, Agricultural and Manufacturing Schedules for Minnehaha County, Sioux Falls City, South Dakota.

1910 Federal Manuscript Schedule, Population, Agricultural and Manufacturing Schedules for Waukesha County, Town of Menomonee, Brookfield, Lisbon, New Berlin, City of Waukesha.

1920 Federal Manuscript Schedule, Population, Agricultural and Manufacturing Schedules for Waukesha County, City of Waukesha, Town of Brookfield, New Berlin,

Federal Manuscript Schedule, Population, Agricultural and Manufacturing Schedules for Waukesha County, Town of New Berlin, 1930.

Federal Manuscript Schedule, Population, Agricultural and Manufacturing Schedules for Waukesha County, Town of New Berlin, 1940.

DESCRIPTION OF 19th & EARLY 20th CENTURY STYLES & FASHION COURTESY OF JOAN SEVERA—RENOUND HISTORIAN OF PERIOD CLOTHING:

"Emily Rathbun," Women's Clothing Styles of the 1850's,

"Beriah Brown," Men's Clothing Styles of the 1850's,

"Parmelia DuBois (Hawks) Sperry," Women's Clothing Styles of the 1850's,

"Agnes (Schaefer) Kau," Women's Clothing Styles of the 1860's,

"Emily Experience Snyder Lumb (c. 1868)," Women's Clothing Styles of the 1860's,

Sarah (Davis) Faulkner (c. 1874)," Women's Clothing Styles of the 1870's,

"Isabelle Searle (c. 1875)," Women's Clothing Styles of the 1870's,

"Frederik Stigler & Mary Schneider's Wedding Day (Oct. 30, 1877)," Women's Clothing Styles of the 1870's,

"Adda S. Lumb (c. 1877)," Children's Clothing Styles of the 1870's,

"Elsie Chapman (c. 1882)," Women's Clothing Styles of the 1880's,

"Michael, Andrew & Otilia Stigler (c. 1883)," Children's Clothing Styles of the 1880's,

"Bertha Buetow's wedding day, (April 5, 1888)," Women's Clothing Styles of the 1880's,

"Amelia (Snyder) Putz (c. 1891)," Women's Clothing Styles of the 1890's,

"Martie and Ellen Sears (Feb 13, 1892)," Women's Clothing Styles of the 1890's,

"Agnes 'Ida' Golemgeske (c. 1907)," Women's Clothing Styles of the 1900's,

"John & Elizabeth Best Family (circa 1907)," Family Clothing Styles of the 1900's.

"Bartz Family (c. 1912)," Family Clothing Styles of the 1900's,

INDIVIDUALS & FAMILIES PROVIDING HISTORIC FAMILY PHOTOGRAPHS
--(listed in chronological order as they appear in this volume):

"Emily Rathbun," courtesy of Merrialyce von Krosigk Blanchard of Salem, Oregon,

"Mary (McCormick) Faulkner," courtesy of Cathryn Larsen of Kenosha, Wisconsin,

"August Blodgett," courtesy of Isabel Wray of Dousman, Wisconsin,

"Lucy Blodgett," courtesy of Isabel Wray of Dousman, Wisconsin,

"Maria Amelia (Boeijink) Bixby," courtesy of Sue Hornbeck Bixby of Troy, Michigan,

"Johann Joseph Nettesheim," courtesy of Gene Nettesheim of Boulder, Colorado,

"Frank D. Faulkner," courtesy of Libbie Nolan of Big Bend, Wisconsin,

"Henry Snyder Jr.," courtesy of Kenneth Eiler of Overland Park, Kansas,

"Emily (Snyder) Lumb," courtesy of Libbie Nolan of Big Bend, Wisconsin,

"William and Alice Bigelow," courtesy of Jeannie Brown of Windsor, California,

"Agnes (Schaefer) Kau," courtesy of Mary Stigler of Brookfield, Wisconsin,

"William and Alice Bigelow (1868)," courtesy of Jeannie Brown of Windsor, California,

"Nellie Murphy (c. 1868)," courtesy of Mark Powers of Woodland, California,

"John, Joseph and Katherine Phillips (c. 1868)," courtesy of Mary Stigler of Brookfield, Wisconsin,

"Deborah A Beaumont (c. 1868)," courtesy of Jeanne Pedriana of Elm Grove, Wisconsin,

"Henry, Thomas & Harriet Lumb (c. 1868)," courtesy of Libbie Nolan of Big Bend, Wisconsin,

"Emily Experience Snyder Lumb (c. 1868)," courtesy of Cathryn Larsen of Kenosha, Wisconsin,

"George Barney (c. 1868)," courtesy of Jen Doane of Clinton, Utah,

"Julia Washburn (c. 1868)," courtesy of Jen Doane of Clinton, Utah,

"Thomas Cleary Family, Walworth County (1868)," courtesy of Dorothy Singer of Kenosha, Wisconsin,

"Virginia Lawrence (c. 1870)," courtesy of Libbie Nolan of Big Bend, Wisconsin,

"Charlotte (Armstrong) Foss (1870)," courtesy of Catherine A. Fanara of Madison, Wisconsin,

"J. M. Meidenbauer (1870)," courtesy of Roy Meidenbauer of New Berlin, Wisconsin,

"Andrew & Catherine (Casper) Schneider (c.1871)," courtesy of Mary Stigler of Brookfield, Wisconsin.

"Christina (Pegler) Schrubbe (c. 1871)," courtesy of Jeanette Pelletier of Bay City, Michigan.

"Benedict, Julia Anna (daughter), and Anna Winzenreid (c. 1871)," courtesy of Elaine Moss of Oconto, Wisconsin.

"Sophia Shaefle (c. 1871)," courtesy of the Williams family of Oconomowoc, Wisconsin.

"Thomas Faulkner Sr. (c. 1871)," courtesy of Cathryn Larsen of Kenosha, Wisconsin.

"Sarah (Davis) Faulkner (c. 1874)," courtesy of Cathryn Larsen of Kenosha, Wisconsin.

"Henrietta 'Hattie' (Bolter) Behling (c. 1874)," courtesy of Evelyn J Nicholson of West Allis, Wisconsin.

"August & Anna Erbe (c. 1875)," courtesy of Helen Joan Davies Carlson of Palmyra, Wisconsin.

"August and Christine Caesar (c. 1875)," courtesy of Elaine Alane of Helenville, Wisconsin

"Isabelle Searle (c. 1875)," courtesy of Cathryn Larsen of Racine, Wisconsin

"Emma Harris (c. 1875)," courtesy of Libbie Nolan of Big Bend, Wisconsin

"John B. Jermark (1877)," courtesy of Judy Lynch of Manhattan, Kansas

"Nathan Baxter (c. 1877)," courtesy of Lola Baxter in care of Lisa Lohry of Waterville, Minnesota.

"Gerhard Reinders' Family (c. 1877)," courtesy of William Joynt, of Elgin Ill., in care of Peter Sjoberg of Rockford, Ill.

"Frederik Stigler & Mary Schneider's Wedding Day (Oct. 30, 1877)," courtesy of Mary Stigler of Brookfield, Wisconsin.

"Adda S. Lumb (c. 1877)," courtesy of Libbie Nolan of Big Bend, Wisconsin,

"Ephraim Beaumont (c. 1878)," courtesy of Jeanne Pedriana of Elm Grove, Wisconsin,

"Mary Winton (c. 1878)," courtesy of Libbie Nolan of Big Bend, Wisconsin,

"Dr. August Schaefle (c. 1878)," courtesy of the Williams family of Oconomowoc, Wisconsin,

"Mabel & Alvin Snyder (c. 1878)," courtesy of Kenneth Eiler of Overland Park, Kansas,

"Mary Louis Potter (c. 1880)," courtesy of Carol Logan of Chico, California,

"Anna Caesar (c. 1880)," courtesy of Elaine Alane of Helenville, Wisconsin,

"William Bradley (c. 1880)," courtesy of Libbie Nolan of Big Bend, Wisconsin,

"Simon Woelfel (c. 1880)," courtesy of Roger and Marian Woelfel of New Berlin, WI.,

"Daniel & Barbara Schley (c. 1881),"
courtesy of Tricia Dingwall
Thompson and extended family
of Bozeman, Montana,

"Robert R. Boness (c. 1882)," courtesy of
Erin Rajek of Schofield, Wisconsin,

"Anna Woelfel (c. 1882)," courtesy of
James Woelfel of Holt, Michigan,

"Elsie Chapman (c. 1882)," courtesy of
Libbie Nolan of Big Bend, Wisconsin,

"Henry Snyder (c. 1883)," courtesy of
Kenneth Eiler of Overland Park, Kansas,

"Michael, Andrew & Otilia Stigler (c.
1883)," courtesy of Mary Stigler
of Brookfield, Wisconsin

"Matthew and Frances Beaumont (c.
1883)," courtesy Jeanne Pedriana
of Elm Grove, Wisconsin

"Rev. Simon Woelfel (c. 1883),"
courtesy of Roger & Marion
Woelfel of New Berlin, WI.,

"George & Magdalena Gebhardt's
adult children & spouses (1884),"
courtesy of Roger & Marion
Woelfel of New Berlin, WI.,

Joseph and Catharina Duckgeischel
(c. 1884)," courtesy of Leanne
Bennett of Waukesha, Wisconsin,

"Jennie Parsons and daughter Mary
(c. 1885)," courtesy of Pat
Nolan, Big Bend, Wisconsin,

"Charles Kreig Family (c. 1885)," courtesy of
Jerry Hartwell of Bowling Green, Ohio,

"Andrew Aikin (c. 1885)," courtesy of
Leanne Bennett of Waukesha Wisconsin,

"Emily and Emma Hodgson (circa
1885)," courtesy of Catheryn
Larsen of Kenosha, Wisconsin,

"Lee Elden (baby)Rufus and Harriet
Faulkner (1886)," courtesy of Cathryn
Larsen of Kenosha, Wisconsin,

"Mathias Gebhardt & Mary Katharina
Woelfel Wedding Day (Nov. 8,
1887)," courtesy of Roger & Marion
Woelfel of New Berlin, Wisconsin,

"John Michael Meidenbauer (c. 1888),"
courtesy of Roy Meidenbauer
of New Berlin, Wisconsin,

"Otto and Caspara Rasmussen wedding
day (1888)," courtesy of Susan
Goodman of Chevy Chase, Maryland,

"Harry Bliemeister (1888)," courtesy of John
Schoenknecht of Wauwatosa, Wisconsin,

"Bertha Buetow's Wedding Day,
(April 5, 1888)," courtesy of Jane
Sylvester of Madison, Wisconsin,

"George Ramstöck (c. 1889)," courtesy of
Hayley Ramstack of Manawa, Wisconsin,

"Charles Krieg (c. 1890)," courtesy of
Jerry Hartwell of Bowling, Ohio,

"Ferdinand William Brunkow (c.
1890)," courtesy of Richard
LaVerne of Sarasota, Florida,

"John K. Meidenbauer (c. 1890),"
courtesy of Roy Meidenbauer
of New Berlin, Wisconsin,

"Amelia (Snyder) Putz (c. 1891)," courtesy of
Kenneth Eiler of Overland Park, Kansas,

"William Caesar & Margaret Veenendaal
Wedding (July 27, 1892)," courtesy of
Elaine Alane of Helenville, Wisconsin,

"Martie and Ellen Sears (Feb 13, 1892)," courtesy of Libbie Nolan of Big Bend, Wisconsin,

"Rufus Elden Faulkner (c. 1892)," courtesy of Catheryn Larsen of Racine, Wisconsin,

"John M. and Anna Meidenbauer (1902)," courtesy of Roy Meidenbauer of New Berlin, Wisconsin,

"Catherine (Casper) Phillips (c. 1888)," courtesy of Lois (Phillips) Alton of Hartland, Wisconsin,

"Fred & Mary Stigler Family (c. 1893)," courtesy of Mary Stigler of Brookfield, Wisconsin,

"Jacob Franz Brandt Family (c. 1893)," courtesy of Leanne Bennett of Waukesha, Wisconsin,

"Karl (Charles), William Henry & Christian Vogel (circa: 1893)," courtesy of Terry Haslam-Jones of Rossendale, England,

"John Christian Dieman (February 1, 1894)," courtesy of Jerry Hartwell of Bowling Green, Ohio,

"Mary Gumm (c.1895)," courtesy of Andrew Dent Pierce of Eugene Lane, Oregon,

"Jarvis Porter Boyce (c. 1895)," courtesy of Debra Woidyla Barham of Clearfield, Utah,

"Albert Veenendaal holding Eddie Krause (c. 1895)," courtesy of Elaine Alane of Helenville, Wisconsin,

"John Schaeffel Family (c. 1897)," courtesy of the Williams family of Oconomowoc, Wisconsin,

"Elm Grove Youth Baseball (c. 1898)," courtesy of Craig Black of Brookfield, Wisconsin,

"Augusta (Bartz) & August Gehrt Wedding, (March 11, 1899)," courtesy of Jan Pace of Waukesha, Wisconsin,

"Albert & Christiana Schrubbe's Wedding (Jan. 13, 1900)," courtesy of Betty Ann Kramer of Clovis, California,

"Frank Berst Family (c. 1900)," courtesy of Jessica Schmus of Oak Creek, Wisconsin,

"Best children (c. 1900)," courtesy of Fred C. Smyth of Whidbey Island, Washington,

"Behrend Sisters (c. 1900)," courtesy of Jonathan Brumfield of Huntsville, Alabama,

"Ida and Anna (Behrend) Meuler (c. 1900)," courtesy of Dorothy Meuler of Oconomowoc, Wisconsin,

"Herman Grundmann Family (c. 1901)," courtesy of Erica Crom of Rantoul, Illinois,

"Andrew Stigler (c. 1902)," courtesy of Mary Stigler of Brookfield, Wisconsin,

"George Stigler (c 1903)," courtesy of Mary Stigler of Brookfield, Wisconsin,

"George Parsons (c. 1904)," courtesy of Libbie Nolan of Big Bend, Wisconsin,

"Lee Elden Faulkner (c. 1904)," courtesy of Cathryn Larsen of Kenosha, Wisconsin,

"Nauertz Family (c. 1905)," courtesy of Kathleen Nauertz-Husz of Milwaukee, Wisconsin,

"Eva May Russell (c. 1905)," courtesy of Libbie Nolan of Big Bend, Wisconsin,

"George E. Cook and John R Schaeffel (c. 1905)," courtesy of the Williams Family of Oconomowoc, Wisconsin,

"John Hoffman Jr. at the University of Wisconsin-Madison (1906)," courtesy of Sally Clarin of Brookfield, Wisconsin.

"Agnes 'Ida' Golemgeske (c. 1907)," courtesy of Jan Pace of Waukesha, Wisconsin.

"John & Elizabeth Best family (circa 1907)," courtesy of Fred C. Smyth of Whidbey Island, Washington.)

"Sadie James & Elizabeth Elias (1908)," courtesy of Wales Village Hall, Wales, Wisconsin.)

"Gottlieb Bartz Family (1908)," courtesy of Jan Pace of Waukesha, Wisconsin.

"William Bishoff & Clara Rynders Wedding (June 30, 1908)," courtesy of Donna Hoff- Grambau of Mount Pleasant, Michigan.

"Charles B. Coleman (c. 1909)," courtesy of Roberta Poetsch of Rochester, Minnesota.

"Robert Hunter Family (c. 1910)," courtesy of Carl L. Borgstram, Town of Ottawa, Waukesha, Wisconsin.

"Albert Beecroft Family (c. 1910)," courtesy of Mark J. Kelly of Texas City, Texas.

"Thomas Michael Blessinger (c. 1910)," courtesy of Georgia Davis Briggeman of Deer Lodge, Powell Co., Montana.

"[Unidentified] Kau brother in Butte, Montana (c. 1910)," courtesy of Georgia Davis Briggeman of Deer Lodge, Powell Co., Montana.

"Heinrich Boldt Family (c.1910)," courtesy of Crystal Keslin of Lubbock, Texas.

"Helen Phillips (circa 1910)," courtesy of a Lois Alton of Hartland, Wisconsin.

"John and son, Valentine, Casper (1912)," courtesy of Lois Alton of Hartland, Wisconsin.

"Bartz Family (c. 1912)," courtesy of Jan Pace of Waukesha, Wisconsin.

"The Ulrich Woelfel Home in Rollhofen, Bayern (1913)," courtesy of Louse Wasserman of Germersberg, Bavaria, Germany.

"Andrew Caesar (c. 1915,)" courtesy of Elaine Alane of Helenville, Wisconsin.

"Horgenbach, Canton Thurgau, Switzerland (c. 1917)," courtesy of Sally Clarin of Brookfield, Wisconsin.

"Edward Barton's Threshing Crew (c.1917)," courtesy of Lois Alton of Hartland, Wisconsin.

"Mary (Kau) Phillip--standing between the 2 girls (1918)," Image courtesy of Lois Alton of Hartland, Wisconsin.

"Henry, Ralph, Rose, and Barbara Blattner (c. 1918)," Image courtesy of Steve and Carol Blattner of Waukesha, Wisconsin.

"Henrich Britting Home in Rollhofen, Bayern (1913)," courtesy of James A. Woelfel of Holt, Michigan.

"Pvt. Clarence Potter (c. 1918)," courtesy of Carol Logan of Chico, California.

"William Phillips (1918)," courtesy of a Lois Alton of Hartland, Wisconsin.

"Vern Bartz Hauling ice (c. 1919)," courtesy of Jan Pace of Waukesha, Wisconsin.

"Karl Kleist (c. 1920)," courtesy of Marlene Connell of Hartford, Wisconsin.

"Elwyn & Evelyn Roberts (circa 1920)," courtesy of Wales Village Hall, Waukesha County, Wisconsin.

"John K. & Anna Meidenbauer (circa 1923)," courtesy of Roy Meidenbauer of New Berlin, Wisconsin.

"Sebina Danford Barney with baby George (c. 1 Big Bend Vernon Historical Society. 925)," courtesy of Jennifer Doane of Clinton, Utah.

HISTORIC FAMILY PHOTOGRAPHS COURTESY OF REGIONAL HISTORICAL SOCIETIES & ORGANIZATIONS

"The Scots of Vernon," courtesy of <u>Big Bend Vernon Historical Society.</u>

"Christina Dunkel," courtesy of the <u>Elmbrook Historical Society.</u>

"Charles Dunkel (c. 1906)," courtesy of the <u>Elmbrook Historical Society.</u>

"Mads Larson (c. 1910)," courtesy of the <u>Hartland Historical Society.</u>

"Beriah Brown," courtesy of <u>Hawks Inn Historical Society, Delafield, Wisconsin.</u>

"Dr. Alfred Castleman," courtesy of <u>Hawks Inn Historical Society, Delafield, Wisconsin.</u>

"Ammi Doubleday Hawks," courtesy of <u>Hawks Inn Historical Society, Delafield, Wisconsin.</u>

"Frances Hawks," courtesy of <u>Hawks Inn Historical Society, Delafield, Wisconsin.</u>

"Nelson Paige Hawks," courtesy of <u>Hawks Inn Historical Society, Delafield, Wisconsin.</u>

"Parmelia DuBois (Hawks) Sperry," courtesy of <u>Hawks Inn Historical Society, Delafield, Wisconsin.</u>

"A Barefoot Host," Courtesy of <u>Hartland Historical Society,</u>

"J. Rolfson Family of Norway (1880)," courtesy of <u>Muskego Historical Society.</u>

"Robert Hunter Family (c. 1910)," Courtesy of <u>Town of Ottawa historian, Carl. L. Borgstram.</u>

"Thomas Spencer Redford holding daughter Maplet (c. 1880)," courtesy of the <u>Sussex-Lisbon Area Historical Society.</u>

"Green Road and the Duplainville Area" by Mildred Wiedeman," Courtesy of the <u>Pewaukee Area Historical Society.</u>

"The Hodgsons' in Los Angeles-- Genealogy," courtesy of the <u>Sussex-Lisbon Area Historical Society.</u>

"John Watson," courtesy of the <u>Sussex-Lisbon Area Historical Society.</u>

"Thomas Spencer Redford holding daughter Maplet (c. 1880)," courtesy of the <u>Sussex-Lisbon Area Historical Society.</u>

"David & Annie Jones," courtesy of <u>Wales Village Hall, Wales, Wisconsin.</u>

"Sadie James & Elizabeth Elias (1908)," courtesy of <u>Wales Village Hall, Wales, Wisconsin.</u>

"Elwyn & Evelyn Roberts (circa 1920)," courtesy of <u>Wales Village Hall, Wales, Wisconsin.</u>

"American Farm Yard in Winter," courtesy of the <u>Wisconsin Historical Society.</u>

PEOPLE FILES: COURTESY OF THE WAUKESHA COUNTY HISTORICAL SOCIETY & MUSEUM:

"John & Dorothy Dodge (c. 1848),"

"George & Ruth Ferry Family (c. 1853),"

"Rueben Gibson, (c. 1856),"

"John & Charlotte Kier (c. 1865),"

"George Robertson, (c. 1865),"

"Catherine Dey, (c. 1865),"

"Captain Abiel Pierce, (c. 1867),"

"Dr. Thomas & Katherine Steel (c. 1878),"

"William Small (c. 1880),"

"Jesse Smith (c. 1882),"

"General George Palmer (c 1886),"

"Ole Olson Jr. (c. 1888),"

"Prucius Putnam (c. 1889),"

"John Frederick Dreyer (c. 1892),"

"William Sherman, Josephine & Dwight Allen Jr., (c. 1892),"

"Howell Sawyer (c. 1893),"

"William Sanner (c. 1895),"

"Katherine Sharpe (c. 1896),"

"Dr. Caleb C. Harris (c. 1900),"

"Katherina Fuhr (c. 1901),"

"Dr. Margaret Caldwell (c. 1902),"

"William Melvin Frazier (c. 1902),"

"Mable Foster and Emma J. Richardson (1903),"

"Florence George (c. 1915),"

"Adda Howie (1928),"

WAUKESHA COUNTY HISTORICAL SOCIETY & MUSEUM: PHOTOGRAPH DESCRIPTORS:

"Captain Abiel Pierce,"

"Perry Family (1868),"

"Jane Howie Robertson (c. 1870),"

"H. R. Elderkin M.D. (1871),"

"Dr. Thomas & Katherine Steel (c. 1878),"

"William Small (c. 1880),"

"Mabel (George)Dockstader (c. 1880),"

"Jennie Parsons and daughter Mary. (c. 1885),"

"William Sherman, Josephine and Dwight Allen Jr. (c. 1892),"

"Elizabeth Foster (c. 1895),"

"Mable Foster and Emma J. Richardson (1903),"

"Spaulding Wagon Accident (1905)."

TRANSPORTATION FILE: COURTESY OF THE WAUKESHA COUNTY HISTORICAL SOCIETY & MUSEUM:

"Milwaukee & Watertown Railroad Directors (c. 1853),"

"Spaulding Wagon Accident (1905),"

WAUKESHA COUNTY HISTORICAL SOCIETY & MUSEUM: PIONEER NOTEBOOK:

"John & Dorothy Dodge.

"*LANDMARK*": A QUARTERLY PUBLICATION OF THE WAUKESHA COUNTY HISTORICAL SOCIETY. COURTESY OF JOHN SCHOENKNECHT, EDITOR:

Aitken, Roy & Chester Wilson. "Bringing in the Sheaves," *Landmark*. v. 10, n. 4, p. 19.

Aitkin, Roy. "Shaping a Shoe," *Landmark*, v. 13, n. 1. (Winter, 1970),

_____. "Summer Ice," *Landmark*, v.12, n. 1, Winter, 1969.

Barney, Celia. "Old Homesteads Their Owners: Barney Home." *Landmark*. v. 5. n. 3, Spring, 1962,

Guthrie Linton, Jean. "Genial Kindly Kier." *Landmark*. v. 34, n. 2, Summer, 1991.

Hennig, Douglas T. "Town of Lisbon Pioneers - Part IV, The Small Family," *Landmark*, v. 28, n. 1 & 2. (Spring-Summer Double Issue, 1985),

Keller, Fred H., "Depression Diaries," *Landmark*, v. 37, n. 1, Spring, 1994. p. 21.

_____. "The Great Civil War—Watson, Soldier and Town Chairman." *Landmark*. v. 32, n. 3, (Autumn, 1989.)

_____. "Thomas Spencer Redford—The Lisbon-Sussex Sesquicentennial," *Landmark*, v. 29, n. 1 (Spring, 1986),

Nolan, Libbie, "A Burned Building, Its Bible and Bell," *Landmark*. v. 28, Nos. 1 & 2, (Spring & Summer, 1985).

_____, "Bed, Board and Blossoms," Landmark. v. 9, n. 3, (Summer, 1966).

_____, "Cow Country USA." *Landmark*. v. 15, n. 4, (Autumn, 1972).

_____, "Early Waukesha Manufacturing," *Landmark*, vol. 18, no. 4, (Autumn-Winter, 1975).

Phillips, Charles R. "Waukesha's Carrie's Nation," *Landmark*, v. 12, Nos. 2 & 3 (Spring & Summer, 1969),

Wellauer, Maralyn. "Waukesha County's Swiss Pioneers," *Landmark*, v.25, n. 4 (Winter, 1982).

Wicklein Edward C., "Two Churches Named Zion," *Landmark*. v. 20, n. 1 (Spring 1977), pp.10-14.